Sport and Brexit

This is the first book to investigate the significance of Brexit for sport, with a particular focus on the regulatory and legal challenges that it poses, and the economic and political stresses that are likely to follow in its wake.

Written by a team of leading researchers working across sport studies, legal studies and political science, and edited by an EU official with nearly two decades of experience working in EU sport policy, the book explains why regulation, and European dis-integration, matter to sport. It examines key topics including free movement, State aid and labour law, and considers the interests of key stakeholders from fans to football clubs to governing bodies.

This is an essential reference for any advanced student, researcher, policy maker, administrator or industry professional working in sport, international law, political science, or international business and management.

Jacob Kornbeck is Policy Officer in the European Commission, a former member of its Sport Unit (2001–14), where he was involved in the elaboration of the White Paper (COM(2007) 391) and the Communication on Sport (COM(2011) 12). An External Lecturer at the German Sport University in Cologne, he has published in the fields of sports law and policy, as well as social policy and social work. He also serves on the boards of the *European Journal of Social Work* (as Book Review Editor) and the *Journal of Data Protection and Privacy*.

Routledge Research in Sport Business and Management

Sport Officiating
Recruitment, Development, and Retention
Lori Livingston, Susan L. Forbes, Nick Wattie, and Ian Cunningham

Sport and Environmental Sustainability
Research and Strategic Management
Edited by Greg Dingle and Cheryl Mallen

Sport and the Pandemic
Perspectives on Covid-19's Impact on the Sport Industry
Edited by Paul M. Pedersen, Brody J. Ruihley and Bo Li

Embedded Multi-Level Leadership in Elite Sport
Edited by Svein S. Andersen, Per Øystein Hansen and Barrie Houlihan

Good Governance in Sport
Critical Reflections
Edited by Arnout Geeraert and Frank van Eekeren

Stakeholder Analysis and Sport Organisations
Edited by Anna-Maria Strittmatter, Josef Fahlén and Barrie Houlihan

Sport and Brexit
Regulatory Challenges and Legacies
Edited by Jacob Kornbeck

Sport Management Education
Global Perspectives and Implications for Practice
Edited by Mike Rayner and Tom Webb

For more information about this series, please visit www.routledge.com/Routledge-Research-in-Sport-Business-and-Management/book-series/RRSBM

Sport and Brexit

Regulatory Challenges and Legacies

Edited by Jacob Kornbeck

Routledge
Taylor & Francis Group
LONDON AND NEW YORK

First published 2022
by Routledge
4 Park Square, Milton Park, Abingdon, Oxon OX14 4RN

and by Routledge
605 Third Avenue, New York, NY 10158

Routledge is an imprint of the Taylor & Francis Group, an informa business

British Library Cataloguing-in-Publication Data
A catalogue record for this book is available from the British Library

Library of Congress Cataloging-in-Publication Data
Names: Kornbeck, Jacob, 1968– editor.
Title: Sport and Brexit : regulatory challenges and legacies / Edited by Jacob Kornbeck.
Identifiers: LCCN 2021040861 | ISBN 9780367755195 (hardback) | ISBN 9780367755218 (paperback) | ISBN 9781003162803 (ebook)
Subjects: LCSH: Sports and state—Great Britain. | European Union—Great Britain. | Sports—Social aspects—Great Britain. | Sports—Political aspects—Great Britain. | Sports administration—Great Britain.
Classification: LCC GV706.35 .S54162 2022 | DDC 796.0941—dc23/eng/20211020
LC record available at https://lccn.loc.gov/2021040861

ISBN: 978-0-367-75519-5 (hbk)
ISBN: 978-0-367-75521-8 (pbk)
ISBN: 978-1-003-16280-3 (ebk)

DOI: 10.4324/9781003162803

Typeset in Goudy
by Apex CoVantage, LLC

MIX
Paper from responsible sources
FSC www.fsc.org FSC™ C013985

Printed in the United Kingdom
by Henry Ling Limited

Contents

Disclaimer

The editor of this volume, **Jacob Kornbeck**, is a Policy Officer in the European Commission, but opinions expressed by him are strictly personal and do not render official positions of the European Commission or of the European Union. The same applies to the choice of contributors and the editorial work performed. Opinions expressed in chapters other than the Preface, Introduction and Conclusion are those of the contributors having signed the chapters in question.

Figures

Tables

Contributors

Emmanuel Bayle is Professor of sports management and Director of the Sport Sciences Institute of the University of Lausanne (ISSUL), Switzerland. He has published several books and articles on governance, management and performance in sports organisations. He currently manages a research project on the performance of international sport federations and has consulted for international sports organisations (UEFA, Rugby Europe).

Simon Boyes is Senior Lecturer and a member of the Centre for Rights and Justice at Nottingham Trent University (NTU), UK. Simon teaches on the International, European and Comparative Law, and Public Law and Human Rights modules on Nottingham Law School's LL.B programmes. Simon's research activities are focused in the areas of sports law and sports regulation. He researches and publishes on a number of sports law topics, predominantly related to legal regulation of sports governing bodies, the relationship between sports self-regulation and the law, as well as the relationship between sport and the law of the European Union.

Alexander Brand is Professor of Political Science/International Relations at Rhine-Waal University, Campus Kleve, Germany. He is one of two principal investigators in the research project EUFOOT ('Becoming European through Football?' sponsored through the German Research Foundation DFG). He is a long-time member of 'Sport and EU', the former Association for the Study of Sport and the European Union. He is an invited member of the Forum Sport Politics at the German Sport University in Cologne. Among his main research interests are foreign policy analysis, the politics of development policy, mass media, discourse and international relations, and sport/football and politics.

Andrea Cattaneo is Lecturer in EU Law at Edge Hill University, UK. He has worked on EU-funded projects exploring the regulation of football agents within the EU (2017–2019) and the development of the EU's Sports Diplomacy Strategy (2018–2021). Andrea has authored a number of works in the area of EU Sports Law. He is a member of the Centre for Sports Law Research and sits on the Board of Sport and EU Association.

Laura Donnellan is Lecturer in Law at the University of Limerick, Ireland where she teaches European Union Law and Sport and the Law. She has published in national and international journals in the areas of sports law and animal welfare in the EU. Laura is a Fellow at the Oxford Centre for Animals Ethics and a Consulting Editor for *The Journal of Animal Ethics*.

Borja García is Senior Lecturer in Sport Management and Policy at Loughborough University, UK. He is a political scientist who specialises in European Union politics. His research expertise focuses in three areas: EU sport policy, the governance of global sport and the political activism of football fans. Borja is a leading academic in the study of the origin and development of EU sport policy, having published in top international journals such as the *Journal of Common Market Studies*, *Journal of European Public Policy* or *Public Administration*. Borja is one of the founders of Sport and EU, the Association for the Study of Sport and the European Union.

Arnout Geeraert is Assistant Professor at Utrecht University's School of Governance, Netherlands and Research Fellow at the Leuven Institute of International and European Studies (LINES) at KU Leuven.

Grant Jarvie is Professor and Director at the University of Edinburgh, UK and a former acting University Principal and Chair at the national Sports Council for Scotland. He chaired the recent Scottish Government review of the Scottish sporting landscape and is a visiting Professor at the University of Toronto, Canada. He is also founding Director of an international think tank.

Zahid Mustafi is a PhD student at the University of Lausanne (UNIL), Switzerland. With an educational background in management and economics, he decided to join UNIL with a specialisation in sports. After receiving his Master's in sport management (prize for the best Master's thesis 2018), and completing his internship in a football club, he began teaching and studying for his PhD in 2019 at UNIL, focusing on the regulation of Swiss professional football under various themes in terms of management, economics, sports and the labour market for football players.

Arne Niemann is Professor of International Politics at the Department of Political Science, Johannes Gutenberg University (JGU) of Mainz, Germany. He is Director of the tri-national, interdisciplinary MA programme in European Studies. His research focuses on the European integration process, European Union politics and particular policy areas of European politics, such as sport. Arne is principal investigator in the research projects EUFOOT ('Becoming European through Football?') and FANZineE ("Football as the basis for social cohesion in Europe"), funded by the German Research Foundation (2018–2022) and the Federal Ministry of Education and Research (2021–2024), respectively. From 2012 to 2015, he was co-editor of the Sport&EU Review.

Leanne O'Leary is Senior Lecturer in Law in the Centre for Sports Law Research at Edge Hill University, UK. Leanne's research interests focus on the interface between sports law and employment law. Leanne is a dual qualified solicitor, CAS arbitrator and member of the Sport Resolutions (UK) Panel of Arbitrators and Mediators.

Henk Erik Meier is Professor for the Social Sciences of Sport at Münster University, Germany. He is a political scientist specialising in comparative policy research. His research expertise focuses on three areas: sport governance, national identity and sport, and the future development of sports. He has published on a broad range of issues, such as women's football and sport broadcasting in top international journals like the *Journal of Common Market Studies, Public Administration* or *European Sociological Review*.

Walter S. Palmer is Director in Alumni Relations at Dartmouth College, USA, a former professional basketball player (NBA, Europe, Latin America) and former leader of European and global athlete trade union organisations. After retirement from the court in 2003, Walter spearheaded the founding of the German basketball players association, Spieler Initiative, SP.IN (2005); the European Elite Athletes Association, EU Athletes (2007); and UNI Sport PRO, now the World Players Association (2012). During that period (2010–2014), he co-chaired the European Sectoral Social Dialogue Committee in the sport sector during its pilot phase. In 2015, he served for a short time as the Deputy Executive Director for International Development and Marketing at the NBA Players Association before starting his own consulting business where he continued to advise player unions from around the world on issues related to organising, governance, career development programming, and anti-doping policy. He is also a board member at the Centre for Sport and Human Rights and a member of the Boston advisory board for the Concussion Legacy Foundation.

Seema Patel is Senior Lecturer in law at Nottingham Law School, Nottingham Trent University, UK. Her research discipline is sports law, with specialised focus on discrimination issues and the regulatory balance between inclusion and exclusion in competitive sport. As an international expert on gender discrimination in sport, Seema has provided extensive media commentary and analysis on the legal implications of gender eligibility rules. Her current academic publications examine the regulatory gaps in the protection of athletes' human rights in sport. Seema has participated in sport policy consultation in her area, and she has also contributed to government inquiries into increasing inclusion in sport.

Stefaan Van den Bogaert is Professor of European law and Director of the Europa Institute at Leiden Law School, Netherlands and serves as Vice-Dean of the Law School. He is Visiting Professor of European sports law at the Free University of Brussels (VUB), Belgium and a member of the editorial board of Common Market Law Review.

Richard Parrish is Professor and Jean Monnet Chair of EU Sports Law and Policy at Edge Hill University, UK where he is Director of the Centre for Sports Law Research. Richard has advised the EU institutions on the development of its EU sports policy, having been a member of the European Commission's Group of Independent European Sport Experts (2010) and a member of EU Commission's High-Level Group on Sport Diplomacy (2015–16). He has authored a number of EU studies for the Commission and Parliament and he was Specialist Advisor to the House of Lords Inquiry 'Grassroots Sport and the European Union.'

Stephen Weatherill is the Jacques Delors Professor of European Law in the University of Oxford, UK and a Fellow of Somerville College. His research and published work cover the wide sweep of EU constitutional and substantive law, including major textbooks.

Preface

As a result of the fortunate circumstances of my professional life, I have been actively involved in the *Bosman* and *Meca-Medina and Majcen* cases. It is therefore only natural that I agree with the finding of this instructive and fascinating collective book that—within the EU and beyond—the regulation and governance of sport have been dramatically reshaped by EU law over the last decades.

And even sport itself: when—in 2005—Arsenal FC, under Arsène Wenger, fielded a team without any Englishmen against Crystal Palace, as a direct result of the *Bosman* ruling, it symbolised the end of the 'kick and rush' and the enthronement of a different way of playing football, in the very country that had codified football.

As a practitioner, I am regularly confronted with the questions of the various stakeholders of professional sport in relation to Brexit. This collective work will enable them to see things much more clearly. This is no small merit!

The game of predictions being closely linked to sport, let us dare to conclude with a little exercise in futurology as to the fact that 'Brexit' will not be, for sport in the UK, synonymous with radical disintegration. That would be far too simplistic a view.

When in 1995 the CJEU decreed the freedom of players at the end of their contract, it took FIFA only five years to globalise this liberalisation of the labour market. It was simply not sustainable to have one set of rules for the EU, the core market of the football industry, and another for the rest of the world.

In 2021, the European Super League case is now before the CJEU. If its ruling frees up the production market—even partially—and thus gives the big EU clubs the freedom to create their own top competition, we bet that the gravitational pull of this new European mega-competition will soon bring the biggest English clubs back into its orbit. Brexit or no Brexit. A volume II will then be necessary, which is all the harm we wish the authors of this book.

Jean-Louis Dupont
Lawyer at the Bar of Barcelona

Préface

Les heureux hasards de la vie professionnelle m'ayant permis de participer activement aux affaires « Bosman » et « Meca Medina et Majcen », c'est tout naturellement que je me rallie au constat de cet instructif et passionnant ouvrage collectif, à savoir que—au sein de l'UE et même au-delà—le droit et la gouvernance du sport ont été spectaculairement refaçonnés par le droit communautaire au cours des dernières décennies.

Et même le sport lui-même: quand—en 2005—Arsenal FC, sous l'égide d'Arsène Wenger, aligne contre Crystal Palace une équipe sans aucun Anglais, fruit direct de l'arrêt Bosman, c'est là tout le symbole de la fin du 'kick and rush' et de l'intronisation d'une autre façon de jouer au football, dans le pays-même qui avait codifié le football.

En tant que praticien, je suis régulièrement confronté aux questionnements des divers acteurs du sport professionnel par rapport au Brexit. Cet ouvrage collectif leur permettra d'y voir bien plus clair. C'est un mérite qui n'est pas mince !

Le jeu des pronostics étant intimement lié au sport, osons conclure par un petit exercice de futurologie quant au fait que « Brexit » ne sera pas, pour le sport au Royaume-Uni, synonyme de désintégration radicale. Ce serait une vision beaucoup trop simpliste.

Lorsqu'en 1995 la CJUE a décrété la liberté des joueurs en fin de contrat, il n'a fallu que cinq ans à la FIFA pour mondialiser cette libéralisation du marché du travail. Il n'était tout simplement pas soutenable d'avoir des règles pour l'UE, marché au coeur de l'industrie du football et d'autres pour le reste du monde.

En 2021, la CJUE est à présent saisie du dossier de la « European Super League ». Si l'arrêt qu'elle prononcera libère—même partiellement—le marché de la production et confère ainsi aux grands clubs de l'UE la liberté de créer leur propre compétition faîtière, nous faisons le pari que la force de gravité de cette nouvelle méga-compétition européenne aura tôt fait de ramener dans son orbite les plus grands clubs anglais. Brexit or no Brexit. Un tome II sera alors nécessaire, ce qui est tout le mal que nous souhaitons aux auteurs du présent ouvrage.

Maître Jean-Louis Dupont
Avocat au Barreau de Barcelone

Part I

Introduction

Chapter 1

Introduction

Sport, Brexit and the regulatory role of the European Union

Jacob Kornbeck

1.1. Introduction

As the title indicates, the present book is a collection of texts about Sport and Brexit. In a timely manner—at a time when numerous aspects of the UK-EU theme are still 'up in the air'—it aims to provide an overview of knowledge on a range of key topics, all of which are linked with the regulatory capacity of the EU. Therefore, it is not a book about all aspects of the politics and policies of Brexit, as seen from a sport perspective, just like it is not a sport management book on how to tackle Brexit-related challenges. The ambition was not to be all things for all people, but rather to investigate key challenges within the regulatory ambit of the Sport and Brexit thematic area. The present introduction will explain this exclusive focus on legal and political aspects of EU regulation and will provide a short chapter overview. In doing so, it will follow a humble approach of recording observations made in the years 2020–2021, in the spirit of the late John Le Carré (1931–2019): 'He left the question unasked; but not, perhaps, unanswered';[1] for the survey provided through the diverse contributions comprised between the front cover and end cover of this book is not driven by theory (although some theories are represented in its pages) but rather by practice.

1.2. Brexit and the art of disentanglement

Brexit marks a monumental change in British politics, law and, ultimately, history. Besides being divisive and objectively unsettling to the business model of the British state as it has been practised for almost half a century, Brexit is also bound to dominate debates in all areas of policy and politics. According to Denis MacShane, seasoned politician and book author, Brexit might not be over in a decade,[2] while Peter Wilding, the reluctant father of the catchy

1 Tinker, Tailor, Soldier, Spy, Chapter 28.
2 MacShane (2019).

DOI: 10.4324/9781003162803-2

locution, feels a bit sad about his creation.[3] Yet the 2019 General Election gave the Johnson administration a strong mandate, effectively removing the need for a second referendum so that, while the Brexit theme lends itself easily to polemics, no matter what camp we are in, Brexit has become a settled fact. It is one with which Remainers and Brexiteers alike will have to live, for better and for worse; yet this they can only do if they manage, very gradually, to grasp its implications. At the time of this writing, it seems difficult to gauge the most likely future scenarios, while what we can engage in with some confidence is stocktaking: drawing up an inventory of 46 years (1973–2019) of British EU membership.

If anything, it seems that Brexit will have proven the pioneers and theoreticians of European integration right, if 47 years (1 January 1973 to 31 January 2020) of *de facto* integration[4] cannot be easily undone, or at least not without considerable transaction costs.[5] Because Europe had come to embrace all aspects of life, albeit to varying degrees,[6] every sector deserves its own Brexit assessment even if, at this stage, we may not be able to chart the voyage with much certainty. Rather, the exercise will be about plotting the course of navigation made so far on the best available maps. By taking stock of what British membership of the European Union has contributed to British life, we shall perhaps be able to make some informed guesses about the future, with all the unavoidable caveats. This book aims to provide such a stocktaking exercise for the sport sector: a sector which is very dear indeed to many Brits. It will look at different aspects of professional as well as amateur (competitive or recreational) (in UK parlance: 'community') sport, in an attempt to isolate, identify and assess the influence which Europe has exerted so far. If some of the initial assumptions behind the integration process were accurate, then the very act of integration should mean that the initially constituent parts of the (then) Communities and (now) Union cannot be easily disentangled. They would have amalgamated gradually, just like eggs in a pan: an image used in the 1960s by a young political activist: 'six eggs in a pan.'[7] The

3 Wilding (2018).

4 For a chronology of British EEC/EC/EU membership until 2012, see Wallace (2012).

5 Cf. Greer (2008), p. 221: 'Path dependency is used to explain why inefficient or suboptimal outcomes persist. They persist, the argument runs, because the transition costs of shifting to a better path are too high. At some time in the past, those involved made decisions and investments that set them along one trajectory. Now, even if they wish they were on a different trajectory, their existing investments bind them to it. This is path dependence because even if the path turns out to be less than optimal, it would be too hard and time-consuming to go back to the fork and take the other path.'

6 For a discussion of the merits—and limitations—of the argument that integration left the UK as an 'awkward' member in a Community/Union which had become purportedly different from what the UK had agreed to join in 1973, see e.g. Richardson and Rittberger (2020).

7 Lauritzen (2008). This was the vision of Peter Lauritzen (1942–2007), who served as the Council of Europe's youth sector for 35 years and who is memorialised through the creation of the Peter Lauritzen Collection (www.coe.int/en/web/youth/peter-lauritzen-collection), a thematic library on

gradual merger of national structures was to proceed pragmatically, as announced by Robert Schuman in his declaration on 9 May 1950. His was not a vision for institutions for their own sake, but rather one of using integration, institutions and a common framework—unheard of until then, with national sovereignty having held sway since 1648—to be used as policy tools.

> Europe will not be made all at once, or according to a single plan. It will be built through concrete achievements which first create a *de facto* solidarity.[8]

What Schuman termed *une solidarité de fait* was and remains an eminently pragmatic concept. While the absence of grandeur made it unpopular with some, evoking grey bureaucrats attending meetings in grey buildings under a grey Belgian sky, the concomitant absence of symbols allowed Member States to retain their national identities, as acknowledged freely by a British lawyer for whom it was a badge of honour to have been dubbed '*un juriste illustre mais perfide*' by a Belgian federalist MEP:[9]

> The genius of the legal order of the Union is that it preserves the national identities of the Member States and their essential state functions, while enabling them to pursue more effectively objectives that they have in common, by accepting the discipline of acting together through common institutions, on the basis of binding rules and under the supervision of the Court of Justice. [. . .] Though I am on record as being critical of some aspects of the Lisbon Treaty and of the recent case law of the Court, my admiration for this most ingeniously paradoxical of legal orders remains undimmed [. . .].[10]

At the same time—and in a rather British way reminiscent both of 18th-century empiricist philosophers and also the piecemeal development of the world's biggest colonial empire—it was and remains a model based on trial and error and, as such, worthy of a pragmatic and praxeological analysis, based first and foremost on how it has so far worked in practice: 'the proof of the pudding.'

Council of Europe premises in Budapest. That Lauritzen did not work for any of the (then) three European Communities (ECSC, EEC, EAEC) or the later European Union (EU) is of little importance, as the early activists of integration shared a certain vision: less of their preferred point of arrival than of the method to get there.

8 The Schuman Declaration—9 May 1950, https://europa.eu/european-union/about-eu/symbols/europe-day/schuman-declaration_en.

9 Dashwood (2010), p. 50: 'Being thought illustrious but perfidious is probably the best compliment I've ever been paid. What I like so much about the EU is how well it is designed to cater for a political reality, which my MEP critic would wish to deny.'

10 *Ibid.*, p. 50.

1.3. A praxeological (not a theory-driven) survey

On Christmas Eve (24 December 2020), British Prime Minister Boris Johnson and European Commission President Ursula von der Leyen announced that an agreement had been reached on a draft EU-UK Trade and Cooperation Agreement (hereinafter: TCA).[11] Approved subsequently by the House of Commons on 30 December 2020 (despite announced resistance within the two major political parties), by the European Parliament on 28 April 2021 and by the Council on 29 April 2021,[12] this seemed to provide at least a modicum of clarity and legal certainty. In particular, it appeared the cherry on the cake after a long and tortuous process comprising the United Kingdom European Union membership referendum (26 June 2016), Prime Minister Theresa May's letter to European Council President Donald Tusk (29 March 2017) invoking Article 50 TFEU and announcing a two-year process (until 29 March 2019), the signature of the Brexit Withdrawal Agreement (24 January 2020) and the transition period referred to earlier. Harrowing it was, interspersed with such thorny incidents as the UK Supreme Court's ruling in the *Miller* case (requiring that Parliament legislate for Article 50 TFEU to be triggered)[13] (24 January 2017) and a controversial prorogation of the UK Parliament (28 August to 14 October 2019) which lead to another landmark Supreme Court ruling in the second *Miller* case (holding the prorogation to have been decided by the Sovereign upon unlawful advice provided by the Prime Minister)[14] (24 September 2019). The world held its breath watching House of Commons debates like never before, including three spectacular defeats for Theresa May's administration whenever the Prime Minister tabled a bill based on a text negotiated with her European counterparts, voting 432–202 (15 January 2019), 391–242 (12 March 2019) and 344–286 (29 March 2019), respectively. When following the resignation of Theresa May (24 May 2019), Boris Johnson was imminently ready to take over, and Queen Elizabeth II remarked that she could not understand why anyone would wish the job of Prime Minister.[15]

11 Trade and Cooperation Agreement between the European Union and the European Atomic Energy Community, of the one part, and the United Kingdom of Great Britain and Northern Ireland, of the other part. OJ L 149, 30 April 2021, pp. 10–2539.

12 Council Decision (EU) 2021/689 of 29 April 2021 on the conclusion, on behalf of the Union, of the Trade and Cooperation Agreement between the European Union and the European Atomic Energy Community, of the one part, and the United Kingdom of Great Britain and Northern Ireland, of the other part, and of the Agreement between the European Union and the United Kingdom of Great Britain and Northern Ireland concerning security procedures for exchanging and protecting classified information. OJ L 149, 30 April 2021, pp. 2–9.

13 Miller & Anor, R (on the application of) v Secretary of State for Exiting the European Union (Rev 3) [2017] UKSC 5, www.supremecourt.uk/cases/uksc-2016-0196.html.

14 R (Miller) v The Prime Minister and Cherry v Advocate General for Scotland ([2019] UKSC 41, www.supremecourt.uk/cases/uksc-2019-0193.html.

15 Bourbon-Parme (2021), pp. 235–236.

Yet far from ushering in an implosion imagined by many commentators (not least of a centre-left or left persuasion[16]), and in the face of the stark bewilderment of the business community,[17] the UK General Election (12 December 2019) bestowed upon the Conservative Party a staggering landslide majority of 80 seats, with numerous inveterate Labour seats turning Conservative for the first time ever: a trend broadly confirmed in the following local and devolved elections (6 May 2021). As the year 2020 opened—a year which was to be marked by an unprecedented worldwide pandemic (Coronavirus/COVID-19) triggering unheard-of confinements of entire populations, with the US Black Lives Matter (BLM) protests spilling over into the UK far more virulently than into other (geographically) European countries—it was clear that Brexit was going to happen, like it or not. There was no need for additional democratic legitimacy through a second, confirmatory referendum, as the GE had largely been won thanks to Prime Minister Boris Johnson's pledge to 'get Brexit done.'[18] While the Supreme Court's *Miller* judgment may have marked a 'constitutional moment'[19] in British history, presumably damaging the reputation of the Tory party and potentially dangerous to the Union with Scotland, the GE brought redemption for the government.

Meanwhile, the remaining EU Member States—the so-called 'EU-27'—were united like never before.[20] If ever the UK had intended to drive a wedge between

16 P. Trowbridge, 'Is it the end of the road for the conservative party?' *The Guardian*, Wednesday 11 September 2019 10.25 BST, www.theguardian.com/commentisfree/2019/sep/11/end-road-conservative-party-boris-johnson-tory.

17 For an outspoken business perspective, see e.g. Anderson (2019).

18 According to Bongardt and Torres (2020), p. 12, this very strategy may account for the Conservative party's success in securing the votes of parts of the Labour electorate who had never previously voted Tory. They do not see the outcome as a rejection of 'Corbynism' but rather of Corbyn's unclear stance on Brexit, including his allusions to a possible confirmatory referendum.

19 Baroncelli and Rosini (2020), p. 82.

20 For an assessment on the fifth anniversary of Brexit, citing politicians, experts and think tank personalities, see J. Rankin, 'Moving on: Why the EU is not missing Britain that much', *The Guardian*, Wednesday 23 June 2021 05.15 BST, www.theguardian.com/world/2021/jun/23/moving-on-why-the-eu-is-not-missing-britain-that-much: 'The EU is still hobbled by deep splits, whether over helping refugees or fixing flaws in the currency union. Many officials see the deepest threat emanating from Hungary and Poland, where powerful ruling parties are weakening independent courts and media, widely seen as an internal "exit" from the rule of law at the heart of Europe. [. . .] Smaller EU Member States were impressed by how the EU has stood behind Ireland in the disputes with the UK over the Irish border, which had raised concern about the peace process, he said. "Small Member States told us what is happening in Ireland shows us that when one country has an existential issue that that is an existential issue for all." Other divisions did not ricochet into Brexit talks. Instead, the process forced the 27 Member States to pay more attention to each other, said Nathalie Loiseau, an MEP, who was France's Europe minister. Loiseau added: "It created more common culture of what it means to have a single market, to have a level playing field, and this will play a role in the future in our relations with the rest of the world." [. . .] While many mourned the British departure, Brexit made it easier for the EU to make progress on long-stalled policies. Soon after the Brexit vote the EU activated common defence plans that had lain on the drawing board for years. [. . .] The coronavirus pandemic also led to an economic step once thought politically

them (e.g. when Theresa May travelled to C&E European capitals in the wake of the 2016 referendum), such hopes had not materialised.[21] That the EU responded to the pandemic by agreeing on a massive (as unparalleled as the pandemic) €750 billion 'Next Generation EU' (NGEU) recovery fund (21 July 2020), despite appreciable resistance from the so-called 'frugal four' (Austria, Denmark, Netherlands, Sweden), might not have been possible had the UK still been a Member State. Significantly, however, the UK had deliberately declined an EU offer to participate in parts of its pandemic response as a befriended third country. The early weeks of 2021 had been dominated by news coverage of negative effects of Brexit-induced border controls, including a dramatic drop in British exports of fish and shellfish, impractical paperwork deterring road haulage companies from accepting consignments as well as the confiscation of British lorry drivers' sandwiches, given that these contained fresh produce of animal origin otherwise requiring physiosanitary inspection (a measure obviously apt to drive up drivers' private costs during missions to Europe, as they could no longer rely on food purchased from UK retailers and packed in their own kitchens), all of which seemed to confirm the impression of a UK adrift. Yet the UK (like the USA and Israel) was soon to embark earlier on its COVID-19 vaccination campaign, making these countries the darlings of the media for some time, with promises of earlier de-confinement and ensuing return of economic growth, all the while the EU's vaccination campaign was beset with initial problems. Member States had indeed given a far-reaching mandate to the Commission to make bulk purchases on an impressive scale, while very soon the EU found itself embroiled in toxic talks with AstraZeneca, an Anglo-Swedish pharmaceutical company, which had flatly declared itself unable to honour its contractual obligations towards the EU, while being able simultaneously (and quite conspicuously) to deliver vaccines to the UK. Even if some commentators saw these differences in performance as indications of British

impossible: joint borrowing from financial markets to fund an €800bn recovery fund. For some, the EU recovery fund underscored the power of France and Germany, the two governments that forged the plan and then put it to the rest. [. . .] "It was always an unspoken truth that Germany and France were primus inter pares, the primary players, but I think Brexit has accentuated that," said Korteweg. "It raises questions particularly for the northern European Member StateMember States that tended to gravitate towards London on particular issues." In response the Dutch government had sought to work more closely with France. "What we see the Dutch doing is actually bandwagoning, saying OK, if you can't beat them join them." [. . .] Given the British role as leader of the EU's awkward squad, obtaining opt-outs and raising red flags, some things are easier without the UK. "There are different states of sorrow," said Riekeles. "We miss the British, but probably less than we thought."'

21 Alongside numerous commentators in the media, Dagnis Jensen and Dahl Kelstrup (2019), p. 36 concede that, 'given the fragmented nature of the EU, its unity in the Brexit negotiations is puzzling.' They explain (*Ibid.*) this apparently surprising finding with reference to 'a common material interest by all Member States in defending the integrity of the single market and the EU's system in line with the rational choice model,' alongside 'shared norms and values' ('the identity model' and, finally, discipline and procedure: 'a set of principles according to which the negotiations must be conducted and subsequently coordinated.'

competence, as well as of a more risk-prone approach favoured by UK and US leaders, the question of multinational companies' loyalties towards their country of origin could not be overlooked.[22]

The materiality and actuality of Brexit was thus evidenced by dissimilar developments and policy choices on either side of the Channel: Europe and Britain had begun to drift apart from each other since the moment at midnight when the UK has exited the EU officially and irretrievably (31 January 2020). Yet when the dust had started settling, legal scholars were already busy scrutinising the TCA in an attempt to ascertain to what extent Europe's regulatory clout would or would not be discontinued in the UK. This was the time for painstaking stock-taking: for charting and plodding a messy reality in light of the incremental legal, political and societal effects of 47 years of British EEC/EC/EU membership, rather than for jumping to apply theories and models and make generalisations of perhaps dubious heuristic value. And such is the philosophy of the present collection of essays: observation, recording and reporting. When the editor's book proposal had returned from peer review, some feedback (for which he is sincerely grateful to the anonymous colleagues who invested their time in the exercise on behalf of Routledge) showed regret for the absence of a strong theoretical underpinning. The present editor pondered the feedback and decided, nevertheless, to go along with a less theory-driven text, assuming that a wide readership could be found for a book relating the unique and often striking details of the regulatory challenges and legacies left for the sport sector to deal with.

This Introduction starts with a quotation from the late David John Moore Cornwell *alias* John Le Carré (19 October 1931–12 December 2020), who passed away a mere 12 days before the EU and the UK agreed, on Christmas eve just before 5 pm, on the TCA. A German linguist, the master of the mercilessly realistic (as opposed to Ian Fleming's James Bond) genre of the British spy novel was also a convinced European, equally opposed to the UK's participation in the US-led invasion of Iraq (2003), which may have been one of the drivers of the Leave result in the EU referendum,[23] and thus of Brexit. Just how uncomfortable this seemingly prototypical English gentleman was with Brexit became abundantly clear in his last novel, *Agent Running in the Field*, a book replete with Brexit references and related diatribe.[24] Yet far from instrumentalising John Le Carré in the name of

22 All of these developments were reported widely by mainstream media outlets. The relevant news reports can be found easily through internet searches. Adding a foonote to each of the points made in this paragraph did not seem warranted and would have burdened the chapter with numerous, very long references.

23 See The Guardian view on the Chilcot report: A country ruined, trust shattered, a reputation trashed. *The Guardian*, Wednesday 6 July 2016 20.04 BST, www.theguardian.com/commentisfree/2016/jul/06/the-guardian-view-on-the-chilcot-report-a-country-ruined-trust-shattered-a-reputation-trashed: 'The gap between the public and the private rationale fed the mistrust which has since—amplified by the banking and MPs' expenses crises—fuelled the Brexit vote.'

24 J. Le Carré, *Agent Running in the Field* (London: Viking, 2019).

anti-Brexit polemics—indeed this book is meant to be un-polemic, fact-based, emotionally detached and dry to the bone within the meaning of Tacitus: '*sine ira et studio*'[25]—the reason to implicate the novelist at this stage is the methodological assertion made in his Cold War masterpiece *Tinker Tailor Soldier Spy*: 'He left the question unasked; but not, perhaps, unanswered.'[26] For while the United Kingdom had finally exited the European Union, officially on 31 January 2020, and while a TCA was in place, in addition to the Withdrawal Agreement, much remained quite literally 'up in the air'—meaning that the exact implications can be hard to define, notwithstanding the rhetoric used by Brexiters and Remainers alike. It is not unreasonable to assume that the Brexit process may last for a decade, exacting increasingly specific sub-agreements sector by sector and adding to a generic 'Brexiternity.'[27] Ironically, this would seem to confirm (albeit in a negative and implicit way) some of the central assumptions of the important (although older) school of European integration research: the 'spill-over'[28] paradigm of the neo-functionalists. For just like European integration, through a dynamics of unintended and unforeseen consequences, has generated needs for additional integration, so may European disintegration, even if it is only partial and limited to one single Member State. Disentangling a country from 47 years of membership (1973–2020) in a political and legal union, with primacy of Union law, direct effect and a wide-ranging harmonisation of laws and technical standards, is bound be a difficult exercise, and it is hardly surprising if many still have difficulty in distinguishing the essential from the trivial, the short-term from the long-term and, crucially, the confirmed from the merely promised (or merely ventilated). In this situation, however, each and every sector of society (be it on the British or the European side) must know that Brexit is going to affect it (even if the Brexit side is likely to be more affected than the European side). The argument that more time is needed for a painstaking analysis to be made may seems intellectually honest

25 Tacitus, *Annales* I.1—a classic reference for disinterested historiographic scholarship

26 J. Le Carré, *Tinker Tailor Solider Spy* (London: Hodder & Stoughton, 1974), Ch. 28.

27 MacShane (2019).

28 For a classic formulation coined by Haas (1958), p. 297 (cf. Rosamond, 2005, p. 244): 'Sector integration [. . .] begets its own impetus toward extension to the entire economy even in the absence of specific group demands and their attendant ideologies. Thus, ECSC [European Coal and Steel Community] civil servants speaking for national governments have constantly found it necessary to "harmonise" their separate policies in order to make it possible for the integrated sectors to function, without necessarily implying any ideological commitment to the European idea.'—For an application to sport, see García García (2008), p. 58: 'The logic of spill-over dictates an almost automatic integration of economic sectors. Therefore, after the first arrival of football to the EU agenda one would expect (following the neofunctionalist argument) the development of a new European policy on sport. This has not happened, though. How can be explained, in the case of football, the changes in direction and intensity of the EU institutions in their treatment of football issues? Or how can be explained the different reactions of competition authorities in 1976 (Donà) and in 1995 (Bosman)? An agenda-setting perspective might help with these weaknesses of the neo-functionalist logic to explain the twists and turns of football's place on the EU agenda.'

and certainly cautious; yet, it cannot do away with the need for some sort of *prima facie* analysis, like the first conversation in a lawyer's chambers, the first consultation of a GP prior to referral to a specialist, or an early brainstorming session in an organisation inviting all attendees to imagine what may be next. What certainly can be provided at this stage are sectoral inventories of the accumulated effects of British EU membership: taking stock of the (frankly extraordinary) legacy, identifying the salience of the rules it has produced and making some cautious guesses about possible implications of the termination of this membership.

1.4. A focus on the regulatory capacity of the EU

Therefore, rather than making uncertain predictions on a large scale, it must be possible (and intellectually defensible) to stake stock of this legacy and say something about the likely outcomes of the rupture which is now being enacted. This is what the present book aims to do, focusing narrowly—yet importantly—on the regulatory role of the Union. For while the European Union may be rightly denounced as a paper tiger in some areas (geopolitics, defence), its regulatory might is an impressive and empirical fact. According to US-based legal scholar Anu Bradford (perhaps betraying her European roots and education?), a 'Brussels effect' is now making itself felt around the world, with standards enshrined in EU legislation becoming increasingly relevant in third countries, too, sometimes leading to emulation at various levels, be it technical standards or even legislation.[29] Despite all the ridicule which parts of the English-speaking media and politics establishment had habitually been reserving for the European integration project and its institutions, sometimes even including voices from otherwise respected academics,[30] there is strong evidence that the regulatory clout of the Union is real. The example of the General Data Protection Regulation (GDPR), widely emulated in South-East Asia,[31] may be a particularly illustrative case, as the GDPR has become known far beyond the narrow confines of the community of EU law buffs and tech geeks; Brexit has left considerable uncertainty regarding the future British data protection regime.[32] Significantly, opting for the EU approach to privacy implies rejecting the rather different US approach. Similarly, rejecting the European rights-based approach to free movement has direct consequences in the

29 Bradford (2020).

30 Gillingham (2016).

31 Greenleaf (2012, 2018, 2021). Note that despite Greenleaf's focus on Council of Europe legislation, this is to a large extent substantially the same as the corresponding EU legislation. The difference is one of enforcement, not of requirements as such, which is why Bygrave (2021) has speculated about a 'Strasbourg effect' comparable to Bradford's 'Brussels effect.' Niebel (2021) anticipates the GDPR to achieve important global influence, which Pauletto (2021) expects to have wider ramifications regarding innovation in various markets, as well as for the global political economy.

32 Vanberg and Maunick (2018).

sport sector, which have not been addressed comprehensively in the generic Brexit negotiations. Concerns of stakeholders relying on easy recruitment in Europe were voiced early on but do not appear to have had any particular influence upon the negotiation outcome.[33] The House of Lords invested time and work into two days of public hearings which revealed, *inter alia*, that access to semi-skilled or unskilled workers may be as crucial to British success in sports, including by hosting international events, as is the ability to recruit high-profile players and athletes with star status; again, these insights gained by legislators do not appear to have had any considerable influence.[34]

The relevance of EU legislation can be gauged from the determination of many Brexiters to escape it, while according to some lawyers, EU law is also expected to retain some of its relevance in the UK for the foreseeable future.[35] No extrapolation and no interpretation of double-speak are needed where Brexiters themselves have made it abundantly clear that escaping the regulatory reach of the Union was a major goal worth fighting—and ultimately even suffering[36]—to achieve. If Union law is 'not merely the Law of the Land but the "Higher Law" of the Land,' within a 'constitutional architecture' which 'may, with very few exceptions, be found only in the internal constitutional order of federal states,'[37] then sincere opponents of the norms enshrined in Union law (e.g. aimed at protecting data subjects, animals, the environment or workers), who saw a relaxed regulatory regime as a necessary prerequisite to economic growth, were objectively right in wishing to escape the reach of EU law, irrespective of whether or not one adheres to the values represented in such EU norms opposed by Brexiters. If British reticence about British EC/EU membership was 'always about control,'[38] then the EU's regulatory role is worthwhile focusing on in any sectoral survey of Brexit and its possible implications. In the case of sport, as we shall learn in this book, the relevance of the regulatory impact (as compared with the economic, cultural or other forms of impact) of EU membership and its termination may even be above average, as the European Union appears to have had an exceptional influence on the shaping

33 Kornbeck (2016, 2018).

34 Kornbeck (2020).

35 Forrester (2018).

36 On the question of whether Brexit is worth a great amount of stressful disruption caused to the workforce, Imad A. Moosa has examined the 'econometrics of Brexit,' asking if this is a case of 'science or a means of expressing confirmation bias?' (Moosa, 2020, p. 58). Admitting that 'common sense and practical experience tell us that the UK will be worse off following Brexit,' and engaging critically with Patrick Minford and Economists for Brexit (*Ibid.*, p. 73) while contending that econometrics may be unable to 'explain what happens in the real world' (76), Moosa nevertheless—perhaps surprisingly (?)—concludes that all the expected 'adverse consequences for the British economy' may nevertheless be 'a price worth paying for sovereignty and independence' (*Ibid.*, p. 76).

37 Weiler (1991), p. 2415.

38 Weinberg (2020), p. 1.

of sports law.[39] Conversely, the single most paradigmatic piece of sport-related case law, *Bosman*, has made its effects felt outside the narrow confines of the sport sector.[40] That the legal chapter in a sports management handbook should include a disproportionate amount of text on the laws of Anglo-Saxon countries compared with other countries (3/4 page for the USA, Canada and Australia each compared with 5 lines on China), may seem disproportionate to some; yet the same book treated the EU ahead of everyone else, preceding even the World Anti-Doping Agency (WADA) and the Court for Arbitration in Sport (CAS).[41] Similarly, it is interesting to note the frequent references made to EU law in a rather succinct, multi-jurisdictional introduction to 'global sports law' by an academic US lawyer.[42] Accordingly, the present book too will take the EU's regulatory role and its relevance to the sport sector rather seriously, and in so doing, will eschew an especial treatment of economic, social, geographic and related aspects, deserving as they may otherwise be. There is a compellingly strong case for a survey of this kind, since in the sport sector, the EU has revealed with abundant clarity its nature of a legal community: integration through law.[43]

This very regulatory capacity of the future Community seems to have been underestimated by the UK even before the EEC started operating. Former US National Security Advisor Zbigniew Brzeziński (1928–2017) cites the memoirs[44] of Sir Roy Denman (1924–2006), one of the British negotiators from 1972–1973 (and a declared Europhile[45]), for having described the British nonchalance towards a European integration project which was deemed unable to take off.[46] A decade later, Prime Minister Margaret Thatcher despatched a British businessman to the Commission. The memoirs of the British co-architect (with Jacques Delors) of the Single Market, Lord Cockfield,[47] testify to this incongruity between objectives and means, between 'the British ingenuity behind the EU single market'[48] and a certain intuitive reserve. He succeeded because he got along well with the Europeans and understood 'that the unification of Europe was more than an economic affair.' Yet

39 See Boyes (2012), Weatherill (2010, 2016, 2017, 2018).
40 Derlén and Lindholm (2016).
41 Shilbury and Ferkins (2020).
42 Ross (2021).
43 See Weiler (1991).
44 Denman (1996).
45 See Bates (2006).
46 Brzeziński (1997), pp. 41–42: '[. . .] as early as the 1955 conference in Messina, which previewed the formation of a European Union, the official spokesman for Britain flatly asserted to the assembled would-be architects of Europe: "The future treaty which you are discussing has no chance of being agreed; if it was agreed, it would have no chance of being applied. And if it was applied, it would be totally unacceptable to Britain . . . au revoir et bonne chance." More than forty years later, the above dictum remains essentially the definition of the basic British attitude toward the construction of a genuinely united Europe.'
47 Cockfield (1994).
48 Anderson (2019).

as helpful as these qualities were in reaching the goals which Thatcher had set for Cockfield, as unwanted were they apparently when they manifested themselves too visibly. This apparent rule came to bear in the case of a 'powerful speech' by Cockfield[49] held in preparation of the pivotal Milan European Council (28–29 June 1985) where Cockfield's White Paper[50] outlining the seven-year (1985–92) programme for the completion of the Single Market was going to be adopted by the Heads of States and Government. Thatcher finally decided not to propose Cockfield for a second mandate: a decision sugar-coated in a personal note to Cockfield, praising his indisputable expertise.[51] She accused him of neglecting issues pertaining to national sovereignty and of 'going native.'[52] Removing him must have been easy, Cockfield being essentially apolitical and unelected, yet his business credentials were solid.[53]

If Thatcher (and the UK) preferred free trade without enforceable Community law underpinning it,[54] Cockfield's White Paper relied unashamedly on the Community method, using Community law with direct effect and primacy over national law to achieve his political aims, even if the Prime Minister liked to think of the Single European Act (SEA) was as 'Thatcherism on a European scale.'[55] The Single

49 FCO preparation for Milan (1985), www.margaretthatcher.org/document/204633

50 Completing the Internal Market: White Paper from the Commission to the European Council (Milan, 28–29 June 1985). COM(85) 350. 14 June 1985.

51 1988 Jul 22 Fr Archive (Thatcher MSS) Personal and party papers, Cambridge Europe: MT to Lord Cockfield (retiring as EC Commission Vice President) [released Jul 2018]. www.margaretthatcher.org/document/209870: 'Dear Arthur [. . .] It will be a sad day when you leave the Commission but I know that you only intended to serve for one term. The Commission's loss will be our gain in that we shall be able to hear once again your wise advice and powerful speeches in the House of Lords.'

52 Thatcher (1993), p. 547; citing Alexandre-Collier (2015), sec. 8: 'Unfortunately [. . .] he tended to disregard the larger questions of politics—constitutional sovereignty, national sentiment and the promptings of liberty. He was the prisoner as well as the master of his subject. It was all too easy for him, therefore, to go native and to move from deregulating the market to reregulating it under the rubric of harmonisation.'

53 Lord (2000), p. 151: 'Arthur (Lord) Cockfield was one of the unlikeliest political entrepreneurs of recent times. Described in Hugo Young's biography of Margaret Thatcher as "eccentric, apolitical and unelected" (Young, 1989, p. 301), he was more of a policy enthusiast than a politician.' Note that Young's book is recommended by Barnier (2021), pp. 322–323 as a source for understanding British mentality and Brexit.

54 According to former British Ambassador to Washington, DC, with a solid previous record of EU neogotiations, 'just as our European partners consistently misread British politics,' so has there been, in the UK, 'a fundamental misreading of the European project, which has never been about markets and free trade,' see Darroch (2020), p. 314. Darroch's assessment may be simplistic, as the European project has very much been about markets and trade, albeit of a different sort than that imagined by many Anglo-Saxons, rather using economic developments as deliberate tools to achieve political means than seeing them as ends in themselves. According to Manners (2002), the EU uses the size and attractiveness of its market to wield 'normative power,' while in the assessment of Geeraert and Drieskens (2017), this 'Normative Market Europe' has extended its normative reach to the sport sector, among many others.

55 Young (1998), p. 333; citing Alexandre-Collier (2015), sec. 8.

Market could not have been achieved without binding legislation and specific governance structures based on majority voting. That Thatcher achieved an objectively good result for the UK at the 1985 (December) Luxembourg summit,[56] owed much to discrepancies between the French, German and British negotiating strategies and wishes,[57] and while 'the UK position was heavily influenced by British frustration over the mismatch between budgetary contributions and CAP payments,'[58] the Community method was allowed to prevail in the creation of the Single Market. 'The internal regulatory capacity of the EU has only continued to grow since.'[59] The legal and technical focus of the Community was already then part and parcel of its DNA, and indeed a natural choice for an organisation that was deemed to work without all the bells and whistles of a full-fledged state: the quest for 'regulatory capacity' seems to have been a natural choice and would serve to explain why such an implausibly small bureaucracy came naturally to prefer legal over other instruments.[60] And yet, even David Cameron could deny the nature of the rules enshrined in Union law, e.g. when insisting that Europeans working in the UK were 'immigrants' rather than 'citizens.'[61] In so doing, he not only went against the advice of many of his own mandarins (as he gladly admits himself), but also denies the applicability of Union law at that time, as well as the fact that free movement of workers was instituted as early as 1957 by the EEC Treaty. (The 1952 ECSC Treaty had only guaranteed that of manufactured steel products.)

Since the Single European Act (SEA), the UK had been embracing market liberalisation through the Single Market while they were rejecting other European

56 Moravcsik (1991), p. 44.
57 *Ibid.*, p. 28.
58 *Ibid.*, pp. 35–36.
59 Bradford (2020), p. 32.
60 *Ibid.*, p. 32.
61 See Cameron (2020), p. 640: 'Much of this was theological. Belgium's Charles Michel opposed everything we were doing' when the UK tried, up to 2016, renegotiating the free movement of workers. 'For him, ever-closer Union was exactly what the EU was about,' while between the UK and its EU partners, Cameron detected what he describes as 'a fundamental misunderstanding' over 'immigration.' Merkel could not see why the UK should have an issue as long as unemployment was low and the country needed workers. She 'and others just didn't see free movement as immigration. As far as they were concerned, if you're from inside the EU you're a worker. If you're from outside the EU, you're a migrant. Indeed, we were constantly told by the central and eastern Europeans that we were not allowed to call them "EU migrants." They were "EU citizens."' Cameron goes on the praise his country's 'multiracial democracy' where 'race, ethnicity, religion and nationality figure less and less,' where some might see EU free movement objectionable 'precisely because it favoured (mainly white) EU migrants over (mainly black and Asian) non-EU migrants.' That Cameron should have published his book in the very year when the BLM protests spilled over so virulently from the US to the UK, with calls for 'decolonisation' of curricula, museums and public monuments does not make him emerge as a particularly prescient statesman, though it does provide an excellent illustration of (some of) the thinking behind the UK's position, and the process which led to the 2016 referendum.

leaders' wishes for a more political union. In addition, the initial ambitions of the integration project, failed to acknowledge 'that markets need laws and government to function,' and that the Single Market 'necessarily led to the deepening of European law to allow it to operate, and this has consolidated the primacy of EU law over national law.'[62] There may also be economic arguments why 'this policy-mix was risky,' including the work of Harvard economist Dani Rodrik, according to whom globalisation and trade liberalisation necessarily leave a minority within highly developed economies less well off, triggering an increased need for domestic compensation.[63] Rodrik's work, in turn, was inspired by that of Yale political scientist David Cameron [sic] which, as early as the 1970s (and no doubt inspired by the first oil shock), found that 'the single most important cause for higher public spending was the exposure of an economy to international trade.'[64]Yet this does not suffice to explain why the same leaders would also insist on denying the quasi-statehood of the Community/Union,[65] in spite of the direct effect and primacy of Community/Union law—and of British resistance to reach of the very same legal order. The UK's successful opt-out from the Social Chapter of the SEA in the Maastricht Treaty may have been an 'almost Pyrrhic victory'[66] through which the UK seemed to gain, while actually relegating itself to a role on the periphery of EU decision-making. Eventually, this 'malign neglect' may have accentuated the 'hard choices that had to be taken anyway.'[67] Because the UK had decided to stay outside the Economic and Monetary Union (EMU) (later the Eurozone), social policy and Schengen, the Single Market came to be perceived as the 'bedrock'[68] of British EU membership; yet, by deciding to leave the EU, the UK jeopardised this very aspect of its membership. Though the UK had initially shown enthusiasm for the Single Market, it became increasingly 'uneasy with its implications' on account of its 'necessarily regulatory nature' including 'sovereignty costs' and the 'EU governance set-up to make it function.'[69] A growing consensus among Britain's EU partners regarding the desirability of deeper integration in an increasing number of policy areas meant that British reticence made the objectives of the EU increasingly irreconcilable with British preferences and interests. The UK thus 'came to dislike' the 'regulatory nature and functions' of the single market, though they were 'critical

62 Sowels (2019), p. 5, sec. 15.
63 *Ibid.*, p. 11, sec. 33, citing Rodrik (2012), p. 57.
64 *Ibid.*, p. 11, sec. 34, citing Cameron (1978).
65 See Weiler (1991), p. 2413 on the direct effect of Community/Union law: 'direct effect operates not only in creating enforceable legal obligations between the Member States and individuals, but also among individuals inter se. Critically, being part of the law of the land means that Community norms may be invoked by individuals before their state courts, which must provide adequate legal remedies for the E.C. norms *just as if they were enacted by the state legislature.*' [emphasis added, J.K.]
66 Di Quirico (2020), p. 47.
67 *Ibid.*, p. 38.
68 Bongardt (2020), p. 152.
69 *Ibid.*, p. 152.

to its functioning,' while the interests of the City (the London-based financial industry) showed themselves incompatible with the political aims of the Eurozone.[70] The City also resented the EU's ambition to extend its regulatory reach to the financial sector.[71] Thus, while the outcome of the 2016 referendum did not conceptually preclude an arrangement which would have permitted the UK to continue enjoying 'privileged access' to the single market, such access would inevitably imply a 'sovereignty cost'[72] such as renouncing the (by Brexiters much advertised) prospect of setting an autonomous UK customs tariff and developing an international trade policy distinguishable from (and less regulation-heavy than) that of the EU.[73] For the City, however, two distinct 'vital interests' must be considered. Whereas a 'relaxed regulatory environment' may be 'what really counts for the prosperity of the City' and something which 'of course can be guaranteed by a friendly government post-Brexit,' this may be a 'necessary but not sufficient condition for the City to maintain its hegemony both domestically and internationally.' The other 'vital condition' is market access, in Europe and worldwide, and such access to the EU's (still important) single market can be denied by the EU if the 'relaxed regulatory environment' appears to undercut the EU.[74]

1.5. Plan of this book

That the inconsistencies implied in choosing an approach like that of Thatcher and Major are bound to depend largely—though not exclusively—on regulatory aspects of the policies enacted is clear from a theoretical and conceptual perspective. How this principle has manifested itself in practice will be seen from the chapters of this book, which are organised in the following sections:

- Part One aims to prepare the ground conceptually prior to the substantive chapters. Apart from the present Introduction (Chapter 1), it includes a discussion of how established and accepted theories of European integration may be used to frame discussions like those unfolding in this book (Chapter 2 by *Alexander Brand, Arnout Geeraert and Arne Niemann*). If we accept the logic of trade-offs between market access and sovereignty, then we nevertheless need

70 *Ibid.*, p. 154.

71 On account of his previous tenure as European Commissioner for Internal Market (2010–14), responsible *inter alia* for regulating the banking sector, the news of Michel Barnier's appointment to the post of EU chief Brexit negotiator triggered some rather negative reactions in the UK. For a summary of some of these, see T. Palmeri & P. Briançon, 'How to annoy a brit—put a Frenchman in charge of Brexit,' *Politico*, July 27, 2016 11:56 am, www.politico.eu/article/michel-barnier-named-as-junckers-brexit-chief-europe-negotiations-consquences-future/

72 Bongardt (2020), p. 154.

73 *Ibid.*, p. 155.

74 Talani (2020), p. 209.

to understand the processes through which the UK negotiated its relationship with the EU at different stages;[75]

- The chapters included in Part Two are dedicated to specific categories of rules laid down in Union law. Four key areas of regulation are presented: free movement (Chapter 3 by *Stefaan Van den Bogaert*), state aid (Chapter 4 by *Andrea Cattaneo*), employment law (Chapter 5, by *Leanne O'Leary*) as well as anti-discrimination in relation to athletes' sex and gender rights (Chapter 6 by *Seema Patel*). These chapters also illustrate the role of EU law in bestowing unnegotiable rights upon individual citizens: a point not wasted upon the UK Supreme Court who, in *Miller*, accorded special importance to this function of the EU legal order in balancing the prerogatives of the legislature against those of the executive.[76]
- Part Three is dedicated to the perspective and experiences of stakeholders, starting with that of athletes' trade unions involved in European social dialogue with their employers (Chapter 7 by *Walter S. Palmer*). Additional complementary perspectives are provided in chapters on football (Chapter 8 by *Stephen Weatherill*) and cricket (Chapter 9 by *Richard Parrish*). While the extension of social dialogue to sports occupations confirms that the single market is the EU's 'vehicle' for achieving 'quality growth' in the sense of 'beyond growth for growth's sake,'[77] the case studies on football and cricket reveal that the interests of different sports may vary considerably, and that the sportspeople in question may not all depend upon the protections guaranteed by EU law (if they are third country nationals anyway).
- While the English Channel may only be a negligible 21 miles (34 kilometres) wide in the Strait of Dover, geography nevertheless remains an unescapable aspect of all things Brexit-related, and geography is the topic of Part Four. After an exploration of the difficulties involved in transporting racehorses in and out of Northern Ireland (Chapter 10 by *Laura Donnellan*), the perspective and challenges of Scotland are presented (Chapter 11 by *Grant Jarvie*). Then follow the Swiss experience as a country which never joined the European Union (Chapter 12 by *Emmanuel Bayle and Zahid Mustafi*) as well as a discussion of the EU's ability to taken on an active and visible global role in the politics and policies of sport (Chapter 13 by *Borja García and Henk Erik Meier*). 'How close the UK will stay to the single market remains to be seen,' while for the EU, 'proximity with the single market is invariably conditioned by regulatory alignment.'[78]
- Part Five, finally, includes two conclusions: first an exhibition of assumptions about the continued relevance of EU law in the UK in the field of sport (Chapter 14 by *Simon Boyes*) and second, the editor's own Conclusion (Chapter 15).

75 Bongardt and Torres (2020), pp. 30–31.
76 Baroncelli and Rosini (2020), p. 67.
77 Bongardt (2020), p. 148.
78 Bongardt et al. (2020), p. 209.

This choice of contributions will inform readers about European integration and disintegration; convergence and divergence between (present and past) EU Member States; sport policy, sport politics and sports law; professional sport, elite sport, competitive sport; amateur sport, recreational sport and community sport; as well as intra-UK diversity and devolution. Apart from confirming some familiar tropes regarding the (not so surprising) impact of a British EC/EU membership spanning from the first oil crisis to the COVID-19 pandemic, as a de facto (albeit sometimes unnoticed) transformation of the UK,[79] the chapters can also be expected to renew interest in observing sport-relevant developments at EU level, since neglecting them can sometimes cost dearly, as it did to some in the case of the 1995 *Bosman* ruling.[80] Finally—and to some readers possibly surprisingly—the ensuing chapters might confirm the tacit admission, by Brexiters, of a relevance of the Union going far beyond its paper tiger image often conveyed in Brexit debates, especially by Brexiters. On some rare occasions such admissions have been explicit and candid, as when Professor Patrick Minford (of the Economists for Brexit network) provided evidence to House of Commons,[81] four years prior to the referendum, invoking with jolly nonchalance, to the obvious consternation of some attending MPs, the option of 'running down' the British car industry, 'just as in the same way we ran down the coal and steel industries.'[82] While Minford did not mince his words (pun unintended) and also defended his ideas in academic fora,[83] other Brexiters have adopted a more cautious communication style, presumably in recognition of the fact that increased insecurity may not have been the preferred outcome for most ordinary Leave voters. Yet their preference for escaping EU regulation pays involuntary respect to the relevance of the Union, its institutions and—above all—its character as a legal community.

79 K. Butler, 'Football, flights and food: How the EU reshaped Britain', *The Guardian*, Friday 1 January 2021 12.30 GMT, www.theguardian.com/politics/2021/jan/01/football-flights-and-food-how-the-eu-reshaped-britain.

80 Tokarski (1998).

81 House of Commons, Session 2012–13. Corrected Transcript of Oral Evidence. To be published as HC 115-iii. House of Commons oral evidence taken before the Foreign Affairs Committee: The Future of the European Union: UK Government Policy. Tuesday 11 September 2012. Professor Patrick Minford CBE. Evidence heard in Public. Questions 107–144, https://publications.parliament.uk/pa/cm201213/cmselect/cmfaff/c115-iii/c11501.htm.

82 *Ibid.*: Q140 Rory Stewart [MP]: 'I am still trying to understand the political implications of this talk of transitional arrangements. Is it not conceivable that what you are really talking about is the collapse of the entire UK car industry and that when we leave the European customs union and go directly into competition with Asian car manufacturers, this transitional arrangement is just a polite way of describing the wiping out of the manufacturing industry? How will that be explained to a public and a political class that are increasingly proud of our development in this kind of manufacturing industry in Britain?' Professor Minford: 'It is perfectly true that if you remove protection of the sort that has been given particularly to the car industry and other manufacturing industries inside the protective wall, you will have a change in the situation facing that industry, and you are going to have to run it down. It will be in your interests to do it, just as in the same way we ran down the coal and steel industries.'

83 Minford (2019).

References

Alexandre-Collier, A. (2015) Euroscepticism under Margaret thatcher and David Cameron: From theory to practice. *Observatoire de la société britannique*, 17, 115–133. https://journals.openedition.org/osb/1778.

Anderson, I. (2019) *F**K Business: The Business of Brexit*. London: Biteback Publishing.

Barnier, M. (2021) *La Grande Illusion. Journal secret du Brexit (2016–2020)*. Paris: Gallimard.

Baroncelli, S. & Rosini, M. (2020) Brexit, sovereignty and devolution: The view of constitutional law. In: Bongardt, A.; Talani, L.S. & Torres, F. (eds) *The Politics and Economics of Brexit*. Cheltenham: Edward Elgar, pp. 56–87.

Bates, S. (2006) Obituary: Sir Roy Denman. *The Guardian*, Friday 21 April 2006 00.01 BST. www.theguardian.com/news/2006/apr/21/guardianobituaries.eu.

Bongardt, A. (2020) UK dithering over Brexit on the European single market and its regulatory model. In: Bongardt, A.; Talani, L.S. & Torres, F. (eds) *The Politics and Economics of Brexit*. Cheltenham: Edward Elgar, pp. 138–161.

Bongardt, A.; Talani, L.S. & Torres, F. (2020) Brexit: What have we learnt? In: Bongardt, A.; Talani, L.S. & Torres, F. (eds) *The Politics and Economics of Brexit*. Cheltenham: Edward Elgar, pp. 204–210.

Bongardt, A. & Torres, F. (2020) Brexit as a question of political rationality: Hard choices for the UK, lessons for EU sustainability. In: Bongardt, A.; Talani, L.S. & Torres, F. (eds) *The Politics and Economics of Brexit*. Cheltenham: Edward Elgar, pp. 11–37.

Bourbon-Parme, T. de (2021) *Boris Johnson. Un Européen contrarié*. Paris: François Bourin.

Boyes, S. (2012) Sports law: Its history and growth and the development of key sources. *Legal Information Management*, 12:2, 86–91.

Bradford, A. (2020) *The Brussels Effect: How the European Union Rules the World*. Oxford: Oxford University Press.

Brzeziński, Z. (1997) *The Grand Chessboard: American Primacy and Its Geostrategic Imperatives*. New York: Basic Books.

Bygrave, L.A. (2021) The 'Strasbourg effect' on data protection in light of the 'Brussels effect': Logic, mechanics and prospects. *Computer Law & Security Review*, 40, 105460.

Cameron, D.R. (1978) The expansion of the public economy: A comparative analysis. *American Political Science Review*, 72, 1243–1261.

Cameron, D.R. (2020) *For the Record*. London: William Collins.

Cockfield, L. (1994) *The European Union: Creating the Single Market*. Chichester: Wiley Chancery Law.

Dagnis Jensen, M. & Dahl Kelstrup, J. (2019) United, house divided: Explaining the EU's unity in the Brexit negotiations. *Journal of Common Market Studies*, 57:S1, 28–39.

Darroch, K. (2020) *Collateral Damage: Britain, America and Europe in the Age of Trump*. London: William Collins.

Dashwood, A. (2010) 40 Years an EU lawyer—apologia Pro Vita Sua. Or: EU Law—A 40-year journey and still motoring. *Cambridge Yearbook of European Legal Studies*, 13, 47–64.

Denman, R. (1996) *Missed Chances*. London: Cassell.

Derlén, M. & Lindholm, J. (2016) Bosman: A legacy beyond sports. In: Duval, A. & Van Rompuy, B. (Hrsg) *The Legacy of Bosman. Revisiting the Relationship Between EU Law and Sport*. Den Haag: Asser Press & Heidelberg: Springer, pp. 31–49.

Di Quirico, R. (2020) The road to Brexit: European integration, the UK ad the failure of the 'malign neglect' strategy toward the EU. In: Bongardt, A.; Talani, L.S. & Torres, F. (eds) *The Politics and Economics of Brexit*. Cheltenham: Edward Elgar, pp. 38–55.

Forrester, I. (2018) European union law in the UK after Brexit. *Judicial Review*, 23:1, 45–64.

García García, B. (2008) *The European Union and the Governance of Football: A Game of Levels and Agendas*. Doctoral thesis, Loughborough University. http://hdl.handle.net/2134/5609.

Geeraert, A. & Drieskens, E. (2017) Normative market Europe: The EU as a force for good in international sports governance? *Journal of European Integration*, 39:1, 79–94.

Gillingham, J.R. (2016) *The EU: An Obituary*. London: Verso.

Greenleaf, G. (2012) The influence of European data privacy standards outside Europe: Implications for globalization of Convention 108. *International Data Privacy Law*, 2:2, 68–92.

Greenleaf, G. (2018) 2017–2018 Further update to graham Greenleaf's Asian data privacy laws—trade and human rights perspectives, 15 November. https://ssrn.com/abstract=3285086.

Greenleaf, G. (2021) How far can convention 108+ 'globalise'? Prospects for Asian accessions. *Computer Law & Security Review*, 40:105414, 1–12.

Greer, S.L. (2008) Choosing paths in European Union health services policy: A political analysis of a critical juncture. *Journal of European Social Policy*, 18:3, 219–231.

Haas, E.B. (1958) *The Uniting of Europe*. Stanford: Stanford University Press.

Kornbeck, J. (2016) "Brexit" et sport: un premier bilan. *Lettre de l'Officiel Juridique du Sport*, 108, 1–3.

Kornbeck, J. (2018) "Brexit" et Sport: deux ans plus tard. *Lettre de l'Officiel Juridique du Sport*, 131, 6–7.

Kornbeck, J. (2020) "Brexit", sport et permis de travail: entre vedettes et main d'œuvre faiblement qualifiée. *Lettre de l'Officiel Juridique du Sport*, 148, 6–8.

Lauritzen, P. (2008) *Eggs in a Pan. Youth work: Speeches, Writings and Reflections*. Strasbourg: Council of Europe Publishing.

Lord, C. (2000) Lord Cockfield: A European commissioner as a political entrepreneur. In: Theakston, K. (ed) *Bureaucrats and Leadership*. Houndsmills: Palgrave Macmillan, pp. 151–170.

Manners, I. (2002) Normative power Europe: A contradiction in terms? *Journal of Common Market Studies*, 40:2, 235–258.

MacShane, D. (2019) *Brexiternity: The Uncertain Fate of Britain*. London: IB Tauris.

Minford, P. (2019) Understanding the UK negotiating position on Brexit. In: Kainer, F. & Repasi, R. (eds) *Trade Relations after Brexit*. Baden-Baden & Oxford: Nomos & Hart, pp. 43–58.

Moosa, I.M. (2020) The econometrics of Brexit: Science or a means of expressing confirmation bias? In: Weinberg, A.; Antoniou, A.S. & Cooper, C.L. (eds) *Brexit in the Workplace: A Psychology of Survival?* Cheltenham: Edward Elgar, pp. 58–79.

Moravcsik, A. (1991) Negotiating the single European act: National interests and conventional statecraft in the European community. *International Organization*, 45:1, 19–56.

Niebel, C. (2021) The impact of the general data protection regulation on innovation and the global political economy. *Computer Law & Security Review*, 40, 105523.

Pauletto, C. (2021) Options towards a global standard for the protection of individuals with regard to the processing of personal data. *Computer Law & Security Review*, 40, 105433.

Richardson, J. & Rittberger, B. (2020) Brexit: Simply an omnishambles or a major policy fiasco? *Journal of European Public Policy*, 27:5, 649–665.

Rodrik, D. (2012 [2011]) *The Globalization Paradox: Democracy and the Future of the World Economy*. New York: W.W. Norton.

Rosamond, B. (2005) The uniting of Europe and the foundation of EU studies: Revisiting the neofunctionalism of Ernst B. Haas. *Journal of European Public Policy*, 12:2, 237–254.

Ross, S.F. (2021) *Advanced Introduction to Global Sports Law*. Cheltenham: Edward Elgar.

Shilbury, D. & Ferkins, L. (eds) (2020) *Routledge Handbook of Sports Governance*. London: Routledge.

Sowels, N. (2019) From the 'thatcherisation of Europe' to Brexit. *Revue Française de Civilisation Britannique*, XXIV-4, online since 25 November 2019, connection on 10 December 2020. http://journals.openedition.org/rfcb/4819.

Talani, L.S. (2020) Brexit and the future of the City of London: Between deregulation and innovation. In: Bongardt, A.; Talani, L.S. & Torres, F. (eds) *The Politics and Economics of Brexit*. Cheltenham: Edward Elgar, pp. 162–180.

Thatcher, M. (1993) *The Downing Street Years*. London: Harper Collins.

Tokarski, W. (ed) (1998) *EU-Recht und Sport*. Aachen: Meyer & Meyer.

Vanberg, A.D. & Maunick, M. (2018) Data protection in the UK post-Brexit: The only certainty is uncertainty. *International Review of Law, Computers & Technology*, 32:1, 190–206.

Wallace, H. (2012) The UK: 40 years of EU membership. *Journal of Contemporary European Research*, 8:4, 531–546.

Weatherill, S. (2010) Bosman changed everything: The rise of EC sports law, the past and future of EU law. In: Poiares Maduro, M.P. & Azoulai, L. (eds) *The Classics of EU Law Revisited on the 50th Anniversary of the Rome Treaty 2010*. Oxford & Portland, OR: Hart Publishing, pp. 480–487.

Weatherill, S. (2016) The lex Sportiva and EU law: The academic lawyer's path before and after Bosman. In: Duval, A. & Van Rompuy, B. (eds) *The Legacy of Bosman: Revisiting the Relationship between EU Law and Sport*. Den Haag: T.M.C. Asser Press & Heidelberg: Springer, pp. 233–250.

Weatherill, S. (2017) *Principles and Practice in EU Sports Law*. Oxford: Oxford University Press.

Weatherill, S. (2018) Sources and origins of EU sports law. In: Anderson, J.; Parrish, R. & García García, B. (eds) *Research Handbook on EU Sports Law and Policy*. Cheltenham: Edward Elgar, pp. 6–23.

Weiler, J.H.H. (1991) The transformation of Europe. *Yale Law Journal*, 100:8, 2403–2483.

Weinberg, A. (2020) A psychology of Brexit. In: Weinberg, A.; Antoniou, A.S. & Cooper, C.L. (eds) *Brexit in the Workplace: A Psychology of Survival?* Cheltenham: Edward Elgar, pp. 1–16.

Wilding, P. (2018) Brexit's my fault: How the word I invented could be an epitaph for the nation's decline. *Sky News*, Thursday 13 December 2018 09:03, UK. https://news.sky.com/story/brexits-my-fault-how-the-word-i-invented-could-be-an-epitaph-for-the-nations-decline-11576816.

Young, H. (1998) *This Blessed Plot. Britain and Europe from Churchill to Blair*. London: Palgrave Macmillan.

Chapter 2

European (dis-)integration theories, Brexit and sport

A double disconnect and tentative remedies

Alexander Brand, Arnout Geeraert and Arne Niemann[1]

2.1. Introduction

What is the contribution of European Integration Theories (EIT)—grand theories and mid-range explanatory approaches—to predicting the impact of Brexit on EU sport policy? Some ideas derived from the main schools of thought in European integration may already frame the debate of Brexit's implications for sport and sport regulation such as Jacob Kornbeck's thoughts on 'spill-over' (owing its popularity to neofunctionalism) and potential future 'spill-back' in the Introduction to this volume. But a more systematic examination of EIT's capacity to enhance our understanding of the post-Brexit shape of sport regulation and governance in Europe, as well as *through* European-level institutions, is still a desideratum.

It is in this sense that we start our foray into EIT, Brexit and sport from the notion of a *double disconnect*. As disintegration presents a rather novel concern for most EITs—just think of the famous slogan of an 'ever closer union'[2]—the non-existence of many such theorised links should not come as a huge surprise. True, the main paradigmatic schools of (European and regional) integration, namely neofunctionalism, intergovernmentalism and postfunctionalism have recently started to conceptualise dynamics of disintegration in the wake of Brexit (and other recent crises).[3] Moreover, neofunctionalism and intergovernmentalism in particular have also been used, undoubtedly, to explain progressive integration dynamics in the field of sport in a separate track of the debate. Yet all in all, these grand theories have not yet been marshalled to gauge what Brexit implies *in the field of sport* (policy and regulation). We observe a first disconnect here, because of this missing link between grand theories engaging Brexit and the same schools of thought extending such reflection to the field of sport governance and regulation.

1 We want to thank Tim-Benjamin Heinrichs for his research assistance.

2 Dinan (1994).

3 Most pronounced in: Schmitter and Lefkofridi (2016), Czech and Krakowiak-Drzewiecka (2019), Hooghe and Marks (2019), Niemann et al. (2020).

DOI: 10.4324/9781003162803-3

On the other hand, various mid-range approaches and concepts (e.g. advocacy coalitions, the principal-agent framework and Europeanisation) were applied successfully to assess and explain integration impulses in the field of (European) sport policy. Such explanatory tools below the level of grand theories did arguably enjoy more prominence in the theory-oriented discussion and analysis of sport regulation and governance throughout Europe. However, scholars making use of these concepts have not yet begun to adjust them to the realities of a European Union *minus* the UK. This we see as a second disconnect: the so far absent discussion of how much of a 'reality shock' Brexit actually presents to the by now routinely applied concepts and mid-range approaches of Europeanisation, EU actorness and the like *in the realm of sport policy*, and whether any adaptation to the perspectives taken is warranted at all.[4]

In what follows, we will briefly sketch the mentioned debates and main literatures. We start by introducing the main grand theories of European integration, in particular in their capacity to theorise (dis-)integration in general, and the likely implications of Brexit on European integration more specifically. In a second step, we explore how both strands of the EIT debate—grand theories and mid-range approaches/concepts—have been deployed to illuminate dynamics in the fields of sport policy, regulation and governance so far. This is guided by an attempt to ask whether one can infer anything substantial about the post-Brexit future in these domains from the existing EIT-inspired literature. Finally, in the remainder of the chapter, we attempt to offer some tentative suggestions on this basis on how to go forward in theorising the likely implications of the specific disintegration in the form of Brexit on sport regulation and sport policy in Europe.

2.2. Main theory schools and the hard case of (dis-)integration

2.2.1. *What do the grand theories say?*

Being perhaps the most long-standing integration theory, *neofunctionalism* assumes that: (1) integration is a process, which evolves over time and takes on its own dynamic; (2) *regional* integration is characterised by multiple, diverse and changing actors who also build transnational coalitions[5]; (3) decisions are taken by rational actors, who nevertheless have the capacity to learn from their experiences in co-operative decision-making[6]; (4) decision-making tends to be incremental, where seemingly marginal adjustments are often driven by the unintended consequences

4 This is not to claim that a discussion of Brexit's likely impact on sport, most notably on British football, has not yet started. To the contrary, cf. Perry and Steenson (2019). However, such analyses and forecasts have not proposed to marshal EIT in an effort to shed light on coming developments.

5 Haas (1964), pp. 68 ff.

6 Haas (1958), p. 291.

of previous decisions; (5) the very integration process is dominated by elites. Early neofunctionalists attached little significance to the role of public opinion. Instead, they assumed a 'permissive consensus' in favour of European integration,[7] but later theorising suggested that politicisation may lead to stagnation or 'spill-back.'[8] The key neofunctionalist conception of change is encapsulated in the notion of 'spill-over,' of which three types are generally distinguished.[9]

Functional spill-over pressures come about when an original objective can be achieved only by taking further integrative actions due to the interdependence of policy sectors and issue areas that cannot be treated in isolation.[10] However, such functional structures do not determine actors' behaviour in a mechanical or predictable manner. Actors must regard functional logics as plausible in order for them to unfold their potential.[11] *Cultivated spill-over* concerns the role of supranational institutions that, concerned with increasing their own powers, become agents of integration because they are likely to benefit from its progression. Once established, they tend to take on a life of their own and are difficult to control by those who created them. And thirdly, *political spill-over* encapsulates the process whereby (national) elites come to perceive that problems of substantial interest cannot be effectively addressed at the domestic level. This should lead to a gradual learning process whereby elites shift their expectations and political activities to a new European centre. Consequently, national elites—both governmental as well as outside government—would come to promote further integration, thus adding a political stimulus to the process.[12]

In contrast, *(Liberal) intergovernmentalism* considers national member governments (as rational, utility-maximising actors) to be the key actors in the integration process. The latter is deemed to progress only when it is in the national interest. Specifically liberal variants of intergovernmentalism define such national interests as being (mainly) tied to the economic preferences of national interest groups.[13] According to such Liberal intergovernmentalism, governmental preferences emerge through domestic political conflict in which groups compete for political influence, national and transnational coalitions form, and new policy alternatives are recognised by governments. As the primary interest of governments is to maintain themselves in office, the support of a coalition of domestic actors is required. Governments' external policy objectives are thus regarded as varying in response to changing pressure from domestic groups, whose preferences are aggregated through political institutions.[14] Due to the imperatives induced

7 Haas (1968), p. xii.
8 Schmitter (1970), Niemann et al. (2020), pp. 4–5.
9 Tranholm-Mikkelsen (1991).
10 Haas (1958), pp. 297, 383; Lindberg (1963), p. 10.
11 Niemann (2006), p. 31.
12 Cf. Haas (1958), chs. 8+9; Lindberg (1963), chs. I+IV.
13 Moravcsik (1998).
14 Moravcsik (1993), p. 481.

by interdependence and the increase in cross-border business opportunities, it is 'primarily the commercial interests of powerful economic producers,' which motivate national preferences.[15] Governments' preferences stay exogenous, i.e. they are largely assumed to be unaffected by the integration process.

At the EU level, Member States consequently develop strategies and bargain with one another to reach substantive agreements that realise those national preferences more efficiently than unilateral actions do. This intergovernmental bargaining process is characterised by 'credible threats to veto proposals, to withhold financial side-payments, and to form alternative alliances excluding recalcitrant governments,' with the outcomes reflecting the relative power of states.[16] In intergovernmental bargaining, outcomes 'reflected the relative power of states [. . .]. Under this perspective, supranational institutions are established by states primarily to address problems of incomplete contracting, compliance and monitoring. They act on behalf of states and can be controlled by them.'[17] In the process of delegating power to institutions, state sovereignty is unaffected or may even strengthen or 'rescue' the nation-state.[18]

The most recently introduced grand theory of European integration is presented by *postfunctionalism*. In their 'postfunctional theory,' Hooghe and Marks[19] seek to include aspects that earlier explanatory frameworks of European integration had failed to address. They suggest that the neofunctionalist and intergovernmentalist focus on elites, interest groups, technocracy and economic interests was justified in the initial phase of European integration. Since the 1990s, however, integration has increasingly extended to policies that affect citizens' identities and that have had a profound impact on people's lives. It thus became more and more difficult for EU institutions, national governments, civil services and interest groups to shield the European integration process from mass politics. Media, political parties and social movements played an increasingly active role in this process, which has been accompanied by a growing level of politicisation. Hence, the 'permissive consensus' that had prevailed in the first few decades of the European Community turned into a 'constraining dissensus' that may obstruct further integration.

According to postfunctionalism, European integration has hence become an identity issue and offers populist parties the chance to achieve electoral success. As a result, EU politics and society gradually becomes polarised on a cultural divide that may also constitute a new sociopolitical cleavage.[20] Countries particularly affected by this tend to be those where exclusive attachment to the national in-group is popular and where institutional procedures open to direct mass public

15 Moravcsik (1998), pp. 3, 20–26.
16 *Ibid.*, p. 3.
17 *Ibid.*, pp. 490–494.
18 Milward (1992).
19 Hooghe and Marks (2009).
20 Hooghe and Marks (2018).

interest articulation (such as referendums on EU treaties or membership) foster Eurosceptic mobilisation.

While neofunctionalism and intergovernmentalism consider European integration as an efficiency-oriented process that may be characterised as mostly cooperative in nature, postfunctionalism points to the disruptive and conflictual tendencies of identity-related polarisation and politicisation. It also highlights the limits and setbacks of an elite-driven technocratic and efficiency maximising process, which seems to leave this newly emerged grand theory with greater potential to theorise disintegration than earlier approaches.

2.2.2. *Explaining Brexit (and its impacts)*

While Brexit, as a case of horizontal disintegration, is a particularly hard case for neofunctionalism, the theory still considerably adds to our understanding of Brexit, in particular due to it taking politicisation more seriously in its more current variants.[21] Whereas crises as such had been viewed as a relatively normal feature of the integration process from the start, early neofunctionalists had not foreseen that politicisation and identity politics might seriously threaten the integration process as such, or even precipitate the exit of a Member State.[22] The assumption was rather that politicisation might question further integration possibly leading to stagnation or even spill-back in particular policy areas, not challenge the process *as a whole*.[23] As a pluralist and transformative theory, neofunctionalism assumes multiple actors who may learn, which in principle implies that also citizens may choose to take (critically) part in a process of increasingly deep functional integration to which they had previously merely acquiesced.

Interestingly, a number of neofunctionalist logics were invoked by Remainers in the run up to the referendum. These might still be relevant for the EU-27 and even perhaps for the future UK-EU relationship. Neofunctionalist pressures pushing for Britain to remain an EU member (and now, after Brexit, in very close cooperation with the Union) included: the functional rationale relating to the benefits of the single market, the economic costs of leaving it, the benefits of other areas of EU integration such as internal security or climate change, and the adverse repercussions likely to result from leaving the EU. In addition, there were other path dependencies—including sub-optimal bargaining positions when negotiating new trade agreements—that made membership sticky and renationalisation costly.[24] Many interest groups in the UK were therefore strongly in favour of remaining within the EU, and later advocated a 'soft Brexit,' which may explain the decision

21 Cf. Niemann et al. (2020).
22 Schmitter (2009).
23 Schmitter (1970).
24 Niemann et al. (2020), pp. 6–7.

for a transition period[25] and will probably continue to support a closer bi-lateral relationship in the future.

In addition, neofunctionalism is a dynamic theory in the sense that a specification of the conditions of spill-over can usefully delimit its scope of application and thus be seen as an exercise in revising it. Several factors can be identified which help to explain why the (functional) rationales for 'Remain' found little traction: (1) When issues are substantially politicised and polarised, as during the Brexit referendum, they tend to be framed in emotive terms beyond the reach of (functional) rationality; (2) When citizens have only limited knowledge of the EU, when successive governments have done little themselves to explain European policy, and when experts are distrusted, understanding the complexities of the pros and cons of membership again becomes problematic; (3) When the bulk of the media campaigns against membership in a simplified manner, often framed in a biased and (sometimes) misleading way, an assessment of the costs and benefits becomes difficult as benefits and functional logics can hardly register; (4) When integration measures stretch the perceived adaptive capacity of societies/economies, such as the decision for early liberalisation of the free movement following Eastern enlargement, they can lead to unintended countervailing dynamics and, in the case Brexit, provide an easy target for hostile nationalistic campaigns; And finally, (5) when the debate is not only one of domestic politics but when 'Brussels' itself becomes the problem, the supranational institutions, one of the main agents of European integration, cannot play any substantive role. An important neofunctionalist dynamic (cultivated spill-over) is thus taken out of the equation.[26]

Several studies suggest that the Brexit referendum was a wake-up call for other European countries, with positive attitudes towards the EU having increased.[27] It is uncertain, though, whether this trend continues and Brexit remains an aberration, and whether this implies that one of the earlier neofunctionalist assumptions may eventually be (at least partly) fulfilled—i.e. that politicisation leads to greater citizen involvement and support for integration.[28] Likewise, it remains to be seen if the exit of its most sceptical member will pave the way towards further deepening,[29] and if so, in which policy fields.

A (Liberal) intergovernmentalist (LI) account also provides a number of insights into the Brexit process. First, it underlines the importance of national interests and national diversities in the integration process. Second, by opening up the black box of the state, LI scholars have rightly indicated that governmental preferences emerge through domestic political *conflict*, even if interest groups (and not citizens/voters) were given a privileged role therein. Third, from

25 Czech and Krakowiak-Drzewiecka (2019), p. 598.
26 Niemann et al. (2020).
27 van Kessel et al. (2020).
28 Niemann et al. (2020).
29 Czech and Krakowiak-Drzewiecka (2019), p. 598.

a LI perspective, Brexit is of an illusory nature—i.e. it mainly has repercussions regarding UK domestic policies and politics but less so for the UK relationship with the EU. For example, then-PM David Cameron did not call the EU referendum due to genuine dissatisfaction with the Union but in a strategic move to appease and quieten the Eurosceptics in his own party.[30] As Hooghe and Marks explain, the 'view that Brexit is epiphenomenal is logically consistent with two core premises of intergovernmentalism',[31] namely that any benefits of cooperation are decided upon and hammered out in intergovernmental bargains, and second that such bargains depend 'not on referendum outcomes but on economic interests, relative power, and credible commitments.'[32] This only ties in with Moravcsik's early prediction of a power asymmetry in favour of the EU, which provided it with greater leverage in the (post-)Brexit negotiations, because the UK has had much more to lose from a no-deal given its greater dependence on trade with the EU than vice versa.[33] Such an asymmetry was only strengthened through the multitude of potential veto players within the political system of the EU (27 *ms* along with the European Parliament), whose assent was and is needed.[34]

Of the three grand theories, however, Postfunctionalism seems to have the most suitable toolkit for conceptualising and explaining Brexit. Here, it becomes a classic example where functional rationality adopted by elites in the arena of interest group and technocratic politics is overcome by an identity logic; and all this through a shift to the arena of mass politics during a process of growing politicisation and polarisation. Several favourable conditions facilitated this process.[35] First, the pre-Brexit period was characterised by unintended integration effects that challenged national identity and self-determination. The very substantial migration to the UK, especially since the decision for early liberalisation of the free movement following Eastern enlargement in 2004, became the decisive issue in the run-up to the referendum and provided an easy target for the nationalistic 'Leave' campaign. Second, there was the rise of a non-mainstream Eurosceptic party, UKIP, which seized on these developments and thus managed to mobilise voters. Third, a binary in-out referendum proved to be a conducive institutional venue. As suggested by Hooghe and Marks:

> [f]ew events reveal so clearly the disruptive effect of a referendum in a climate of politicization. Far from resolving tensions in the Conservative party, the referendum exacerbated them. The vote provided just a single *bit* of information. It presented voters with the simplest possible choice on a profoundly

30 Moravcsik (2016).
31 Hooghe and Marks (2019), p. 1123.
32 *Ibid.*
33 Moravcsik (2016).
34 Cf. Hooghe and Marks (2019), p. 1123.
35 For the whole argument, cf. Schimmelfennig (2018).

complex issue. A dichotomous choice says nothing about the trade-offs, the compromises needed to realize them, or the likely consequences.[36]

In that sense, Brexit may so far be the clearest case of the emergence of a 'constraining dissensus'; however, this constraint is one which is bound to the confluence of quite a few specific conditions, trends and political decisions. It remains to be seen how much this stands a chance of being replicated elsewhere, or sending existential ripple effects through the EU. Even as integration as such might not be fundamentally challenged for the moment, the rules of the game within the politics of European integration may have already changed profoundly.[37]

2.3. Grand theories, mid-range approaches and concepts in EIT addressing sport policy and governance

2.3.1. Grand theories and EU sport policy

As stated in the beginning of this chapter, EIT's inroads into making sense of Brexit and its impact have developed recently and *in parallel* to the obviously much more long-standing efforts to apply EIT to the area of sport governance and regulation. So far, a substantive discussion of the role of Brexit for this policy field *from the perspective of EIT* is consequently lacking. It is thus warranted to briefly ascertain how EIT have approached sport policy in and through the EU before Brexit. In particular, neofunctionalism and intergovernmentalism have already been successfully employed to explain important aspects of the emergence and development of EU action in the field of sport. Nonetheless, neither can fully account for the dynamics that drive and constrain this action.[38] The main reason is that EU integration in the field of sport has unfolded in different phases, in which either the EU institutions or the Member States appear to have taken control.

The dynamics behind the EU's initial encounters with sport provide strong support for neofunctionalism's propositions.[39] It is indeed appealing to argue, as Parrish has, that the EU became involved as a consequence of a functional spillover from internal market laws into the field of sport.[40] Although sport was not considered a competency or a jurisdiction upon inception, it naturally came under the scope of EU law as it developed from an amateur activity into a commercial industry.[41] In particular, several rulings of the Court of Justice of the EU (CJEU) argued that sport-related activities fall subject to EU law insofar as they constitute

36 Hooghe and Marks (2019), p. 1124.
37 Czech and Krakowiak-Drzewiecka (2019), p. 600.
38 Cf. Parrish (2003), Barani (2005), Meier (2009).
39 Meier (2009), p. 11.
40 Parrish (2003), p. 33.
41 Cf. García (2007).

an economic activity within the meaning of the Treaty; the much mediatised *Bosman* ruling may have proved to be a 'watershed'[42] here. Not only did it unearth the far-reaching effects of the application of EU internal market law on sport governing bodies such as FIFA and UEFA, it also empowered the Commission to act more decisively in ensuring that these sport governing bodies comply with EU law. From a neofunctionalist perspective, the ruling, a deregulatory measure and, thus, an example of *negative integration*, triggered a functional spill-over into prescriptive and encouraging measures associated with *positive integration*. Unhappy with what was perceived as an (overly) technocratic approach to sport, the Member States and the European Parliament indeed called upon the Commission to take initiatives to safeguard the current sport structures, maintain the sociocultural function of sport, and provide legal certainty for sport governing bodies.[43] This would eventually result in the emergence of an EU sport policy facilitated and propelled by the creation of a Sport Unit within the Directorate-General Education and Culture in 1998 and an EU sporting competence introduced by the Lisbon Treaty in 2009.

The development of such an EU sport policy was, much in line with neofunctionalist tenets, cultivated by community-level institutions that promoted EU integration in the field of sport by using their delegated authority.[44] Partly building on this European Parliament's support,[45] the Commission acted as a policy entrepreneur. These activities culminated in the 2007 White Paper on Sport, which was accompanied by 53 specific actions,[46] and the 2011 Communication on the European Dimension in Sport.[47] Apart from covering issues such as physical activity and social dialogue, a functional spill-over from negative integration towards policies aimed at encouraging good governance could also be discerned. It is the result of increased litigation by disgruntled stakeholders against their sport-governing bodies following *Bosman*, which both exposed democratic deficits in international sport governance and caused an overflowing Commission caseload.[48]

There is somewhat less empirical evidence of political spill-over in the field of sport.[49] However, it is worth pointing out that sport-governing bodies and their stakeholders seem to have encouraged EU action on matters of public order, such as match-fixing and doping, and the promotion of physical activity and grassroots sport, as long as such measures did not encroach on their autonomy. On the other hand, recent corruption scandals in international sport governance have

42 Parrish (2003), p. 9.
43 *Ibid.*
44 Geeraert (2016).
45 Vermeersch (2009).
46 European Commission (2007).
47 European Commission (2011).
48 Meier (2009), p. 32; Geeraert (2016), p. 116.
49 Cf. Parrish (2003); Meier (2009); Geeraert (2020).

prompted a desire on the part of the Member States to use the European level to promote good governance and integrity in sport.[50]

EU integration in the field of sport also shares clear intergovernmentalist characteristics. True, the Member States and their governments may have only rarely been the key drivers behind such integration. Most notably, they did not appreciate nor expect the CJEU's ruling in *Bosman* and the Commission's subsequent increased regulatory practice in sport cases.[51] Yet an intergovernmentalist would argue that the Member States have allowed integration in sport to progress only if and when it was in their national interest. They have controlled the Commission both in its application of EU law on sport-governing bodies as well as in its execution of sport policies.[52]

Even though the Commission thus had acted as a policy entrepreneur in sport, the Member States at the very least had given it a 'soft political mandate' for doing so.[53] In turn, the Commission indeed always sought to ensure that it had 'solid political support' from the governments before issuing and executing sport-specific measures. With the entry into force of the Lisbon Treaty, the EU may have been assigned a sporting competence; indeed, the strategy behind adopting such a sporting competence was, however, 'empowering the EU in order to restrain it.'[54] Echoing Liberal intergovernmentalism's emphasis on interest groups as determining factors of the Member States' preferences, this strategy was shaped by lobbying efforts of a transnational coalition of sport stakeholders.[55]

2.3.2. Mid-range theories of EU governance in the field of sport

Over the years, EU scholars shifted their focus from explaining the process of integration towards understanding the EU as a political system and the dynamics of governance within. Likewise, in the first comprehensive theoretical study of the EU and sport, Parrish argued that, rather than drawing on EIT grand theories, 'an approach is needed that is best able to capture the real nature of EU governance.'[56] Others have followed suit and applied theories of EU governance to explain the day-to-day working of the EU in the field of sport.

Parrish himself introduced Sabatier's *Advocacy Coalition Framework* to explain the development of EU sport law and policy.[57] He argued that a 'sports policy subsystem' had emerged in the EU, which is composed of two actor coalitions that

50 Geeraert (2016).
51 Cf. García (2007).
52 Geeraert and Drieskens (2015); Geeraert (2016).
53 Parrish and Miettinen (2008), p. 35.
54 García and Weatherill (2012), p. 248.
55 *Ibid.*
56 Parrish (2003), p. 35.
57 Parrish (2003, 2011); Sabatier (1998); also Yilmaz (2018).

attempt to steer sport policy in a direction consistent with their respective belief systems. Whereas the Single Market advocacy coalition was to emphasise the economic aspects of sport and thus advocated a regulatory approach to sport, the sociocultural coalition stressed the social, cultural and educational roles of sport, which therefore differs from normal economic sectors and thus deserves a tailored (i.e., more 'generous') approach.[58] Drawing on insights from rational choice institutionalism, Parrish argued that the status quo in EU sport policy can be seen as an equilibrium that is a function of strategic interactions between the rival advocacy coalitions, which utilise institutions and institutional venues as critical resources in their pursuits.

An appreciation of complexity has informed *multi-level governance* approaches, which set out to explaining the nature of the EU as a polity in which decision-making capabilities are shared rather than monopolised. Consequently, nested governments continuously negotiate at supranational, national, regional and local tiers.[59] Several authors have explored the consequences of such multi-level dynamics for policy-making in European sport governance. They emphasise how sport policy output is 'crowded and difficult'[60] and determined by activities in a 'myriad of policy-specific subsystems.'[61] Taken together, sport- governing bodies and their stakeholders as well as the EU's interactions with these bodies can be conceived of as forming a multi-level governance system.[62] Within this system, the EU acts as a 'metagovernor' and shapes the interactions between sport governing bodies and their stakeholders.[63]

Yet another line of inquiry into the EU and sport draws on theories of EU governance that are informed by rational choice institutionalist assumptions. Scholars in this tradition assume that actors in the field of sport policy and regulation behave strategically to attain their (pre-established) goals and are both empowered and constrained by formal institutions in their pursuits.[64] Meier and García, for instance, draw on veto player theory to make causal predictions about the consequences of granting sport governing bodies veto power within EU sport policy-making.[65] They argue that the latter would be undesirable since it could result in bargaining deadlock. Geeraert and Drieskens' *principal-agent (PA)* analysis of the EU's control of FIFA and UEFA[66] also relies on assumptions of rational actor behaviour; yet, it significantly broadens traditional dyadic PA conceptions by employing a triangular principal-supervisor-agent

58 Weatherill (2003), p. 92.
59 Hooghe and Marks (2004).
60 García (2008), p. 123.
61 Parrish (2003), p. 202.
62 García (2008); Geeraert et al. (2013).
63 Geeraert (2014).
64 See e.g. Parrish (2003), García (2008), Meier and García (2012).
65 *Ibid.*
66 Geeraert (2016), Geeraert and Drieskens (2015).

model. In doing so, they are able to demonstrate that, whereas football stakeholders and public authorities as principals lack control options over FIFA and UEFA (the agents), they may rely on the CJEU and the Commission (the supervisors) to exercise control on their behalf. These 'supervisors' are capable of controlling FIFA and UEFA by deploying three instruments (monitoring, sanctioning and steering) that are applied through two control routes: the EU law route and the EU sports policy route. In turn, within this triangular principal-supervisor-agent set-up, FIFA and UEFA can mitigate EU control through a range of strategies. Next to directly engaging with the Commission, they can seek to manipulate the preferences of the European Parliament and the Member States in an effort to decrease the Commission's incentive to control. Similarly, by manipulating the preferences of football principals, FIFA and UEFA can prevent their recourse to the CJEU and the Commission. A constant interplay between FIFA and UEFA, their principals and their supervisors therefore dictates whether or not the CJEU and the Commission can deploy the control instruments at their disposal. As this makes clear, any serious conceptual engagement with EU governance in the field of sport has to grapple with a multitude of vectors and thoroughly complex systems of the making and moulding of decisions.

2.3.3. Concepts addressing consequences of European integration and the EU as an actor in global sport governance

By the end of the 1990s, EU scholars started exploring the implications of the EU's development into a political system in terms of its impact on national policies[67] as well as global governance.[68] Sport and EU scholars consequently applied related concepts and frameworks to study the increasing impact of the EU on both domestic and global sport governance.

A first group of scholars focused their attention on *Europeanisation* effects in the field of sport policy. The 'Europeanisation-of-sport' literature has, to a large extent, exhibited a 'Europeanisation-of-football' bias to this day.[69] Starting from a conventional understanding of Europeanisation as a process of change in the domestic arena resulting from the European level directions and demands,[70] it first pointed toward the fact that actors at the domestic level are not merely receivers but also creatively adapt to pressures from EU institutions, as much as they seek to influence them in the future. This has been true for football in the wake of the CJEU's *Bosman* ruling

67 Brand and Niemann (2007).

68 Brand et al. (2013).

69 See for exceptions: Sakka and Chatzigianni (2012), Gasparini (2020). For the discussion of football, cf. Niemann et al. (2011), Brand et al. (2013).

70 Cf. Schmidt (2002).

much as in the case of the Commission looking into broadcasting rights around the turn of the century.[71] Europeanisation, however, also received (and continues to receive) significant impulses from transnationalising forces, be it the formation of transnational lobby networks or the creation of a de facto pan-European football league.[72] The main point in this strand of literature arguably is that the protagonists (top-level association and club representatives in particular) have changed their frame of reference: to quite some extent their frame of action, attention and reference has become Europeanised. More recently, this argument has been advanced to include football fans across Europe, and by that a significant share of the wider European public, which are nevertheless 'affected' by sport and football in particular. The guiding question then becomes, whether we can also witness forms of 'subjective Europeanisation,' or even a subconscious Europeanisation of identities through investing time and emotion into a by now thoroughly Europeanised game.[73]

As previously internal policies gradually took external dimensions and external competences, such as the Common Foreign and Security Policy, were successively added to the Treaties, the EU developed into an important global actor. Scholars consequently have developed theoretical frameworks to explore and explain the EU's external action. Many of these are relevant for the analysis of the EU and sport as well. Indeed, the EU's significant impact on global sport governance occurred through interactions with external private actors, namely sport governing bodies. Scholars in this camp have borrowed analytical concepts from International Political Economy to explain the EU's (in-)effectiveness as a global regulator.[74] Drawing on this literature, García and Meier postulated that the EU's market size and regulatory capacity, and the broader political opportunity structure are important determinants of its influence on the global regulation of sport.[75] Geeraert's and Drieskens' holistic analysis of the EU's market power in global sport governance generally confirmed these findings yet also stressed the importance of cohesiveness in the Member States' respective positions and actions.[76]

Further addressing the question of EU actorness in the realm of sport, these two authors also employed three components of general actorness (as defined by Bretherton and Vogler): opportunity, presence and capability to explore and explain the EU's evolving participation in global sport governance.[77] Their analysis revealed that the EU's actorness within the field is established, but not guaranteed. Whereas the EU has been able to shape the perceptions, expectations and behaviour of sport-governing bodies because of its market power (presence), the sport world's successful defense of its autonomy (opportunity) as well as a lack of

71 Niemann and Brand (2008).
72 Brand et al. (2013), Niemann and Brand (2020).
73 Weber et al. (2020).
74 Young (2014).
75 García and Meier (2017).
76 Geeraert and Drieskens (2017), Geeraert (2016).
77 Geeraert and Drieskens (2018).

consensus between the Member States on the need for EU interventions in sport (capability) have prevented it from fully capitalising on its potential.

Whether the nature or identity of the EU as a global power is anchored in being a 'Normative Power,' which is able to determine what is normal by projecting a catalogue of norms into international politics,[78] or a 'Market Power' (combining a comparatively large regulated market with 'institutional features and interest group contestation'[79]) is subject of an ongoing debate among EU scholars. With a view on sport policy, Geeraert and Drieskens have argued for an integrated perspective in which normative and market dynamics alternate and intertwine to produce a 'Normative Market Europe' as a significant force in global sport governance.[80] Although its market power has allowed it to become significant force in this domain, it is its dominant focus on dispersing liberal norms that truly makes the EU a unique species there.

2.4. Brexit and sport: which place for EIT?

Where does all this leave us as regards assessing likely implications of Brexit for sport policy and regulation in, and through, the EU? Can Brexit be considered a 'rupture' which may put the regulatory clout of the EU in sport into question, as Kornbeck asks in the Introduction to this edited volume?

A few caveats are in order. First, one might ask how different and how similar sport policy (as well as adjacent regulation) is to the EU policy areas that are commonly assessed under a post-Brexit perspective. It is safe to assume that different policy fields and nexuses will not be affected in a homogeneous manner. Second, in assessing any impact, we need to be clear about which kind of impact we allude to. Brexit might have very different kinds of consequences for the EU as an organisation, the relationships among the remaining 27, the future EU-UK relationship, and the EU's role vis-à-vis external actors (say, in global sport governance). Third, we may not use Brexit and 'disintegration' as wholly interchangeable phenomena or concepts. We should reserve the latter term for a significantly declining level of transactions, authentic forms of re-nationalisation of community competences, and a discernibly weakened sense of community only.[81] Whether this is going to materialise as a result of Brexit still remains to be seen.

EIT has only begun to tackle likely effects of Brexit on sport governance and regulation, if at all. Should we heed to Jones' advice that the existing explanatory frameworks of integration are 'ill-equipped to go in reverse'?[82] We recommend to not act precipitately here and suggest that insights from EIT might indeed guide

78 Cf. Manners (2002), pp. 239–241.
79 Damro (2012), p. 696.
80 Geeraert and Drieskens (2017), p. 79.
81 Börzel and Risse (2018), p. 6.
82 Jones (2018), p. 440.

our inquiry into post-Brexit EU sport policy to quite some extent. Admittedly, neofunctionalists also address spill-back, but mostly it makes us aware of how deeply entrenched and sticky Community-level policies became over time—difficult to unravel, even if a party leaves the multi-level decision-making system.

What is more, crises—exogenous but also endogenous ones—might trigger further integrative steps, if only to cushion or preserve achievements; and the exit of a country (until very recently only an abstract idea) which had not been a key driver behind integration might even strengthen the internal coherence of the remaining parties. This might prove true, to some extent, for sport policy as well due to the fact that UK governments usually were not much in favour of a grand role of the EU in sport and occasionally also politicised this issue. It is in this sense that neofunctionalism even provides a few hints at non-disintegrative impulses flowing from Brexit.

In a surprisingly similar vein, liberal intergovernmentalism thematises Brexit as an 'illusion' meaning that even in light of a formal departure, the future relationship between the community and the country, which has exited, can be assumed to remain close and, in myriad ways 'coordinated,' in the face of Brexit-imposed frictions. It is not too far-fetched to then assume a great deal of continuity in basic aspects of EU-UK relations, and also in many sport domains. The example of leading British football clubs and their efforts to establish farm teams throughout the continent with which to trade talented players in the future in an effort to prevent post-Brexit regulations, not least those newly installed by the FA, somewhat points into such a direction.

Postfunctionalism, in its capacity to describe the centrifugal forces in integration, may be brought in to gauge how much politicised sport and sport-related regulation can become as a policy field, or how much this arena might be affected by overall polarisation and EU fatigue. Most likely, we are to observe shifts and changes to Europeanisation dynamics of sport as a result of Brexit. This is particularly expectable for the more subjective and identity-related forms of Europeanisation, those in the minds of spectators and sport fans in particular. Here, Brexit might become a central point of reference for Eurosceptics all over the EU, including those in sport industries and among sport fans, in challenging *any* EU authority. Finally, in terms of actorness in global sport governance, the EU's market power in sports, and thereby one pillar of its strength, is certain to decrease at least in the short to mid run, because of Brexit, but certainly not to the extent that it is rendered impotent. Ultimately, the effect of Brexit will only be felt meaningfully as soon as the UK steps up to challenge the EU and its positions in sport governance. This, however, seems rather unlikely at the moment.

References

Barani, L. (2005) The role of the European court of justice as a political actor in the integration process: The case of sport regulation after the Bosman ruling. *Journal of Contemporary European Studies*, 1:1, 42–58.

Börzel, T. & Risse, T. (2018) A litmus test for European integration theories. *KFG-Working Papers*, 85. www.polsoz.fu-berlin.de/en/v/transformeurope/publications/working_paper/wp/wp85/WP_85_Boerzel_Risse_WEB.pdf.

Brand, A. & Niemann, A. (2007) Europeanisation in the societal/trans-national realm: What European integration studies can get out of analysing football. *Journal of Contemporary European Research*, 3:3, 182–201.

Brand, A.; Niemann, A. & Spitaler, G. (2013) The two-track Europeanisation of football: EU-level pressures, transnational dynamics and their repercussions within different national contexts. *International Journal of Sports Policy and Politics*, 5:1, 95–112.

Czech, S. & Krakowiak-Drzewiecka, M. (2019) The rationale of Brexit and the theories of European integration. *Oeconomia Copernicana*, 10:4, 589–602.

Damro, C. (2012) Market power Europe. *Journal of European Public Policy*, 19:5, 682–699.

Dinan, D. (1994) *Ever Closer Union*. London: Palgrave Macmillan.

European Commission (2007) White paper on sport (2007), COM (2007) 391 final. (perhaps only in the footnote?)

European Commission (2011) Developing the European dimension in sport, COM (2011) 12 final. (perhaps only in the footnote?)

García, B. (2007) UEFA and the European Union: From confrontation to cooperation? *Journal of Contemporary European Research*, 3:3, 202–223.

García, B. (2008) *The European Union and the Governance of Football: A Game of Levels and Agendas*. PhD thesis, Loughborough University.

García, B. & Meier, H.E. (2017) Global sport power Europe? The efficacy of the European Union in global sport regulation. *Journal of Common Market Studies*, 55:4, 850–870.

García, B. & Weatherill, S. (2012) Engaging with the EU in order to minimize its impact: Sport and the negotiation of the treaty of Lisbon. *Journal of European Public Policy*, 19:2, 238–256.

Gasparini, W. (2020) The Europeanisation of sport. In: Porro, N.; Martelli, S. & Testa, A. (eds) *Sport, Welfare and Social Policy in the European Union*. London: Routledge, pp. 69–74.

Geeraert, A. (2014) New EU governance modes in professional sport: Enhancing throughput legitimacy. *Journal of Contemporary European Research*, 10:3, 302–321.

Geeraert, A. (2016) *The EU in International Sports Governance. A Principal-agent Perspective on EU Control of FIFA and UEFA*. London: Palgrave Macmillan.

Geeraert, A. (2020) The autonomy of the Olympic and sport movement. In: Chatziefstathiou, D.; Garcia, B. & Séguin, B. (eds) *Routledge Handbook of the Olympic and Paralympic Games*. London: Routledge, pp. 250–264.

Geeraert, A. & Drieskens, E. (2015) The EU controls FIFA and UEFA: A principal-agent perspective. *Journal of European Public Policy*, 22:10, 1448–1466.

Geeraert, A. & Drieskens, E. (2017) Normative market Europe: The EU as a force for good in international sports governance? *Journal of European Integration*, 39:1, 79–94.

Geeraert, A. & Drieskens, E. (2018) Playing a different game: The EU's normative engagement in international sports governance. In: Schunz, S.; Damro, C. & Gstohl, S. (eds) *The European Union's Evolving External Engagement. Towards New Sectoral Diplomacies?* London: Routledge, pp. 216–236.

Geeraert, A.; Scheerder, J. & Bruyninckx, H. (2013) The governance network of European football: Introducing new governance approaches to steer football at the EU level. *International Journal of Sport Policy and Politics*, 5:1, 113–132.

Haas, E. (1958) *The Uniting of Europe*. Stanford: Stanford University Press.

Haas, E. (1964) Technocracy, pluralism and the new Europe. In: Graubard, S. (ed) *A New Europe?* Boston: Houghton Mifflin, pp. 62–88.

Haas, E. (1968) *The Uniting of Europe*, 2nd edition, Stanford: Stanford University Press.

Hooghe, L. & Marks, G. (2004) *Multi-Level Governance and European Integration*. Lanham: Rowman and Littlefield.

Hooghe, L. & Marks, G. (2009) A postfunctionalist theory of European integration: From permissive consensus to constraining dissensus. *British Journal of Political Science*, 39:1, 1–23.

Hooghe, L. & Marks, G. (2018) Cleavage theory and Europe's crises: Lipset, Rokkan and the transnational cleavage. *Journal of European Public Policy*, 25:1, 109–35.

Hooghe, L. & Marks, G. (2019) Grand theories of European integration in the twenty-first century. *Journal of European Public Policy*, 26:8, 1113–1133.

Jones, E. (2018) Towards a theory of disintegration. *Journal of European Public Policy*, 25:3, 440–451.

Lindberg, L.N. (1963) *The Political Dynamics of European Economic Integration*. Stanford: Stanford University Press.

Manners, I. (2002) Normative power Europe: A contradiction in terms? *Journal of Common Market Studies*, 40:2, 235–258.

Meier, H.E. (2009) Emergence, dynamics and impact of European sport policy. In: Gardiner, S.; Parrish, R. & Siekmann, R.C.R. (eds) *EU, Sport, Law and Policy: Regulation, Re-regulation and Representation*. The Hague: T.M.C. Asser Press, pp. 7–34.

Meier, H.E. & García, B. (2012) Abandoning hopes for veto power: Institutional options for sport governing bodies in the European Union. *International Journal of Sport Policy and Politics*, 5:3, 421–443.

Milward, A.S. (1992) *The European Rescue of the Nation-State*. London: Routledge.

Moravcsik, A. (1993) Preferences and power in the European Community. A liberal intergovernmentalist approach. *Journal of Common Market Studies*, 31:4, 473–524.

Moravcsik, A. (1998) *The Choice for Europe*. Ithaca: Cornell University Press.

Moravcsik, A. (2016) The great Brexit kabuki—a masterclass in political theatre. *Financial Times*, 8 April (perhaps only in the footnote?)

Niemann, A. (2006) *Explaining Decisions in the European Union*. Cambridge: Cambridge University Press.

Niemann, A. & Brand, A. (2008) The impact of European integration on domestic sport. The case of German football. *Sport in Society*, 11:1, 90–106.

Niemann, A. & Brand, A. (2020) The UEFA champions league: A political myth? *Soccer & Society*, 21:3, 329–343.

Niemann, A.; Edwards, E. & Jakobi, P. (2020) Still not yet obsolete? A neofunctionalist account of Brexit. *Mainz Papers on International and European Politics (MPIEP)*, 25. https://international.politics.uni-mainz.de/files/2021/04/Niemann-Edwards-Jacobi_MPIEP_No25.pdf

Niemann, A.; García, B. & Grant W. (eds) (2011) *The Transformation of European Football. Towards the Europeanisation of the National Game*. Manchester: Manchester University Press.

Parrish, R. (2003) *Sports Law and Policy in the European Union*. Manchester: Manchester University Press.

Parrish, R. (2011) Social dialogue in European professional football. *European Law Journal*, 17:2, 213–229.

Parrish, R. & Miettinen, S. (2008) *The Sporting Exception in European Union Law*. The Hague: T.M.C. Asser Press.
Perry, K. & Steenson, M. (2019) A post-Brexit impact: A case study on the English premier league. *Journal of Sports & Entertainment Law*, 10:1, 1–50.
Sabatier, P. (1998) The advocacy coalition framework: Revisions and relevance for Europe. *Journal of European Public Policy*, 5:1, 98–130.
Sakka, S. & Chatzigianni, E. (2012) Enhancing Europeanisation through European sport-related programmes: The case of Greece. *Choregia*, 8:8, 32–56.
Schimmelfennig, F. (2018) Brexit: Differentiated disintegration in the European Union. *Journal of European Public Policy*, 25:8, 1154–1173.
Schmidt, V.A. (2002) Europeanization and the mechanics of economic policy adjustment. *Journal of European Public Policy*, 9:6, 894–912.
Schmitter, P. (1970) A revised theory of regional integration. *International Organization*, 24:4, 836–868.
Schmitter, P. (2009) On the way to a post-functionalist theory of European integration. *British Journal of Political Science*, 39:1, 211–215.
Schmitter, P. & Lefkofridi, Z. (2016) Neo-functionalism as a theory of disintegration. *Chinese Political Science Review*, 1:1, 1–29.
Tranholm-Mikkelsen, J. (1991) Neo-functionalism: Obstinate or obsolete? *Millennium*, 29:1, 1–22.
van Kessel, S.; Chelotti, N.; Drake, H.; Roch, J. & Rodi, P. (2020) Eager to leave? Populist radical right parties' responses to the UK's Brexit vote. *The British Journal of Politics and International Relations*, 22:1, 65–84.
Vermeersch, A. (2009) *Europese spelregels voor sport. Overzicht van het Europees sport- beleid in wording en de toepassing van het Europees recht op sport*. Antwerp: Maklu-Uitgevers.
Weatherill, S. (2003) Fair play, please! Recent developments in the application of EC law to sport. *Common Market Law Review*, 40:1, 51–93.
Weber, R.; Brand, A.; Niemann, A. & Koch, F. (2020) Non-elite conceptions of Europe: Europe as reference frame in English football fan discussions. *Journal of Contemporary European Research*, 16:3, 293–319.
Yilmaz, S. (2018) Advancing our understanding of the EU sports policy: The socio-cultural model of sports regulation and players' agents. *International Journal of Sport Policy and Politics*, 10:2, 353–369.
Young, A. (2014) Europe as a global regulator? The limits of EU influence in international food safety standards. *Journal of European Public Policy*, 21:6, 904–922.

Part II

Rules

Chapter 3

The end of free movement after Brexit

What does this mean for the English game?

Stefaan Van den Bogaert

3.1. Introduction

In what has been termed as a sporting fairytale, Leicester City football club won the 2015–2016 English Premier League, becoming English football champions for the first time in the club's history. Especially after only narrowly escaping relegation the previous season, the victory of the team, a cosmopolitan ensemble of players from all over the globe, including countries such as Algeria, Australia, Belgium, Denmark, England, France, Ghana, Germany, Poland or Wales, captained by a Jamaican defender and managed by an Italian, came as a complete surprise. Gary Lineker, former Leicester and England striker and famous talk show host, had even famously promised that he would present BBC's *Match of the Day* in his underwear if Leicester won the title.[1]

One month later, on 23 June 2016, a majority of British citizens, many of whom had undoubtedly marvelled at Leicester's title run, reminiscing the victory of a footballing David against the Goliaths from Manchester or Liverpool, caused another shock, albeit of a totally different nature and magnitude this time, voting in a popular referendum for the departure of the United Kingdom from the European Union. Undoubtedly, a combination of factors has contributed to the *Leave* campaign unexpectedly gaining the upper hand in the referendum.[2] Evidently, popular dissatisfaction about the EU immigration rules, who were perceived to enable workers from all EU Member States to freely enter the UK labour market, take British jobs and benefit from the UK social system, was an important argument for many people to vote for Brexit. Unsurprisingly, however, all Premier League teams, more or less all equally multiculturally composed as Leicester City, had expressed themselves in favour of *Remain*.[3]

1 Match of the Day presenter keeps Twitter promise, www.bbc.com/sport/football/37074641.
2 See van Middelaar (2018).
3 According to the Premier League's chairman, Richard Scudamore, the campaign to leave the EU was 'completely incongruous' with the 'openness' he felt was represented at the summit of the English football pyramid: www.espn.com/soccer/english-premier-league/story/2897686/premier-league-chief-richard-scudamore-backs-remain-in-eu-referendum.

DOI: 10.4324/9781003162803-5

Despite the *Leave* campaign winning the vote with only a relatively small margin, the referendum being only consultative, the breakdown of the voting above all displaying an utterly divided nation along different lines, and the government being caught completely off guard by the outcome and clueless about the way forward, the mantra of the Conservative government has since then unwaveringly been 'Brexit means Brexit.' UK Prime Ministers may have come and gone, the withdrawal negotiations may have been cumbersome, with the remaining EU-27 Member States continuing to form one united front, and it may have taken much longer than anticipated on the basis of the two-year period envisaged by Article 50 TEU to exit the EU; but in the end, on 31st January 2020, Brexit was a fact. For the first time in the history of the European Union, a Member State had actually withdrawn from the Union. Albeit that, even when the UK had formally left the bloc, the Withdrawal Agreement, which entered into force on 1 February 2020, provided that EU law firmly continued to apply to and in the UK during a transitional regime which lasted until 31 December 2020.[4] This interim period allowed the EU and the UK to negotiate a partnership for the future. A trade and cooperation agreement was eventually reached, but only on Christmas Eve 2020, one week before the expiry of the deadline when all hope seemingly had vanished.[5] Even though several provisions of this vast agreement, containing more than thousand pages, annexes included, need to be further elaborated and crystallised, the agreement has already provisionally entered into force and governs the EU-UK relations as from 1 January 2021.

Even with the new EU-UK Trade and Cooperation Agreement in place, which was hailed as a big success by the main negotiators, the unmistakable fact remains that big changes occurred on 1 January 2021. On that date, the UK did leave the EU Internal Market and Customs Union, as well as all EU policies and international agreements. As an immediate and far-reaching consequence, the free movement of persons, goods, services and capital between the UK and the EU has come to an end. EU citizens no longer have the right to work, study or live in the UK, and vice versa. Border checks will apply, and EU citizens will need visas for long-term stays in the UK.

Inevitably, the end of free movement is going to have a big impact on sports, especially in the UK, but also in the EU. Sport is often viewed as a paradigm of freedom of movement. At this stage, it is of course too early to tell what the precise consequences will be for the sports industry. Many sports associations are still grappling to come to terms with the new reality. It is already possible however, to chart some major changes that are in any event going to happen. This paper is going to do this for football. After all, football is the most popular global sport and

4 Dougan (2020).

5 Trade and Cooperation Agreement between the EU and the European Atomic Energy Community, of the one part, and the United Kingdom of Great Britain and Northern Ireland, of the other part [2020] OJ L 444, pp. 14–1462.

the biggest sporting industry. The English Premier League is widely regarded as the world's leading football competition.[6] And even on Netflix, football is branded as the English game.

Before zooming in on the changes after Brexit, it is worth looking back, in the first paragraph, at what once was and now is lost, at least for the UK, in terms of the right to freedom of movement for sportsmen and women in the EU. In the second paragraph, the impact of Brexit for the English game will be analysed. In the end, some conclusions will be drawn.

3.2. When the UK was still an EU Member State: sport and freedom of movement[7]

3.2.1. The essence of the right to free movement[8]

The rules on free movement were already enshrined in the original Treaty of Rome, establishing the European Economic Community. Together with the Treaty competition rules, they constitute the fundamental pillars of the European integration process. Their ultimate objective is to realise the EU internal market, defined as an area without internal frontiers within which the free movement of goods, persons, services and capital is ensured.[9] This involves the elimination of all obstacles to intra-Community trade, 'in order to merge the national markets into a single market bringing about conditions as close as possible to those of a genuine internal market.'[10] Originally, these rules applied only between the six Founding Fathers of the European Communities, the three Benelux countries, as well as France, Germany and Italy. When the UK acceded to the European Communities in the first enlargement of 1973, together with Ireland and Denmark, the free movement rules also became applicable in the UK as part of the *acquis communautaire*.

Over the years, the rules on free movement of persons and services have intersected with the world of sport.[11] These rules have been conferred to all EU citizens. Essentially, they entail the right for a national of any Member State of the European Union to freely move within the territory of other Member States, stay there, accept offers of employment and receive equal treatment vis-à-vis host state nationals as regards employment, the provision of services, remuneration or other conditions of work and employment.

Initially, the competence of the European institutions to intervene in the world of sport and subject rules and practices of sporting associations to the Treaty free

6 The Premier League currently tops the UEFA Association coefficient: www.uefa.com/memberassociations/uefarankings/country/#/yr/2021
7 Van den Bogaert (2005), chapter 6.
8 Craig and de Burca (2020).
9 Article 26 TFEU.
10 Case 15/81 *Schul*, ECLI:EU:C:1982:135, para. 33.
11 Articles 45, 49 and 56 TFEU.

movement rules was contested. Sport did not figure in the Treaty of Rome. Based on the principle of conferral, the associations claimed the right of self-regulatory autonomy and immunity from EU judicial intervention into their sporting affairs. The Court of Justice of the EU was, however, quick to reject these claims and dispel any lingering doubts as to the applicability of the Treaty already in *Walrave*, the first clash between sport and European law, firmly stipulating that sport is subject to European law insofar as it constitutes an economic activity within the meaning of the Treaty.[12] Building on this principled statement, which was reaffirmed in *Donà* two years later,[13] and reiterated ever since by the Court of Justice in all sports-related cases, it was long assumed that amateur sport did not come under EU law scrutiny. Gradually, it became clear, however, that also amateur sportsmen did enjoy (some form of) free movement protection. Firstly, sport could be considered as a social advantage for a migrating or self-employed worker within the meaning of Article 7(2) Regulation 492/2011.[14] Later, the introduction of the concept of European citizenship considerably strengthened the position of amateur athletes under EU law. But it was only recently, however, in *TopFit and Biffi* that the Court of Justice expressly acknowledged for the first time that EU citizens can rely on Articles 18 and 21 TFEU in connection with the practice of a (competitive) amateur sport in the society of the host Member State. According to the Court, it was clear from Article 21(1) TFEU, read in conjunction with Article 165 TFEU, that practising an amateur sport, in particular as part of a sports club, allows an EU citizen residing in a host Member State 'to create bonds with the society of the state to which he has moved and in which he is residing or to consolidate them. That is also the case with regard to participation in sporting competitions at all levels.'[15] As a result, an Italian national was entitled to participate in the German national athletics championships.

The Treaty provisions on freedom of movement also have direct effect. This entails that they can be directly relied upon in national proceedings by EU citizens who claim to be hindered in the exercise of their free movement rights. In *Walrave*, the Court established that 'the prohibition of discrimination based on nationality applies not only to the actions of public authorities, but also to rules of any other nature aimed at regulating in a collective manner gainful employment and the provision of services.'[16] It motivated this decision by holding that the exercise of the right to freedom of movement for persons 'would be compromised if the abolition of state barriers could be neutralised by obstacles resulting from the exercise of their legal autonomy by associations or organisations not governed by public law,'[17] and that limiting application of the free movement rules to acts of a public

12 Case 36/74 *Walrave and Koch v UCI*, ECLI:EU:C:1974:140, para. 4.

13 Case 13/76, *Donà v Mantero*, ECLI:EU:C:1976:115, para. 12.

14 Case 59/95 *Reed* ECLI:EU:C:1986:157, para. 28

15 Case C-22/18 *TopFit & Biffi*, ECLI:EU:C:2019:495, paras. 34–35.

16 *Walrave*, para. 17.

17 *Ibid*, para. 18.

authority would also 'risk creating inequality in its application.'[18] Later, in the specific context of Article 45 TFEU, the Court would even go one step further still and state that the prohibition of discrimination on grounds of nationality applies to private persons as well.[19] In essence, this means that individual sportsmen and women can invoke their free movement rights in national proceedings against sporting associations, and certainly athletes who are to be regarded as workers can also invoke their rights against sport clubs.[20]

Also more generally, the Treaty provisions relating to the fundamental freedoms have almost invariably been given a wide interpretation in the case law of the Court of Justice. First of all, the Court made it immediately clear that when any given sporting activity, regardless of its nature, has 'the character of gainful employment or remunerated service,' it comes within the scope of Articles 45 of 56 TFEU, as the case may be.[21] This enabled the Court, in particular, to qualify professional or semi-professional football players as workers or service providers within the meaning of the Treaty.[22] A good illustration of the fact that the hurdle relating to the applicability of the Treaty provisions is generally easily taken is *Deliège*. In this case, concerning a dispute about the non-selection of a Belgian judoka to participate in an international tournament, the Court stated that in determining whether sporting activities constitute a genuine and effective economic activity, a decision which was ultimately left to the national judge, it was first important to note that the national court had referred 'among other things to grants awarded on the basis of earlier sporting results and to sponsorship contracts directly linked to the results achieved by the athlete.'[23] Furthermore, It must also be taken into account that sporting activities 'are capable of involving the provision of a number of separate, but closely related, services which may fall within the scope of Article 56 TFEU, even if some of those services are not paid for by those for whom they are performed.'[24]

The wide coverage of the Treaty free movement rules is also exemplified by the judgment in *Bosman*, in which the Court held that these provisions 'are intended to facilitate the pursuit by Community citizens of occupational activities of all kinds throughout the Community, and preclude measures which might place Community citizens at a disadvantage when they wish to pursue an economic activity in the territory of another Member State.'[25] Therefore, the Treaty rules do not only cover directly or indirectly discriminatory measures; they also cover provisions 'which preclude or deter a national of a Member State from

18 *Ibid*, para. 19.
19 Case C-281/98, *Angonese*, ECLI:EU:C:2000:296, para. 36.
20 Lindholm and Parrish (2020).
21 *Walrave*, para. 5
22 *Donà*, para. 12.
23 Joined case C-51/96 and C-191/97 *Deliège*, ECLI:EU:C:2000:199, para. 51.
24 *Deliège*, para. 56.
25 Case C-415/93 *Bosman*, ECLI:EU:C:1995:463, para. 94.

leaving his country of origin in order to exercise his right to freedom of movement constitute an obstacle to that freedom, even if they apply without regard to the nationality of the workers concerned.'[26] The primary result of Bosman's crusade against the football establishment was that out-of-contract football players were now entitled to freely move to another club in another Member State, without a transfer sum being due. Unquestionably, this is by far the most influential decision of the Court of Justice relating to sport based on the Treaty free movement rights.[27]

Having said this, the scope of the free movement provisions is not unlimited. Most importantly, in *Walrave*, the Court qualified the composition of national sport teams, in particular national teams, as a question of purely sporting interest which as such has nothing to do with economic activity and therefore escapes EU law scrutiny. It added, however, that this restriction on the scope of the Treaty must remain limited to its proper objective.[28] Furthermore, in *Deliège*, the Court observed that, although selection rules have the effect of limiting the number of participants in a tournament, 'such a limitation is inherent in the conduct of an international high-level sports event, which necessarily involves certain selection rules or criteria being adopted.'[29] Therefore, such rules do not in themselves constitute a restriction on the freedom to provide services prohibited by Article 56 of the Treaty.

Moreover, the right to freedom of movement is not absolute. The Court did show receptiveness to the argument that sport is special, acknowledging the aims of encouraging the recruitment and training of young players and of maintaining a certain balance between clubs by preserving a certain degree of equality and uncertainty as to results or of ensuring the regularity and proper functioning of sporting competitions as legitimate objectives in the general interest, capable of justifying *prima facie* restrictive measures.[30] To be acceptable under EU free movement law, however, these restrictive measures must ultimately still pass the proportionality test. In *Olympique Lyonnais*, for instance, the Court accepted that a scheme providing for the payment of compensation for training where a young player signs a professional contract with another club than the one which trained him can be justified by the objective of encouraging the recruitment and training of young players, provided that the scheme is suitable to ensure the attainment of this goal and does not go beyond what is necessary to attain it. In this case, the Court ruled that the French scheme at issue went beyond what was necessary to

26 *Bosman*, para. 96.

27 See, *inter alia*, the contributions from M. Ilesic, S. Weatherill, S. Van den Bogaert, and G. Infantino & P. Mavroidis on *Bosman* in Maduro and Azoulai (2010); or the Special Issue: 20 Years After Bosman—The New Frontiers of EU Law and Sport (2015) *Maastricht Journal of European and Comparative Law* 22:2.

28 *Walrave*, paras. 8–9.

29 *Deliège*, para. 64.

30 *Bosman* para. 106; Case C-176/96 *Lehtonen*, ECLI:EU:C:2000:201, para. 53.

ensure the objective pursued, for the payment Lyonnais requested from Newcastle for the transfer of Olivier Bernard, a 'former joueur espoir' from Lyonnais, was actually not compensation calculated in relation to training costs, but consisted of damages in relation to the total loss suffered by the club by the breach of contract, unrelated to the real training costs incurred.

3.2.2. The specific case of nationality discrimination in sport

As the Treaty freedom of movement rules are in essence a specific expression of the general prohibition of discrimination on grounds of nationality laid down in Article 18 TFEU, it does not come as a surprise that a substantial part of the case law of the Court of Justice of the EU relating to free movement and sport concerns instances of nationality discrimination.[31] Until now, the Court of Justice has always adopted a robust and orthodox approach vis-à-vis nationality discrimination in sports: it is prohibited as incompatible with European law. The first time the Court had to deal with this issue was in the case of *Donà v Mantero*. The Court firmly rejected rules allowing only nationals to take part in matches organised by the responsible national federation as contrary to Articles 18, 45 and 56 TFEU. As a result, sporting federations were no longer entitled to exclude foreign EU sportsmen completely from participating in official matches at club level. That did not mean, however, that federations set the door wide open for foreign athletes. To the contrary, many, if not all federations, continued to set limitations on the number of foreigners to be recruited and/or fielded in official matches. These restrictions varied from one federation to another, from one sport to another, from one season to another, from one level to another, etc.

The Court's subsequent dismissal of the UEFA'3 + 2' nationality clause in *Bosman* as incompatible with Article 45 TFEU—the lesser known aspect of the *Bosman* ruling—forced the sporting associations to fully liberalise the EU sports employment market for sportsmen from EU/EEA countries. English football club Manchester United is entitled to play with 11 Dutchmen. In the wake of the *Bosman* ruling, many EU/EEA athletes have made use of their free movement rights. As a result, a typical team squad in many a sporting discipline in the EU is nowadays composed of a mixture of home state nationals, EU citizens and also third-country nationals. The 2010 UEFA Champions League final between Bayern Munich and Internazionale perfectly illustrates this point. The starting 11 of the German 'Rekordmeister' counted five German nationals, two EU citizens and three third-country nationals; the Portuguese coach of the *nerazzurri* fielded no Italians, only foreigners: two EU citizens and no less than nine (!) third-country

31 See e.g. S. Weatherill (1989), Van den Bogaert (2018).

nationals. In the 2020–21 Premier League season, no less than 61(!) different nationalities were represented.[32]

Not even *Bosman* did signal the definitive end of nationality clauses at club level, however. The Treaty free movement rights only concern EU/EEA citizens. Many sporting associations decided to hold on to quota with regard to third-country nationals. In 2003, in *Kolpak*, the Court was invited for the first time to express its opinion on the legality of such nationality requirements.[33] The Court stipulated that a professional handball goalkeeper of Slovak nationality who was legally employed in Germany could rely on Article 38(1) of the Association Agreement concluded between the European Communities and Slovakia, which confers the right to equal treatment to Slovak nationals as regards working conditions, remuneration and dismissal in the EU in relation to the host Member State's nationals, to challenge a rule of the German handball federation, providing that clubs were entitled to field only two non-EU/EEA nationals in official matches. Two years later, in the case of *Simutenkov*, involving a Russian footballer playing for a team in Spain's second division who complained about the fact that the Spanish football federation had issued a license as a non-EU player, subjecting him to the quota for non-EU/EEA nationals, the Court confirmed the approach in *Kolpak* and allowed Simutenkov to base his claim for an EU license directly on Article 23(1) of the Partnership Agreement concluded between the European Communities and Russia.[34] The potential impact of the *Kolpak* and *Simutenkov* decisions is far-reaching.[35] For non-EU/EEA sportsmen to be able to successfully challenge nationality clauses, it suffices that the following four cumulative criteria are met: (i) they must be legally employed in a host EU Member State; (ii) an international agreement establishing a partnership or association must be concluded between the EU and its Member States and the country of origin of the non-EU/EEA athletes concerned; (iii) the international agreement must contain an equal treatment provision as regards working conditions, remuneration and dismissal in the host EU Member State; and (iv) that provision must be directly effective. The EU has concluded international agreements containing a similar equal treatment clause with a large number of third-countries.[36] To give but one example: in 2000, the EU and its Member States have concluded the Treaty of Cotonou, a partnership agreement between the EU and 78 ACP (Africa—Caribbean—Pacific) countries. And arguably, several of the equal treatment clauses in these international agreements may fulfil the criteria for direct effect, enabling legally employed third-country national sportsmen to rely on them before the courts of the host Member

32 See https://fbref.com/en/comps/9/nations/Premier-League-Nationalities. England is the nation which is best represented (244 players), followed by France (36), Spain (29), Ireland (28) and Brazil (27).

33 Case C-438/00 *Kolpak*, ECLI:EU:C:2003:255

34 Case C-265/03 *Simutenkov* ECLI:EU:C:2005:213.

35 Dubey (2005), Van den Bogaert (2004).

36 Hillion (2008).

State, so as to render the nationality clauses inapplicable to them.[37] In view of the foregoing, the practical relevance or effectiveness of nationality clauses has inevitably diminished from a legal point of view. Many 'foreign' athletes do enjoy some form of free movement protection under EU law.

3.3. Brexit: the end of free movement

On 1 January 2021, this picture has dramatically changed, at least from a legal perspective. As a result of the UK's departure from the EU internal market, the free movement rules no longer apply to and in the UK. Also, no new arrangements have been made in the EU-UK Trade and Cooperation Agreement.

Evidently, the free movement rules continue to apply in the remaining 27 EU Member States. Portuguese forward Ronaldo still has the right, protected by Article 45 TFEU, to return from Juventus Turin in Italy to Real Madrid in Spain, for example. Conversely, UK nationals no longer have the right to move to a Member State of the EU, and EU citizens no longer have the right to move to the UK. Ronaldo no longer has the right to return to Manchester United. EU citizens wishing to travel to the UK must comply with the immigration rules of the UK. Likewise, UK nationals travelling to a Member State of the EU must fulfil the immigration conditions set by that particular Member State. If they subsequently also want to visit another Member State, they can no longer just go there, as before, when they could still rely on the free movement rules; instead, they must also comply with the immigration rules of that second Member State.

3.3.1. What does this mean in practice, particularly in the UK?

To start with, there are of course EU citizens who were already living in the UK before 31 December 2020. Their rights and status remain the same until 30 June 2021. To stay in the UK after that date, they must in principle apply to the EU Settlement Scheme.[38] If their application is successful, they will be given either settled or pre-settled status, depending on how long they have been living in the UK at the moment of the application. Settled status is usually given to applicants who have been resident in the UK for a continuous period of five years. Belgium's Kevin De Bruyne, who has been playing for Manchester City since August 2015, has thus been living long enough in the UK to qualify for settled status. People

37 Article 13(3) of the Cotonou Treaty stipulates that 'the treatment accorded by each Member State to workers of ACP countries legally employed in its territory, shall be free from any discrimination based on nationality, as regards working conditions, remuneration and dismissal, relative to its own nationals.' The Court of Justice, however, has not yet ruled on the possible direct effect of this provision.

38 www.gov.uk/settled-status-eu-citizens-families.

who have received settled status can stay in the UK as long as they like. They can also apply for British citizenship if they meet the eligibility criteria. EU citizens who have not been continuously resident in the UK for five years by 31 December 2020 will usually get pre-settled status. They can stay in the UK for five more years from the date they got pre-settled status. As soon as they have accumulated five years' continuous residence, they can apply for settled status. People with settled or pre-settled status have, in particular, the right to work in the UK, use the NHS for free, enroll in education or study in the UK, or travel in and out of the UK.

For EU citizens planning to visit, work, study or settle in the UK after 31 December 2020, the UK has introduced a new points-based immigration system.[39] Specifically for football, the English Football Association (FA), the Premier League and the English Football League (EFL) have agreed on a separate plan for entry requirements for overseas players post-Brexit.[40] Footballs' Governing Body Endorsement (GBE) proposal was endorsed by The Home Office in December 2020. The criteria provide the framework for Premier League and EFL clubs to sign overseas players after 31 December 2021.

3.3.2. *What are the most important features of this new system?*

Firstly, and most importantly, post-Brexit, Premier League and EFL clubs can no longer freely sign players from the EU. EU citizens who want to play in the Premier League or EFL are required to gain a Governing Body Endorsement, just like all other overseas players without the right to work in the UK. The GBE will operate on the basis of a rather complex and detailed points-based system, where points are scored for senior and talented young players based on:

- Senior and youth international appearances;
- Quality of the selling club, based on the league they are in, league position and progression in continental competition;
- Club appearances, based on domestic league and continental competition minutes.

How does it work?[41] A club must obtain a GBE from the FA before a player is permitted to play any football for the club. A formal application for a GBE can be made at any time during the season. A GBE will only be granted for a limited period of three years or the length of the player's contract (whichever is shorter),

39 www.gov.uk/guidance/new-immigration-system-what-you-need-to-know.

40 www.thefa.com/news/2020/dec/01/gbe-points-based-system-launched-011220.

41 The Football Association—Governing Body Endorsement Requirements for Men's Players, 2020/2021 season, available at www.thefa.com/news/2020/dec/01/gbe-points-based-system-launched-011220

but it can be extended. A player is not eligible to play for his club beyond the expiry date of the GBE.

The FA will automatically grant a GBE if a player has accumulated enough international appearances in the last two years.[42] Alternatively, a player will earn a GBE if he achieves 15 or more points on the basis of the other criteria.[43] If a player only achieves between ten and 14 points, an Exceptions Panel may still consider the application on the basis of evidence that exceptional circumstances prevented the player from achieving the required 15 points.

In practice, this new GBE system will not pose too many problems for the top players from the EU—or from elsewhere—to come to the UK.[44] If the likes of Manchester United or Liverpool want to sign Mbappé from France or Haaland from Norway, and they can convince these players to cross the Channel, the new rules will not stand in the way of a transfer. After all, any player over the age of 21 from a country ranked in the FIFA top 50 who has played in more than 70% of his country's international matches over the last two years will automatically receive a GBE. Likewise, any player from a club in a so-called 'band 1 league' (the English Premier League, the German Bundesliga, the Spanish La Liga, the Italian Serie A and the French Ligue 1) who appears at least once on the match day squad list in the domestic competition, already gets 12 of the 15 points required for a GBE. If his club were to qualify for the group stages of the UEFA Champions League, the player would gain five more points. Depending on how well the club performs in the Champions League, these five points may become eight if the club reaches the stage of the quarterfinals, or even ten if it gets to the final. And that is without even taking into consideration how many minutes the player has actually played.

The message is clear: this new system is designed to ensure that the Premier League and EFL clubs continue to have virtually unrestricted access to most top EU players, even after Brexit. This is unsurprising. The Premier League has global appeal, to both players and fans. Premier League matches are broadcast all over the world. This represents enormous financial value. Evidently, the FA, the clubs and the UK government were not going to let Brexit jeopardise this leading position on the football ladder.

Be that as it may, lower down the footballing ranks, it becomes more complicated to gain enough GBE points. Established football nations such as Greece, 2004 European champions, or Bulgaria, 1994 World Cup semi-finalists, have respectively slipped to places 51 and 71 on the FIFA World ranking. This means that even Greek or Bulgarian internationals who have played all games of their country for the last two years only get two points towards a GBE. Furthermore, the Greek and Bulgarian leagues are categorised as band 4 and 6 leagues. Only

42 Para. 24 GBE system.

43 In accordance with paras 31–39 of the GBE system.

44 The Guardian, *Football and Brexit: a guide to the new rules and their impact on clubs*, 28 December 2020, www.theguardian.com/football/2020/dec/28/football-and-brexit-a-guide-to-the-new-rules.

six and two points respectively are awarded for playing in these leagues. Based on their actual appearances in the domestic competition, players can earn maximum another six or two points. This means they still fall short of qualifying for a GBE. In the example about Greece, the player could get to the required 15 points by winning the title in Greece, or by qualifying for the UEFA Champions league or the Europa league. In the Bulgarian example, that would not even suffice; arguably, progression to the final stages of the European cup competitions will be required (reaching the final of the Europa league means seven points; the final of the CL is worth ten points). For players from these countries, or for players from lower-tier clubs in higher-ranked countries, it thus will not be so easy, or even possible at all at a given moment in time, to transfer to a club in the UK after Brexit.

Secondly, the UK's exit from the EU means that clubs will not be able to sign players from overseas until they are 18. Under Article 19 on the protection of minors of the FIFA Regulations on the Status and Transfer of Players, international transfers of players under the age of 18 are in principle prohibited.[45] Only a limited number of exceptions apply to this rule, e.g. when the player's parents were to move to the UK for reasons not linked to football.[46] Another exception specifically concerns transfers within the territory of the EU or EEA.[47] Within the EU, transfers of players aged between 16 and 18 are permitted, provided the new club fulfils a number of minimum conditions relating to the quality of football education and/or training, guarantees about academic or schooling or vocational education and/or training and optimal living circumstances. As long as the UK belonged to the EU, English clubs have frequently made use of this opportunity to sign young talents from the European continent. This door has now been closed. Talented young players from countries such as the Netherlands or Germany will no longer be transferred to a club in the UK, at least not before they turn 18.[48] Nothing prevents in principle these players from being transferred in the meantime to Italy or Spain, of course. In an industry where scouts of top clubs travel to all corners of the world in search for talents and compete for the signature of a young talent, this change might be considered by some English clubs as a setback.

Thirdly, in the Premier League the number of overseas Under-21 players a club can sign was limited to three in the January 2021 transfer window and will be limited to six per season moving forwards. According to the FA, this enables the recruitment of the world's best young players to train and play with home-grown talent. Under the application of the Home-grown Players rule in England, there must be at least eight home-grown players in a squad of maximum 25 players.

45 https://resources.fifa.com/image/upload/regulations-on-the-status-and-transfer-of-players-june-2020.pdf?cloudid=ixztobdwje3tn2bztqcp

46 Article 19.2(a) FIFA Regulations.

47 Article 19.2(b) FIFA Regulations.

48 Brexit heeft ook ingrijpende gevolgen voor sportwereld, met name het voetbal, 24 December 2020, https://nos.nl/collectie/13852/artikel/2361933-brexit-heeft-ook-ingrijpende-gevolgen-voor-sportwereld-met-name-het-voetbal.

A player qualifies as home-grown if he plays at least three years for an English team before the age of 21. The home-grown rule applies irrespective of the nationality of the player. In the past, this has allowed English clubs to classify international star players such as Cesc Fabregas from Spain or Paul Pogba from France as home-grown. Undoubtedly, the application of the home-grown rule, in combination with the prohibition of international transfers of minors, will further increase pressure on signing overseas players at the age of 18. At the same time, the combined application of these rules will result in clubs ensuring opportunities for young and local players, which is one of the other explicitly acknowledged objectives of the new system.[49]

Last, but certainly not least, it must be observed that these new entry requirements only apply to the men's game, and even more specifically to clubs in the Premier League or the English Football League. Clubs in other leagues within the men's football pyramid are not permitted to contract overseas players, thus including EU nationals, unless these players have obtained a visa outside the GBE system which permits them to play football in the UK, and the player's employment by the club complies with the terms and conditions of their visa and the relevant Immigration Rules.[50]

Separate, albeit similar arrangements have also been made for the women's game and for managers. Without going into too much detail, the women need to earn more points (24) to obtain a GBE.[51] The 'Auto Pass' threshold for international appearances is also set at a higher level, in that a player must have played 70% of international matches for her national team that must be ranked furthermore in the FIFA top 20, before she will automatically qualify for a GBE. There is also a greater emphasis on playing in the top-level competitions, both domestically and internationally. Currently, the Netherlands are the reigning European Champion and vice World Champion. The Dutch league, however, is not considered to be a top-tier competition. It will be difficult for a non-international from the Netherlands, or any other country outside the world's top eight leagues, to obtain a GBE. Also, there are no criteria for U21 players. Arguably, these differences can be explained by the fact that the women's game is still in a phase of (rapid) development, but still, one cannot but fail to notice them.

Conversely, the rules for managers in the men's game are more straightforward and easier to satisfy than for players: they must hold a UEFA professional license or equivalent and have managed either a club in any band 1–5 competition or an international team from the world's top 50 for a cumulative period of 36 months or a continuous period of 24 months in the last five years.[52]

49 This should also lead to safeguarding the England teams.

50 Para. 3 of the Men's GBE system.

51 The Football Association—Governing Body Endorsement Requirements for Women's Players, 2020/2021 season, www.thefa.com/news/2020/dec/01/gbe-points-based-system-launched-011220.

52 The Football Association—Governing Body Endorsement Requirements for Men's Team Manager, season 2020/2021, www.thefa.com/news/2020/dec/01/gbe-points-based-system-launched-011220.

3.4. Conclusion

Brexit is an unprecedented event in the history of the European Union. It may be too early to estimate the precise repercussions, but that the departure of the UK from the EU will yield important consequences across all sectors of society, including sport, is a fact. For one, the free movement of persons, generally perceived as one of the greatest achievements of the EU integration process, has come to an end. The single fact that EU citizens no longer have the right to play in the UK, the home of football, potentially has devastating consequences for the competitiveness and the attractiveness of the Premier League, perhaps the best football league in the world. To avoid these, a new entry requirement system has been introduced for overseas players in the UK. These new FA rules are detailed and complex. They require additional paperwork and administrative costs. And most importantly, they accommodate fewer people. The best players and the most promising young talents from the EU will still be able to play in the Premier League. That is the main objective of the new rules. For the other players, it will become harder, or even impossible, to play in the UK. This may be a pity, for themselves, just as well as for the (especially smaller) UK clubs who now perhaps lose the opportunity to sign the still undiscovered diamond from anywhere in Europe. But it does not necessarily have to be a bad thing for the English game. Where opportunities go, new opportunities come. In fact, the game could in a way become 'more English' again, as clubs will increase their focus on recruiting the best home-grown talents. And this is also one of the main objectives of the new rules. Interesting times lie ahead . . .

References

Craig, P. & de Burca, G. (2020) *EU Law. Text, Cases & Materials*, 7th edition. Oxford: Oxford University Press.

Dougan, M. (2020) So long, farewell, auf Wiedersehen, goodbye: The UK'S withdrawal package. *Common Market Law Review*, 57:3, 631–704.

Dubey, J.P. (2005) Case note on Kolpak. *Common Market Law Review*, 42, 499–522.

Hillion, C. (2008) Case note on Simutenkov. *Common Market Law Review*, 45, 815–833.

Lindholm, J. & Parrish, R. (2020) Horizontal direct effect of union citizenship and the evolving sporting exception: TopFit. *Common Market Law Review*, 57:4, 1283–1304.

Maduro, M. & Azoulai, L. (eds) (2010) *The Past and Future of EU Law: The Classics of EU Law Revisited on the 50th Anniversary of the Rome Treaty*. Oxford: Hart Publishing.

Van den Bogaert, S. (2004) . . . And another uppercut from the court of justice to nationality requirements in sports regulations. *European Law Review*, 29, 267–275.

Van den Bogaert, S. (2005) *Practical Regulation of the Mobility of Sportsmen in the EU Post Bosman*. Alphen an der Rijn: Kluwer (European Monographs 48, Kluwer Law International).

Van den Bogaert, S. (2018) Sport, free movement and nationality. In: Anderson, J.; Parrish, R. & Garcia, B. (eds) *Research Handbook on EU Sports Law and Policy*. Cheltenham: Edward Elgar, pp. 360–381.

van Middelaar, L. (2018) Brexit as the European union's 'Machiavellian moment'. *Common Market Law Review*, 55:Special issue, 3–28.

Weatherill, S. (1989) Discrimination on grounds of nationality in sport. *Yearbook of European Law*, 9, 55–92.

Chapter 4

Brexit, sport and EU State aid law

Andrea Cattaneo

4.1. Introduction

4.1.1. General remarks

Sport is an area that attracts significant interest in domestic politics. From investing in sporting infrastructures, to bailing out clubs in financial difficulties, to using sport brands as instruments to advance policy objectives, the connection between sport and the state is often in the public domain.[1] The discussion has even greater prominence in times of economic crisis, where states may have other pressing objectives to pursue, and directing funding to sport may be perceived as an outrageous waste of public expenditure.

Public investments in sport can also affects markets where operators are in competition amongst each other. This is true at domestic level, where entities that receive public funding may compete with privately funded operators. However, as elite sport is one truly international industry, competition in the market for organising and commercially exploiting sporting events goes beyond State barriers.

In the context of competitive markets, provisions are required to ensure that states are not offering unlawful advantages to entities established within their territory, to such an extent that is capable of distorting the competition. Under the umbrella of the World Trade Organisation, rules regulate the granting of subsidies by signatories to domestic companies. A similar set of principles apply also within the European Union. In a heavily integrated market, ensuring that undertakings do not receive unfair advantages is instrumental for the functioning of the internal market. As sporting entities engage in economic activities, they are subject to state aid rules. Within European Union law, a consistent set of principles have emerged in relation to the application of State aid rules in the area of sport.

1 For an overview of the involvement of the state in sport, see Houlihan (1991).

DOI: 10.4324/9781003162803-6

As the United Kingdom (UK) has left the EU, the EU-UK Trade and Cooperation Agreement (TCA)[2] regulates their relationship, with the objective of guaranteeing a level playing field between the UK market and the EU-27 single market. In this regard, the United Kingdom has also committed to adopt a new system regulating state subsidies.

This chapter will illustrate the general notions and principles regulating the granting of subsidies at international level and within the EU, and subsequently focus on the policies, decision practice and case law of EU Courts and institutions in relation to State aid and sport. Finally, this chapter will look at the new Subsidy control instruments adopted under the TCA and discuss their possible impact in the area of sport.

4.1.2. Levelling the playing field and WTO

In their relationships with competitors, States attempt to mitigate frictions and ensure greater uniformity of conditions of inter-State competition, through the regulation of the labour market and movement of goods, and the enforcement of competition policy.[3] The ability of a State to depart from the regulatory power of the competitor can translate into lower standards in goods and labour regulations and the granting of subsidies to attract investors in the domestic market. To ensure transparency and reduce tensions, systems to regulate the granting of subsidies are implemented.

In the area of subsidies, the EU encounters significant constraints in ensuring a level playing field when dealing with third countries. Effectively, this requires the ability to identify and act upon illegal subsidies when granted through State resources to undertakings that are not established within the territory of the EU but that operate within it. While these subsidies are capable of distorting the competition within the EU internal market, to the same extent of an aid granted by a Member State, they would not be caught by EU State aid rules.[4] Therefore, the EU's preferred method of ensuring a level playing field with its competitors is by including provisions to that effect when negotiating bilateral agreements.[5]

For the EU and third countries, the reference system for subsidy regulation is provided by the World Trade Organisation. Under the WTO Agreement on Subsidies and

2 Trade and Cooperation Agreement Between the European Union and the European Atomic Energy Community, of the one part, and the United Kingdom of Great Britain and Northern Ireland, of the other part. OJ L 444, 31 December 2020, pp. 14–1462.

3 Hölscher and Stephan (2009).

4 EU Commission, *White Paper on levelling the playing field as regards foreign subsidies*, COM/2020/253 final.

5 See, for example, Association Agreement between the EU and Ukraine, at Article 262, and the Comprehensive Economic and Trade Agreement (CETA) between the EU and Canada, at Article 8.

Countervailing Measures ('SCM Agreement'),[6] a measure which offers an advantage to domestic undertakings against their foreign competitors may constitute an illegal subsidy. The measure, which must be comprised under an exhaustive list of 'financial contributions,' does not necessarily require a cost to be borne by a public authority.[7] Therefore, both substance and form will be assessed in this context—while, as it will be mentioned later, EU State aid rules primarily focus on the impact of the measure rather than its denomination. Effectively, subsidies that fall under WTO rules may not necessarily constitute relevant measures under EU State aid rules.

In terms of enforcement, under Article XVI of the SCM Agreement, WTO Member States are not required to notify the granting of the subsidy, but merely ensure its compatibility with the rules. However, if a Member State can establish the existence of a subsidy, the injury to its domestic industry and the causation between the two, it can impose a countervailing duty on the granting State.[8] This instrument is very effective, as it allows a State to unilaterally impose duties against another State and await a possible challenge before the dispute resolution mechanism.[9] Alternatively, a WTO member can file a complaint against the granting State through the Dispute Settlement Mechanism. This mechanism will first compel the parties to undertake a negotiation and, failing this, the offending party will be subjected to a Panel Scrutiny, and—if necessary—an appellate decision. When the State is considered in breach, the complainant is entitled to retaliate with trade sanctions.[10]

The WTO rules offer minimum standards and a general framework that States are free to improve in their attempt to ensure a level playing field. This is an important objective both for the EU and for its trading partners. In particular, while the EU State aid policy has primarily an internal dimension, as it aims to prevent conducts unduly distorting the competition within the internal market, it also has a significant impact on its partners. The exceptions built into the EU Treaties[11] and through secondary legislation[12] allow Member States to use public funding in the pursuit of specific public policy objectives. However, such use of public funding is inherently capable of hindering the access to the market from third countries: as these conducts award an advantage to domestic undertakings, they necessarily create obstacles for foreign undertakings that are active on the EU market but cannot access similar benefits.

6 Agreement on Subsidies and Countervailing Measures, World Trade Organisation.
7 Ehlermann and Goyette (2006).
8 Article 11 *et seq*, Agreement on Subsidies and Countervailing Measures, World Trade Organisation.
9 Damro (2013).
10 Article 17, Agreement on Subsidies and Countervailing Measures, World Trade Organisation.
11 Article 107(2) and 107(3) TFEU.
12 See, for example, Commission Regulation (EU) No 651/2014 of 17 June 2014 declaring certain categories of aid compatible with the internal market in application of Articles 107 and 108 of the Treaty, [2014] OJ L 187/1 and Commission notice on the de minimis rule for State aid [1992] OJ C 213/2.

Therefore, in the relationship between the EU and the UK, the notion of level playing field has gained significance. In its 2018 Guidelines, the EU Council stressed how, in light of the geographic proximity and economic interdependence between the EU and the UK, the aim of the negotiations was to prevent any unfair competitive advantage that the UK could potentially enjoy by undercutting the levels of protections within its market.[13] In the Political Declaration, a non-binding document agreed in 2019 setting the general principles pursued by the parties through their negotiations, the UK and the EU stated that the underlying objective of the negotiation was to ensure open and fair competition. This could be achieved through regulatory convergence in areas such as competition, social and environmental standards, and State aid.[14] This objective was finally confirmed in the TCA, where parties recognised that their trading relationship required conditions that ensure a level playing field.[15]

Within this context, the negotiation aimed to set up a subsidy regime that could be enforced domestically, through the creation of an independent authority for the UK and a dispute settlement mechanism.

4.1.3. EU State aid law

EU State aid policy aims to regulate the intervention of the Member States on the internal market and prevent them from using subsidies to encourage investments and benefit undertakings in their territory, at the expense of those located in another Member State. This objective requires stricter procedural rules than the discipline provided for by the WTO.[16]

EU State aid rules can be found in Article 107–109 TFEU. Under the first paragraph of Article 107 TFEU, any measure, granted by a Member State or through State resources that is capable of distorting the competition within the internal market by favouring certain undertakings or the production of certain goods, will be incompatible with the internal market.[17] A measure will therefore be a State aid if, regardless of its form and denomination, it constitutes a means for public authorities to provide a selective advantage to its recipient, where no adequate return corresponds to such advantage.[18] The undertaking is therefore selected on the basis of specific characteristics and receives a benefit that would not be

13 European Council, *Guidelines on the framework for the future EU-UK relationship*, 23 March 2018, at 12.

14 Political Declaration setting out the framework for the future relationship between the European Union and the United Kingdom, 2019/C 384 I/02, points 17 and 77.

15 Trade and Cooperation Agreement, Chapter 1 Article 1.1.

16 Ehlermann and Goyette (2006).

17 To give examples that will be discussed in the chapter, measures that can constitute State aid are special tax rates, loans with low interest rates, direct subsidies, preferential rental or selling rates and stadium construction through public funding.

18 Sinnaeve (2001), p. 75.

available under normal market conditions. Essentially, this require the investigating authority to compare the beneficiary of the aid with other operators engaged in similar activities in the same market,[19] and to assess whether the intervention of the State is outside the logics followed by a private operator.[20] Finally, the measure will only be caught if it is likely to cause a distortion within the market and has an effect on inter-state trade. The focus here is on the effects of the aid: even measures granted to undertakings active only within the territory of one Member State can distort inter-state trade if they make it more difficult for competitors to access the relevant market.[21]

Under certain circumstances, State aid will be exempted from the prohibition of Article 107. When the measure offers individual consumers support of a social character, or when it makes good damage caused by natural disaster or exceptional occurrences, the aid will be considered compatible with Article 107(2). Furthermore, under Article 107(3), aid promoting the economic development of certain regions, or certain economic activities, and aid aiming to promote the execution of a project of common European interest or to remedy a serious disturbance in the economy of a Member State may be considered compatible with the internal market. This provision guarantees a degree of flexibility that Member States can use to identify areas where the granting of aid may be legitimate. However, a State aid granted under Article 107(3) must be necessary in order to correct a specifically identified market failure; it must be appropriate to address the objective of common interest and administered in a transparent way.[22] Therefore, any distortion caused will be outweighed by the positive effects triggered by the measure, effectively allowing the Commission to exercise a balancing test between the objective pursued and the restriction caused.[23]

Under Article 108(3) TFEU, Member States must notify the Commission their intention to grant the aid and suspend the granting, pending the approval of the institution. Where such a notification has not occurred, and in any event in which the Commission deems the aid unlawful,[24] the Member State may be ordered to recover the aid.[25] The collateral effect of Article 108 TFEU is to empower National

19 Case C-487/06 P *British Aggregates v Commission* [2008] ECR I-10515, at 82.

20 EU Commission, Notice on the notion of State aid as referred to in Article 107(1) of the Treaty on the Functioning of the European Union, C/2016/2946, OJ C 262, 19 July 2016, pp. 1–50, at 4.2.

21 Case C-280/00 *Altmark Trans and Regierungspräsidium Magdeburg* [2003] ECR I-07747, at 78.

22 EU Commission, State aid action plan—Less and better targeted State aid: a roadmap for state aid reform 2005–2009 (Consultation document) {SEC(2005) 795}, COM/2005/0107 final, at 20.

23 *Ibid*, at 11.

24 Council Regulation No 659/1999 of 22 March 1999 laying down detailed rules for the application of Article 108 TFEU OJ L 83/1, 27 March 1999, Art 1(f). The obligation of prior notification does not subsist in relation to a series of measures that the Commission has exempted either because they fall below a certain *de minimis* threshold, or through General Block Exempting Regulations (GBERs).

25 Case 70/72, *Commission v Germany* [1973] ECR 813, a t13. Under Article 263 TFEU, the decision by the Commission can be brought before the Court of Justice for annulment.

Courts faced with a claim that State aid has been granted, to assess whether the measure constitutes such an aid that requires to be notified to the Commission.[26]

4.2. EU State aid and sport

4.2.1. Introduction

Public intervention in sport is as a politically sensitive matter. Whether it forms part of a structured investment programme to develop local facilities and enhance public participation, or it constitutes a means to subsidise professional clubs, there may be a number of reasons convincing public authorities to direct funding to the sporting sector.[27] These decisions, however, are likely to attract the interest of third parties, which may inform the Commission of measures that affect their position on the market, and request that the Commission take a Decision on their legality.[28] Citizens may also voice their concerns for the use of public funds, although they would not be entitled to initiate any investigation of the Commission.[29]

In any event, the granting of State aid is likely to provide an advantage to undertakings involved in a range of relevant markets, such as the market for the organisation and exploitation of sporting events, the market for the construction of sport facilities, and the market for hospitality services, just to name few examples.[30] The State that decides to distribute public funds has to identify the objective pursued and those who benefit from the measure, as well as the most appropriate way to curb any distortive impact the decision may have on the market.

The brief analysis that follows demonstrates that the approach to State aid cases of EU institutions differ depending on whether the measure provides primarily an economic advantage to private undertakings, or whether it is framed as a necessary intervention for the benefit of the whole community. This approach effectively implements the guidelines already set by the Commission in its Staff Working Document attached to the White Paper on Sport.[31] In this regard, public contributions to the construction of sport facilities may be comprised under general objectives of public policies, while aid to professional sports clubs need to be granted under market conditions to avoid undue distortions of the competition.[32]

26 Case C-354/90, *FNCEPA v. France* [1991] E.C.R. 1–5505, at 10–14. See also Commission notice on the enforcement of State aid law by national courts, OJ C 85, 9 April 2009.
27 Traupel (2014).
28 Council Regulation (EU) 2015/1589 of 13 July 2015 laying down detailed rules for the application of Article 108 of the Treaty on the Functioning of the European Union, OJ L 248, 24 April 2015.
29 Only interested parties have a right to have their complaint examined by the Commission. See *Ibid*, Article 12.
30 Nicolaides (2015).
31 EU Commission, Staff Working Document—The EU and Sport: Background and Context—Accompanying document to the White Paper on Sport {SEC(2007)932}, COM(2007) 391 final.
32 *Ibid*, at 3.2.2.

4.2.2. State aid and sport participation

Under Article 165 TFEU, the action of the EU is aimed at promoting European sporting issues, and in particular the structure based on voluntary activity and the social and educational function of sport. Such an objective underlies the approach of the Commission when public measures are granted to financing sporting infrastructures for the benefit of the public.[33]

In this light, the General Blocking Exemption 615/2014 (GBER II) and its amendments exempt State aid specifically granted for the construction or renovation of sporting and multifunctional facilities from the requirement of prior notification.[34] Where these measures are below a certain threshold,[35] they are used for sport and multifunctional facilities granting open and non-discriminatory access to the public, and if the process of assigning the construction or renovation the facilities to third parties has been fair, open and transparent, the distortion caused on the market will be acceptable.

The adoption of this Regulation and its amendments must be seen alongside a series of Decisions of the Commission, through which the funding of structures aiming at promoting sports participation was effectively recognised as forming part of the public duty of Member States.[36] In these cases,[37] the institution accepted the argument that the failure of the market in supplying private investors to finance the construction or renovation of the facilities had an impact on the public participation in sport, and, in turn, on the protection of health and well-being of the citizens.[38]

The investigations concluded that the measures were likely to provide a selective advantage to private undertakings, some of which were professional sport

33 Kornbeck (2019).

34 Commission Regulation (EU) 2017/1084 of 14 June 2017 amending Regulation (EU) No 651/2014 as regards aid for port and airport infrastructure, notification thresholds for aid for culture and heritage conservation and for aid for sport and multifunctional recreational infrastructures, and regional operating aid schemes for outermost regions and amending Regulation (EU) No 702/2014 as regards the calculation of eligible costs, C/2017/4213, OJ L 156, 20 June 2017. The Regulations expressly lists investment aid, including aid for the construction or upgrade of sport and multifunctional recreational infrastructure, and operating aid for sport infrastructure. See GBER II, Art 55(7).

35 Calculated in reference to eligible costs and possible operating profits from the investment. Furthermore, for aid not exceeding € 2 million, the maximum amount of aid may be set at 80% of eligible costs. See *Ibid*, at 10–12.

36 Communication from the Commission to the European Parliament, the Council, the European Economic and Social Committee and the Committee of the Regions, Developing the European Dimension in Sport, SEC(2011) 68 final, at 3.4.

37 Case SA.31722—Hungary, Supporting the Hungarian sport sector via tax benefit scheme, C(2011)7287 final; Case SA.35135 (2012/N)—Germany Multifunktionsarena der Stadt Erfurt; Case SA.35440 (2012/N)—Germany Multifunktionsarena der Stadt Jena; Case SA.33618 (2012/C) which Sweden is planning to implement for Uppsala arena; Case SA.37109 (2013/N)—Belgium Football stadiums in Flanders.

38 Case SA.31722, at 87.

clubs,[39] and that they were capable of distorting a market where undertakings from different Member States operate. However, they were also necessary to pursue a legitimate objective, and proportionate through restrictive conditions limiting the distortion caused. The reference to the social and educational dimension of sport, as well as its ability to improve the health and wellbeing of the public were therefore considered in exempting the various aid under Article 107(3)(c) TFEU.

The Decisions on funding for sporting infrastructures fit perfectly within the orthodox approach to State aid: the balancing test confirmed by the Court of Justice in *Magic Mountain Kletterhallen*[40] and *Hamr Sport*.[41] In this regard, sport is not necessarily seen in its economic dimension, but as instrumental to pursue public policy objectives, falling under the duty of public authorities. The measures are aimed at addressing a specifically identified failure of the market, which translates into an obstacle to fulfil a responsibility of the state towards the public.[42] To this aim, the Commission can therefore exercise a degree of discretion in assessing the balance between the necessary distortion of the competition caused by the aid, and the extent of the market failure that the measures address.[43]

Such a discretion is apparent when professional sport clubs are recipients of the aid. In the Aid to host the UEFA Euro Championship 2016,[44] French public authorities granted funding for a total of more than €1 billion for the construction or renovation of arenas mainly used by professional football clubs. The Commission applied Article 107(3)(c) and exempted the aid, accepting that it was addressed to remedy the failure of the market in providing the funding necessary to host international sporting and cultural events.[45] Notwithstanding the control system introduced by French authorities to ensure that the use of the funding was proportionate and limited to what was strictly necessary, the Commission refrained from thoroughly scrutinising it. In its assessment, the institution did not require an exact balance between the distortion created and the market failure addressed.

39 Case SA.37109 (2013/N), at 3.

40 Case T-162/13 *Magic Mountain Kletterhallen GmbH and Others v European Commission* [2016] ECLI:EU:T:2016:341.

41 Case T-693/14 *Hamr—Sport a.s. v European Commission* [2016] ECLI:EU:T:2016:292.

42 See Decision of the Commission in Case C4/2008 *Investment of the Municipality of Rotterdam in the Ahoy Complex*, at 67, Case SA.35135 (2012/N) at 13 and 14, Case SA.35440 (2012/N) at 15 and 16, and Case SA.33618 (2012/C) at 26 and 48.

43 Nicolaides (2018).

44 Decision of the Commission on Aide d'Etat SA 35501 (2013/N)—France Financement de la construction et de la rénovation des stades pour l'EURO, 2016 C(2013) 9103 final.

45 SA 35501, at 275

4.2.3. State aid and professional sports

While aid schemes instrumental to pursue public policy objectives may be regarded favourably by the Commission, a different approach was adopted in relation to aid granted to professional football clubs. In a set of Decisions, the Commission examined the legality of State aid granted by public authorities to football clubs, either to alleviate their financial difficulties, or to apply a more favourable taxation regime or through a commercial deal. In these instances, the Commission adopted a more analytical approach, where the economic assessment of the aid and its effects takes precedence over objectives of public policy.

In the investigations involving Dutch football clubs, the Commission scrutinised the decisions of public authorities to provide support to their local clubs through loans, waiver of debts or commercial arrangements favourable to the clubs.[46] In its Decision, the Commission considered whether the behaviour of the public authority could be compared to that of a private market operator. The Commission accepted that, in the event that the financial difficulties of the clubs were to worsen, their creditors, including the municipalities granting the aid, would have not been able to recover their money. The measures were not providing an advantage to the clubs, as private investors could have adopted a similar approach.[47]

Another set of investigations concerned aid granted by public financial institutions to Spanish football clubs in the form of guarantees and counter-guarantees.[48] As private investors were reluctant to guarantee the debt of the clubs, and no restructuring plan was in place to ensure that the public expenditure could be effectively recovered, the Commission held that the measures were illegal.[49] The Decision was however annulled by the General Court, as the Commission failed to demonstrate how the economic value of the guarantees and counter-guarantees resulted in an illegal advantage for the clubs.[50] In the absence of a thorough economic analysis of the market, the claim that a private market operator would have behaved differently was unsubstantiated.[51]

Finally, the tax regime granted by the Spanish authorities to a selected group of football clubs[52] and the swap of lands between Real Madrid and the municipality

46 Decision of the Commission to open an investigation in the case State aid SA.33584 (2013/C) (ex 2011/NN).

47 Decision of the Commission on the Measure SA.41613–2015/C (ex SA.33584–2013/C (ex 2011/NN)), at 57–58.

48 Decision of the Commission in Case SA.36387 Aid to Valencia football clubs, at 9–12.

49 European Commission, Press Release IP/16/2401, State aid: Commission decides Spanish professional football clubs have to pay back incompatible aid, Brussels, 4 July 2016.

50 Case T-766/16 *Hércules Club de Fútbol v Commission* [2019] ECLI:EU:T:2019:173.

51 Cases T-732/16 *Valencia Club de Fútbol v Commission* [2020] ECLI:EU:T:2020:98 and T-901/16 *Elche Club de Fútbol v Commission* [2020] ECLI:EU:T:2020:97.

52 Decision of the Commission to open an investigation in the case State aid SA.29769 (2013/C) (ex 2013/NN)—Spain State aid to certain Spanish professional sport clubs.

of Madrid[53] were put under the lens by the Commission. In the first case, the EU institution held that a reduced tax regime, for which only a small group of clubs qualified, constituted an illegal advantage. The Decision was then annulled by the General Court, which held that the Commission considered only the reduced tax rate, without taking into account the impact of the corresponding limited tax deductions.[54] However, the Court of Justice upheld the decision of the Commission.[55] The Court found that the tax rate was applied to profits, while deductions were calculated on extraordinary reinvestments of such profits, which were not certain when the measure was adopted. In order to consider the deductions, the Commission would have had to wait until the profits were made and reinvested. This would have meant postponing the assessment in a way contrary to Article 108(3) TFEU: from the moment of the adoption of the measure—ex-ante—to the time in which all the effects had been produced—ex-post.[56]

In the other case mentioned above, the Commission held that the terms of an agreement between the club and the municipality of Madrid constituted an illegal form of State aid.[57] Once again, the Decision was annulled by the General Court, which criticised the analysis of the Commission that ignored to give account of all the elements of the agreement.[58]

In relation to this set of aid, the Commission, rather than considering the societal dimension of sport, focused exclusively on the economic impact of the aid granted. As the measures were not pursuing public policy objectives, the relaxed balancing test adopted by the Commission in cases involving financing for sport infrastructures was not applied. Rather, the institution implemented a more analytical approach, which requires it to fully satisfy its burden of proof. The Commission therefore needs to substantiate its analysis with reference to the entire spectrum of characteristics of the sports markets and its investors, to demonstrate that an unlawful advantage has been granted. This assessment is, however, undertaken within the framework of Article 108(3) TFEU, where a prior notification is required for aid schemes and evaluation ex post is only referred to the assessment of the extent of the possible recovery of the aid.

4.2.4. State aid, sport and COVID-19

During the course of the COVID-19 pandemic, a number of Member States have notified the Commission with their intention to administer supporting measures

53 Decision of the Commission to open an investigation in the case State aid SA.33754 (2013/C) (ex 2013/NN)—Spain Real Madrid CF.

54 Case T-865/16 *Fútbol Club Barcelona v Commission* [2019] ECLI:EU:T:2019:113, at 38.

55 Case C-362/19 P *European Commission v Fútbol Club Barcelona* [2021] n.y.p.

56 *Ibid*, at 86.

57 Commission Decision on State aid, SA.33754 (2013/C) (ex 2013/NN) implemented by Spain for Real Madrid CF.

58 Case T-791/16 *Real Madrid Club de Fútbol v Commission* [2019] ECLI:EU:T:2019:346, at 122.

to the sporting industry. There is no doubt that other measures will have been submitted to the Commission and examined by the institution by the time this chapter has been published. Far from providing an overview of the measures approved, this section aims to assess how the measures fit within the current discussion.

The Commission has defined the COVID-19 outbreak as an extraordinary event and has stated that the spread of the virus and the adoption of necessary measures to contain it have severely impacted undertakings in various sectors.[59] Therefore, the Commission has adopted a Temporary Framework, allowing Member States to grant measures below a certain threshold, necessary to 'remedy the liquidity shortage faced by undertakings' and reduce the impact of the disruptions caused by the pandemic.[60] In some cases, Member States have taken advantage of the Temporary Framework and adopted measures in support of the sporting industry. The UK sport sector has also benefitted from the application of the Temporary Framework.[61] With a series of measures adopted in November 2020, the UK Government has granted a series of loans to national governing bodies and clubs affected by the restrictions imposed to tackle the spread of the pandemic.[62] These measures, alongside more general support mechanisms made available by the UK, were allocated on the basis of the requests made and the evidenced submitted of the applicant, and the process was overseen by an independent body.

Member States have also notified supporting measures under Article 107(2)(b), as necessary to make good the damage caused by the exceptional occurrence presented by the pandemic. The French Government notified the intention to grant subsidies to professional sports associations and clubs, and to events' organisers.[63] The measure was available where the applicants could demonstrate that restrictions imposed to public attendance to events had an impact on the sale of tickets, and/or the sale of food and drinks at sporting events. To ensure that the measure was limited to what was necessary to address the consequences of the restrictions, a range of caveat were introduced limiting the size of the aid and placing strict conditions linking the actual loss incurred with the calculation of the grant.

59 Communication from the Commission to the European Parliament, the European Council, the Council, the European Central Bank, the European Investment Bank and the Eurogroup, Coordinated economic response to the COVID-19 outbreak, COM/2020/112 final.

60 Communication from the Commission—Temporary framework for State aid measures to support the economy in the current COVID-19 outbreak, OJ C 91I, as amended by Communication from the Commission C(2020) 2215 final of 3 April 2020 on the Amendment of the Temporary Framework for State aid measures to support the economy in the current COVID-19 outbreak, OJ C 112I, and successive amendments.

61 European Commission, Press Release IP/20/603: State aid: Commission approves £50 billion UK " umbrella" scheme to support the economy in the coronavirus outbreak, Brussel 6 April 2020.

62 UK Government, Press Release: Government announces £300 million Sport Winter Survival Package to help spectator sports in England 19 November 2020.

63 Aide d'État SA.59746(2020/N)—COVID 19—Compensation des clubs sportifs et organisateurs d'évènements sportifs—France.

The disruptions caused by the pandemic and the measures adopted to contain its spread have also created a serious disturbance in the economy of Member States. In another series of aid approved by the Commission, Member States issued supporting measures under Article 107(3) (b).[64]

In approving the measures, the Commission has recognised that the spread of the virus has caused disruptions falling outside the normal functioning of the market[65] and that specific sectors and areas have been severely affected by the restrictions imposed to contain the spread of the pandemic.[66] In particular, undertakings active in the market for exploiting events with spectators have had their economic activity reduced or eliminated through administrative measures accompanied by sanctions.

The decisions reflect the flexibility that forms part of the EU State aid policy, allowing states the ability to refer to the economic needs of a sector in times of severe disturbances. While these measures have considered the economic dimension of sport, future measures may also be needed to ensure that, once the restrictions will be finally lifted, the public will be able to return to effectively enjoy the wider spectrum of societal benefits of sport.

4.2.5. Subsidies under the EU-UK TCA

Measures adopted by the UK before and during the transition period are subject to EU State aid rules, provided that proceedings have commenced before four years from the end of the transition period. In regard to these proceedings, the decisions of the Commission and the judgments of the Court remain binding on the UK.[67]

From the end of the transition period, measures granted by the United Kingdom fall outside the jurisdictional reach of the EU Commission.[68] The institution will lose its investigative powers, and interested parties will not be able to file complaints about State aid measures applied in the UK.[69] Instead, the UK-EU

64 State Aid SA.59340 (2020/N)—Czech Republi c COVID-19: Aid for sport entities and organisations-CZ, State Aid SA.60265 (2020/N)—Croatia, COVID-19: Aid to the tourism and sport sectors and State Aid SA.60212 (2020/N)—Slovakia COVID-19: Aid for professional sport clubs.

65 SA.59746(2020/N), at 53, and SA.60212 (2020/N) at 37.

66 SA.59746(2020/N), at 49.

67 Agreement on the withdrawal of the United Kingdom of Great Britain and Northern Ireland from the European Union and the European Atomic Energy Community. OJ C 384 I, 12 November 2019, pp. 1–177, Articles 92(1) - 95(1).

68 However, under Article 10 of the Ireland/Northern Ireland Protocol, EU rules will remain applicable to the EU Member States and the UK in respect of measures capable of having effect on the trade between Northern Ireland and the European Union. See Protocol on Ireland/Northern Ireland, Agreement on the withdrawal of the United Kingdom of Great Britain and Northern Ireland from the European Union and the European Atomic Energy Community, OJ L 29, 31 January 2020.

69 EU Commission, Notice to Stakeholders, Withdrawal of the United Kingdom and EU Rules in the Field of State Aid, 18 January 2021, at 3.

TCA regulates the relationship between the UK and the EU after the transition period. Under Article 366, the agreement imposes the UK an obligation to introduce a subsidy regime. The definition of subsidy under the terminology chosen in the TCA and the principles related to their assessment broadly mirrors the notions developed under EU law. A subsidy will be caught by the provision when it will have an effect on trade and investments between the EU and the UK.[70] The exceptions to the general prohibition are also similar to those included in Article 107(2) and (3) TFEU.[71]

The TCA sets out general principles that must inform the subsidy regime implemented by the UK, which will have to be transposed into a fully-fledged regime. In essence, these principles replicate the general approach to EU State aid: subsidies must be justified as an appropriate, necessary and proportionate instrument to pursue a specific public policy objective and address an identified market failure, or social difficulties that would not otherwise be remedied. The subsidies constitute an incentive to change the behaviour of the recipient, and any distortion of the competition between the EU and the UK is limited and, in any event, outweighed by the positive effects.[72]

However, the system presents necessary differences with the past. First of all, should disputes arise between the UK and the EU in relation to the granting of subsidies, the TCA provides for a mechanism that include a consultation stage, and following that, an arbitration procedure.[73] Disputes arising between the parties can only be related to subsidies that have an effect on trade between the EU and the UK. However, in the context of trade frictions caused by the UK withdrawal from the EU, assessing the impact of subsidies on trade might prove difficult in the short term.

Measures that have only local impact will fall outside the scope of application of the TCA, as was the case under EU State aid rules anyway.[74] In relation to these, the UK will have to decide how to deal with subsidies that affect only the UK internal market. While this does not raise concerns for the EU counterpart, the UK may have to introduce a system that prevents a subsidy race between public authorities within its internal market, comprised by four nations with devolved powers.

Furthermore, under the TCA, UK public authorities are not mandated to notify the measures before adopting them, but the UK has committed to establish an independent authority to oversee the regime.[75] Instead of an ex-ante control

70 Trade and Cooperation Agreement, Chapter 3, Article 363.1.

71 *Ibid*, Article 364.

72 *Ibid*, Article 366 These principles are to regulate the conduct of public authorities during the interim period before the full implementation of the new subsidy regime.

73 *Ibid*, Article 375.

74 See State aid SA.38208 (2014/NN) (ex 2014/CP)—United Kingdom Alleged State aid to UK member-owned golf clubs.

75 Trade and Cooperation Agreement, Chapter 3, Article 371.

system, the UK has to grant domestic courts the power to review the compliance of measures with the principles established under the TCA, and to award necessary remedies, including orders to recover the subsidy.[76]

On the basis of this principles, it must be noted that a system in which every subsidy can potentially be reviewed by the courts is neither efficient, as it overburdens the judiciary, nor effective, as it leaves the beneficiaries exposed to recovery decisions. In practice, the regime in the UK may therefore have to include a clearance system by the independent authority, effectively bringing the UK closer to the EU ex-ante control system.[77]

However, the absence of an ex-ante system, and the standstill obligation as its corollary, can provide greater flexibility to the regime. Removing one layer from the procedure can reduce the possibility of political influences over the decision and the length of proceedings. Furthermore, as opposed to the WTO system where only States can take action, the involvement of domestic courts offers competitors and third parties an avenue to obtain redress in case they have suffered damages from an unlawful aid.

In this regard, it is worth reminding that under Article 108 TFEU national courts have jurisdiction to assess whether measures granted by public authorities constitute a type of aid that should be notified to the Commission.[78] In the UK, State aid claims have in the past been heard within judicial review procedures, in which the judiciary assesses the conduct of public authorities under the grounds of legality, rationality and adherence to procedural requirements.[79]

In two important cases, UK courts had to assess the use of public funding in relation to sport. In the first one, the tender for the use of the London Olympic Stadium to West Ham FC was discussed multiple times in court.[80] In the 2013 case, the High Court held that there was no unfairness, irrationality or illegality in the decision to award the use of the arena to one football club, to ensure its multi-functional nature.[81]

76 Under Article 372.2 the EU can appear as an intervening party in any court action in the UK concerning the subsidy rules.

77 George Peretz QC, The subsidy control provisions of the UK-EU trade and cooperation agreement: a framework for a new UK domestic subsidy regime, *UK State Aid Law Association Blog*, 30 December 2020, https://uksala.org/the-subsidy-control-provisions-of-the-uk-eu-trade-and-cooperation-agreement-a-framework-for-a-new-uk-domestic-subsidy-regime-by-george-peretz-qc/ (accessed 1 March 2021).

78 Although any challenge to a decision to approve or prohibit a State aid can be brought only to the CJEU. See Case C-188/92 *TWD Textilwerke Deggendorf GmbH v Germany* [1994] ECR I-833.

79 Peretz (2016).

80 See *The Queen on the Application of Leyton Orient Football Club Limited v London Borough of Newham* [2011] EWHC 3047 (Admin) and *The Queen on the Application of Leyton Orient Football Club Ltd v London Legacy Development Corporation v West Ham United Football Club* [2013] EWHC 3653 (Admin).

81 *The Queen on the Application of Leyton Orient Football Club Ltd v London Legacy Development Corporation v West Ham United Football Club* [2013] EWHC 3653 (Admin), at 33–34.

In *Sky Blu Sports*,[82] the Court of Appeal assessed the conduct of the Coventry Council, which granted a loan to Arena Coventry Limited (ACL), a joint venture managing the lease of the local stadium. As the local football club, versing in financial difficulties, stopped paying rent for the use of the stadium, the Council intervened to cover the ACL's debts with the banks. This case is not too dissimilar from the Decisions involving the Dutch football clubs mentioned above: the Court had to consider whether the Council acted as a private market operator. In its assessment, the Court stressed that not all market operators have the same objectives. Provided that the public authority has conducted a sound analysis of the relevant factors, the final decision can present acceptable degrees of variation.[83] The established approach guarantees a margin of discretion to public authorities, which reflects the difficult task of imposing a legal assessment over political decisions. Essentially, only when there is no other plausible explanation for granting the measure, this will be classed as unlawful State aid.[84]

Although the cases discussed analysed measures amounting to State aid, the assessment required was limited to decide whether the measures had to be notified to the Commission. As opposed to this, under the UK subsidy regime, the assessment of the Court will not be based on whether it constituted an aid that should have been notified, but whether, having given consideration to all the circumstances of the case, it constituted an illegal subsidy.

Therefore, on the one hand established case law on assessing State aid is already part of the UK domestic legal order, and the principles developed can be used as guidelines for future proceedings. On the other, the tasks undertaken by the domestic courts under Article 108 TFEU were substantially different from the assessment that will be required to them in the future. Furthermore, the adoption of rules and terminology departing from *the acquis communautaire* may constitute an incentive for courts to avoid an over-reliance on previous case law.

4.3. Conclusion

The EU approach to State aid in sport has consistently developed through two fundamental lines: one more flexible in relation to aid necessary to pursue public policy objectives, the other more strict for measures granted to professional clubs.

82 *The Queen (on the application of) Sky Blue Sports & Leisure Limited, Arvo Master Fund Limited v Coventry City Council v Arena Coventry Limited, Trustees of the Alan Edward Higgs Charity* [2016] EWCA Civ 453.

83 *Assicurazioni Generali SpA v Arab Insurance Group (Practice Note)* [2003] 1 WLR 577 at 16.

84 *The Queen (on the application of) Sky Blue Sports & Leisure Limited, Arvo Master Fund Limited v Coventry City Council v Arena Coventry Limited, Trustees of the Alan Edward Higgs Charity* [2016] EWCA Civ 453, at 25, citing the EU Commission Communication on the application of Articles 92 and 93 of the EEC Treaty and of Article 5 of the Commission Directive 80/723/EEC to public undertakings in the manufacturing sector (OJ C 307/3) at 29.

UK courts and public authorities have also had experience in dealing with State aid granted to the sport sector. In this regard, the chapter has identified similarities in the preference for funding of multifunctional arenas and the support issued to sport through the Temporary Framework.

Insofar as the TCA will regulate the relationship between the two partners, the subsidy regime of the UK is likely to maintain a close connection with the EU State aid system. The principles of interpretation and application of State aid rules form part of the UK legal order already. In the absence of clear statutory rules that introduce a different discipline, the binding nature of the case law might restrain the development of alternative approaches and confirm the application of these principles at national level. Aside from the dispute resolution mechanism, the natural consequence of this is that the divergence between the EU State aid system and the UK subsidy system will be limited in the short period, constrained by the geographical proximity of the markets and the case law developed by the UK courts.

However, the length and range of the disputes arising from the decisions to award the tenancy of the Olympic Stadium demonstrates the level of interests and public concerns that these types of measures attract in the UK. Such an interest will increase the pressure to build and enforce a solid subsidy regime. Once this regime is fully operational, the divergence between EU State aid rules and UK subsidy regulations will have to be assessed further.

Bibliography

Damro, C. (2013) EU state aid policy and the politics of external trade relations. *Journal of Industry, Competition and Trade*, 13:1, 159–170.

Ehlermann, C.D. & Goyette, M. (2006) The interface between EU state aid control and the WTO disciplines on subsidies. *European State Aid Law Quarterly*, 5:4, 695–718.

Hölscher, J. & Stephan, J. (2009) Competition and antitrust policy in the enlarged European union: A level playing field? *Journal of Common Market Studies*, 47, 863–889.

Houlihan, B. (1991) *The Government and Politics of Sport*. London: Routledge.

Kornbeck, J. (2019) HEPA as 'le geste sportif'? Structures versus activities in public policies for the promotion of sport and health-enhancing physical activity. In: Scheuer, C. & Dreiskamper, D. (eds) *Schola Ludens Europaea: Papers dedicated to Roland Naul*. Aachen: Meyer & Meyer, pp. 183–215.

Nicolaides, P. (2015) A critical analysis of the application of state aid rules to sport. *Maastricht Journal of European and Comparative Law*, 22:2, 209–223.

Nicolaides, P. (2018) A more economic approach to the control of state aid. In: Nascimbene, B. & Di Pascale, A. (eds.) *The Modernisation of State Aid for Economic and Social Development*. Wiesbaden: Springer, pp. 63–75.

Peretz, G. (2016) State aid and judicial review. *Judicial Review*, 21:3, 195–203.

Sinnaeve, A. (2001) Competition policy, state aid and state enterprises. In: Hawk, B. (ed) *Annual Proceedings of the Fordham Corporate Law Institute: International Antitrust Law and Policy*. Huntington, NY: Juris Publishing, pp. 67–88.

Traupel, T. (2014) Football and state aid: Really the greatest pastime in the world? *European State Aid Law Quarterly*, 13:3, 414–425.

Chapter 5

Sport, employment law and Brexit

Leanne O'Leary

5.1. Introduction

Over the past forty years, national employment law in the United Kingdom (UK) has developed under the influence of two European legal orders: the European Union (EU) and the Council of Europe. Both legal orders have benefited the employment interests of athletes. *Mutu and Pechstein v Switzerland*[1] and *Ali Riza and Others v Turkey*[2] ruled on the compliance of sports arbitration tribunals with Article 6 of the European Convention on Human Rights (ECHR) and the right of athletes to a fair hearing. In the EU legal order, the recognition of athletes' right of free movement under Article 45 TFEU opened up employment opportunities for athletes and increased competition for athletes' services, with flow-on positive effects for wages in some sports. The cases of *Union Royale Belge des Sociétés de Football Association v Bosman*[3] and *Deutscher Handballbund eV v Kolpak*,[4] for example, have been instrumental in removing federation-imposed restrictions to employment for athletes in another Member State.

The UK withdrew from the EU on 31 January 2020, or exit day as it is defined in the European Union (Withdrawal) Act 2018 (EUWA 2018). Insofar as employment law is concerned, an immediate effect has been the loss of free movement rights for British citizens, changes to the way employers employ workers from the EU and changes to membership of European Works Councils.[5] On exit day, all other employment rights derived from the EU remained the same. The immediate effect for athletes has been the loss of free movement

1 App Nos 40575/10 and 67474/10 (ECtHR, 2 October 2018).
2 App Nos 30226/10 and 4 Others (ECtHR, 28 January 2020).
3 Case C-415/93 [1995] ECR I-4921.
4 Case C-438/00 [2003] ECR I-4135. *Deutscher Handballbund eV v Kolpak* [2003] ECR I-4135.
5 Directive 2009/38/EC of the European Council of 6 May 2009 on the establishment of a European Works Council or a procedure in community-scale undertakings for the purposes of informing and consulting employees [2009] OJ L 122/28. The Employment Rights (Amendment) (EU Exit) Regulations 2019 removes the right of employees in the UK to set up a new European Works Council post exit day.

DOI: 10.4324/9781003162803-7

rights and immigration restrictions for those providing services and working in competitions based in other Member States, issues which are discussed elsewhere in this chapter.

This chapter will focus on the effect of Brexit for the legal recognition of professional athletes as workers or employees and the rights of players' associations that represent the collective interests of athletes. Section 5.2 discusses the legal effect of EU employment law following Brexit and the concept of 'retained EU law' introduced by the EUWA 2018. Section 5.3 considers the legal tests applicable to determining employee and worker status, highlighting the difficulty faced by some athletes of a traditional construction of an employment contract, and Section 5.4 outlines the effect of Brexit for national trade union law. The chapter concludes that any legislative development at an EU level regarding worker status, which benefits those athletes currently excluded from employment protection, will not benefit athletes in the UK. Any post–exit day Court of Justice of the European Union (CJEU) decision on the issue will likely be persuasive in a case before a UK court. The legal status of athletes under a contract with a club, federation or competition organiser will depend on the development of the concept of employee and worker under national law. Brexit will have no effect on the legal rights of players' associations to represent athletes.

5.2. EU employment law and Brexit

Owing to the social and political importance attached to national employment law and the different approaches across Member States to employment regulation, the power provided to the EU to harmonise laws in this area is narrow. Article 153 TFEU provides the EU with a competence in the sphere of employment law to adopt directives in areas such as health and safety, working conditions, information and consultation of workers and social security and social protections amongst others. The competence expressly excludes the right to pay and the right to strike.[6] During the period in which the UK was a member of the EU, EU employment law influenced the shape of workers' rights in the UK and, arguably, influenced the UK to adopt *'a socially liberal and protective framework that it might not otherwise have adopted.'*[7] EU-derived employment law: created or extended workers' rights on working time, equality, consultation and business transfers;[8] broadened access to an Employment Tribunal for workers when access might otherwise have been denied;[9] and

6 Article 153(5) TFEU.

7 Grant (2020). See also Countouris and Ewing (2019).

8 See The Transfer of Undertakings (Protection of Employment) Regulations 2006 SI2006/246; The Equality Act 2010; The Working Time Regulations 1998 SI 1998/1833; and The Transnational Information and Consultation of Employees Regulations 1999 SI 1999/3323.

9 *Benkharbouche v Secretary of State for Foreign and Commonwealth Affairs and Libya v Janah* [2017] UKSC 62, a case concerning an embassy's immunity from employment law claims under the State

widened protection for atypical workers engaged through an agency or in part-time or fixed-term employment.[10] Most EU employment law measures have taken the form of a directive (although there are relevant employment rights provided in the Treaty too, such as equal pay).

The UK is a dualist legal system under international law and for the European Treaties to have legal effect, the European Communities Act 1972 (and subsequent legislation) was enacted to incorporate EU law into national law.[11] Between 1 January 1973 and 31 January 2020 EU regulations, directives, decisions of the CJEU and other law had binding legal effect in the UK. However, the status of EU law in national law changed on 31 January 2020. The EUWA 2018 repealed the European Communities Act 1972 and introduced the concept of 'retained EU law.' EU law in force in national law prior to exit day continues to apply until such time as the Government changes the law or the courts interpret the law in a different direction.[12]

The EUWA 2018 creates a new body of domestic law called retained EU law that is divided into three categories:

- EU-derived legislation that was implemented in national law prior to exit day.[13] This category of retained law is already incorporated in domestic legislation as either an Act of Parliament or a statutory instrument (e.g. The Working Time Regulations 1998 that implemented the Working Time Directive or the Equality Act 2010 that implements the Equal Treatment Directive);
- EU legislation (regulations or other instruments of direct effect that were not implemented in national law before exit date as primary or secondary legislation);[14] and
- Other rights and obligations that have effect because of the European Communities Act 1972. This is a broad provision that captures rights set out in the European Treaties, for example, that had direct effect in the UK.[15]

Immunity Act 1974 and in which an embassy was denied immunity from EU-derived employment law claims on the basis of article 47 of the Charter of Fundamental Rights of the European Union.

10 See The Agency Workers Regulations 2010 SI 2010/93, Part Time Workers (Prevention of Less Favourable Treatment) Regulations 2000 SI 2000/151, and The Fixed-Term Employees (Prevention of Less Favourable Treatment) Regulations 2002 SI 2002/2034.

11 European Communities Act 1972 (now repealed), s2.

12 See the European Union (Withdrawal) Act 2018 (EUWA 2018), ss 2–7 and the European Union (Withdrawal Agreement) Act 2020. Although the UK left the EU on 31 January 2020, under the terms of the UK-EU Withdrawal Agreement it entered a transition period which preserved the legal status quo, subject to a few exceptions, until the end of the transition period on 31 December 2020.

13 EUWA 2018, s 2.

14 EUWA 2018, s 3 and s 7(6). This category is divided into "principle" and "minor" and conditions for how these can be modified or changed are outlined in the EUWA 2018.

15 EUWA 2018, s 4.

There are some aspects of EU law that were not retained in national law on exit day, such as: The Charter of the Fundamental Rights of the European Union,[16] the principle of supremacy of EU law[17] and the *Francovich*[18] principle of state liability. CJEU decisions decided before exit day are a part of retained EU law and will likely be followed when deciding cases involving retained EU law, unless the Government has changed the law. The Supreme Court will not be bound by pre–exit day CJEU decisions and may depart from them in accordance with its own rules of precedent.[19] Additionally, UK courts may '*still have regard to*' CJEU decisions that are made post–exit day[20] but are no longer bound to follow them. It is likely that CJEU cases will become persuasive, just as cases from any other jurisdiction are persuasive when raised in a national court.

The UK Government now has the power to determine the country's employment law and policy direction, subject only to the "level playing field" provisions in the EU-UK Trade Agreement.[21] Under the level playing field provisions, insofar as they relate to employment law, the UK is able to determine its own labour laws and policy under the condition that it will not weaken or reduce labour and social standards or levels of protection below the levels in place at the end of the transition period, if that would impact on investment and trade.[22] The practical effect of the level playing field provisions for national employment law and policy will only be known as the EU-UK relationship develops over time. The consensus view, however, is that although there are areas of EU employment law that are less favoured (for example, holiday pay calculation, the 48-hour maximum working week and protections for agency workers), it is likely that existing employment rights will largely remain intact.[23] Employment rights derived from national

16 EUWA 2018, s5(4). See Barnard (2019) who argues that the Charter will have a legacy effect through the general principles of law and judicial interpretation, but will be considerably weaker.

17 EUWA 2018, s 5(1).

18 Case C-6/90 *Francovich v Italy* and Case C-9/90 *Bonifacti v Italy* [1993] ECR I-5357 which confirmed that a Member State could be liable to an individual for failing to implement an EU directive.

19 EUWA 2018, s 6(4). Under the European Union (Withdrawal) Act 2018 (Relevant Court) (Retained EU Case Law) Regulations 2020 some other courts, including the Court of Appeal, in England and Wales have been provided with the power to depart from pre–exit day case law as well.

20 EUWA 2018, s 6(2).

21 Trade and Cooperation Agreement Between the European Union and the European Atomic Energy Community, of the One Part, and the United Kingdom of Great Britain and Northern Ireland, of the Other Part ('EU-UK Trade Agreement') OJ L 149, 30 April 2021, pp. 10–2539, Articles 386–387.

22 EU-UK Trade Agreement, Article 387(2).

23 Teague and Donaghey (2018). The Government's attempt in January 2021 to conduct a review of employment legislation was abandoned after it became public: 'Kwarteng confirms Government Review of UK Employment Law,' *ft.com* (19 January 2021), www.ft.com/content/ab8d876c-bc65-441e-8b04-051d3be124c9 (accessed 4 March 2021); and 'Employment rights review scrapped by business secretary,' *BBC.com* (28 January 2021), www.bbc.co.uk/news/business-55842992 (accessed 4 March 2021).

law such as unfair dismissal, the entitlement to a redundancy payment and the national living wage are not affected by Brexit.

The working conditions of some athletes far exceed the minimum statutory protections, and where an employment dispute arises, alternative dispute resolution procedures in the sport's regulatory framework may resolve the dispute rather than an Employment Tribunal. The services provided by some athletes and the contracts under which these are provided may form a working relationship to which employment legislation will apply. Any changes to national employment laws brought about by Brexit potentially affect the working conditions of athletes and changes to trade union laws affect the legal environment in which players' associations represent the interest of athletes collectively. Employment rights provided in national law are available only to those individuals who are categorised as employees or workers. The following section considers the legal status of athletes in the UK and whether Brexit will affect that status, if at all.

5.3. Legal status of athletes

There is no sport-specific legislation in the UK regarding the status of athletes. To rely on employment rights and protections in national law an athlete must establish employee or worker status. National law recognises three categories of legal status: employee, worker and independent contractor. An employee is employed under a contract of service, whereas an independent contractor is engaged under a contract for service.[24] Worker is defined separately in some statutes and generally works under a contract to provide services personally. In doing so, a worker may be in a subordinate or dependent position or may be someone who is in a sufficient arm's length and independent position from their employer '*as to be treated as being able to look after themselves.*'[25]

A wide range of statutory employment protections apply to employees. The law will also imply specific terms into a contract of employment e.g. an implied term on the part of the employer to provide work for those in certain occupations or those who need to be doing work in order to maintain work skills[26] or the implied term of mutual trust and confidence.[27] A higher duty is owed to employees under

24 See the definition of employee and employment contract in the Employment Rights Act 1996, ss 230(1)-(3).

25 *Bryne Brothers (Formwork) Ltd v Baird* [2002] ICR 667 para 17(4).

26 See *Herbert Clayton and Jack Waller Ltd v Oliver* [1930] AC 209 (HL) and *William Hill Organisation v Tucker* [1999] ICR 291.

27 See *James-Bowen and Ors v Commissioner of Police of the Metropolis* [2018] 1 WLR 4021 (SC) citing *Malik v BCCI* (1997) IRLR 462 (HL) in which the mutual obligation is described as the obligation on, "*an employer and employee not, without reasonable and proper cause, to engage in conduct likely to destroy or seriously damage the relationship of trust and confidence required between an employer and employee*": *James-Bowen*, para 16. In the sports context, see *McBride v Falkirk Football and Athletic Club* [2012] IRLR 22 (EAT Scotland).

health and safety laws.[28] Workers are entitled to protection from discrimination, to receive the national minimum wage and to benefit from statutory provisions regarding rest breaks and annual leave, but they are not entitled to a redundancy payment or to bring a claim of unfair dismissal upon termination of a contract; those benefits are available only to employees. Cases involving gig economy workers have illustrated the difficulties with distinguishing between a worker and an independent contractor.[29] Some employment rights are extended to workers. Independent contractors or self-employed people do not have employment rights.

It has been left to the courts to determine the legal status of a party to a contract, applying tests developed at common law and taking into account the circumstances of each individual case. In the context of modern working relationships, with a greater variation in work patterns and practices, and business models developing around technology (e.g. the 'gig economy') and automation, the line between employee and worker or worker and independent contractor has become increasingly blurred.[30] As Lord Denning once asserted, it is '*often easy to recognise a contract of service when you see it, but difficult to say wherein the difference lies.*'[31] The label the parties attach to the relationship or the fact a written contract has been signed is not determinative of the relationship. A written contract is only one factor in determining legal status and the courts may look behind the written contract and enquire into the circumstances in which the relationship is conducted to determine '*the true agreement.*'[32] To establish employee status, it is generally considered that there must be a mutual obligation, a degree of control exerted by one person over another, and terms consistent with an employment contract such as personal service.[33]

Difficulties with defining worker or employee are not unique to the UK.[34] Employment law regulation worldwide makes a distinction between employees whose relationship is often characterised by an imbalance of power and require greater statutory protection, and independent contractors who do not. Access to employment rights requires a classification under the contract as employee or worker, and the legal construction of the contract of employment has typically been influenced by the concepts of subordination, continuity and the requirement

28 Health and Safety at Work etc Act 1974.

29 *Uber BV and Others v Aslam and Others* [2021] UKSC 5.

30 See the *Good Work: The Taylor Review of Modern Working Practices* (July 2017).

31 *Stevenson Jordan and Harrison Ltd v McDonnell and Evans* [1952] 1 TLR 101, 111.

32 *Autoclenz v Belcher* [2011] ICR 1157 (SC), para 35; and *Uber BV* (n 29) para 85.

33 *Ready Mixed Concrete (South East) Ltd v Minister of PNI* [1968] 2 QB 497. For a definition of mutual obligation, see *HMRC v Professional Game Match Officials* [2020] UKUT 0147 (TCC), paras 67–70 (appeal pending) that confirmed football umpires in the Championship, League 1 and League 2 are self-employed contractors and not employees. Note the current debate that the requirement for mutuality of obligation is limited only to establishing whether a contract exists at all: Freedman (2020), p. 210.

34 See the preamble to the International Labour Organisation Employment Relationship Recommendation 2006 (No 198).

of a bilateral contract only.[35] If an individual in a subordinate working relationship is not able to benefit from employment protections because of their legal classification under a private contract, it creates opportunities for exploitation and reduces the efficacy of employment laws.[36]

Relying only on a private contract that may be drafted by the more dominant party, usually the putative employer, to regulate access to employment protections, results in factually identical work relationships being underpinned by different types of contract. For example: in the situation of a professional club football match between an English football club and a club from Croatia, the players on the English team may be considered employees and players on the other side may be independent contractors.[37] So too across competitions such as the National Collegiate Athletics Association football competition in which players are classified as 'student athletes' and in the National Football League where players are considered employees of the teams that they represent. The legal status of athletes falls within a policy and regulatory debate that is occurring at a national and international level to define a broader scope of employment law protection that is more in keeping with the nature of modern work practices.[38]

The concept of worker is preferred to that of employee in most EU legislation and although it is used in different contexts, it is generally considered that a worker provides services in a contractual relationship that is hierarchical and characterised by subordination. The CJEU defined worker in *Allonby v Accrington and Rossendale College*[39] as, '*a person who, for a certain period of time, performs services for and under the direction of another person in return for which he receives remuneration.*'[40] The CJEU has also emphasised that when determining whether a hierarchical relationship characterised by subordination exists, it is necessary to take account of '*the objective situation of the individual concerned,*' all the circumstances of their work, the terms of the contract and how the obligations are performed in practice, the interpretation of which should be supported by the objectives of the relevant legislation.[41] The express terms of the contractual documents are not conclusive and where there is a conflict between the terms and the actual relationship, an interpretation based on the actual relationship is to be preferred.[42] Under EU law,

35 Countouris (2019), pp. 8–10.

36 *Ibid.*

37 For a discussion, see Duval and van Maren (2017).

38 See ILO Recommendation 198; Countouris (2019), Freedman (2020). Countouris notes an emerging consensus that reform is required and suggests a broader conceptualisation of the notion of the employment relationship as a 'universal work relation' that captures those covered by a subordinate employment contract, but also those less subordinate, continuous or formalised personal relations that are currently excluded: Countouris (2019), pp. 15–18.

39 Case C-256/01 [2004] ECR I-873.

40 *Ibid*, para. 67.

41 Case C-610/18 *AFMB Ltd v Raad van bestuur van de Sociale verzekeringsbank* [2020] ICR 1432, paras. 60–62.

42 *Ibid*, paras. 58–59.

in various contexts, a football player,[43] handball player[44] and basketball player[45] have been considered workers.

In national law 'worker' has a specific statutory definition, examples of which are set out in the National Minimum Wage Act 1996, the Employment Rights Act 1996 and the Working Time Regulations 1998. A 'worker' works under a contract of employment or provides services personally for another party, who is not a client or customer.[46] Worker status extends the categories of employment rights to working individuals whose degree of dependence is the same as an employee. In a series of cases arising before the Supreme Court, the test for determining worker status has developed in a manner consistent with EU law. Some of the cases concerned claims involving EU-derived employment rights and others involved employment rights derived from national law.[47]

Subordination is a factor for establishing worker status, but it is not a '*freestanding and universal characteristic of being a worker*.'[48] In *Bates van Winkelhof v Clyde and Co LLP and Anor*,[49] the Supreme Court held that an equity partner in a law firm was a worker. Although Bates van Winkelhof was not in a subordinate relationship with other partners in the law firm, she was integrated into the business of the entity to whom personal services were provided and had an inability to market those services to anyone else. This gave rise to dependency on a particular relationship and rendered the person vulnerable to exploitation.

The contract terms are only one element for consideration of worker status. In *Uber BV and Others v Aslam and Others*,[50] the Supreme Court put aside the terms of a contract that claimed Uber drivers were independent service providers, in favour of an interpretation that Uber drivers were workers for the purposes of the Working Time Regulations 1998, National Minimum Wage Act 1998 and the Employment Rights Act 1996. The Supreme Court emphasised that the features of a working relationship—which it identified as subordination and/or the dependency of workers and control—and the bargaining power of the putative

43 *Bosman* (n 3) and Case C-325/08 *Olympique Lyonnais SASP v Bernard* [2010] 3 CMLR 14.

44 *Kolpak* (n4).

45 Case C-176/96 *Lehtonen v Fédération Royale Belge des Sociétés de Basket-Ball ASBL* [2000] 3 CMLR 409; and Case C-265/03 *Simutenkov v Ministerio de Educacion y Cultura and Anor* [2005] ECR I-2579.

46 National Minimum Wage Act 1998, s 54(3); Employment Rights Act 1996, s 230(3); Working Time Regulations 1998, reg 2(1).

47 *Carmichael v National Power plc* [1999] 1 WLR 2042 (tour guides engaged on an 'as and when required' basis were not workers); *Hashwani v Jivraj* [2011] UKSC 40 (arbitrator engaged to provide arbitration services not a worker); *Autoclenz Ltd* (n 32) (car valeters held to be workers); *Bates van Winkelhof v Clyde & Co LLP and Anor* [2014] 1 WLR 2047 (equity partner in a law firm considered a worker); *Pimlico Plumbers Ltd v Smith* [2018] UKSC 29 (plumber held to be a worker); and *Uber* (n 29) (drivers in the gig economy held to be workers).

48 *Bates* (n 47) para 39.

49 *Ibid.*

50 *Uber* (n 29).

employer meant that the terms of a written contract cannot be taken as the starting point in determining whether an individual is a worker, or as conclusive of the relationship between the parties. The bargaining power that favours the employer in a working relationship was an influential factor in the decision because an employer is '*very often in the position to dictate such contract terms and the individual performing the work has little or no ability to influence those terms.*'[51] The *Uber* case is another in a growing list of authorities that demonstrate the courts' willingness to protect those with a weaker bargaining power in an employment relationship.[52]

Athletes provide their skills and services in a non-standard work environment. It is not an office or a factory but a stadium, track or road, and an athlete's training or performance schedule does not fit within the usual 9 am to 5 pm work routine. Training for, and participating in, sport may not be perceived as work. A sport's regulatory rules may define athletes as amateur or a status other than worker. There may also be difficulties establishing continuity in certain sports where an athlete is temporarily part of a team for an event, e.g. a World Championship or the Olympic Games, and in some cases there may be more than one party to the athlete's contract depending on how the sport is organised. Those factors can militate against a finding of worker status for athletes, when the traditional concept of an employment contract is applied, namely: subordination, continuity and bilateralism. Commercialism in sport has contributed to a growth in revenue for some sports organisations, and many elite athletes are now able to earn an income from sport. Increasingly, athletes are providing services under a contract in which their legal status may fall within the legal definition of employee or worker, even if the terms of the contract or the sport's regulatory rules or public perception consider otherwise.

Only a few high-profile, talented athletes will be in a position to negotiate the terms on which they provide services on an equal basis with a club, team or federation. Generally, an athlete will be in a weaker bargaining position and unable to negotiate the terms on which his or her services are provided. Also, the terms may be determined within a regulatory decision-making process that does not involve the athlete, or the terms may be set down by a party who is not in a direct contractual relationship with the athlete. *Uber* confirms that for individuals providing services in an atypical environment who are not in a position to negotiate the terms of a contract, the contract terms are not determinative. The circumstances of the relationship and the purpose of the legislation under which the right is asserted are all relevant factors for consideration.

Athletes in a number of countries have endeavoured to establish worker or employee status in order to rely on employment protections in disputes with a

51 *Ibid*, para 76.

52 See *R(on the application of UNISON) v Lord Chancellor* [2017] UKSC 51, *Autoclenz Ltd* (n 32) and Alan Bogg (2018).

federation, sports club or other competition entity, or with establishing worker status for the purposes of trade union recognition, with varying degrees of success. In the United States of America (USA), student athletes were unsuccessful in establishing worker status so as to form a trade union and engage in collective bargaining.[53] In Canada, a group of 'amateur' rugby players successfully established that they were employees of Rugby Canada for the purposes of collective bargaining.[54] In Austria, a synchronised swimmer successfully argued that she was a worker of the Austrian National Olympic Committee for the purposes of workers' compensation.[55] In the UK, a player employed by a football club has been held to be a worker.[56]

The challenges of establishing worker status for some athletes are demonstrated in the case of *Varnish v British Cycling Federation (trading as British Cycling)*.[57] Jessica Varnish, a former professional cyclist with the Great Britain Cycling Team claimed unfair dismissal, sex discrimination, victimisation and unlawful detriment against British Cycling and UK Sport. Unfair dismissal and unfair detriment are national law rights that arise under the Employment Rights Act 1996; and sex discrimination and victimisation claims arise under the Equality Act 2010 which implements the Equal Treatment Directive. As a preliminary issue, in order to proceed with her claims, Varnish had to establish employee or worker status.

At the relevant time, Varnish was a member of British Cycling's Podium Programme. She had a four-year fixed-term written Athlete Agreement with British Cycling which expressly stated that it was not an employment contract and that participation in British Cycling's Podium Programme did not create an employment relationship. Under the Athlete Agreement, British Cycling agreed to

53 *Northwestern University and College Athletes Players' Association* (Case 13-RC-121359, National Labor Relations Board, Decision on Review and Order, 17 August 2015), overturning a previous Decision and Direction for Election by the Regional Director for Region 13 (Chicago, Illinois) in *College Athletes Players' Association v Northwestern University* (Case 13-RC-121359, 26 March 2014).

54 *Canadian Rugby Union—Federation Canadienne De Rugby ('Rugby Canada') v United Steel Paper & Forestry, Rubber Manufacturing, Energy, Allied Industrial and Service Workers International Union Local I-1937* (British Columbia Labour Relations Board ("BCLRB") No B2/2019, 9 January 2019) upheld by the British Columbia Labour Relations Board following an application for leave and reconsideration in *Canadian Rugby Union—Federation Canadienne De Rugby ('Rugby Canada') v United Steel Paper & Forestry, Rubber Manufacturing, Energy, Allied Industrial and Service Workers International Union Local I-1937* (BCLRB No B88/2019, 5 July 2019) (decision under appeal).

55 International Labour Organisation, *Decent Work in the World of Sport: Issues Paper for Discussion at the Global Dialogue Forum, Geneva* (20–22 January 2020) para. 37.

56 *Walker v Crystal Palace Football Club Ltd* [1910] 1 KB 87. The definition of 'workman' applicable in that case for the purposes of the Workman's Compensation Act 1906 has some similarity with the definition of employee under the Employment Rights Act 1996; cf *Jessica Varnish v British Cycling Federation (t/as British Cycling)* [2021] ICR 44 (EAT).

57 *Varnish* (n 56).

develop a performance plan and provide a package of services (e.g. access to the services of a coach and sports psychologist, team clothing and equipment, sports science support, medical services, etc.) which had a value of up to £700,000. Membership to British Cycling's Performance Podium Programme could be suspended or terminated for performance-related or disciplinary reasons. In return, Varnish agreed to comply with the performance plan, train with the GB squad, wear team clothing and engage in contractual appearances, amongst others. She was required to obtain the prior written consent of British Cycling before working in any media capacity, and she also agreed not to engage in personal commercial work with any third party without the prior written consent of British Cycling. Owing to her inclusion in British Cycling's Performance Podium Programme, Varnish was eligible to apply to UK Sport (an executive non-departmental public body that distributes National Lottery funding to sports to support Olympic and Paralympic medal success) for a means-tested grant known as an Athlete Performance Award. The funding provides financial support for athletes while training.

Varnish argued that she was employed by British Cycling, UK Sport or both under a tri-partite arrangement. British Cycling argued that the contract was not a contract of service or a contract personally to execute any work or labour but a contract under which the primary or dominant purpose was to train, support and assist Varnish. The Employment Tribunal agreed with British Cycling, and the decision was upheld on appeal. A significant reason for the finding was the restrictive approach to the concept of work that both Tribunals adopted. Whilst the Employment Tribunal accepted that British Cycling exercised a high degree of control in the relationship, mutuality of obligation and personal service were not present, so as to establish an employment relationship. The absence of personal service to do work militated against a finding of worker status. In the Tribunal's view, Varnish did not provide work or skill in consideration for wages which were relevant to the concept of mutuality of obligation and personal performance. She was personally performing a commitment to train in anticipation of gaining selection to compete for Team GB at the Olympics; she was not performing work provided by British Cycling. Moreover, the benefits and services provided to support the training were not remuneration awarded in exchange for work or skill performed. The funding received from a third party was a non-repayable grant based on the assessment of likely future potential and not past factors, wages or remuneration.

The *Varnish* decision demonstrates the difficulties that some athletes need to overcome to establish employee or worker status when the main regulatory device to circumvent employee and worker status is the contract between the parties. It demonstrates the rigidity with which the courts can approach the interpretation of the contract of service to the exclusion of some individuals from employment protections. Varnish's working pattern and work arrangements did not fall within the concept of the standard employment relationship that the contract of services was designed to capture.[58] *Varnish* was decided before *Uber*, and in light of that case, it may be that a different outcome could be drawn. The Athlete's Agreement expressly stated that it was not an employment agreement and in so doing limits or excludes the application of employment legislation to a category of individuals who are dependent on British Cycling for their participation in events that generate commercial opportunities for them and revenue for British Cycling.

The capacity of an athlete to benefit from employment legislation depends on the contract terms, the way in which the relationship is carried out, and the context in which athletes provide those services. The issue for athletes globally is the conceptualisation of athletes as workers. The construction of worker status under EU law and national law is the same and, following Brexit, is unlikely to change in the short term. To the extent that EU law develops in a way that recognises all athletes as workers, then those UK athletes who are not currently considered workers will be excluded from that benefit. If sport-specific legislation is introduced at a European level that provides worker status for athletes, it will have no legal effect in the UK; although, future CJEU decisions regarding worker status will likely be persuasive in domestic cases. Overall, it is difficult to predict the direction of employment law. The next section considers the effect of Brexit for players associations.

5.4. Trade union law and Brexit

Athletes in several professional sports in the UK have organised collectively and formed trade unions (better known as players associations) to represent their employment interests. Football has a long-established collective bargaining relationship that pre-dates the Premier League and a well-resourced players association, unlike other professional sports such as rugby union, cricket, rugby league or netball. The collective bargaining model that exists in the Premier League through the Professional Football Negotiating and Consultative Committee (PFNCC) does not exist in other professional sports.[59]

As trade unions, players associations are subject to collective labour laws that regulate trade union recognition, collective bargaining and industrial action, the principal statute of which is the Trade Union and Labour Relations (Consolidation) Act 1992. All statutes and legal rules that regulate the collective labour relationship are national laws. EU employment law has been influential in shaping individual employment rights in the UK. It has, however, had no influence on wage setting, trade union recognition or the national laws governing strike action because the EU does not have competence to legislate in the areas of collective bargaining, the right to organise, right to strike and other forms of industrial action. Brexit is, therefore,

58 Countouris (2019), p. 8.
59 For more information, see O'Leary (2017), chapter 8.

unlikely to have a significant effect on collective bargaining and trade union laws in the UK or the day-to-day collective representation of athletes.[60]

It is also unlikely to alter the engagement of players associations with their European counterparts such as EU Athletes or FIFPRO and other international affiliates. Membership to these European and international trade union associations has provided a source of support for the development of national players associations, a collective voice at a European-level and has enabled some players associations to participate in initiatives that support professional athletes. Brexit will not affect affiliation to these international trade unions or receipt of benefits that membership provides, although any involvement in European projects may be dependent on the funding terms for the project.

Article 399 of the EU-UK trade agreement refers to multilateral labour standards and agreements. It provides a commitment on the part of each of the EU and the UK to respect, promote and implement the internationally recognised core labour standards as defined in the ILO Conventions (e.g. freedom of association and the effective recognition of the right of collective bargaining); ratify the fundamental ILO Conventions on labour rights; and promote social dialogue amongst workers and their employers, amongst other things.[61] While on the face of it the clause may provide encouragement for the UK Government to implement more favourable trade union laws, commentators are critical of such clauses which are typically included in trade agreements and have reportedly had little effect.[62]

5.5. Conclusion

The UK Government now has the power to determine the direction of employment law and policy, subject only to the level playing field provisions in the trade agreement. The effect for individual employment rights, including the determination of employee and worker status, will only become apparent as the EU and UK trade relationship develops. At the time of writing, the test for worker status in national law is consistent with the test applied under EU law. There is no indication that sport-specific legislation regarding the legal status of athletes will be introduced at an EU-level and if it were, it will be of no effect in the UK. The UK Government has indicated that it is considering legislative changes to the definition of worker in national law; there are no UK Government plans to legislate specifically for the status of athletes.[63] Whether athletes who provide services in

60 For a discussion of the effect of BREXIT on employment law and labour relations law generally, see Teague and Donaghey (2018).

61 EU-UK Trade Agreement (n 21) Article 399.

62 Nicola Countouris, Lord John Hendy QC, Keith Ewing (*Institute of Employment Rights*, 7 January 2021), www.ier.org.uk/comments/collective-bargaining-promises-in-brexit-deal-are-nothing-but-hot-air/ (accessed 29 March 2021).

63 See the Taylor Review (n 30) and the Government's response in HM Government, *The Good Work Plan* (December 2018) which sets out the Government's proposal to clarify worker status.

an atypical work environment and who may currently be excluded from employment protections because of their status will benefit from the change is unknown.

Brexit will have no effect for trade union laws and for the representation activities of players associations because trade union regulation arises under national law only. Of far greater concern for trade union rights is the potential repeal of the Human Rights Act 1998 (HRA1998), which the Conservative Government has indicated it may do.[64] The HRA 1998 has provided an additional legal avenue for unions to challenge legislative incursions or employer practices that limit the right to collective bargaining and strike action.[65] Repealing the HRA 1998 would limit trade union legal challenges in an already restrictive collective labour rights regime in the UK.

References

Barnard, C. (2019) So long, farewell, auf Wiedersehen, Adieu: Brexit and the charter of fundamental rights. *Modern Law Review*, 82:2, 350–366.

Bogg, A. (2018) The common law constitution at work: R (on the application of UNISON) v lord chancellor. *Modern Law Review*, 81:3, 509–538.

Countouris, N. (2019) *Defining and Regulating Work Relations for the Future of Work*. Geneva: International Labour Office. www.ilo.org/wcmsp5/groups/public/—ed_dialogue/documents/publication/wcms_677999.pdf.

Countouris, N. & Ewing, K. (2019) *BREXIT and Workers' Rights*. London: Institute of Employment Rights. www.ier.org.uk/product/brexit-and-workers-rights/.

Duval, A. & van Maren, O. (2017) The labour status of professional football players in the European Union: Unity in/and/or diversity? *European Labour Law Journal*, 8:3, 258–278.

Freedman, J. (2020) Employment status, tax and the gig economy—improving the fit or making the break? *King's Law Journal*, 31:2, 194–214.

Grant, J.L. (2020) Great Britain and Brexit: A forecast of the future of employment protection during corporate insolvency. *International Insolvency Review*, 29:1, 61–82.

O'Leary, L. (2017) *Employment and Labour Relations Law in the Premier League, NBA and International Rugby Union*. Heidelberg: Springer.

Teague, P. & Donaghey, J. (2018) Brexit: EU social policy and the UK employment model. *Industrial Relations Journal*, 49:5–6, 512–533.

64 In December 2020 the Government established a review into the Human Rights Act 1998 (HRA 1998) to consider the relationship between the ECtHR and domestic courts; and the impact of the HRA 1998 on the relationship between the judiciary, government and the executive: *Independent Review into the Human Rights Act 1998* (December 2020), Terms of Reference.

65 See, for example, *Secretary of State for Justice v Prison Officers Association* (2020) ICR 1257 (CA) and *National Union of Rail, Maritime & Transport Workers v United Kingdom* (2015) 60 EHRR 10.

Chapter 6

Sport and Brexit

Athletes' sex and gender rights

Seema Patel

6.1. Introduction

6.1.1. General remarks

This chapter investigates the impact of Brexit upon athletes' sex and gender equality and human rights. As the curtain closes on the UK's membership with the European Union (EU), attention turns to the aftermath of this separation. Whilst the discussion has centred on the financial and economic factors, equality and human rights for minorities have been to some extent invisible during this divorce.[1] Even less consideration has been made of the impact upon the protection of athletes from sex and gender inequality in sport. An examination of Brexit in this context offers a useful insight into the unique position of athletes' rights and sheds light on the power struggle that is currently taking place between sport interests and human rights.

This chapter will briefly outline the historic context of sex and gender issues in sport, exploring the tensions between inclusion and exclusion in an environment that is driven by the treatment of athletes according to their physical and non-physical differences. The current legal landscape of equality and human rights provisions that seek to protect individuals from sex and gender discrimination will then be mapped out, examining how those rights apply to sport and drawing upon examples of athletes who have asserted their rights in the courts and sought to challenge discriminatory treatment.

This chapter will evaluate how equality and human rights for minority groups in the UK might be protected post-Brexit and whether those changes will affect the current restrictive position of athletes seeking to gain protection from equality and human rights legislation when their rights have been threatened.

1 Danisi et al. (2019).

DOI: 10.4324/9781003162803-8

6.1.2. Position of athletes' sex and gender rights

The concept of sex denotes the biological and physical characteristics that are usually determined at birth. Gender relates to the subsequent social consequences for an individual and is representative of a person's sense of identity. The traditional notions of sex and gender, where fixed biological and cultural assumptions defined a man or woman, are currently being challenged and transformed to encompass a much broader and fluid spectrum of gender identity.[2] Indeed, gender diverse groups, such as individuals with sex variations or trans people, have often been misplaced along this spectrum which has affected inclusion in society. The value and importance of equality, human rights and non-discrimination principles are therefore essential for the protection of gender diverse groups.

In the context of sport, sex and gender identity presents a curious conundrum because sport creates conditions which separate athletes according to their human differences and ability. Sporting activity is therefore divided along sex and gender lines, as a way of ensuring fairness in competition and protecting the essence of sport. The inclusion or exclusion of athletes may therefore be viewed as legitimate when in the pursuit of this aim, even when exclusion is incompatible with principles of human rights.[3] The biological view that men enjoy physiological advantages over women justifies the sex segregation across and within the male and female categories of sport. Sport-governing bodies have introduced eligibility rules to support this this science-based division, which have evolved from sex testing to gender verification and eligibility criteria based upon hormone levels.

However, in recent times, sport has struggled to justify this rationale as it is increasingly clear that sex and gender cannot be strictly categorised, or that eligibility rules cannot be arbitrarily formulated without threatening the human rights of the athlete. This balance struggle has been magnified by the case of South African sprinter Caster Semenya who was prohibited from competing after failing to satisfy the International Association of Athletics Federations (IAAF, now World Athletics) Eligibility Regulations for the Female Classification (Athletes with Differences of Sex Development [DSD]) (2018 Regulations). The 2018 Regulations require 'biologically male' athletes with 46 XY DSD, who have naturally excessive testosterone levels, to reduce their level through hormone treatment. Athletes who do not meet the criteria and who did not wish to undergo treatment are invited to compete in non-restricted female events or male competitions. Semenya filed arbitration proceedings to the Court of Arbitration for Sport (CAS), challenging the validity of the 2018 Regulations on both legal and scientific grounds. The CAS Panel concluded that the 2018 Regulations were discriminatory but were a necessary, reasonable and proportionate means of achieving the aim of protecting

2 Patel (2021).
3 Patel (2015).

female athletes in certain events. Following the judgment, Semenya appealed to the Swiss Federal Supreme Court (SFT) but was dismissed, holding that the CAS decision was compatible with principles of Swiss public order. She seeks to appeal against the 2018 Regulations to the European Court of Human Rights (ECtHR).

This case has firmly placed the rights of gender diverse athletes in the spotlight and prompted a review of sport gender policies by sports bodies, with significant questions around the ability of sport to recognise and protect equality and human rights in the formulation of their rules. A strong equality and human rights framework exists to protect sex and gender rights in society, particularly at the European level. Yet the application of these provisions to sport is vague, and it is opined elsewhere that the *Semenya* case emphasises the regulatory gaps in the protection of athlete gender rights in sport, with an incapacity to deal with human rights issues in the complex sport regulatory system.[4]

Having outlined the current climate of sex and gender discrimination in sport, it is worth mapping the pre-Brexit landscape of rights and principles that exist to protect minorities from sex and gender discrimination and that promote equality and human rights. In doing so, it will be possible to identify the holes that post-Brexit might leave in this structure and the overall effect upon vulnerable athletes rights.

6.1.3. The landscape of equality and human rights provisions

Equality and non-discrimination form part of the emphasis on human dignity that underpins the entire construction of modern human rights regimes. The principle of equality is found within the rule of law, and it is considered a protectable legal right.[5] Equal treatment and protection from discrimination on the grounds of sex and gender is located within a range of international, regional and domestic discrimination laws that impose legal standards and place obligations on the states who are signatories to them, to take appropriate measures to ensure the protection of human rights. Overarching recognition within the framework derives from international law where the right to equality and freedom from discrimination on the basis of sex and gender are recognised by the Universal Declaration of Human Rights 1948 (UDHR), the International Covenant on Civil and Political Rights 1976 (ICCPR) and the International Covenant on Economic, Social and Cultural Rights 1976 (ICESCR). At this level there is a strong commitment to non-discrimination and gender equality in sport (The Convention on the Elimination of All Forms of Discrimination Against Women 1979 [CEDAW] [Article 10(g)], the Beijing Declaration and Platform for Action 1995; The Brighton plus Helsinki 2014 Declaration on Women and Sport, the UNESCO International Charter of

4 Patel (2021).
5 Patel (2015).

Physical Education, Physical Activity and Sport [2015 revised] and the Yogyakarta Principles Plus 10 [supplementing the Yogyakarta Principles 2006]). The United Nations (UN) and the United Nations Human Rights Council (UNHRC) have been integral to supporting the protection of gender rights in sport, and an increasing range of non-legally binding soft law tools are being implemented at the international level to encourage non-state actors to comply with human rights and to encourage states to more closely regulate non-state actors.[6]

At the European level, the Council of Europe enacted the European Convention on Human Rights 1950 (ECHR) which implements several principles of the UDHR and contains fundamental civil and political rights, such as freedom from discrimination on any ground, including sex (see Article 14 ECHR and Protocol No. 12 ECHR). In the European Union (EU), equality and equal treatment are key principles that have been recognised through the enactment of EU Treaties, Directives and Regulations, judgments of the Court of Justice of the European Union (CJEU) and informal declarations, statements and movements that improve gender equality. The institution has actively encouraged states to consider equality between men and women when formulating and implementing laws, regulations, administrative provisions, policies and activities (TFEU Article 10). EU legislation has improved standards for gender parity in relation to equal pay, women's pregnancy and maternity rights, pension schemes, part-time workers, equal treatment and safe workplaces.

EU law offers a wide defence through the enforcement of primary and secondary legislation stemming from the Charter of Fundamental Rights of the European Union 2009 (EU Charter).[7] Article 6(1) TEU gives full legal status to the EU Charter and formally codifies rights and principles for EU citizens in one single document, with equality and non-discrimination represented in Title III. The EU Charter overlaps civil and political convention rights but offers further protection by preserving a broad range of fundamental rights such as economic and social rights into primary EU law. It applies to EU Member States when they are implementing EU law and represents a constitutional boundary during this process. The EU Charter has framed rights in an inclusive manner[8] and has played a significant part in transforming the culture and practice of the European institutions.[9]

6 Patel (2021); see also United Nations Human Rights Council, 'The elimination of discrimination against women and girls in sport, resolution 40/5 UN human rights council' (2019), https://ilga.org/downloads/Elimination_of_discrimination_against_women_and_girls_in_sport.pdf (accessed 20 April 2021); see also United Nations Human Rights Council, 'Report of the United Nations high commissioner for human rights, intersection of race and gender discrimination in sport, A/HRC/44/26 United Nations high commissioner for human rights' (2020), www.ohchr.org/EN/HRBodies/HRC/RegularSessions/Session44/_layouts/15/WopiFrame.aspx?sourcedoc=/EN/HRBodies/HRC/RegularSessions/Session44/Documents/A_HRC_44_26_AEV.docx&action=default&DefaultItemOpen=1 (accessed 20 April 2021).

7 McCorkindale (2018).

8 Danisi et al. (2019), p. 2.

9 De Schutter (2010), p. 26.

The CJEU rulings have acknowledged the value of fundamental rights through its development of robust decisions which have confirmed the protection of specific minority rights including women and gender reassignment. The CJEU has led in the protection of those who are not explicitly covered and encouraged a wider interpretation of the term 'sex' to include other identities such as trans people.[10]

At EU level, there is an increased willingness to engage with sport policy and regulation. The EU have demonstrated a competence in sport as reinforced by Article 165 TFEU and in the EU White Paper on Sport.[11]In assessing the compatibility of sports rules with Community law in various cases, the CJEU judgments imply that a balance between individual and sporting interests is possible by encouraging good governance which recognises the specificity of sport through a more sensitive and autonomous application of EC law.[12] The CJEU are also increasingly progressing the horizontal applicability of EU law,[13] but no cases have concerned sex or gender discrimination in sport at this level. The EU White Paper includes within the definition of specificity, 'separate competitions for men and women'.[14] Despite the strong commitment to equality and equal treatment in the EU, gender divisions are considered specific to sport and therefore exempt from EU law under this current regime. This blanket protection of the sex categories of sport reinforces a generalisation of sex and gender and a misinterpretation of the rights of athletes at stake. The human rights implications of this assumption are explored elsewhere.[15]

The ECtHR have also been prepared to intervene in the sport regulatory space, as evidenced in various cases.[16] In *Mutu and Pechstein v. Switzerland*,[17] the judges offered commentary on the validity of CAS proceedings and reinforced that they must be compatible Convention rights. Semenya has referred her case to the regional ECtHR, in a fight for her human rights; yet thus far, no ECtHR cases have concerned sex or gender discrimination in sport. Despite some shortfalls in the EU system, a strong dialogue is emerging, and there is increasing awareness of securing athletes rights by ensuring that sport regulates fairly and responsibly.

Domestic equality and human rights in the UK are guarded in three primary ways: through EU law protection encapsulated in the EU Charter; through the Human Rights Act 1998 (HRA) which gives effect to the ECHR; and through human rights decisions and judgments of the domestic courts. The UK have historically led in the recognition of equality and non-discrimination, particularly

10 Lembke (2016).
11 European Commission (2007). White Paper on Sport. COM (2017) 391 final. 11.07.2007.
12 Chappelet (2017).
13 Lewandowski (2020).
14 European Commission (2007), p. 13.
15 Patel (2021).
16 Fédération Nationale des Syndicats Sportifs (FNASS) and others v. France [ECtHR 29 May 2018] App. Nos. 48151/11 and 77769/13.
17 Mutu and Pechstein v. Switzerland [ECtHR 2 October 2018] App no 40575/10 and 67474/10.

in the areas of sex (Sex Discrimination Act 1975), disability (Disability Discrimination Act 1995) and race (Race Relations Act 1975). This proactive engagement has influenced CJEU judgments, and references from the UK to the CJEU have strengthened EU equality jurisprudence. That said, the UK and EU have shared a reciprocal relationship when it comes to equality rights, and the EU has played a critical role in the establishment of an effective gender regime which provides minority groups with an appropriate standards of rights. As emphasised, this has been achieved through the development of primary and secondary legislation, through social dialogue and business influence,[18] and through the persuasive domestic and CJEU judgments.[19] For instance, the European courts have been influential in securing domestic protection for women in relation to discrimination, sexual harassment and equal pay.[20] Domestic legislation has been formulated in response to compliance with EU law.[21] The Equality Act 2010 (EA) consolidates and repeals previous legislation in specific areas and shields protected characteristics which include disability, gender reassignment, race, sex, age, marriage and civil partnership, pregnancy and maternity, religion or belief and sexual orientation.

As a member of the Council of Europe, the HRA gives national effect to the ECHR by imposing an obligation on public bodies to comply with Convention rights. Article 14 of the UK Human Rights Act 1998 (HRA) prohibits discrimination in the enjoyment of human rights (Not a free-standing right, see Protocol No. 12 ECHR). The HRA demonstrates the domestic internalisation of human rights treaties and recognises the rights of the ECHR as an integral part of domestic law. Rulings of the ECtHR have driven stronger recognition of gender rights in the UK. For instance, the Gender Recognition Act 2004 (GRA), recently reviewed, affords trans people the right to apply for legal recognition of their acquired gender (s. 1[3] and Schedule 1 GRA). It was introduced in response to decisions of the ECtHR which criticised the UK position on trans people and prompted revisions to the statutory framework.

It is suggested that the EU Charter reflects the rights of the HRA but offers supplementary safety for minorities, with additional rights recognised and with a broad interpretation of its implementation.[22] The EU Charter represents a statutory boundary for domestic equality rights, as well as underpinning the entire domestic regime.[23]

The application of non-discrimination domestic provisions to sport is limited by the exemption clauses often contained within domestic equality legislation that permit discrimination if it is a gender-affected activity.[24] A sport is gender-affected

18 Fredman et al. (2018), p. 4.
19 Wintemute (2016), Jolly (2018).
20 See Wintemute (2016), p. 389.
21 *Ibid.*, p. 388.
22 Lock (2017), p. 5.
23 Jolly (2018).
24 See section 195 Equality Act 2010; section 19 Gender Recognition Act 2004.

if the physical strength, stamina or physique of average persons of one sex or gender would put them at a disadvantage to average persons of the other sex or gender. This restriction is justified to ensure safe and fair competition and was used by the IAAF in *Semenya v IAAF* to contend that civil and common law legal systems offer a margin of appreciation to sport bodies when determining what is necessary and proportionate to achieve legitimate objectives.[25] In the context of domestic human rights there is a general reluctance to regard sports bodies as fulfilling a public function for the purpose of imposing human rights law.[26] Although the UK courts have considered that sports bodies may be quasi or hybrid public authorities, that is, private bodies that exercise public functions, the position remains constricted,[27] with limited influence from the EU. The ability of an athlete to access the courts is narrow as evidenced in a judicial review case concerning a British female canoeist who argued that the London Organising Committee for the Olympic Games (LOCOG) had failed to carry out an equality impact assessment in accordance with the EA. This was rejected by the court on the grounds that the LOCOG were a private entity.[28]

Overall, there is a firm commitment to sex and gender rights in the international human rights framework. These rights have been prominent at the European level and certainly influenced UK law in securing minority rights. Yet in the context of sport the application of these provisions to athletes is rather weak and there is a general uncertainty around how human rights provisions might apply to the sport gender rules, and how they are enforced upon sports bodies to ensure compliance.[29] The next section considers the impact of Brexit upon this human rights landscape and examines whether a weaker or stronger application to sport might emerge from the EU-UK separation.

6.2. The impact of Brexit

6.2.1. *General remarks*

There is a general agreement that a detailed evaluation of minority equality rights, particularly sex and gender issues, have been invisible from the Brexit dialogue, which has largely focused on financial pressures and economic matters.[30] Although an Equalities Analysis 2017 was published to accompany the EU (Withdrawal) Act 2018, which facilities the UK exit from the EU, it concluded that the effect

25 CAS 2018/O/5794 *Mokgadi Caster Semenya v. The International Association of Athletics Federation (IAAF)* and CAS 2018/O/5798 *Athletics South Africa v. The International Association of Athletics Federation (IAAF)*, para. 303.

26 Boyes (2000).

27 *Ibid.*

28 The Queen (On the application of Samantha Rippington) v LOCOG, Order of 6 February 2013.

29 Patel (2021).

30 Fredman et al. (2018), p. 3; Hepburn (2020b), p. 25; MacLeavy (2018a); Danisi et al. (2019).

on equality would be minimal due to existing domestic law protections against discrimination.[31] However, in the absence of any purposeful equality impact assessment to review the potential consequences of Brexit upon minority rights, this analysis was criticised for failing to clarify the position on equality and non-discrimination rights.[32] This had led to continued uncertainty around the force of Brexit upon equality and non-discrimination.

What is strikingly obvious is that the UK are no longer bound by EU law, which means that there is no longer an obligation to comply with EU equality and non-discrimination obligations that are not already enshrined within UK law. Thus, the impact of Brexit on the protection of fundamental rights in the UK is determined by how sensibly those fundamental rights are extracted from the UK structure.[33] The outcome of future trade agreements may well include commitments to fundamental rights but are not yet formalised. Instead, the UK exit from the EU represents a significant risk to sex and gender equality because there will be no other institution influencing the progression of those agendas on domestic law.[34] As evidenced above, despite the UK's pre-EU membership introduction of non-discrimination legislation, the EU has ensured minimum standards of protection and symbolised constitutional protection for equality in the UK, with no formal written constitution of its own.[35] Gender equality provisions in the UK have been inspired by secondary EU legal instruments relating to maternity discrimination, sexual harassment and discrimination at work, flexible working provisions, equal pay for equal work and shared parental leave. Post-Brexit, there will be no regulatory net to safeguard these provisions and prevent them from being reduced or lost in the future.[36]

6.2.2. EU charter

The EU (Withdrawal) Act 2018 converts EU law into domestic law and outlines retained EU law. The EU Charter, which acted as the regulatory safety net, is excluded from this category and therefore no longer binding. It is worth reiterating that the EU Charter bolstered equality rights through assurance that law is applied and interpreted in a way that is consistent with fundament rights.[37] It is likely that minority groups will be most affected by the loss of the EU Charter, which recognised non-discrimination as a free-standing right and offered access

31 UK Parliament, 'Equality analysis, European Union (Withdrawal) bill' (2017), https://assets.publishing.service.gov.uk/government/uploads/system/uploads/attachment_data/file/629244/European_Union__Withdrawal__Bill_equality_analysis.pdf (accessed 28 April 2021).

32 Hepburn (2020b), p. 45.

33 McCorkindale (2018), p. 131.

34 MacLeavy (2018b).

35 Jolly (2018).

36 Fredman et al. (2018), p. 4; Women's Budget Group (2019).

37 *Ibid.*, p. 5.

to the jurisprudence of the CJEU.[38] The Women's Budget Group (WBG) has conducted extensive research into the economic impacts of Brexit on gender equality and found that the poorest women, black and minority ethnic (BAME) women and disabled women are likely to be most affected by losses, cuts and reductions as a consequence of the EU Charter extraction.[39] This concern is supported by the Equality and Human Rights Commission (EHRC) who identified EU-derived employment rights and the EU Charter's free-standing right to non-discrimination as areas of particular concern.[40] Although many rights from the EU Charter have been transposed into domestic law, other minority rights contained in secondary legislation may not have been and are in danger of being neglected post-Brexit.[41]

The strength of the EU Charter remedial force will also be squeezed, weakening the remedies available for minorities. The EU Charter no longer takes primacy over domestic law where they conflict and can no longer instruct domestic courts to disapply domestic legislation and adhere to EU law. The justification for this removal is that the underlying fundamental rights and principles that exist independently will be retained and will not be impacted by this removal.[42] This may indicate little change to the protection of fundamental rights after Brexit because the EA and common law may absorb the responsibilities of the EU Charter. Unless the EA is specifically repealed, anti-discrimination rights will continue to be applicable in the UK after Brexit.[43] However, it is advocated that this is not a 'complete solution'[44] because without binding impact of EU law, there is no security that the EA or other non-discrimination provisions will be exempt from repeal in the future.[45] Post-Brexit there is an 'increased scope for deregulation' which will negatively impact upon minority rights.[46]

Indeed, the EA satisfies the minimum requirements of EU law but without the protective EU net there is increased latitude for significant reform in this area.[47] There are potentially some gaps in the protection offered by the EA which may be further exposed post-Brexit.[48] The future is tentative, and the UK may not follow or apply future EU advances in equality and non-discrimination, which leaves

38 Hepburn (2020b).
39 Women's Budget Group (2019).
40 Equality and Human Rights Commission, 'Equality and human rights commission, opinion on EU (withdrawal) bill—EU charter of fundamental rights', 5 January 2018, www.equalityhumanrights.com/sites/default/files/eu-withdrawal-bill-legal-advice-jason-coppel-qc.pdf (accessed 28 April 2021).
41 Hepburn (2020a), p. 163; Lock (2017); Fredman et al. (2018), p. 4.
42 McCorkindale (2018), p. 129.
43 Lock (2017), p. 2.
44 Fredman et al. (2018), p. 5.
45 *Ibid.*; Hepburn (2020b).
46 Women's Budget Group (2019).
47 Wintemute (2016), p. 397.
48 O'Cinneide (2016).

some of the EU derived rights 'frozen in time'.[49] The future relationship between the UK and EU is hazy, and it is unknown whether future agreements will include any arrangement for minimum rights for minority groups.

6.2.3. *Role of the courts*

Another area of ambiguity post-Brexit is the influence of the CJEU and the interpretation of equality and non-discrimination principles by the courts. The CJEU will no longer be part of the UK legal system, and the Supreme Court will become the highest legal authority.[50] As explained, the judgments of the CJEU have advanced equality throughout the EU by acting as a 'progressive and purposive interpreter of the fundamental right to equality'.[51] A number of UK minority rights would have been exposed without the guidance of the CJEU.[52] Membership to the EU has qualified UK citizens to access the direct effect of EU law where their rights have not been sufficiently protected at a domestic level. However, CJEU rulings on equality matters will no longer be binding in the UK; UK citizens will lose the benefit of direct effect, and references to the CJEU by the UK courts for preliminary rulings will cease to be possible. References have not only resulted in clarifications for UK law, but UK contributions to CJEU case law have equally been key to the EU equality agenda.[53]

In determining how the CJEU judgments will be interpreted, the EU (Withdrawal) Act suggests that the UK courts may have regard for CJEU decisions in limited relevant circumstances (European Union [Withdrawal] Act 2018 Explanatory Notes Section 6 Interpretation of Retained EU Law). Brexit gives the Supreme Court the freedom to derogate from EU case law and adopt an alternative interpretation of retained EU equality and non-discrimination principles, which might be inconsistent with the CJEU.[54] With the potential to effectively ignore CJEU rulings, the future of equality and non-discrimination protection in the courts is a concern.

6.2.4. *Human Rights Act 1998*

The impact of Brexit on the HRA remains unclear but for now there is a commitment to the ECHR, and the UK remain bound by Convention rights. The Council of Europe and the EU are distinct which leaves the HRA currently in place. Public bodies and those bodies fulfilling public functions continue to comply with

49 Hepburn (2020a), p. 151; Lock (2017), p. 15.
50 Fredman et al. (2018).
51 Jolly (2018).
52 *Ibid.*
53 Fredman et al. (2018), p. 4.
54 *Ibid.*, p. 6.

the ECHR and are still subject to the HRA.[55] This was solidified throughout the EU-UK Trade Agreement 2020. As a founding member of the Council of Europe, the UK support the promotion of human rights, democracy and the rule of law across the continent. That said, the relationship has been strained at times,[56] and it is further unknown how the rights contained in the ECHR have been or will be replicated in the UK following Brexit.

The biggest impact on human rights post-Brexit will stem from the removal of the EU Charter. Equality protection of the HRA is not as expansive as the EU Charter. In terms of enforcing human rights, the mechanisms are weaker with the HRA than the EU Charter which can disapply domestic legislation. Although the judgments of the ECtHR are legally binding on the states, the UK courts are required to consider the judgments of the ECtHR where it is deemed to be relevant.[57] There is no obligation to apply the ECtHR case law.[58] If the courts find that the disputed provision or legislation is incompatible with the ECHR, it can issue a declaration of incompatibility. The declaration of incompatibility does not alter the validity of the disputed legislation or provision, and it is the decision of the Government to amend the legislation or provision as recommended.

There is uncertainly around whether the HRA is repealed in light of Brexit. It is fair to assume that the future of equality and human rights legislation is subject to the government in power at the time.[59] There has been continuous consultation around the replacement of the HRA for a British Bill of Rights, which might give the UK more legislative control.[60] This has been left open as something that might happen in the post-Brexit era. The idea that the ECHR weakens the supremacy of the UK has long been debated. If the UK exited the Council of Europe and were no longer signatories to the ECHR, this would further endanger the protection of fundamental human rights for minorities and represent a complete disengagement with Europe.[61]

Overall, the ramifications of Brexit on equality and human rights for minority sex and gender groups is largely speculative because they have not been addressed in a committed manner by the Government. The available academic commentary is varied but most submit that Brexit leaves a void in the future championing of domestic minority rights, particularly those not explicitly covered by legislation. Although there may be opportunities for reform and review of minority rights post-Brexit, there is little evidence of strengthening the network of protection.[62]

55 Wintemute (2016).
56 Donald and Leach (2020).
57 House of Lords, *The UK, the EU and a British Bill of Rights* (The European Union Committee, 2016), https://publications.parliament.uk/pa/ld201516/ldselect/ldeucom/139/139.pdf (accessed 20 April 2021).
58 House of Lords (2016).
59 Wintemute (2016).
60 Clear (2019).
61 *Ibid.*
62 Dustin et al. (2019).

6.3. Implications for sport

The above analysis implies that sex and gender equality rights are potentially under threat post-Brexit. Brexit aside, the application of these provisions to sport has been weak and ambiguous which has left athletes in a vulnerable position. The reason for this treatment is partly explained by the complex relationship between sport and the law in which sport is often considered a private body immune from legal intervention; the lack of enforceability of equality and human rights provisions to sport; and the curious nature of sex and gender in sport where divisions based upon human differences form the essence of sport. The ability of athletes to successfully assert their rights in court is limited and seldom has a court strengthened athletes' rights. Although the case did not concern sex and gender, professional footballer Jean-Marc Bosman successfully challenged the infringement of his EU rights by football transfer rules in the CJEU.[63] This is a rare example of a court confirming the position that sport cannot operate above the law and does highlight the positive value of EU law in sport.

Against this background, although the position of athletes sex and gender rights is already weak, Brexit may indirectly dilute athletes rights further by losing the influence of EU legislation and sport policy dialogue which has at least signaled an appetite to address sport issues. The position is further stretched by the loss of any future EU advancements in sport and equality on UK law and policy.

Brexit represents a departure from the broader global gender equality movement that goes beyond the borders of the UK. Although the current system for protecting athletes' sex and gender rights is imperfect and needs reform, it is unequivocal that collectivity is required to improve the regulation of athletes' sex and gender rights. Brexit is at odds with underlying notions of equality and human rights because it creates a sense of segregation and division.

In light of the *Semenya* case and the trans athlete sport policy debates, firmer international solutions are being sought to rectify the global gaps in the protection of athletes' sex and gender rights.[64] That said, the EU offers a middle ground between the state and domestic institutions, and the international system with better access for individual human rights breaches. It was previously suggested that given its recognition of fundamental rights under the EU Charter, there is scope for the EU to offer firmer guidance on the application of equality law to sport gender policies.[65] For instance, the promotion of good governance in sport possibly encourages the safeguarding of athletes' rights. However, with the UK-EU bridge dismantled, any such development will no longer apply to the UK, and this will permanently alter the structural framework of equality and human rights.

63 *Union Royale Belge des Societe de Football Association ASBL v Jean-Marc Bosman* (C-415/93) ECR I-4921.

64 Patel (2021).

65 Patel (2015).

As long as the UK membership to the Council of Europe remains intact, there is potential for continued activism through this European channel.[66] The Council of Europe have demonstrated a commitment to protecting the integrity of sport, which could be expanded to encompass athletes' sex and gender rights. The binding power and enforceability of the Council of Europe tools upon sports bodies will require strengthening and force to be effective.

6.4. Conclusion

The impact of Brexit on equality and human rights is unlikely to be instant and will surface in the future as the fallout unravels itself. This chapter has identified that minority rights are in a potentially weak position post-Brexit. Without the constitutional protection afforded by EU law, the EU Charter and the CJEU jurisprudence, those rights are at risk of being exposed or reduced. An evaluation of the landscape of sex and gender equality and human rights provisions demonstrates the significant influence that the EU has had on securing minority rights and stabilising the entire international regime at the regional level.

Equality and human rights protection for all minority groups are non-negotiable values that requires dedicated attention in future discussion and law making and should not be side-lined by economic and financial matters. Instead, such rights should be integral rather than peripheral to the post-Brexit setting and a key focus shift is necessary.

In the context of sport, this chapter has outlined the current vulnerability of athletes' sex and gender rights, and the uncertainty around the application of equality and human rights provisions to sport to protect athletes. Pre-Brexit, there were significant regulatory gaps in the protection of athletes' gender rights, and it is argued that these deficiencies need to be rectified through international reform. A collective movement is encouraged to ensure that minority athletes are treated fairly and sports bodies operate consistently. Although these underlying issues extend beyond the Brexit debate, the post-Brexit environment is likely to weaken their position indirectly with the loss of EU competence in sport policy and wider equality commitments. Human rights recognition will continue through the Council of Europe, but Brexit alters the structure of the equality and human rights framework and symbolises a distancing from the broader gender equality movement that is playing a key part in defending athletes' rights.

References

Boyes, S. (2000) The regulation of sport and the impact of the human rights act 1998. *European Public Law*, 6:4, 517–530.

66 *Ibid.*

Chappelet, J.L. (2017) Beyond governance: The need to improve the regulation of international sport. *Sport in Society*, 21:5, 724–734.

Clear, S. (2019) UK human rights act is at risk of repeal—here's why it should be protected. *The Conversation*, 12 February. https://theconversation.com/uk-human-rights-act-is-at-risk-of-repeal-heres-why-it-should-be-protected-111368 (Accessed 20 April 2021).

Danisi, C.; Dustin, M. & Ferreira, N. (2019) Queering Brexit: What's in Brexit for sexual and gender minorities? In: Dustin, M.; Ferreira, N. & Millns, S. (eds) *Gender and Queer Perspectives on Brexit*. Gender and Politics Series. London: Palgrave Macmillan, pp. 239–272.

De Schutter, O. (2010) *International Human Rights Law*. Oxford: Oxford University Press.

Donald, A. & Leach, P. (2020) *Engaging with Europe after Brexit: Time to reset the UK's Relationship with the Council of Europe*. The Foreign Policy Centre. https://fpc.org.uk/engaging-with-europe-after-brexit-time-to-reset-the-uks-relationship-with-the-council-of-europe/ (Accessed 28 April 2021).

Dustin, M.; Ferreira, N. & Millns, S. (2019) Conclusion: Brexit, gender justice and the Overton window. In: Dustin, M.; Ferreira, N. & Millns, S. (eds) *Gender and Queer Perspectives on Brexit*. London: Palgrave Macmillan, pp. 463–472.

Fredman, S.; Young, A. & Campbell, M. (2018) *The Continuing Impact of Brexit on Equality Rights, UK in a Changing Europe*. London. https://ukandeu.ac.uk/wpcontent/uploads/2018/04/The-continuing-impact-of-Brexit-on-equalityrights.Pdf (Accessed 20 April 2021)

Hepburn, E. (2020a) Uncharted waters: The social and equality impacts of Brexit. *Scottish Affairs*, 29:2, 141–178.

Hepburn, E. (2020b) *Social and Equality Impacts of Brexit. Report to the Scottish Government*. Edinburgh: Scottish Government. www.gov.scot/binaries/content/documents/govscot/publications/research-and-analysis/2020/01/social-equality-impacts-brexit/documents/social-equality-impacts-brexit/social-equality-impacts-brexit/govscot%3Adocument/social-equality-impacts-brexit.pdf

Jolly, S. (2018) Your right to equality is currently protected. After Brexit it won't be. *Prospect Magazine*. www.prospectmagazine.co.uk/magazine/your-right-to-equality-is-currently-protected-after-brexit-it-wont-be.

Lembke, U. (2016) Tackling sex discrimination to achieve gender equality? Conceptions of sex and gender in EU non-discrimination law and policies. *European Equality Law Review*, 2016:2, 46–55. www.equalitylaw.eu/downloads/3938-european-equality-law-review-2-2016 (Accessed 28 April 2021).

Lewandowski, W. (2020) The implications of the recent jurisprudence of the court of justice of the European union for the protection of the fundamental rights of athletes and the regulatory autonomy of sporting federations. *Tilburg Law Review*, 25:1, 55–66.

Lock, T. (2017) Human rights law in the UK after Brexit. *Public Law*, Brexit Special Issue 2017, 117–134.

MacLeavy, J. (2018a) Women, equality and the UK's EU referendum: Locating the gender politics of Brexit in relation to the neoliberalising state. *Space and Polity*, 22:2, 205–223.

MacLeavy, J. (2018b) Gender equality: Adrift in the Brexit backwash. *LSE Brexit* blog, 27 July. https://blogs.lse.ac.uk/brexit/2018/07/27/gender-equalityadrift-in-the-brexit-backwash/

McCorkindale, C. (2018) Brexit and human rights. *Edinburgh Law Review*, 22:1, 132–138.

O'Cinneide, C. (2016) *Equality Rights in a Post-Brexit United Kingdom*. Bright Blue Human Rights Project. https://humanrights.brightblue.org.uk/blog-1/2016/7/29/equality-rights-in-a-post-brexit-united-kingdom (Accessed 20 April 2021)

Patel, S. (2015) *Inclusion and Exclusion in Competitive Sport: Socio-Legal and Regulatory Perspectives*. London: Routledge.

Patel, S. (2021) Gaps in the protection of athletes gender rights in sport- a regulatory riddle. *The International Sports Law Journal*. Online first. https://doi.org/10.1007/s40318-021-00182-2

Wintemute, R. (2016) Goodbye EU anti-discrimination law? Hello repeal of the equality act 2010? *King's Law Journal*, 27:3, 387–397.

Women's Budget Group (2019) *What Does Boris Johnson's Brexit Deal Mean for Women?* Analysis from the Women's Budget Group. https://wbg.org.uk/wp-content/uploads/2019/10/WBG-BJ-deal.pdf.

Part III

Stakeholders

Chapter 7

Brexit and social dialogue in sport

Walter S. Palmer

7.1. Introduction

During my 17-year career as a professional basketball player in the United States (NCAA and NBA), Europe and Latin America, I experienced first-hand the asymmetric power dynamic between clubs and leagues, and players that substantially influenced my sphere of rights and freedoms.[1] During my four years of college basketball at Dartmouth, the NCAA capped my potential compensation at the cost of tuition, denied my status as an employee and classified me as a 'student-athlete' to sidestep responsibility for any potential workers' compensation claims.[2] In Europe and Latin America, I had an employment contract but found many of the individual terms, such as salary and bonus, to be unenforceable and the collective terms, like work schedules and anti-doping rules, to be non-negotiable. In the NBA, my experience was much more positive. I had an employment contract that was part of a collective bargaining agreement. Through my membership in the players union, I was an active participant and stakeholder in the governance of the sport. Upon my retirement from professional sport in 2003, the sum of these experiences, both positive and negative, inspired me to become a labour organiser and devote years of my life to promoting social dialogue and collective bargaining in sport. In my view, collective bargaining is the ideal form of governance for commercialised elite sport. Unfortunately, resistance from politically influential sport organisations remains high. It is not a coincidence that the emergence of the European Union and the growth in the number of independent athlete unions and associations around the world has gone hand in hand. Faced with a campaign by sport organisations to maintain their monopsonistic control of the market[3] for athlete labour and intellectual property (codeword, 'autonomy'), the EU provides

1 Lewandowski (2020).
2 T. Branch, 'How the myth of the student athlete was born', *Deadspin.com*, 20 February 2014, https://deadspin.com/how-the-myth-of-the-ncaa-student-athlete-was-born-1524282374.
3 Z. Carter, 'The woman who shattered the myth of the free market', *New York Times Opinion—Guest Essay*, 4 April 2021, www.nytimes.com/2021/04/24/opinion/joan-robinson-economy-monopoly-labor.html?referringSource=articleShare.

DOI: 10.4324/9781003162803-10

elite athletes with an arena for action that is somewhat shielded from the well-honed strategies of co-optation and/or threat of exclusion that sport organisations use to deal with challenges at the level of the nation-state. The transnational governance of the EU provides a legal and regulatory framework within which elite athletes can have some hope of balancing the scales. As long-time Spanish professional basketball player, national team member and player association President, Jose Luis Llorente, so eloquently expressed it at a press conference just before the 2010 EU Sport Forum in Madrid, 'We must stand together for the fundamental rights of athletes as citizens and employees in Europe to ensure they're protected. The law is the law'.[4] Athletes, both individually and collectively, have been a driving force towards the horizontal application of EU law to sport by bringing cases to the European Court of Justice to establish the applicability of the fundamental freedoms and competition law. Elite athletes are also beginning to challenge the misclassification of many athletes as independent contractors by sport federations and collectively organising for the purpose of engaging in social dialogue. Where athletes are recognised as workers, they are organising into unions and consolidating in representative organisations at the European and global level for the purpose of sectoral social dialogue. Much has been written about the judicial review of sport regulations and the actions of the European Court of Justice in a variety of cases including *Walrave*,[5] *Bosman*[6] and *Meca-Medina* which have all confirmed that 'economic activities in the context of sport fall within the scope of EC law'.[7] In that context, this chapter will focus on the European Union's role in promoting social dialogue and how that may, or may not, be undermined by Brexit.

7.2. What is social dialogue?

Social dialogue can be defined as all forms of 'negotiation, joint working, or even simple exchanges of views' between two 'social partners'—the representatives of workers and those of the employers—and is a term that encompasses all forms of industrial relations and collective bargaining.[8] The social dialogue landscape for elite athletes in the European sport sector is complex. Historically, working conditions were unilaterally determined by clubs, leagues and sport governing bodies. Over time, some athletes have been able to organise collectively and be involved in the determination of their status and working conditions.[9] Even in instances

4 Via spinbb.net "Athletes send strong message for workers' rights to EU Commission" 4.19.2010, retrieved 3 May 2021.

5 Case 36–74. *B.N.O. Walrave and L.J.N. Koch v Association Union cycliste internationale, Koninklijke Nederlandsche Wielren Unie and Federación Española Ciclismo*. 1974 01405.

6 Case C-415/93. *Union Royale Belge des Sociétés de Football Association v Bosman* [1995] ECR I-4921.

7 Case C-519/04 P. *David Meca-Medina and Igor Majcen v Commission of the European Communities* [2006] ECR 2006 I-06991

8 Via https://fia-actors.com/policy-work/social-dialogue-and-collective-bargaining/

9 O'Leary (2017), p. 464.

where the employment relationship between an athlete and their club is clear, significant aspects of the regulatory environment that influence the employment relationship are determined by international federations whose rules are very difficult to influence no matter how well organised athletes may be at the national level. For the many athletes who are not recognised as workers it is even more difficult (many Olympic athletes are considered independent contractors by their federations).

Today, there is a range of different examples across Europe of social dialogue between associations of elite athletes and their leagues or sport governing bodies.

In Ireland, for example, the athletes in some of the most popular sports in the country, men and women's Gaelic football, hurling and camogie, are not recognised as workers but the Gaelic Players Association (GPA) and Gaelic Athletic Association (GAA) have a robust structured dialogue and negotiate over a share of revenue to be applied to player programming. The players association is well funded and structured. Its board recently voted to merge with the Women's Gaelic Players Association (WGPA) to form one unified players body.

In Germany, many elite team sport athletes have labour contracts with their clubs but the extent of collective organisation is very limited with no examples of active collective bargaining (*Tarifverhandlungen*). Even the country's professional football players do not have a collective bargaining agreement. The Vereinigung der Vertragsfußballspieler e.V. (VDV)[10] was founded to provide financial and legal advice to players. It is recognised by DFL (Deutsche Fußball Liga) and the DFB (Deutscher Fußball Bund) but has not engaged in collective bargaining. Germany remains one of the very few countries in Europe without a football players union recognised by the global federation of football players unions, FIFPRO. In the mid-2000s the author founded a basketball players association with members of the national team called Spieler Initiative. From the outset, the new players union faced intense resistance from the league and national federation.[11] After overcoming a lawsuit that challenged its status as a union, it was successful in electing the first workers councils (*Betriebsräte*) in sport and beginning collective bargaining discussions with one of the clubs.[12] These discussions never progressed beyond the beginning stages, and the association is currently not active. In Germany, elite athletes working in individual sports are considered independent contractors by the clubs and federations. Being defined as such, they are not able to organise in unions. However, Athleten.de,[13] a new association representing athletes who are members of national federations in

10 Via VDV website, www.spielergewerkschaft.de/en/home.htm retrieved 9 May 2021.

11 Via spinbb.net, "BBL challenges SP.IN's union status . . . again" 3 February 2009, retrieved 7 May 2021.

12 Via spinbb.net "First collective bargaining session in Bamberg", 23 January 2008, retrieved 9 May 2021 www.spinbb.net/index.php?id=aktuelles00&no_cache=1&tx_ttnews%5Bpointer%5D=60&tx_ttnews%5Btt_news%5D=292&tx_ttnews%5BbackPid%5D=282

13 Via www.athleten.de, retrieved https://athleten-deutschland.org/ueber-uns/ 9 May 2021.

Germany, was recently founded to make dialogue between athletes and their federations possible. It advocates for changes in the German and international sport system to benefit the athletes. The association receives funding from the German government. It's current CEO, Johannes Herber, is a former professional basketball player and served as a player representative for SP.IN during the court case referenced above.

The United Kingdom has a long history of social dialogue. It saw the founding of the first players union in the world, the Professional Footballers Association (at first, the Players' Union), in 1907. It wasn't until 1961 that players finally forced the abolishment of the £20 maximum salary through the threat of industrial action. The next major step came in 1963 when the High Court ended the retain-and-transfer system, ruling in favour of the player George Eastham, supported by the PFA. The PFA continues to have input into the standard players contract, and both management and the players are thriving financially. While social dialogue is much more extensive than in Germany, collective bargaining in sport is 'characterised by voluntary agreements between employers and unions' that are only enforceable if they are incorporated into a contract of employment.[14] There are player associations in a variety of different sports, as well as a national federation of player unions, the Professional Players Federation (PPF). The unilateral imposition of a salary cap in 2015 by Premiership Rugby with the seeming acquiescence of the Rugby Players Association (which received substantial funding from the league), in what would seem to be a clear violation of antitrust norms,[15] raises serious concerns about whether or not a precedent might be set if the practice were to continue. Despite these difficulties at the collective level, the UK has the most developed system of extending employee rights beyond the employment contract when compared to countries in the EU.[16] The UK uses a targeted approach to establishing differing rights and responsibilities in employment law for employees and workers.[17] Recently, Uber drivers were granted certain employment rights as workers in the UK.[18] Unfortunately, when it comes to sport, it seems that Employment Tribunals in the UK may be very reluctant to apply this flexible approach to athletes. The recent case of Jess Varnish, a cyclist for the British Cycling Federation, was denied status as a worker after claiming unfair dismissal, sex discrimination, victimisation and unlawful detriment. As a result, she was not able to proceed with her claims.

In Sweden, top athletes are generally recognised as employees with the top sports of football and ice hockey organised in players associations. The general

14 O'Leary (2017), p. 464.

15 Ravi Mehta, 'All in a day's work: Salary caps in the cross-hairs of UK and EU sports regulation', *Sports Law Bulletin*, 2 December 2019.

16 Risak and Dullinger (2018), p. 15.

17 *Ibid.*, p. 5.

18 A. Satariano, 'In a first, Uber agrees to classify British drivers as "Workers"', *The New York Times*, 16 March 2021, www.nytimes.com/2021/03/16/technology/uber-uk-drivers-worker-status.html.

trade union, UNIONEN, handles collective bargaining agreements in ice hockey and football on behalf of those associations.

In France, collective bargaining is organised centrally, and sectors wishing to deviate from the standards negotiated at the national level must come to an agreement separately. Although sport was one of the last sectors to adopt a collective agreement, this structure finally gave sport employers the impetus needed to engage in social dialogue and collective bargaining with player associations in most of the major sports including football, basketball and handball. In a recent development, women handball players in France became the first women athletes in France to conclude a collective agreement that gave them additional rights related to maternity leave (one year instead of three months) and increased their minimum salary from 1,561 euros to 1,650 euros.[19]

Social dialogue and collective bargaining at the national level has improved working conditions, created legal certainty, shielded leagues from antitrust liability and created conditions that allowed clubs, leagues and players to thrive financially. In the United Kingdom, 'EU law in force prior to exit day will continue to apply until the Government changes the law or the courts interpret the law in a different direction'.[20] It is commonly felt that the EU has had a positive influence on the UK when it comes to workers' rights.[21] Despite a lack of competence in the Treaty regarding the right to pay and the right to strike, the EU has influence over national labour law through Directives and how it defines the term 'worker' in primary and secondary law.[22] In 2019, the Commission issued a *Directive on Transparent and Predictable Working Conditions in the European Union* that recognises, 'in order adequately to frame the development of new forms of employment, workers in the Union should also be provided with a number of new minimum rights aiming to promote security and predictability in employment relationships while achieving upward convergence across Member States and preserving labour market adaptability'.[23] The Directive did not contain a definition of the term 'worker'. The European Trade Union Institute issued a report leading up to the passage of the Directive titled, 'The Concept of "Worker" in EU Law', that described the potential dangers of an explicit definition as there may still be more progress to be made through the interpretation of current laws by the European Court of Justice. The report noted that 'the ECJ has not yet used economic factors to extend the scope of application beyond

19 Via Archyde.com, 'Handball players have their collective agreement, a first for French women's sport', 15 March 2021.

20 Leanne O'Leary, 'Sport, Employment Law and Brexit' (in this volume).

21 *Ibid.*, p. 2.

22 Martin Risak & Thomas Dullinger, *The Concept of "Worker" in EU Law: Status Quo and Potential for Change*, Report 140 (Brussels: European Trade Union Institute, 2018), p. 5.

23 Directive (EU) 2019/1152 of the European Parliament and of the Council of 20 June 2019 on transparent and predictable working conditions in the European Union. OJ L 186, 11.7.2019, pp. 105–121.

those persons working not in a relationship of "personal" subordination but in one based on some form of economic dependency, since they are not really performing on the market but are working in person for only one or a very small number of contractual partners'. This certainly describes many athletes and also identifies a potential gap in status that might open up between elite athletes in the European Union and those in the UK who would not have the benefit of this evolving definition. The European Social Dialogue might offer a way for athletes in the United Kingdom to continue to harmonise their conditions with those of athletes on the continent but much depends on whether the process is restarted (outside of football) and how labour standards progress in the UK over the next few decades.

7.3. The European social dialogue in the sport sector

The European social dialogue is a specific process at EU level that is a 'major instrument for establishing supranational forms of governance'.[24] In accordance with Articles 151–156 TFEU, a European Sectoral Social Dialogue Committee (ESSDC), made up of the employer and employee social partner organisations, would have several important functions. First, the Commission would be required to consult the social partners twice when there is a legislative proposal in the social policy field—the first time, regarding their views on the possible direction of Union action, and the second regarding the content of the proposal. The social partners may also start formal negotiations autonomously. They have nine months to reach an agreement during which the Commission may not continue with its own proposal.[25] If the social partners come to an agreement, Article 155(2) TFEU states that it 'shall be implemented' either through the 'voluntary route' where the responsibility for implementation lies with the national members of the European social partner organisations. Voluntary agreements are not generally binding and would not, therefore, have a direct effect.[26] It is also possible for the social partners to submit a proposal to have their agreement submitted to the Council of the European Union for implementation as a Directive under the conditions set out in Article 153 TFEU.

The 1957 Treaty of Rome gave the Commission the task of 'promoting close cooperation between Member States with regard to the right of association and collective bargaining'. The Single European Act (1986), the Treaty of Amsterdam (1997) and the Lisbon Treaty (2009) built upon each other establishing a legal basis for 'community wide social dialogue' underlining the role of the social

24 Keller (2018).
25 Article 154 TFEU
26 Michele Colluci and Arnout Geeraert, 'The "Social dialogue" in European Professional Football'

partners while respecting their autonomy and diversity (Article 152 TFEU).[27] This single framework for social dialogue at the European level led to framework agreements on parental leave (1995), part-time work (1997) and fixed-term work (1999). The initiative to form a European Sectoral Social Dialogue Committee (ESSDC) in the European Football Sector was begun in the early 2000s when uncertainty on the part of governing bodies in sport about the future of the European Union's role in sport was at a high point. At the time, the EU did not have a specific competency in the field of sport but the European Commission, in the wake of the *Bosman* decision, had played a key role in negotiating a new set of transfer rules to replace those abolished by *Bosman*.[28] The Commission, recognising this history, the limitations of its own competences under the Treaty when it came to sport (both before and after 2009), and the potential role that European Social Dialogue could play, included support for the European Social Dialogue in the European Sport Sector as a priority in the White Paper on Sport (2007) and the Pierre de Coubertin action plan. In 2017, the European Parliament, addressing growing concerns about governance in sport, included an article welcoming the efforts of the Commission and all concerned stakeholders to promote social dialogue in sport as it could 'provide a balance between the fundamental and labour rights of sportspeople and the economic nature of sport'.[29]

Normally, ESSDCs are bipartite (employers and employees) or tripartite (including the Commission). In the case of the ESSDC in football, a nod was given to the 'specificity' of sport, and UEFA was given the role of chairing the Football ESSDC meetings.[30] Subjects for discussion must first pass through UEFA's Professional Football Strategy Council (that includes FIFPRO [players], ECA [clubs], EL [leagues—previously the EPFL]) giving UEFA *de facto* control over the ESSDC.[31] UEFA must 'comply fully with the Statutes, regulations, directives and decisions of FIFA bodies at any time as well as the decisions of the Court of Arbitration for Sport (CAS)';[32] therefore, the chances that the ESSDC in football will approve any meaningful agreements that might have an effect on players in the United

27 Fact Sheets on the European Union, 'European parliament, social dialogue via', www.europarl.europa.eu/factsheets/en/sheet/58/social-dialogue.

28 Colluci and Geeraert (2011).

29 Text adopted by the European Parliament on 2 February 2017,'An integrated approach to Sport Policy: good governance, accessibility and integrity' an excerpt of which reads: 'Welcomes the efforts of the Commission, and of all concerned stakeholders, to promote social dialogue in sport, which is an excellent opportunity to provide a balance between the fundamental and labour rights of sportspeople and the economic nature of sport by involving all stakeholders, including social partners, in the discussion and conclusion of agreements; acknowledges the responsibility of sporting organisations to commit to developing a culture of transparency; insists that the EU should actively promote minimum employment and labour standards for professional athletes across Europe', via www.europarl.europa.eu/doceo/document/TA-8-2017-0012_EN.html.

30 *Ibid.*, p.

31 *Ibid.*, p. 16.

32 FIFA Statutes Art. 14(1)

Kingdom is very slim. Only in the case that the stakeholders change their previous strategy of attempting to achieve a binding agreement for the entire UEFA territory (55 member associations vs. 27 EU countries) and look instead at a Directive that only affected the 27 EU countries would players in the UK be, potentially, in a disadvantageous position. Although it is conceivable that this approach might be put forward by one or another of the social partners as a way to break a potential impasse, the chances are quite slim that UEFA would be able to overcome global regulatory dynamics and its interest in preserving a level playing field[33] to back such an approach. Additionally, Brexit seems to guarantee that future efforts within the football ESSDC will take a broader voluntary approach to implementation due to the prominent position played by the PFA within FIFPRO, the Premier League within the EL, and prominent clubs from the UK within ECA.

After 2007, representatives from player associations in the UK, as members of the European Elite Athletes Association (EU Athletes), also participated in the effort to establish an ESSDC for the broader sport sector. Based on an agreement by the social partners, UNI Europa and the European Association of Sport Employers (EASE), the sector was made up of three subsectors: professional sport, not-for-profit sport and active leisure. After a series of projects to build the capacity of the social partners, a pilot phase was established for the ESSDC that began in December 2012.[34] Much was achieved during the pilot of the ESSDC in the sport sector. The social partners officially recognised each other, built their capacity, approved a joint work program and signed joint statements on the European social dialogue and health and safety, a joint recommendation on minimum requirements of employment contracts in the sport sector and established guidelines on working time, and health and safety.[35] The social partners also drafted and distributed 'guides' to organising and engaging in social dialogue. From the employee perspective, these guides, published in a variety of EU languages, were instrumental in the formation of several player associations at the national level. After five years, the pilot phase ended without transitioning to a formal ESSDC. This can be attributed to a variety of factors including lack of progress in achieving representativeness on both the employer and employee sides across all sports in the professional sport sub-sector, and generally in the other two sub-sectors. Unlike the ESSDC in the football sector, governing bodies were not included in the professional sport sub-sector.

Whereas player associations in the UK will continue to be members of the employee social partner organisations (EU Athletes, UNI Europa), their representatives would most likely be included as observers in any future efforts to establish a broader EU social dialogue. However unlikely, any Directives that might

33 Craig Farrell, 'UEFA's financial fair play plan to level playing field & inhibit teams spending', *Bleacherreport.com*, 28 May 2010.

34 Pierre (2013).

35 Via EUAthletes.org https://euathletes.org/resources/essdc/.

arise out of any future process would not apply to the UK. and would need to be implemented in collective bargaining, such as it is, at the national level in the UK. The official absence of the UK from this process in the future should make little difference as to the impact of any outcomes on the overall global governance of sport. The very existence of a ESSDC provides credibility to both players associations and the issues of clubs and leagues that are often subsumed by the overwhelming influence of sport federations at the national and international level. Therefore, it is regrettable, from the perspective of elite athletes, that the initiative was not successful (so far) in the broader sport sector. The trend, however, that the initial EU social dialogue projects unleashed provide some hope for the mid to long term as the number of independent athlete associations continues to grow with consolidation and increasing influence of athlete social partners at both the European and global levels. The continued existence of the ESSDC in football is important as a precedent and example. It remains a forum where the social partners (plus UEFA) can react to emerging issues and trends.

7.4. Social dialogue as a tool for sport governance

As we have seen in some cases at the national level, social dialogue has the potential to transform sport governance. The current model of sport governance, where an organisation holding a dominant market position regulates the market in a way that infringes upon the fundamental and economic rights of its workforce, creates unacceptable levels of legal and economic risk for all stakeholders. Instead of sport organisations requiring a legislative or special exemption from the law in order to mitigate these risks, collective bargaining can provide some measure of legal stability. Collectively bargained standards take precedence over unilaterally imposed sport regulations; however, due to the globalised nature of those regulations, many, such as anti-doping regulations, may be very difficult to access through national level labour relations in Europe. It is through judicial review and social dialogue at the European level that athletes have a chance to counterbalance the influence of international federations and the Olympic Movement in their daily working lives. The business model of the IOC's global sport governance structure is designed to limit competition, keep labour costs extremely low and control athlete intellectual property. From the perspective of governing bodies, this system has, for the most part, proven to work extremely well. Olympic revenues have increased almost exponentially to over $1.4 billion a year, of which only 0.5% went to athletes directly.[36]

The IOC appears to have figured out how to protect its business model from laws at the national level that might challenge its hegemony. Wellesley University

36 Cheri Bradish, Rob Koehler, & Andrew Bailey, 'Olympic commercialization and player compensation: A review of Olympic financial reports', *Report by The Ted Rogers School of Management in Partnership with Global Athlete*, 6 December 2019, p. 1.

Professor Quinn Slobodian in his book, *Globalists: The End of Empire and the Birth of Neoliberalism*, describes a neoliberal strategy of the 'encasement of markets through transnational governance' to 'inoculate capitalism against the threats of democratic pressures (i.e. demands for redistributive justice) by building global extra-economic institutions and frameworks that would commit nations to capitalist imperatives'.[37] There are parallels to be seen in the approach taken by the International Olympic Committee to build a system of global institutions and regulations that protect the market for athlete labour and intellectual property for their own benefit. The World Bank's 'infamous structural adjustment programs which require countries receiving loans to commit to liberalised policies'[38] mirror the pressure brought to bear by the IOC in negotiations over the host city contract for the Olympic Games. This 'separate territory'[39]of global sport regulations are asserted through the Olympic Charter, implemented through the rules of international federations, the Host City Contract, the World Anti-Doping Code, and enforced through unilaterally imposed licenses and participation agreements for athletes that include mandatory arbitration clauses. In 2013, Thomas Bach, the President of the International Olympic Committee, addressed the General Assembly of the United Nations and declared: 'Sport [is] truly the only area of human existence which has achieved universal law, but to apply this universal law worldwide, sport has to enjoy responsible autonomy. Politics must respect this sporting autonomy.'[40] The collective autonomy of the social partners and collective bargaining is a recognised legal concept that could help sport achieve legal certainty but, instead, the Olympic Movement launched its own global campaign for a special form of 'sporting autonomy'. The UN was intensely lobbied for several years and, perhaps by coincidence, the 2018 Winter Games were held in the home country of the then-Secretary General, Ban Ki Moon, who now serves as Chair of the IOC Ethics Committee. The politics of the European Union, as an institution, is another matter. While the Olympic Movement opened an office in Brussels to lobby European institutions, UEFA appears to be the party that has had the most success.[41] The normal levers that sport has over the nation-state do not work as well when applied to a 'regional democratic organisation' like the EU. It does not field a team at the Olympics or have national team athletes under its influence. The emergence of the European Union changed the rules of the game. The withdrawal of the UK will have little effect on the position of the EU in the Olympic Movement's global strategy to control the market for athlete labour.

37 S. Isra, 'Neoliberal encasement infrastructure: The case of international organization sovereign immunity', *The Law and Political Economy Project*, 12 April 2019.

38 *Ibid.*, p. 2.

39 Parrish.

40 IOC Press Release, 'Historic milestone: United Nations recognizes autonomy of sport', 3 November 2014, via www.olympic.org/news/historic-milestone-united-nations-recognises-autonomy-of-sport (accessed 9 May 2021).

41 UEFA's success in lobbying the EU would be a topic for another book.

Aside from the European Social Dialogue, there is another important dynamic that might expand athlete access to collective bargaining that was unleashed by a competition law complaint filed with the European Commission by two Dutch speed skaters against the International Skating Union in June 2014. At issue were federation rules prohibiting skaters from competing in events that were not organised or promoted by the ISU.[42] First the Commission ruled in the skaters' favour in 2017, and then the General Court confirmed that decision in December 2020. There is potentially a huge market for elite athlete labour, and private event organisers want in on the action. Private event organisers appear to be prepared to bid against competitions controlled by federations for the services of elite athletes. They may also be more willing to partner with athletes in new ways, including collective bargaining. For an example of how this dynamic might play out we can look to the current dispute between the Euroleague and International Basketball Federation, FIBA. Both organisations have filed antitrust complaints against the other with the European Commission. In 2017, the Euroleague supported the formation of the Euroleague Players Association (ELPA). The ELPA states on its website that 'through Collective Bargaining with Euroleague Basketball and the Euroleague clubs, ELPA will seek to achieve a higher level of protection of players' individual and collective rights and to improve the working conditions, economic benefits and job security of all its members'. One of the areas of dispute between the Euroleague and FIBA has to do with the scheduling of windows for national team games. As the Euroleague looks to expand, it needs access to its players during the entire playing season. If the Euroleague were to agree in a collective bargaining agreement (CBA) with its players to a schedule that conflicted with FIBA's calendar, the CBA would take precedence and the Euroleague players would be committed to play for the Euroleague. FIBA's antitrust complaint should not be successful on topics where the Euroleague and its players could come to an agreement. The threat of a CBA gives the Euroleague and the players powerful leverage in future discussions with FIBA and is an example of how other private competitions might benefit from social dialogue, perhaps kicking off a virtual cycle. FIBA's reluctance to recognise national team players as employees precludes its ability to negotiate a similar agreement with national team players but that would not be out of the question. It seems unlikely, however, given the decades long resistance and the commitment to the overall strategy of market encasement referenced in this chapter.

7.5. Prospects for the future

With the withdrawal of the United Kingdom, stakeholders must assess whether or not EU institutions will change their approach to sport. Whilst the United

42 Ben Van Rompuy, 'Dutch speed skating duo files EU antitrust complaint against the international skating union', *Law in Sport*, 19 November 2014.

Kingdom will certainly lose influence, Brexit should have little effect on the European Social Dialogue's potential for transforming international sport governance. The IOC's globalist 'encasement' strategy was designed to deal with nation-states, and a weakened United Kingdom will only find its own national laws and standards more susceptible to influence by sport authorities who will assert the imperatives of global sport regulations. Brexit also does not bode well for the individual athlete in the United Kingdom. With the Jess Varnish decision, it seems clear that athletes in the UK will not be able to take advantage of any progress that might be made in the future regarding an expansion of the definition of worker in the EU.

Indirectly, however, support for the European Social Dialogue by the European Commission touched off a consolidation of collective athlete representation. The European Elite Athletes Association was founded in 2008, representing more than 25,000 athletes from 17 European countries. EU Athletes membership in UNI Europa, the European region of UNI Global Union, prompted interest, discussions and the eventual launch of a global sector within UNI Global Union for professional athletes. What is now the World Players Association was founded in 2012 and represents over 80,000 professional athletes from around the world. At each level, national, European and global players have engaged, or sought to engage, in negotiation.

As described by the International Labour Organisation (ILO), the main goal of social dialogue itself is to promote consensus building and democratic involvement among the main stakeholders in the world of work. Successful social dialogue structures and processes have the potential to resolve important economic and social issues, encourage good governance, advance social and industrial peace and stability and boost economic progress.[43] Last year, a global social dialogue was established at the ILO with the global employee and employer social partner organisations from the sport sector as participants. This process is the answer to Mr. Bach's claim of 'sporting autonomy' except it is one grounded in the true collective autonomy of the social partners and labour relations. In this global context, the European Union will maintain its influence and ability to drive long-term trends towards the embedding of its fundamental principles in global sport, while the UK, as it seems will be the case in so many other areas, will continue its self-imposed decline.

7.6. Conclusion

Bill Simmons, a popular commentator on sports in the United States, coined an idea he calls the 'Ewing Theory'—a theory where a team sometimes plays better without their star player.[44] Clearly, filling the Ewing role, representatives from

43 International Labour Organization website www.ilo.org/ifpdial/areas-of-work/social-dialogue/lang-en/index.htm

44 Bill Simmons, 'Ewing theory 101', *ESPN.com*, 9 May 2001.

the UK have played key roles in many of the European Commission sponsored projects related to the European Social Dialogue over the years. Their presence often created an interesting dynamic in meetings due to the high opinion that UK representatives had of their labour relations system in sport, despite its obvious shortcomings. Their absence may give the French, German, Scandiavian or other approaches to labour relations in sport a chance to emerge for the benefit of all parties.

Common wisdom was that the EU would be damaged by Brexit. Michel Barnier, the chief negotiator for the EU, called Brexit, 'an act of mutual weakening'. New York Times journalist, Roger Cohen, described it as, 'an act inspired by an imaginary past, borne aloft by an imaginary future, turbocharged by social media and enabled by the withered hold of truth'.[45] Articles assessing the extent to which Brexit represented an existential crisis for the EU have appeared with regularity. However, after a gruelling year of dealing with a global pandemic, opinion may be shifting. COVID-19 gave the now 27 Member States a new focus. The unprecedented crisis has 'reignited the Franco-German motor of closer union'.[46] Tools of centralised economic governance that were previously questionable became acceptable in the face of an unprecedented public health emergency. Additionally, a 'rule of law conditionality' to access EU funds was approved by the EU Parliament. For now, it seems the European transnational democratic experiment will emerge from the COVID-19 crisis with a renewed purpose and strengthened mandate. For those working in the European sport sector, it is an interesting time to examine the implications of this response to the pandemic on the governance of sport. If Brexit is brushed aside and the EU becomes more ready to assert itself, what impact will this have on the relationship between the European Union and the organisations that govern sport? Will the European Union send a clear signal to sport that the best way to achieve legal certainty around the specific elements of sport that may require a derogation from EU law is to engage in the European Social Dialogue process with social partners representing elite athletes? The answer is still unclear as the ending of the pilot for the ESSDC in the broader sport sector is still fresh in the Commission's mind. It may take a new regime or another crisis related to sport governance for a reassessment and reprioritisation. When, eventually, the EU Social Dialogue returns as a priority, the good work done during the pilot phase, in terms of lessons learned, will serve the parties well. It may mean a tighter focus on what previously were considered sub-sectors: professional sport, not-for-profit sport and active leisure. Meanwhile the ESSDC in the football sector carries on.

45 R. Cohen, 'Brexit's silver lining for Europe', *New York Times*, 31 December 2020.
46 *Ibid.*

References

Colluci, M. & Geeraert, A. (2011) The 'social dialogue' in European professional football. *Comparative Labour Law and Policy Journal*, 33:2, 203–234.

Keller, B. (2018) *Sectoral Social Dialogue in Professional Football: Social Partners, Outcomes and Problems of Implementation*, Working Paper 2018.04. European Trade Union Institute. www.etui.org/sites/default/files/18%20WP%202018%2004%20Sectoral%20social%20dialogue%20football%20Keller%20Web%20version.pdf.

Lewandowski, W. (2020) The implications of the recent jurisprudence of the court of justice of the European union for the protection of the fundamental rights of athletes and the regulatory autonomy of sporting federations. *Tilburg Law Review*, 25:1, 55–66.

O'Leary, L. (2017) *Employment and Labour Relations Law in the Premier League, NBA and International Rugby Union*. Heidelberg: Springer.

Pierre, J. (2013) Social dialogue in the sports sector at EU level. *Transfer*, 19:4, 581–595.

Risak, M. & Dullinger, T. (2018) *The Concept of 'Worker' in EU Law: Status Quo and Potential for Change*, Report 140. Brussels: European Trade Union Institute.

Van Rompuy, B. (2014) Dutch speed skating duo files EU antitrust complaint against the international skating union. *Law in Sport*, 19 November. www.lawinsport.com/topics/item/dutch-speed-skating-duo-files-eu-antitrust-complaint-against-the-international-skating-union

Chapter 8

Nationality-based restrictions in football after Brexit

The law, politics and economics

Stephen Weatherill

8.1. Introduction

Brexit was sold as a means for the UK to take back control from the EU. A whole range of opportunities, deceptions and disappointments crowd around that creaking process, but the subject matter of this Chapter provides a concrete case study into the consequences of Brexit. EU law offered no scope for either the UK government or the governing bodies of the sport to distinguish between nationals of an EU Member State who are professional footballers on the basis of their nationality. For over 20 years the most prominent clubs in Europe, though rooted in Leagues operating at national level, have been in effect pan-EU enterprises, able to select among the pool of footballing EU nationals with no regard for origin. Restrictions apply only to third country nationals. The UK has now itself become a third country. No longer do the EU rules forbidding nationality discrimination apply to it. So the UK has freedom to chart its own direction in the matter of the eligibility of players from outside the UK. Questions arise, as they arise in every nook and cranny of policy making in the wake of Brexit, about the impulses that will shape the UK's exploitation of this newfound freedom. Brexit, one may surmise, brings a promise of freedom on paper but in practice just what scope and what appetite is there for action undisciplined by transnational rules or indifferent to transnational opportunities? That is the inquiry pursued in this Chapter.

To that end it first briefly sketches the applicable EU rules in order to understand the model from which the UK is now free to depart. It then reflects on the several different constituencies whose interests are likely to be most influential in determining which choices are made. These are most of all the leading clubs, the English Premier League, the governing bodies of the four associations to be found in the UK and, ultimately, the UK government. These actors have different motivations; moreover none is a monolith, and internal compromises are likely to emerge. The paper concludes by sketching the shape of the new model announced in December 2020 and effective from January 2021, but according to an assumption that this is simply the first iteration of a long drawn-out process of contested reform.

DOI: 10.4324/9781003162803-11

8.2. The requirements of EU law

The question of the compatibility of nationality-based rules with EU law provided the Court of Justice with its very first opportunity to engage with sport. This was *Walrave and Koch* v *Union Cycliste Internationale*.[1] The litigation was provoked by a requirement introduced by cycling's governing body, the UCI, that the pacemaker in the world championships for paced cycling should hold the same nationality as the cyclist. Such a rule obviously discriminates on the basis of nationality. EU law clearly prohibits any discrimination on the basis of nationality: that prohibition was at the time contained in Article 7 EEC; its successor today is Article 18 TFEU. The question, entirely novel at the time, was whether that discrimination fell within the scope of application of the EU's Treaties. It did. The Court stated that:

> Having regard to the objectives of the Community, the practice of sport is subject to Community law only in so far as it constitutes an economic activity within the meaning of Article 2 of the Treaty.[2]

Professional sport is clearly an economic activity and one of increasing significance. The Court had set the ball rolling for EU sports law. But it concluded that, notwithstanding this point of principle of enduring constitutional importance, the rules in question did not offend against the demands of EU law. In *Walrave and Koch* the Court concluded that EU law's prohibition of nationality-based discrimination 'does not affect the composition of sport teams, in particular national teams, the formation of which is a question of purely sporting interest and as such has nothing to do with economic activity'.[3] Selection on the basis of nationality for a representative team—in any sport, not simply paced cycling—is nationality-based discrimination, but it is not *unlawful* nationality-based discrimination.

Twenty years later the Court completed the picture. Having accepted in *Walrave and Koch* that nationality may determine the composition of a *national* team, the Court in *Bosman* resisted the claims advanced by the governing bodies that a similar connection should be respected within the *club* game.[4] At club level, in contrast to national representative level, an obligation to discriminate on the basis of nationality was neither necessary nor inherent in the scheme of the sport. It was incompatible with EU law.

Neither *Walrave and Koch* nor *Bosman* contain entirely satisfactory legal reasoning. Their appeal to rules of purely sporting interest which have nothing to do with economic activity as a means to curtail the incursion of EU law into sporting autonomy is unpersuasive, because in reality few sporting rules are devoid of

1 Case 36/74 EU:C:1974:140.
2 *Ibid.*, Para 4.
3 *Ibid.*, at 8.
4 Case C-415/93 *Bosman* EU:C:1995:463.

economic implications. Only subsequently in *Meca-Medina and Majcen v Commission*[5] would the Court shift its analytical focus to a more realistic case-by-case examination of the place of organisational rules in sport under EU law, and away from a preoccupation with the unhelpful notion of the 'purely sporting' rule. On this model sport enjoys a 'conditional autonomy' under EU law: sport, when it comes into contact with EU internal market law, is allowed to pursue its own model of regulation on condition that a sufficiently compelling explanation is provided for the patterns chosen.[6] But despite their intellectual inadequacies the outcome in *Walrave and Koch* and in *Bosman* suggests that international representative football is existentially defined by nationality discrimination, whereas club football is not. And so EU law does not call into question the former but forbids nationality discrimination in club football.

It was therefore immediately required in the wake of *Bosman* that in club football all players holding the nationality of an EU Member State should be treated in the same way. The relevant provision of the Treaty is today Article 45 TFEU on the free movement of workers, supplemented by the anti-discrimination norms found in both Article 18 TFEU and Article 21(2) of the EU Charter of Fundamental Rights. *Walrave and Koch* had long ago established that Article 45 binds both public authorities and private parties acting collectively, so it prevented both Member State governments and governing bodies in sport from discriminating on the basis of nationality in setting rules governing the eligibility of players in club football. It quickly became entirely normal for leading clubs, especially but not only in England, to field sides with few, and even sometimes no, players eligible to play for the association of which the club was a member.

So, since December 1995, players in the EU fall into two categories as a matter of law—they are either EU nationals and entitled to play in any country on the same terms as locals or else they are third country nationals who can be subject to restrictions imposed by a state pursuant to its policy on immigration and/or by the sport's governing bodies. Quotas, work permits and the like are applicable only to third country nationals—although even here a footnote is required to acknowledge that the privileged group comprises also non-EU EEA nationals and, to a limited extent, nationals able to benefit from non-discrimination norms contained in Association Agreements between the EU and third countries.[7]

UEFA operates rules which are tied to players' origins. These are the so-called 'home-grown' rules, which require that a certain percentage of players in a squad meet the definition. The aim is to encourage the development of young players. But, in order to avoid violation of EU law, the 'home-grown' rules are not explicitly linked to nationality. UEFA's current system deems a player 'home-grown' where registered with a club for three seasons between the ages of 15 and 21. This

5 Case C-519/04P EU:C:2006:492.
6 See Weatherill (2017).
7 Case C-438/00 *Deutscher Handballbund eV v Maros Kolpak* EU:C:2003:255.

entails that a player can count as home-grown in one jurisdiction having played his or her football and received his or her training up until the age of 18 in another.[8] There is room to argue that such rules are vulnerable to challenge on the basis that they cause *indirect* discrimination on the basis of nationality,[9] but they have been written with care to eliminate any whiff of *direct* discrimination based on nationality. That has been clearly forbidden in club football ever since the Court's ruling in *Bosman*.

8.3. After Brexit—what changes and what does not

Sport is predominantly regulated by its governing bodies, typically global in their reach and equipped with expertise in their own particular field. It is the creation of neither national governments nor the EU. The *lex sportiva* is a contested concept but it is a useful shorthand expression apt to capture the characteristic development of private transnational ordering within sport.[10] It is neither national nor international law. It is helpfully understood as 'internal' sports law, and it co-exists with the application to sport of the laws of states and of international organisations such as the EU, which counts as 'external' sports law. A solid body of law and practice focuses on the attempts of governing bodies in sport to immunise their practices from review from the outside, whether through formal routes such as mandatory submission of sporting disputes to arbitration or, less satisfactory from the perspective of governing bodies seeking autonomy, by pleading before ordinary courts that the law should be interpreted and applied with sensitivity to sport's peculiarities.[11] The intellectual heart of sports law in both principle and practice is inquiry into the sustainability of such claims to autonomy.

It is important to grasp that much of the existing pattern of governance in sport will be entirely unaffected by Brexit. Brexit concerns the relationship between the UK and the EU. Football's governing bodies in the UK are not leaving UEFA or FIFA. The rules of those organisations will continue to provide the primary basis for the organisation of football in the UK. So matters such as the transfer system, rules against multiple ownership of clubs, the prohibition of third party ownership of players and Financial Fair Play must comply with EU law and each has been assessed, and in some instances adjusted, in order to ensure such compliance.[12] But nothing in EU law directly addresses such practices. They are affected only where they impinge on the functioning of the internal market. Moreover all those rules are the product of 'internal' sports law. None is mandated by state law.

8 For UEFA's own explanation see www.uefa.com/news/newsid=943393.html (accessed 22 February 2021).

9 See Downward et al. (2014), Weatherill (2017), Chapter 8.10.

10 See e.g. Duval (2020), Hock and Gomtsian (2018).

11 Weatherill (2017) Chapter 2.

12 *Ibid.*, Chapters. 9, 10.

Nationality rules are different. EU law directly and explicitly forbids nationality discrimination within the scope of the Treaties, so withdrawal from the EU opens up space for discrimination which was previously closed; and whereas national governments do not typically concern themselves with rules on player transfers, they do typically impose nationality-based rules governing immigration and eligibility for work.

So Brexit does not change the practices of UEFA or FIFA—the *lex sportiva* or 'internal' sports law. But it does allow the UK government to change rules based on nationality. And given that a major animating theme of the case for Brexit has been the elimination of the advantages enjoyed by migrant EU nationals, some change is inevitable. The question is only how much.

8.4. An international league played in England

Brexit releases room for a policy that distinguishes between British athletes and 'foreigners'. The scope for such differentiation is dramatically at odds with the nature of the English Premier League. There is more to football in the UK than the English Premier League, but it seizes the lion's share of attention as arguably the world's most popular league. It offers a vivid illustration of the point that EU law requires the opening of labour markets and the elimination of local preference. Players from across the EU are commonly found in the squads of all 20 clubs in the Premier League, and in law their entitlements stood on an equal status to those of British nationals. It is normal that the majority of players in a team are not British; it is far from unknown that none is British. Writing in *The Times* in October 2017, the former England manager Sam Allardyce explained that 'The Premier league is not like the Bundesliga or La Liga'.[13] His point: 'We still call it the English league, but in reality it is now an international league that is played in England'. In achieving this, *Bosman* was transformative because it required the lifting of quotas based on nationality which were previously the norm in both domestic and international club competitions.[14] Once that bar was removed, at a time of furious commercialisation of the sport consequent on regulatory and technological changes in the broadcasting sector in particular, the leading English clubs were active in acquiring the best talent across the EU with no regard for nationality. The patterns to be found in other professional football leagues in the UK are not as eye-catching but they share the easy assumption that British players enjoy no special status.

The opportunities and the threats posed by Brexit did not go unnoticed during the referendum campaign in the first half of 2016.

13 *The Times*, 30 October 2017, *The Game*, page 11.
14 See generally Lanfranchi and Taylor (2001).

The BBC Sport website published a comment on 31 March 2016 which claimed that Brexit, and the elimination of the right of EU nationals to work in the UK on the same terms as British nationals, 'could lead to more than 400 players losing the right to play in the UK'.[15] It identified over 100 Premier League players from across the EU who would not meet the government's requirements which at that time applied to third country nationals wishing to play in the UK. A similar story, it was explained, would apply in the lower tiers of English football, while none of the 53 EU nationals from a Member State other than the UK who were active at the time in the Scottish Premiership would qualify for a permit on the basis of their international career alone.

The BBC Sport report recognised that the issue was first raised in January 2016 by Karren Brady, vice chair of West Ham United and a Conservative life peer. She said in a letter released to the press that:

> Indeed, there are nearly 200 Premier League footballers alone who have benefited from this arrangement [under EU law]. Leaving the EU could have a big impact on foreign players, as independent analysis has shown that two-thirds of European stars in England would not meet automatic non-EU visa criteria and therefore might be forced to leave. Losing this unhindered access to European talent would put British clubs at a disadvantage compared to continental sides.

This argument was plainly intended to strengthen the case in favour of the UK remaining in the EU, a cause which Brady supported. With gloomy hindsight one can see it as consistent with too much of the Remain campaign in 2016, which was shot through with negative projections which seemed unrealistic to many voters inclined to vote Leave. However, many of the warnings issued by those advocating Remain—concerning the UK's weak bargaining position, the refusal of the EU to abandon its commitment to a level playing field in its single market, the disinterest of third countries to offer the UK a special deal and so on—have turned out to be entirely realistic. So the question arises whether Brexit really will lead to the tarnishing of the English Premier League's remarkably successful business model. Will it, in Sam Allardyce's words, cease to function as 'an international league that is played in England'?

8.5. The incentives and the actors

The UK has just one seat at the United Nations, but for reasons associated with the historical origins of the sport in organised form, it has four members of FIFA—England, Northern Ireland, Scotland and Wales.

15 www.bbc.co.uk/sport/football/35919247 (accessed 22 February 2021). For subsequent calculation see Perry and Steenson (2019).

As a member of both UEFA and FIFA, each national association is responsible for the conduct of the sport within its own jurisdiction, in which official leagues, clubs and players are all subject to their supervision. This is the pyramid structure of sporting governance. On this model, then, the English FA (Football Association) is the governing body responsible for the conduct of the game in England, which includes oversight of the English Premier League, which is connected by a system of promotion and relegation to the three Divisions of the English Football League (EFL) which are in turn connected in the same way to lower leagues; the Northern Irish FA, known as the Irish Football Association, is responsible for the semi-professional Irish League; the Scottish FA is the governing body of the game in Scotland, where the Scottish Professional Football League comprises four Divisions, with at its apex the Premiership which is connected by promotion and relegation to three further Divisions; and the Welsh FA runs a single Division covering all of Wales, although the most popular clubs in Wales have always played instead in the English leagues.

All four national associations have the national team as the centrepiece of their activities, with participation in the Finals of the FIFA World Cup the most glittering prize. They also have other roles such as organising the principal national cup competitions, among which the English FA Cup is the most high-profile.

From a purely formal perspective the most powerful actors are the national associations. But in the economic and political reality the most powerful entity by far in this family tree is the English Premier League. It was created in 1992 precisely in order to pursue a more aggressive model of profit-making than leading clubs felt the FA was able to deliver. It is a limited company, and each of its 20 clubs is a shareholder. It is in principle subject to the overall regulatory oversight practised by the FA as the legitimate governing body for English football under the pyramid structure of governance at the apex of which sits FIFA, but the truth is that the Premier League's commercial clout far exceeds that of the FA.

As a rough summary, one may suppose that the national associations, whose flagship project is the national team, will be attracted by post-Brexit changes which prioritise the eligibility for club football of players who are qualified to play for the national team. Demand for British players will diminish in the EU-27, but it will increase in the UK. This, they would hope, would not simply increase the size of the pool of players playing top-flight football on which the national team could draw but also, by inducing leading clubs to develop young domestic players rather than acquire fully-formed overseas players, improve the quality of players in that pool. The need to protect national teams was an argument advanced in *Bosman* in defence of discrimination in club football but it was swept aside on the basis that the reduction in players' chances of finding employment within the Member State of which they are nationals would be compensated for by the new prospects of employment in other Member States.[16] The case for discriminating

16 Case C-415/93 (n 4) para 134. In fact this argument is unconvincing, see Weatherill (2017), Chapter 8.6.

in order to promote the national team now re-emerges, as the UK is freed of the demands of EU law.

A separate argument—the economics to which the title of this paper nods—asks whether such a strategy is wise. It distorts the market for players. Restricting access to the labour market on the basis of nationality will grant an advantage to those players that hold the 'right' nationality which is not the result of their talent. It will grant them artificially enhanced power in the market for wages. The result might not be better local players, but instead better paid and lazier local players, and moreover players less exposed to overseas players of the highest quality from whom they could learn. That would harm the quality of the competition and would not deliver the anticipated benefits to the national team.

By contrast the clubs, and most of all those in the English Premier League, are likely to prefer to keep the labour market as open as possible. The Premier League wants to attract star players based on ability not nationality. Insofar as British players would replace EU-27 players not because they are better but because they are British the product would be provided by lower quality players, and become less appealing.

At levels below the Premier League the concern would not be to retain access to the very best players but rather to keep the pool from which players could be drawn as deep as possible, so that even in the lower Leagues one can identify rationales for resisting the introduction of new nationality-based restrictions.

A fully satisfying account would want to look beyond the 'FA' and the 'Premier League' and excavate the motivations of individuals and the pattern of influence and lobbying. To take one simple example, the clubs of the Premier League and the FA are not wholly independent: the Premier League is represented on the FA Board. So to depict this as simply 'club v country' is misleading. There are certainly other groups whose interests are likely to be affected—such as players and fans—but whose voice will be weaker. And other actors such as sponsors and broadcasters are likely to channel their preferences in discreet ways. But, pending a more nuanced examination which lies beyond the ambitions of this Chapter, what is at stake is predominantly a contest between an open regime favourable to the aspirations of the Premier League clubs and a more constrained regime protecting British players.

The UK government is the ultimate decision-maker. Although the glitter of the Premier League might induce one to suppose it will readily extract preservation of the current easy patterns of migration enjoyed by high-earning players from outside the UK, it would be unwise to be complacent. Exemption from tightening up of rules governing immigration will be sought by a great many sectors of the economy unable to function to maximum effect without access to imported labour and talent, but the nativist urge impelling Brexit will inevitably affect governmental policy, however economically damaging it may be.

8.6. The new arrangements

After the referendum in June 2016, manoeuvring was initially furtive. Rumours reached the media, doubtless a result of strategic leaking, and tended to confirm the basic schism between the aspirations of the FA and the Premier League. In June 2018 it was reported that the FA was exploring means to 'increase the playing time for domestic footballers' while the Premier League 'will resist any moves to make it more difficult for players from the EU to gain a UK visa post-Brexit'.[17] Two months later the same newspaper repeated that the FA saw Brexit as an opportunity 'to allow greater numbers of young English players a chance in the first teams of the top-flight clubs' while the Premier League was reported as eager for 'all players of every nationality to be allowed work permits simply because they have been offered a contract'.[18] In November 2018, there was talk of compromise around an increase in the number of home-grown players required in a squad,[19] while the Premier League issued a statement reasserting 'that Brexit should not be used to weaken playing squads in British football, nor to harm clubs' ability to sign international players'.[20]

The tortured process of the UK's withdrawal, which was finally confirmed only by the General Election of December 2019, allowed some breathing space but once the UK finally left the EU at the end of January 2020 the search for a new regime became urgent during the transitional period ending at the end of 2020 during which the UK remained aligned to the EU's rules.

In February 2020, one learned that the FA remained keen 'to introduce curbs on the number of foreign players at top clubs' in order to 'force clubs to develop more local talent that will boost the England national team', while the Premier League suggests such proposals 'will harm one of the country's great international exports'.[21]

In Autumn 2020, newspaper reports claimed that the Premier League was willing to assist lower league clubs faced with financial pressures consequent on COVID-19 on condition that they agreed (inter alia) to support the quest to expand the number of permits made available to non-British players.[22] This particular initiative, which also included controversial plans to restructure the Premier League itself in a way that would strengthen the power of the largest clubs,

17 'FA wants Brexit loan rules to help native players', *The Times*, 15 June 2018.

18 'FA determined to slam the gate shut on EU journeymen', *The Times*, 14 August 2018.

19 'Clubs set to fight FA "homegrown" quota proposals', *The Times*, 14 November 2018.

20 'Premier league statement on Brexit and access to talent', 21 November 2018, www.premierleague.com/news/916592 (accessed 22 February 2021).

21 'English football divided over post-Brexit visas for players', *Financial Times*, 21 February 2020.

22 E.g. 'Premier league's "blackmail" over bailout for EFL clubs', *The Times*, 30 September 2020; 'Premier league clubs ready to provide funds for those in football league', *The Guardian*, 2 October 2020.

appears to have died a quick death, as wrangles emerged once it had been made public, but the specific issue of permits could not go away.

At the beginning of December 2020, the FA announced the entry requirements for overseas players that would apply within its jurisdiction from 1 January 2021. Media attention understandably focused on the fate of the best clubs and the best EU players, but the rules went further. Carefully written documents covered playing criteria for men and women, as well as managers, assistant managers, directors of football and performance mangers.[23] These were the product of agreement by the FA, the Premier League and the EFL, duly submitted to the UK government by the FA and approved by the relevant department, the Home Office.

The headline is that, as one would have expected, Premier League and EFL clubs will no longer be able to sign players from the EU on the same basis as British players. An endorsement will be required, just as has long been required in the UK of non-EU players from third countries. A 'points-based' system governs eligibility, and the criteria are founded on senior and youth international appearances, the status of the selling club and club appearances. The criteria are necessarily detailed. For example, for male players, their elucidation stretches over 18 pages, spelling out the method of calculation. Some players will automatically gather enough points, others will be subject to a process for examining exceptions where they fall just below the threshold. Special provision is made in the Premier League for overseas under-21 players. A club may sign three in the January transfer window and six per season in future. This, the FA explains, 'enables the recruitment of the best players from around the world to train and play together with home-grown talent'.[24] It acknowledges too that under FIFA's rules the UK's withdrawal from the EU means that clubs are subject to a ban on international transfers of players under the age of 18—this was previously overridden within the EU/EEA by EU/EEA law, as is explicitly recognised by FIFA's rules on transfers.[25] Outside the EU, this ban seems to prevent English clubs acquiring players aged under 18 from Scotland as much as from Spain and Sweden. It will eliminate not only the buying of such players but also the ease with which non-nationals can be converted into home-grown players. This will probably accentuate the attention paid to training and developing local players under the age of 18, while at the same time excluding British clubs from a market for under-18 talent in the EU-27 in which their principal rivals in Spain, Italy and Germany will remain active. It will also close off the EU-27 market to under-18 British players. All this will change once again in the event of Scotland leaving the UK and joining the EU. As with Brexit generally there lurk shoals of unplanned consequences.

23 www.thefa.com/news/2020/dec/01/gbe-points-based-system-launched-011220 (accessed 22 February 2021).

24 *Ibid.*

25 Art 19(2)(b) FIFA Regulations on the Status and Transfer of Players.

The general intent is plainly to keep the gate open for star players, but not for journeymen and women. It is the Premier League that will provide the most high-profile testing ground for the changes, but the impact is likely to be much more visible lower down the leagues. The brilliant Belgian and the superb Swede will land enough points to qualify but the same is not likely to be true of the ordinary Austrian or the plodding Pole. Similarly the canny Croat coach will qualify where the patchy Portuguese may not.

It took precisely three days into 2021 for the new rules to come under fire. West Bromwich Albion manager Sam Allardyce complained that three intended transfer targets had to be abandoned since the players would not qualify for a work permit.[26] This is admittedly slim evidence of likely trends, and relegation-haunted football managers are highly skilled at finding convenient excuses, but the point was immediately clear: things are different now.

8.7. Conclusion

The arrangements announced in late 2020 are emphatically not the end of the story. On their own terms, they make clear that periodic review is anticipated as the new system beds down, but more generally the point of Brexit is to permit the UK to make its own choices, inter alia on immigration and eligibility for work, unaffected by the requirements of EU law. Combined with the fundamental constitutional rule that Parliament is free to make and unmake laws at any time, this entails that the current rules can be changed at any time, should political preferences so dictate. One may therefore expect that the relevant actors will continue to lobby, plan and seek coalitions to advance their interests.

Richard Masters, the Premier League's chief executive, was quoted on the FA website at the time of the December 2020 deal: 'The Premier League has worked with the FA to come to an agreement to ensure no part of Brexit should damage the success of the Premier League, or the prospects of the England teams'.[27] But one suspects the Premier League will remain wary. *The Guardian* described the deal as 'a controversial move that could have seismic effects on the recent dominance of English clubs over their European rivals',[28] and any slide in the Premier League's economic pre-eminence and (a related though not identical issue) any hint that its leading clubs are losing ground in the competition to win at European level will certainly induce lobbying aimed at allowing English clubs to shake off the newly imposed work permit restrictions to which clubs in the EU-27, home to all

26 www.sportinglife.com/football/news/new-rules-affecting-baggies-plans/188019 (accessed 22 February 2021).

27 www.premierleague.com/news/1922063 (accessed 22 February 2021).

28 www.theguardian.com/football/2020/dec/01/work-permits-for-eu-players-and-no-under-18-signings-in-post-brexit-regulations (accessed 22 February 2021).

the other major Leagues, are not subject thanks to the application of EU law. And once again what Brexit really means will come into question.

References

Downward, P.; Parrish, R.; Pearson, G. & Semens, A. (2014) An assessment of the compatibility of UEFA's home grown player rule with Article 45 TFEU. *European Law Review*, 39:4, 493–510.

Duval, A. (2020) What lex Sportiva tells you about transnational law. In: Zumbansen, P. (ed) *The Many Lives of Transnational Law*. Cambridge: Cambridge University Press, pp. 319–458.

Hock, B. & Gomtsian, S. (2018) Private order building: The state in the role of the civil society and the case of FIFA. *International Sports Law Journal*, 17, 186–204.

Lanfranchi, P. & Taylor, M. (2001) *Moving with the Ball: The Migration of Professional Footballers*. London: Bloomsbury.

Perry, K. & Steenson, M. (2019) A post-Brexit impact: A case study on the English Premier League. *Harvard Journal of Sports and Entertainment Law*, 10, 1–53.

Weatherill, S. (2017) *Principles and Practice in EU Sports Law*. Oxford: Oxford University Press.

Chapter 9

You're out! Brexit and cricket

Richard Parrish

9.1. Introduction

In 2008, the England and Wales Cricket Board (ECB) provided evidence to a House of Commons enquiry on the European Commission White Paper on Sport.[1] In the oral submission, committee member Adrian Sanders MP asked Giles Clarke, Chairman of the ECB, for his reaction to the European Court's judgment in *Kolpak*,[2] a judgment initially wrongly interpreted by Clarke as enhancing the free movement rights of non-EU athletes.[3] In response, Clarke complained that 'we have a situation where English cricket cannot be allowed to manage its own affairs because [. . .] a Slovakian handball player wished to play in the second division of the German Handball league.' In the written submission, the ECB bemoaned 'the absence of any meaningful legitimate means of limiting unqualified cricketers.' In short, the ECB considered membership of the EU constrained its ability to take steps to protect the interests of the England national team, and this was damaging as it was responsible for driving 80% of the ECB's income.[4]

In 2016, the *Take Back Control* campaign was influential in persuading 52% of the British public to vote to leave the EU.[5] Whilst a desire to take greater control over immigration might have been a factor in this outcome, it was not the arrival of non-English cricketers that was on people's minds. Nevertheless, in 2021 the ECB took advantage of its apparent newfound freedom to make amendments to its player eligibility rules to seek to limit the participation of players not qualified to represent England.

1 *European Commission White Paper on Sport*, Seventh Report from the Culture, Media and Sport Committee, Session 2007–08, HC 347, 14/05/08.

2 Case C-438/00 *Deutscher Handballbund eV v Maros Kolpak* [2003] ECR 1–4135.

3 In his oral evidence, Clarke stated 'that decision in the European Court [. . .] provided the right of free movement of labour from citizens of a country signing the Cotonou Agreement'. As explained later in this chapter, it did not.

4 See fn.1.

5 It should be noted that a majority of those in Scotland and Northern Ireland voted 'Remain'.

DOI: 10.4324/9781003162803-12

This contribution seeks not to speculate on the extent to which regulatory control of cricket has been restored to the ECB following Brexit. The 'Indianisation of cricket' is more of a challenge for cricket administrators than judges in Luxembourg.[6] Rather, this chapter reflects on the ECB's resigned view that EU law stumped its attempts to protect the England national team. Brexit might be perceived as offering cricket greater control, but it was not in fact needed to do so. EU sports law, note the plural in sports, contained sufficient flexibility for the specific needs of a range of sports to be taken sensitively into account in the exercise of Treaty functions such as free movement and competition law. Whilst this analysis might have a redundant feel now the UK has left the EU, other sports are facing similar issues to cricket. Those sports should consider what *is* possible under EU law, rather than passively accepting what is *not*.

9.2. The organisation of cricket

It is perhaps beyond the scope of this contribution, or indeed my abilities, to describe the laws of cricket. It is best to tackle its organisational structure instead. The world governing body of cricket is the International Cricket Council (ICC), formed in 1909.[7] The ICC has 104 member nations, but only 12 of them play the 'long-form' of the international game, Test Cricket, which can last for five days. The most prominent test playing nations are, in alphabetical order, Australia, England, India, New Zealand, Pakistan, South Africa, Sri Lanka and the West Indies.

The ICC organises a number of tournaments including the Cricket World Cup (a one-day version of the game) and the ICC T20 World Cup (an even shorter version more attractive to television broadcasting). Cricket in England and Wales is governed by the ECB, a full member of the ICC. Scotland is an associate member. Cricket Ireland is a full ICC member and the governing body for cricket on the island of Ireland thus covering both the Republic of Ireland and Northern Ireland. Within the EU, only Latvia, Lithuania, Poland, Portugal and Slovakia are not members of the ICC, all the remaining EU states being associate members.

The ECB regulates a number of competitions in England and Wales including staging the men's domestic long-form version of the game, the County Championship, consisting of 18 professional clubs (Counties). Along with a number of other competitions based on the shorter version of the game, these competitions act as a source of talent for the national team, selection to which is restricted to England-eligible players. The ECB oversees international men and women's cricket—the England team. International cricket is the main source of income for cricket in England and Wales, and so the strength and success of the national

6 Gupta (2010), quoted in Malcom (2021).

7 Formed originally as the Imperial Cricket Conference, it changed its name in 1965 to the International Cricket Conference before adopting its current title in 1989.

team is paramount. This heightens the importance of developing and maintaining a sufficiently good pool of England qualified players. Consequently, the number of non-England eligible players has been, for over half a century, regulated through a quota system. Questions of nationality and nationalism have been prominent.

9.3. Cricket: them and us

Cricket is an 'imperial game' with a deep-seated association with nationalism.[8] The English exported the game to countries of the empire—Australia, New Zealand, West Indies, India, Pakistan, Sri Lanka, Bangladesh, South Africa and Zimbabwe.[9] As anti-imperialist sentiment grew in those countries, cricket turned from a tool for anglicisation to a focal point for nationalist resistance.[10] Great cricketing rivalries, such as that between England and Australia, have become legendary.[11] Following independence from Britain and the partition of India and Pakistan in 1947, cricket has been at the heart of tension between the two countries, and even considered a potential solution as witnessed by the use of 'cricket diplomacy' to ameliorate estranged relations.[12] In apartheid South Africa, only white players were selected to play for the national team and only white opponents were selected, resulting in cricket's world governing body suspending South Africa from international cricket.

Cricket has even been suggested as a test of national (dis)loyalty, as advocated by former British cabinet minister, Norman Tebbit. In 1990, Tebbit claimed there was a lack of loyalty among UK members of the Asian and Caribbean communities and questioned whether those wanting India, Pakistan or the West Indies to prevail when playing England were 'harking back to where you come from, or where you are.'[13] Tebbit's view reflects a pronounced 'them and us' mentality in cricket and highlights that cricket has acquired a perceived purity that extends to questions about who should be allowed to play it. But the national purity of the game has often be compromised in the pursuit of performance.[14] English cricket has been greatly enriched by the presence of players born outside the UK, many of whom have served as captain. Indeed, five players from England's 2019 ICC men's World Cup victory were born outside the UK.

8 Malcom (2021).
9 To those disputing the English origins of cricket, I refer to James Wilson who wrote: 'it is virtually certain that, even if some of its antecedents were imported, any game recognizable as cricket evolved in England.' See Wilson (2014), p. 20.
10 Fraser (2005), pp. 326–327.
11 See for example the brutal 'bodyline' series between Australia and England in 1932/33.
12 Murray (2018), pp. 70–72.
13 Quoted in Fraser (2005), p. 306.
14 For discussion see, Wilson (2014), pp. 193–223.

The UK's membership of the EU gave the 'them and us' and purity debate a new twist. As Giles Clarke implied in his evidence to the House of Commons, who are they are to tell us how to run a sport they don't even play? Membership of the EU entailed acceptance of the EU's *acquis communautaire*, a body of laws including the principles of free movement and non-discrimination. The *acquis* asked questions, not of who could represent England, but who could be excluded from playing the club version of the sport. The *acquis* has been a challenge for sport generally. Sport is organised on a national segmentation model which is based on national leagues and national championships with the best athletes representing national teams. The EU, based on the single market model, is organised differently.

The *acquis* made it more difficult for cricket administrators to adopt nationality-based eligibility restrictions on who could play County cricket, the club form of the game that produces talent for the England national team. This is not a bad thing, some might say, given the destructive forces of nationalism in sport and society. It might also be argued that the presence of overseas players in domestic cricket drives up standards which flows through into a more competitive national team. For example, despite the presence of non-England qualified players in domestic cricket in England and Wales, the England national team won the Cricket World Cup in 2019. However, the claim expressed by Clarke is that a diminishing pool of England-eligible talent at County level could undermine the success of the England team which could, in turn, progressively suffocate the redistributive flow of funds down the pyramid. The issue facing cricket is not a desire to retain the *national purity* of cricket as an expression of English nationalism, but rather a need to promote *national performance*.

9.4. Cricket and European law: *Bosman* and *Kolpak*

In the same year as UK accession to the EEC, a District Court in Utrecht referred a dispute in motor-paced cycling to the European Court of Justice, and in doing so brought the relationship between sport and the EU a step closer. The Luxembourg Court held that the practice of sport is subject to EU law only insofar as it constitutes an economic activity and that the Treaty's prohibition on nationality discrimination 'does not affect the composition of sport teams, in particular national teams, the formation of which is a matter of purely sporting interest and as such has nothing to do with economic activity.'[15] The purity of English cricket was ensured. A day after the judgment in *Walrave*, the England national team took to

15 Case 36/74 *Walrave & Koch v. Association Union cycliste internationale* [1974] ECR 1405, paras. 4 and 8.

the field in Perth, Western Australia, fielding three players born outside England, and were trounced by Australia.[16]

For the Advocate General in *Walrave*, it was 'common sense' for national teams to consist only of nationals of that country, but the situation regarding nationality restrictions in club sport remained open.[17] Two years later in *Donà*, the Court turned its attention to this question and found that rules limiting participation in football matches solely to the nationals of the state in question conflict with EU law unless such rules excluded foreign players from participation in certain matches for reasons which are not of an economic nature, which relate to the particular nature and context of such matches and are thus of sporting interest only.[18] This was tested, somewhat spectacularly, nearly 20 years later in *Bosman*.[19]

In *Bosman* the Court first condemned the practice that required an acquiring club to pay a transfer fee to secure the services of a player, even though that player was no longer under contract with the releasing club.[20] As a sport not operating a transfer system, this aspect of the judgment caused few ripples in cricketing circles. More significant was Bosman's success in arguing that the use of nationality quotas in European club football amounted to restriction on a worker's freedom of movement. Three 'purely sporting' justifications presented by UEFA, the Belgian Football Association and some Member States, were rejected by the Court and the quota system was ended. The first was that the quota system served to maintain the traditional link between each club and its country.[21] The second concerned quotas being necessary to ensure a pool of talent eligible to play for the national team.[22] The final justification, accepted in principle by the Court, asserted the need to maintain a competitive balance between clubs.[23]

In dismissing the second justification, that nationality quotas are necessary to protect national teams by maintaining a sufficient talent pool for national selectors to select from, the Court viewed sport through the lens of football and in doing so made an 'error.'[24] It pointed out that national players, whose opportunities are reduced by the presence of overseas players, can themselves benefit from the liberalised European labour market that *Bosman* helped create.[25] Indeed, subject to linguistic barriers and culinary preferences, footballers could take their pick from any number of national labour markets, all of which had professional leagues. The

16 Those three players were Colin Cowdrey (India), Tony Greig (South Africa) and Mike Denness (Scotland).
17 Case 36/74 *Walrave*, Opinion of Advocate General Werner, para. 1426.
18 Case 13/76 *Donà v Mantero* [1776] ECR 1333.
19 Case C-415/93 *Union Royale Belge Sociétés de Football Association and others v. Bosman and others* [1995] ECR I-4921.
20 Case C-415/93 *Bosman*, para. 114.
21 *Ibid.*, para. 123.
22 *Ibid.*, paras. 133–134.
23 *Ibid.*, para. 136 & para. 106.
24 Weatherill (2017), p. 182.
25 Case C-415/93 *Bosman*, para. 134.

error was the generalisation. Cricket is different to football. The UK possesses the only professional cricket league in Europe. A European labour market in cricket does not exist.

The position facing cricket was compounded further by the Court in *Kolpak*.[26] This case, the principles of which were confirmed by the Court in *Simutenkov*[27] and *Kahveci*,[28] concerned the EU's relations with third countries, in this instance the Slovak Republic prior to its accession in 2004. Maros Kolpak, as Giles Clarke had observed, was a Slovak handball player, keeping goal for German second division handball club TSV Ostringen. At the time, the Slovak Republic was not a Member State of the EU, although it had entered into a pre-accession Association Agreement with it. This agreement provided that treatment accorded to workers of Slovak Republic nationality legally employed in the territory of a Member State shall be free from any discrimination based on nationality, as regards working conditions, remuneration or dismissal, as compared to its own nationals.[29] Mr Kolpak claimed he had suffered discrimination based on his nationality as the German Handball Federation (DHB) issued him with an overseas (non-EU/EEA) player's licence limiting his possibilities for selection as clubs were only permitted to field two such players.

The Court of Justice agreed with Mr Kolpak. Having established the horizontal effect of Article 38, it went on to find that it precluded discriminatory rules being applied to individuals who are already lawfully employed by a club established in a Member State.[30] In that regard, it is worth pointing out that *Kolpak* did not extend, as Giles Clarke had stated in his oral evidence to the House of Commons, a general right of market access to third country nationals.[31] The DHB attempted to justify the application of the overseas rule on exclusively sporting grounds; namely, its purpose was to safeguard training organised for the benefit of young players of German nationality and to promote the German national team.[32] This was rejected by the Court. Whilst acknowledging the legitimacy of measures based on nationality in the context of national team selection, it repeated its reasoning in *Bosman* that this could not extend to club competitions. In that regard, the Court observed that the argument regarding the protection of the national team was undermined as clubs in Germany were free to field an unlimited number of nationals from EU/EEA states.[33]

26 Case C-438/00 *Deutscher Handballbund eV v Maros Kolpak* [2003] ECR 1–4135.
27 Case C-265/03 *Simutenkov v Ministerio de Educación y Cultura and Real Federación Española de Futbol* [2005] ECR I-2579.
28 Case C-152/08 *Real Sociedad de Fútbol SAD, Nihat Kahveci v Consejo Superior de Deportes, Real Federación Española de Fútbol* [2008] ECR I-6291.
29 Article 38(1) of the EU / Slovak Republic Association Agreement, no longer in force.
30 Case C-438/00, *Kolpak*, para. 58.
31 *Ibid.*, para. 42. For Giles Clarke's evidence, see fn.1.
32 Case C-438/00, *Kolpak*, para. 52.
33 *Ibid.*, para. 56.

The question of the protection of the interests of the national team received no further assessment. Indeed, the Advocate General was equally dismissive arguing that, 'it should be pointed out that up-and-coming young German players are not restricted to playing for a German club. They likewise have the chance to engage in this high-performance sport with foreign clubs.'[34] This is a repetition of the reasoning in *Bosman*, described above, regarding reciprocal labour market opportunities across the territory of the EU—but the European labour market in handball is considerably less developed than in football, and even less so in cricket.

9.5. Cricket and non-nationals

Overseas players have never had unfettered access to playing domestic cricket in England and Wales. However, under pressure from the counties, residency requirements were lifted in the late 1960s with counties permitted to employ one such overseas star, although in practice counties often employed one overseas player per format of game in which they competed.[35] Nottinghamshire duly recruited legendary West Indian Garfield Sobers who, in 1968, dispatched the hapless Malcolm Nash for six consecutive sixes in one over at Swansea and became the first player ever to do so in first-class cricket. In 1992, Yorkshire Cricket Club, who even extended eligibility restrictions to those not born in Yorkshire, let alone the UK, unveiled their first ever overseas player, the great Sachin Tendulkar from India. They persuaded him to pose for a photo-shoot wearing a cloth cap and holding a pint of English beer.

Bosman put paid to EU/EEA nationals being classified as 'overseas' players, but the effect of the judgment was limited. By 2003, 22 'EU (*Bosman*) players' were registered in county sides, most emanating from cricket-playing nations but holding an EU passport.[36] Following *Kolpak*, representative pathways for England-eligible players were reduced further, particularly as the EU had entered into association agreements with some prominent cricket playing countries including South Africa and those from the West Indian countries. In 2004, South African Claude Henderson became the first Kolpak player to sign for a county (Leicestershire), and in order to escape being classed as an overseas player, he was required by the ECB to set aside his international representative ambitions. This requirement became a source of annoyance in those countries suffering the Kolpak player drain, and it was one that damaged the fortunes of South Africa.[37]

34 Opinion of Advocate General Stix-Hackl, Case C-438/00 *Kolpak*, para. 69.

35 See Greenfield et al. (2017), p. 1752.

36 Boyes (2005).

37 The absence of Kolpak players from the South Africa team has been cited as a reason for South Africa's poor performance during England's 2020 tour.

Soon a mini industry had sprung up with a sports agency circulating the names of players willing to sign Kolpak contracts.[38] By 2008, there were 60 Kolpak players in county cricket,[39] and in a match in 2008 between Northamptonshire and Leicestershire, 12 of the 22 players were such players.[40] Although the presence of these players may well have improved the quality of competition, opportunities for England-eligible players were reduced and, to repeat an earlier point, taking advantage of opportunities offered by a liberalised European labour market does not apply to cricket regardless of the view of the Court in *Bosman*.[41] Although counties that recruited Kolpak players must have considered the impact on England-eligible players, and hence the strength of the England team, their business model was understandable. Why rely on developing young England-qualified players when ready-made overseas alternatives could be recruited and success expedited?

The reason why this is important to cricket is that the sport has developed a somewhat unhealthy over-reliance on revenues generated by the success of the England men's national team.[42] Cricket is one sport, amongst many, where income generated through national team activity, such as ticketing and broadcasting sales, is fundamental to the financing of the rest of the sporting activity. In cricket, the England team subsidises the professional club level and provides significant investments to the grassroots. It also finances investment into the England women's and England disability teams, and the success of the England national team is important for driving playing and volunteering participation in the sport. This is not so much the case in football where the existence of continuing club v country disputes highlights the antipathy to which club administrators and even fans feel towards the national game.[43] Cricket therefore has a specificity, the full extent of which was never fully explored under EU law. It became subsumed by EU *sport* law, not EU *sports* law (plural).[44] If any sport could have made a coherent case for the introduction of nationality-based restrictions, it was cricket; yet, the reaction of the ECB revealed a resigned caution and deference to the demands of EU law.

38 See Greenfield et al. (2017), p. 1757.

39 Wilson (2014), p. 222.

40 'Cricket South Africa admit they are powerless to stop England player drain', *The Guardian*, 12 December 2016.

41 The lack of such opportunity is not compensated for by the existence of opportunities to play cricket outside the EU. For example, in theory at least, EU / third country agreements contain reciprocal non-discrimination provisions. Furthermore, in recent years a growth of short-form tournaments across the world, particularly in the Indian Premier League (IPL), offers the best talent significant playing and commercial opportunities.

42 See fn.4.

43 See for example '*L'Affaire Oulmers*' in which a club and its trade body challenged FIFA mandatory player release rules. See Case C-243/06 *SA Sporting du Pays de Charleroi, G-14 Groupment des Clubs de Football Européens v. Fédération Internationale de Football Association (FIFA)* reference for a preliminary ruling from the Tribunal de Commerce de Charleroi lodged 30 May 2006

44 Rather annoyingly, a point already made by Weatherill (2017), p. 185.

The ECB was not the only governing body to consider a re-regulation of the labour market following *Bosman* and *Kolpak*. For the 2006/07 season, UEFA, the European governing body of football, introduced the 'Home-Grown Player Rule,' a rule requiring football teams entering European club competitions to name eight 'home-grown' players in their 25-man squad. Fearful of the European Court's condemnation of its 3 + 2 quota in *Bosman*, the new regulation scrupulously avoided reference to nationality as part of the eligibility. The logic was clear: *Bosman* closed off the purely sporting justification for directly discriminatory nationality restrictions leaving only the Treaty derogations as an inapplicable last defence.[45] By couching the new regulation with reference to location of training and not nationality, UEFA hoped to avoid such legal dead-ends. It calculated that should the regulation be challenged on the grounds of *indirect* discrimination due to the likelihood that more nationals than non-nationals would meet the criteria, a number of defences including those cited at paragraph 106 of *Bosman* could be invoked in justification, subject to proportionality control.[46]

The ECB's response to *Kolpak* was similarly nuanced. In addition to the requirement that Kolpak players renounced any claim to an international call-up with their home country, the ECB introduced a system of financial incentives in an attempt to dissuade counties contracting Kolpak players. The problem was that the level of incentives did not generally outweigh the benefits of fielding Kolpak players and ultimately, this intervention tip-toed around the issue, which was a desire by the ECB to see more England-eligible players playing cricket in England and Wales for the sake of the survival of the sport as a whole. Did EU law really preclude cricket from adopting more stringent nationality-based eligibility conditions? Whilst Brexit has rendered this question hypothetical for cricket, there are plenty of other sports falling within the scope of EU law that face similar questions.

9.6. Justifying nationality discrimination

Bosman has come to frame the debate on questions of nationality discrimination in sport. The case has fogged the minds of sports administrators who only seem to consider what is *not* possible under EU law. However, the application of *Bosman* to cricket is problematic. Unlike footballers, cricketers cannot take advantage of a European labour market and also unlike football, the success of the national team is more than of mere interest to spectators; it is fundamental to the viability of the sport.

Within its jurisprudence, the Court has recognised that some sporting rules are just too important to be so easily dismissed by the Treaty. For example, the

45 Article 45 TFEU entails a right to the free movement of workers, subject to limitations justified on grounds of public policy, public security or public health.

46 For discussion see Downward et al. (2014).

Court has long acknowledged EU law does not preclude rules or practices justified on non-economic grounds which relate to the particular nature and context of certain sports matches, such as matches between national teams from different countries, as long as such a restriction on the scope of the provisions in question remains limited to its proper objective and cannot be relied upon to exclude the whole of a sporting activity from the scope of the Treaty.[47]

Indeed, later in *TopFit*, the Court removed reference to 'non-economic' grounds from this mantra, thereby widening further the scope for professional sport to seek added protections.[48] It should also be noted that the reference to 'matches between national teams from different countries' is cited as an example, implying that justifications can potentially also relate to other sporting contexts, such as the exclusion of non-nationals from sporting competitions.

TopFit concerned the exclusion of an Italian national living in Germany from full participation in the German amateur athletics championships on the basis of his nationality. The issue before the Court therefore concerned direct nationality discrimination. The Court identified inconsistencies in the approach of the German Athletics Association to the question of the exclusion of non-nationals and so found that the athlete in question did receive differential treatment on account of his nationality. However, the Court offered guidance on circumstances in which a non-national could be legitimately excluded from participation in a sporting event. It stated, 'as has been held with regard to the composition of national teams, it appears to be legitimate to limit the award of the title of national champion in a particular sporting discipline to a national of the relevant Member State and consider that nationality requirement to be a characteristic of the title of national champion itself.'[49] Therein lies scope for directly discriminatory measures based on nationality to find shelter under EU law beyond the Treaty derogations.

It is a matter of debate whether in practice this was already the case. For example, in *Deliège* and *Meca-Medina* the Court declined the invitation to identify a restriction of free movement and competition, respectively, by pointing to the importance of the contested rules for the achievement of legitimate sporting objectives. For example, in *Meca-Medina*, the Court considered that the restrictive effects of proportionate anti-doping rules are inherent in the pursuit of sporting objectives, including fairness. Admittedly, neither case concerned the application of nationality-based rules, but the framework was there for cricket to make the case that excluding some non-nationals from domestic competitions was inherent in the pursuit of the national teams' legitimate interests.

47 See Case C-415/93, *Bosman*, para. 76; Cases C-51/96 & C-191/97, *Deliège v Ligue francophone de Judo et disciplines Associeés Asb*, para. 43 & Case C-519/04 P *David Meca-Medina and Igor Macjen v Commission* [2006] ECR I-6991, para. 26.

48 Case C-22/18, *TopFit e.V. and Daniele Biffi v. Deutscher Leichtathletikverband e.V.* [2019], EU:C:2019:497, para. 49.

49 Case C-22/18, *TopFit*, para. 50.

Regardless of the route taken—*TopFit* or *Meca-Medina*—EU law demands restraint on the grounds of proportionality. The total exclusion of non-nationals from domestic cricket was unlikely to be accepted, but a limited overseas quota, carefully connected to the pursuit of legitimate objectives specific to the needs of the sport, are on firmer ground. Cricket operated such as system, but chose not to apply it to Bosman and Kolpak players for fear of rebuke. It is submitted that this approach was too timid, but, ultimately, Brexit has denied us the opportunity to test this theory.

9.7. Conclusion: taking back control

Following the ending of the Brexit transitional period, the ECB's player registration regulations for domestic cricket were amended resulting in both Bosman and Kolpak players having their registration cancelled with effect from 1 January 2021 with the ECB refusing further applications from these players, unless, in the case of EU nationals, they could evidence having settled status or pre-settled status. These amendments applied regardless of whether the player was in receipt of a visa permitting work. Bosman and Kolpak players can continue to play domestic cricket but are categorised as 'overseas players,' for which two places in a starting 11 are reserved. The impact of these steps on the success of the England national team is yet to be seen, but the personal cost to the Kolpak players should not be dismissed. Having renounced their international careers, Brexit has now ended many domestic county careers as well.

A leave vote in the 2016 referendum was not required for English cricket to take back control and take steps to safeguard the viability of the national team. Solutions were available, such as the adoption of more stringent visa requirements to limit the number of Kolpak players, although these could not be applied to Bosman (EU) players. It is further submitted that these Bosman players were not in fact untouchable. It is understandable why *Bosman* deterred sports administrators from pursuing nationality-based eligibility rules. But, whilst the principles established in *Bosman* had general application to sport, it was essentially a football case. The labour market analysis discussed at paragraph 134 of the judgment confirms this. Since then, *Deliège*, *Meca-Medina* and reference to the 'specific nature of sport' contained in Article 165 TFEU have offered new judicial opportunities for a more mature conversation on the role of non-nationals in sporting competitions. *TopFit* confirmed the trajectory of this discussion by recognising that the exclusion of non-nationals from sport is potentially permitted under EU law if such rules are justified by objective considerations which are proportionate to the legitimate sporting objective being pursued. Cricket had reasonable grounds to argue that, given its specificity, protecting the interests of the national team is one such legitimate objective. The total exclusion of non-nationals would likely have been considered a step too far by the Court of Justice, but a limited overseas quota, such as the one cricket had operated for years, would likely have found favour. Ultimately, Brexit rendered that debate irrelevant for cricket, but for other sports, there is still much to play for.

References

Boyes, S. (2005) Caught behind or following-on? Cricket, the European union and the Bosman effect? *Entertainment and Sports Law Journal*, 3:1, 1–10.

Downward, P.; Parrish, R.; Pearson, G. & Semens, A. (2014) An assessment of the compatibility of UEFA's Home-grown player rule with article 45 TFEU. *European Law Review*, 39:4, 493–510.

Fraser, D. (2005) *Cricket and the Law: The Man in White is Always Right*. London: Routledge.

Greenfield, S.; Osborn, G. & Rossouw, J.P. (2017) Beyond Kolpak: European union law's unforeseen contribution to the movement of African cricketers. *International Journal of the History of Sport*, 33:15, 1748–1766.

Gupta, A. (2010) India: The epicentre of global cricket? In: Rumford, C. & Wagg, S. (eds) *Cricket and Globalization*. Newcastle: Cambridge Scholars, pp. 41–59.

Malcom, D. (2021) Cricket, Brexit and the anglosphere. *Sport in Society*. Online first. www.tandfonline.com/doi/abs/10.1080/17430437.2021.1876030

Murray, S. (2018) *Sports Diplomacy: Origins, Theory and Practice*. London: Routledge, pp. 70–72.

Weatherill, S. (2017) *Principles and Practice in EU Sports Law*. Oxford: Oxford University Press.

Wilson, J. (2014) *Court & Bowled: Tales of Cricket and the Law*. London: Wildy, Simmonds & Hill Publishing.

Part IV

Geography

Chapter 10

The tripartite agreement on the transfer of racehorses between the United Kingdom, the Republic of Ireland and France

The implications of Brexit

Laura Donnellan

10.1. After Brexit—what changes and what does not—Introduction

New Year's Day 2021 saw the dissolution of the tripartite agreement (TPA) on the transfer of equidae between the United Kingdom (UK), the Republic of Ireland (ROI), and France. The original TPA, which dates to the 1960s, provided for the free movement of high health horses (3H) between the three countries without the need for formal veterinary inspections. Until 1990, the TPA operated outside the confines of EEC Law; however, a Council Directive on the movement of equidae incorporated the TPA by way of a derogation granted to Member States. The TPA was amended in 2005 to broaden its scope to include all equidae, except those being transported for slaughter. Equidae could freely move between the three countries without health checks so long as each animal had a passport. An amendment and codification of the 1990 Directive in 2009 necessitated an overhaul of the TPA in 2014.

In the lead up to the UK leaving the EU, there was much debate as to the effect it would have on the TPA. In December 2020 it became clear that the TPA would cease to exist from 1 January 2021 and that the movement of equidae would become increasingly cumbersome with import controls being imposed. From January 2021 until 30 June 2021, the movement of equidae into the UK will require an Export Health Certificate (EHC) and equidae will constitute goods; as such, the importer will have to submit documentation in advance of the arrival of the equidae to the point of entry. From 1 July 2021, the formalities will increase including a specific border control post which will limit the entry points for equidae.

The border between the ROI and Northern Ireland (NI) impacts upon the transfer of equines. Horseracing is an all-island activity. On 1 January 2021, a bipartite agreement between the ROI and Northern Ireland came into force which operates along similar lines as that of the TPA. A similar agreement was concluded between the ROI and France.

DOI: 10.4324/9781003162803-14

This chapter will begin with a discussion on the origins of the TPA, its subsequent amendments and its incorporation into EEC and now EU secondary legislation. The financial implications of Brexit and horseracing will be considered. It will proceed to examine the formalities now required for the movement of racehorses based in the EU who travel to the UK for races and the corresponding administrative and veterinary requirements placed on British racehorses competing in races taking place in the EU. The chapter will assess the newly created bipartite agreement between the ROI and NI and the effect this agreement has on the transfer of horse between NI and the UK. Regard will also be given to the recent bipartite agreement between the ROI and France. The discussion will proceed to examine the EU's Animal Health Law and its possible extension to include 3H status from third countries. The chapter will conclude with an exploration of possible future directions.

10.2. After Brexit—what changes and what does not—The origins of the tripartite agreement

10.2.1. Introduction

The original TPA on the transfer of horses for racing, breeding and competition predates the accession of the UK and the ROI to the then European Economic Community (EEC). Both countries became Member States on 1 January 1973. The agreement dates to the 1960s and provided for the free movement of horses between France, the UK and ROI without the need for formal veterinary inspections.[1] Up until 1990, the TPA operated outside the confines of EEC Law; however, that changed with the introduction of Council Directive 90/426/EEC on animal health conditions governing the movement and importation from third countries of equidae which provided for a derogation under Article 6. The TPA subsequently came within the ambit of this derogation.[2]

France, the UK and the ROI revised the TPA in 2005 to broaden its scope to include all equidae, except those being transported for slaughter.[3] Under the

1 There is no copy of the original agreement available online. Some sources refer to the TPA coming into force in the 1970s while others refer to the 1960s. Given that Ireland and the UK joined the EEC on 1 January 1973, it seems more likely that the TPA dates to the 1960s. The Thoroughbred Industries Brexit Steering Group Industry Update and position statement for second phase of negotiations—January 2020 refers to the 1960s, www.britishhorseracing.com/wp-content/uploads/2020/01/Brexit-Update-January-2020.pdf.

2 Council Directive 90/426/EEC of 26 June 1990 on animal health conditions governing the movement and import from third countries of equidae, OJ L 224, 18.8.1990, pp. 42–54.

3 It replaced previous versions of the TPA, Article 11 of the tripartite agreement between France, Ireland and the United Kingdom Concerning the Movement and Trade of Equidae 2005. The text of the TPA was accessed at www.equinerescuefrance.org/wp-content/uploads/2010/12/TPA-ENGLISH-PDF.pdf.

2005 TPA, equidae could freely move between the three countries without health checks so long as each animal had a passport.[4] The purpose of the TPA was twofold. In the first instance, it was a contract between the three Member States wherein the animal health conditions governing the movement of equidae between the signatory countries were defined.[5] Secondly, it mandated that the signatory countries establish requirements in relation to the notification of each other of outbreaks of certain diseases, and of the control measures that would be put in place.[6] If there was a confirmed outbreak of a disease listed in Annex I of the TPA, the signatory country had to notify the others within 24 hours.[7] This was communicated through the Animal Disease Notification (ADNS) System, email or fax.[8]

10.2.1. The 2014 tripartite agreement

The horse meat scandal in 2013 coupled with fears relating to biosecurity prompted a revision of the 2005 TPA. Originally, the TPA applied to sport horses only. However, difficulties arose between the ROI and NI in the transfer of equidae in general, so it was decided to extend the TPA to all equidae moving between the three signatory countries. The 2005 TPA resulted in horses being transferred for slaughter; however, this was not disclosed by the horse-dealers. In Ireland, horses are not generally bred for food. Paragraph 4 (1) of the 2005 TPA stipulated that passports were required for horses; however, in the ROI there were enforcement issues owing to a lack of trained personnel and facilities at the ports. Many horses were passing through ferry ports and border crossings without microchip numbers and passports being checked. Consequently, many horses destined for slaughter were moving from ROI to the UK and France in breach of the terms of the TPA. This was despite the requirement that horses destined for slaughter had to be notified through the Trade Control and Expert System (TRACES) and health certificates had to accompany these animals.[9] Thus, the 2005 TPA created a loophole

4 *Ibid*, para. 4 (1). The particulars relating to the passport were provided for under 93/623/EEC: Commission Decision of 20 October 1993 establishing the identification document (passport) accompanying registered equidae as amended, OJ L 59, 3.3.2015, pp. 1–53. This Decision was repealed by Commission Implementing Regulation (EU) 2015/262.

5 *Ibid*, TPA 2005.

6 *Ibid*.

7 *Ibid*, para. 5. The list includes African horse sickness and glanders. For a discussion of glanders see, Donnellan (2016).

8 The legal basis for the ADNS system is found under Council Directive 82/894/EEC of 21 December 1982 on the notification of animal diseases within the Community, OJ L 378, 31.12.1982, pp. 58–62. The most recent amendment was under 2012/737/EU, OJ L 329, 29.11.2012, pp. 19–22. For more information see European Commission, *Animal Disease Notification System (ADNS)*, https://ec.europa.eu/food/animals/animal-diseases/not-system_en.

9 TRACES is the acronym for the Trade Control and Export System. TRACES is a centralised database for tracking the movement of animals and products of animal origin and non-animal origin from both within and outside the EU, https://ec.europa.eu/food/animals/traces_en.

whereby these lower grade animals were being moved without any traceability. The updated TPA addressed the lacuna, came into force on 18 May 2014 and was drafted in accordance with Article 6 of Directive 2009/156/EC.

In the period between the 2005 TPA and the 2014 TPA, Directive 2009/156/EC had come into force.[10] The 1990 Directive had been amended on several occasions, and thus the 2009 Directive in the interests of 'clarity and rationality' necessitated the codification of the original Directive.[11] Chapter II of the Directive details the Rules for the Movement of Equidae between Member States.[12] Article 3 provides that the competent authorities in the Member States may grant general or limited exemptions in respect of equidae used for sporting, recreational or cultural purposes. Article 6 of Directive 2009/156/EC replicates the text of Article 6 of the 1990 Directive as it provides:

> Member States which implement an alternative control system providing guarantees equivalent to those laid down in Article 4(5) as regards movements within their territory of equidae may grant one another derogations from the provisions of the second sentence of Article 4(1) and Article 8(1)(b) on a reciprocal basis.
>
> They shall notify the Commission thereof.

Article 4 (1) of Directive 2009/156/EC provides that equidae must show no clinical sign of disease at inspection and an inspection must be carried out 48 hours in advance of the embarkment or loading of the animal. This applies only to horses registered in a studbook or likely to be registered in a studbook. Article 8 (1) (b) requires that a health certificate complying with Annex III accompany the transportation of equidae for breeding, production and slaughter.

Under the 2014 TPA, the movement of 3H became traceable between the ROI, France and the UK.[13] Such horses are 'of demonstrably higher health status than the general horse population, and therefore at lower risk of transmitting disease'.[14] The agreement referred to an 'Approved TPA Body' which included sports

10 Council Directive 2009/156/EC of 30 November 2009 on animal health conditions governing the movement and importation from third countries of equidae Text with EEA relevance, OJ L 192, 23.7.2010, pp. 1–24.

11 *Ibid*, Preamble (1).

12 Articles 3–10. Chapter III of the Directive deals with Rules for Importation of Equidae from Third Countries.

13 Under the category of 'high health' status, such equines must be subjected 'to regular veterinary supervision to ensure that a genuine high status health status is maintained', para. 4.1 TPA 2014, Tripartite Agreement Between France, Ireland and the United Kingdom concerning the Movement and Trade of Equidae, May 2014, The TPA is available at: www.lawinsider.com/contracts/3UwoyY4zald.

14 British Horseracing Authority, 'Tripartite agreement 2014 briefing', www.britishhorseracing.com/wp-content/uploads/2014/03/TPA-Briefing.pdf.

associations and industry federations.[15] These bodies were required to give assurances as the high health status of the equidae and the traceability of horses covered by the TPA. The Approved TPA Bodies were listed in Annex III.[16] The UK and ROI listed bodies were Weatherbys\Thoroughbred Breeders and the Irish Thoroughbred Breeders Association, the British Horseracing Authority Association (BHA) and the Irish Turf Club and the British Equestrian Federation (BEF) and Horse Sport Ireland (HSI), each representing a specific category of movement. Weatherbys' Thoroughbred Breeders Association were responsible for sales, breeding and training of thoroughbreds, non-thoroughbred registered and Autre Que Pur-Sang (AQPS, the French term for 'other than thoroughbreds').[17] The Irish Thoroughbred Breeders Association authorised the movement of thoroughbreds for sales and breeding. The BHA and the Irish Turf Club oversaw the movement of thoroughbreds and non-thoroughbred registered for racing and training. The BEF and HSI, both Fédération Équestre Internationale (FEI) affiliated governing bodies, were responsible for the movement of equestrian for competition. The relevant French-approved TPA Bodies were not listed on the English version of the agreement.

From 18 May 2014, the transfer of horses between Ireland and France and the UK and France was restricted to the following:

- Thoroughbred horses being moved for racing, breeding, training or moving to a sale;
- Sporting horses competing in a FEI sponsored competition; and
- Non-registered thoroughbred horses.

The agreement was divided into two parts with one part concerning the transfer of horses between the UK and France and the second part relating to movements of equidae between the ROI and France.[18] The movement of horses between ROI and the UK was unaffected by the 2014 amendments as both countries had a shared health status for horses. The amendments related only to movements between the ROI and France and the UK and France. Horses moving between the ROI and the UK only had to be accompanied by a passport, which was required under the 2005 TPA. The movement of horses between France and ROI and France and the UK (and vice versa) had to be accompanied by a health certificate issued by a veterinary surgeon, as required under Article 4 (5) of Council Directive 2009/156/EC.[19] Horses classified as 'high status' which were moving between

15 TPA 2014 (n. 13) para. 2.5.

16 *Ibid.*

17 *Ibid.*

18 TPA 2014 (n.13) para. 1.2.

19 In Ireland, the veterinary certificate would be issued by the Department of Agriculture, Food and the Marine or in the UK by the Department for the Environment, Food and Rural Affairs (Defra).

France and the ROI and the UK and France (and vice versa) came within the exemption under Article 6 of the 2009 Directive.

The exemptions under the TPA as provided for under Article 6 of Directive 2009/156/EC were listed under paragraphs 3.1 and 3.2. Paragraph 3.1 distinguished between the movement of equidae, other than those destined for slaughter, between the UK and France and ROI and France. The 2014 TPA introduced the concept of the DOCOM, defined as a 'commercial document generated by an Approved TPA Body' or designated third party (an agent or transporter) that stated, 'the proposed movement including the premises of origin and the premises or event to which it is proposed the equidae is to be moved'.[20] The document would attest to the 3H status of equidae, and the details would be logged on the TRACES database. Paragraph 3.2 provided that horses with 3H status, which had been sanctioned by an Approved TPA Body, was accompanied by a DOCOM and a valid passport, would be exempt from the following requirements of Directive 2009/156/EC:

(a) Inspection and certification within 48 hours before embarkation or loading prior to movement of equidae between the signatory Member States; and
(b) For equidae to be accompanied by a health certificate or a health attestation.

The DOCOM was valid for ten days and would be obtained from an approved shipper by completing a Consignor Declaration form (CONDEC).[21] The DOCOM was not required for the movement of equidae between the UK and the ROI as they were 'considered as a single epidemiological unit for equine health purposes'.[22] It was only required between the UK and France and the ROI and France. If a horse were in France for longer than ten days, a return DOCOM would be required from an approved French shipper.[23]

10.3. After Brexit—what changes and what does not—Brexit and the TPA: the implications

10.3.1. Introduction

As the 2014 TPA was based on the derogation under Article 6 of Directive 2009/156/EC and thus predicated on EU Law; during the 21-month transition period the TPA remained in force. In late 2020, there was still hope in some

20 TPA 2014 (n 13) para. 2.6 and Annex II.
21 British Horseracing Authority, 'Tripartite agreement 2014 briefing', p. 2, www.britishhorseracing.com/wp-content/uploads/2014/03/TPA-Briefing.pdf.
22 *Ibid.*
23 *Ibid.* A shipper would apply to the relevant Approved TPA Body for approval depending on the category of movement. If the movement related to competition horses, the application would be made to the BEF in the UK or the HSI in the ROI.

quarters that the TPA could be preserved. On 24 December 2020, the EU and UK concluded a Trade and Cooperation Agreement (TCA).[24] Although the fundamental freedoms of persons, services, capital and goods are no longer applicable to the UK, the Agreement provides that there will be zero tariffs and quotas on all goods that are in conformity with the relevant rules of origin.[25] Animals that have been born and raised in the EU/UK will be considered to be 'wholly obtained in either the EU or the UK'.[26]

The original TPA pre-dated the membership of the ROI and the UK to the then EEC, thus the agreement at that time was intergovernmental in nature. The relevant authorities in the ROI and the UK may have considered a bipartite agreement as a post-Brexit solution; however, this would have been subject to the approval of the other 26 Member States. The fact that a pre-accession agreement existed was irrelevant as the ROI being a Member of the EU is bound by EU law and EU law is supreme and supersedes any conflicting domestic legislation.[27]

The importance of the TPA is evident from the following statistic: the TPA 'covers close to 90% of all horse movements within the EU'.[28] Between the UK and the ROI, horseracing contributes €7.25 billion per annum to the economy.[29]

24 European Commission, 'EU-UK trade and cooperation agreement: Protecting European interests, ensuring fair competition, and continued cooperation in areas of mutual interest', 24 December 2020, https://ec.europa.eu/commission/presscorner/detail/en/ip_20_2531.

25 *Ibid.* The Trade and Cooperation Agreement also 'establishes a new framework for law enforcement and judicial cooperation in criminal and civil law matters'. The rule of origins provides that the 'origin of goods is not determined by where goods are shipped from'. Rather 'origin' is a customs term which describes the economic nationality of a product, see KPMG Brexit Response Team, 'VAT and customs: rules of origin', 26 January 2021, https://home.kpmg/ie/en/home/insights/2021/01/brexit-deal-agreed-vat-and-customs-rules-of-origin.html.

26 *Ibid.*

27 Laura Donnellan, 'The tripartite agreement on the transfer of racehorses & Brexit', *The Economics of Sport*, 18 October 2017, www.sportseconomics.org/sports-economics/the-tripartite-agreement-on-the-transfer-of-racehorses-brexit.

28 Danielle Rossingh, 'How Brexit could derail $7 billion horse racing industry', *CNN.com*, 7 March 2018, https://edition.cnn.com/2018/03/07/sport/brexit-thoroughbred-breeding-horse-racing-intl/index.html.

29 This is according to page 11 of a dossier from 2020 titled 'Protecting the EU Equine Industry and Equine Health and Welfare' prepared by The European Taskforce for Brexit and EU Animal Health Law, a collaboration of the key European Sport Horse and Thoroughbred horse racing and breeding industries and formed by the International Sport Horse Confederation (IHSC)—constituted jointly by the Fédération Equestre Internationale (FEI) and the International Federation of Horseracing Authorities (IFHA). The link for the dossier is available at: https://inside.fei.org/fei/your-role/veterinarians/biosecurity-movements/intl-movements. The figure is based on two Deloitte Reports, one on British horseracing (Economic Impact of British Horseracing 2013 [Deloitte/British Horseracing Authority 2013]) and one on Irish Horseracing (Economic Impact of Irish Breeding and Racing 2017 [Deloitte/Horse Racing Ireland 2017]). The task group came to the figure after considering inflation since the reports were published. For British horseracing, the amount generated of £3.45 billion was based on 2012 figures, and the Irish amount of €1.84bn per annum was based on 2016 figures.

According to the BHA, 22,000 horses move in and out of the UK every year with the total amount in trade estimated at £300 million.[30] On average, every year 20,000 equidae moved (both temporary and permanently) between the UK, the ROI and France.[31]

The Thoroughbred Industries Brexit Steering Group (TIBSG) was established in early 2017 and includes senior representatives of the BHA, the Thoroughbred Breeders' Association, the Racehorse Owners Association and Weatherbys.[32] The TIBSG's remit is to examine the challenges that Brexit presents as well as looking into opportunities outside the EU, in particular, the Middle East.[33] According to the TIBSG's Briefing Note, the annual economic impact of the European Thoroughbred horseracing industry is €12 billion, and it employs 155,000 people directly in various roles.[34] Each year, around 22,000 foals are bred in the EU, which amounts to €760 million in sales, with many of these foals being sold outside of the EU.[35] A 2017 report on the *Economic Impact of Irish Breeding and Racing* by Deloitte was commissioned by Horse Racing Ireland (HRI), and it highlighted the importance of the free movement of equidae and the threat posed by Brexit, as 'any restrictions arising from Brexit, could therefore potentially damage the Irish Breeding and Racing industry (and its British and French counterparts)'.[36]

Apart from the restrictions on the movement of equidae, the cessation of the TPA and the withdrawal of Britain from the EU has an impact on the free movement of persons who work in the industry. EU citizens, excluding Irish citizens, who were resident in the UK up until 31 December 2020 have until 31 June 2021 to apply for settled status.[37] UK citizens residing in the ROI will continue to enjoy the right of free movement due to a series of bilateral agreements dating back to 1922 under the Common Travel Area (CTA) between the ROI and the UK.[38] The CTA pre-dates membership of the EEC/EU, and thus it is not governed by EU Law.[39] In 2019, a Memorandum of Understanding (MOU) was signed by both governments

30 Robin Mounsey, an official spokesperson for the BHA quoted by Business Insider UK, http://uk.businessinsider.com/bha-horseracing-expert-brexit-eu-impact-300m-thoroughbred-trade-2017-3.

31 Dossier (n 29) 3.

32 BHA, 'The UK leaving the EU: Racing industry guidance', www.britishhorseracing.com/regulation/brexit/.

33 BHA, 'Brexit and European racing-briefing note', www.britishhorseracing.com/wp-content/uploads/2018/11/Brexit-briefing-Sep-2018.pdf.

34 *Ibid.*

35 *Ibid.*

36 Deloitte/HRI, *Economic Impact of Irish Breeding and Racing 2017*, 32, www.hri.ie/uploadedFiles/HRI-Corporate/HRI_Corporate/Press_Office/Economic_Impact/HRI%20Report.pdf.

37 UK Gov, 'Apply to the EU settlement scheme (settled and pre-settled status)', www.gov.uk/settled-status-eu-citizens-families/applying-for-settled-status.

38 Government of Ireland, 'The common travel area', www.dfa.ie/brexit/getting-ireland-brexit-ready/brexit-and-you/common-travel-area/.

39 While the CTA has been referenced in legislation, there is no legislation governing the agreement.

to confirm that Brexit would not affect the CTA.[40] Had the 1990 Directive and its subsequent amendment under the 2009 Directive not included the derogation which brought the TPA within the ambit of EU Law, the TPA would arguably have operated along a similar line as the CTA, and the agreement could have been amended to be a bipartite agreement between the UK and the ROI.

10.3.2. Movement of equidae to and from the UK from 1 January 2021 to 30 June 2021

The UK Government's Border Operating Model (BOM) was published in December 2020.[41] There are three stages outlined in the BOM with stages one and three applying to equines. From January 2021 until 30 June 2021, the movement of equines into Britain will require an Export Health Certificate (EHC), and equidae will constitute goods and as such the importer will have to submit documentation in advance of the arrival of the equine to the point of entry.[42] The EHC must be obtained by the exporter from the competent authority of the EU country of origin.[43] All unregistered equines are required to undertake pre-export blood tests and must adhere to residency and isolation requirements prior to importation.[44] Of particular importance to racing, registered equines are not required to meet any blood testing, residency or isolation requirements.[45] The British based importer is required to submit advance notification of the arrival of the 'goods' using the Import of Products, Animals, Food and Feed system (IPAFFS).[46]

Under Stage One, equines can enter at any point of entry, however, under Stage Three there will be an established point of entry with an appropriate Border Control Post (BCP). Checks on documents will be carried out remotely while identity and physical checks on equines will not be mandatory for all horses, but rather on a risk-led basis at the point of destination.[47] An identity check will require a visual inspection of the consignment to verify that it aligns with the information on the

40 Memorandum of Understanding between the Government of Ireland and the Government of the United Kingdom of Great Britain and Northern Ireland concerning the Common Travel Area and associated reciprocal rights and privileges, 8 May 2019.

41 Border and Protocol Delivery Group, *The Border with the European Union Importing and Exporting Goods* (London: HM Government UK Transition, 2020).

42 *Ibid* slide 82. More information on the EHC can be accessed at www.gov.uk/guidance/get-an-export-health-certificate/.

43 *Ibid* slide 82.

44 *Ibid* slide 82. Unregistered equines must be kept on a holding in the country or a country with similar health status for 40 days prior to travel. Slide 82 provides more information on the requirements.

45 *Ibid* slide 82. Thoroughbreds are considered to be registered equines, BHA (n 32). The BHA adds that 'transporters and/or shipping agents can assist in much of the process of both importing and exporting horses'.

46 *Ibid* slide 82. A UK Government Guidance to IPAFFS is available here www.gov.uk/guidance/import-of-products-animals-food-and-feed-system.

47 *Ibid* slide 83.

official documents.[48] A physical check will include an inspection of the means of transport, the condition of the equine, and officials may take samples for analysis.[49]

10.3.3. Movement of equidae to and from the UK from 1 July 2021

From 1 July 2021, the formalities will increase including a specific BCP which will limit the entry points for equidae.[50] There are plans to add more BCPs to the three currently in operation at the following airports: Heathrow, Prestwick and Stansted.[51] According to the BHA:

> British racing does not believe that these checks on thoroughbred horses need to be made at UK ports of entry. We have proposed to government that there are digital solutions, underpinned by high animal health standards, which would allow such checks to be conducted away from ports. The UK Government, in line with its position on reciprocation, has been clear that the level of checks imposed will be dependent on those required by the EU.[52]

The requirements of pre-export blood tests, residency and isolation for unregistered horses under Stage One is also required under Stage Three.[53] As with Stage One, registered horses will not be subjected to such requirements.

10.3.4. The current situation

As the situation is constantly evolving, the impact of the changes that will take place from July 2021 have yet to be gauged. What is clear is that what was possible under the TPA will never be replicated again. The movement of equidae between the three signatory countries was straightforward, more cost efficient and not beset by dogmatic formalities. It is interesting to note that the Stage One requirements have not put off Irish trainers sending their Irish-based horses to the UK to race; the dominance of Irish competitors and winners in Cheltenham was highlighted in an article which stated that '[o]f the 91 places up for grabs, Britain filled just 36 of them (39%) with the Irish taking up 54 (59%) from 40% representation, with Easysland (2nd) the sole representative from France'.[54] A month after Cheltenham, Rachel Blackmore, an Irish jockey, became the first female jockey to

48 *Ibid* slide 83.
49 *Ibid* slide 83.
50 *Ibid* slide 163.
51 BHA (n 32).
52 *Ibid*.
53 Border and Protocol Delivery Group (n 41) slide 163.
54 Matt Hulmes, 'Can Britain bounce back in racing rivalry with Ireland after a dismal Cheltenham?' *The Sportsman*, 22 March 2021, www.racingpost.com/news/fair-and-balanced-trade-deal-agreed-as-brexit-negotiations-come-to-an-end/464968.

win the Grand National on her mount, the Irish-bred and based Minilla Times at Aintree on 10 April 2021.

The Chief Executive of Horse Racing Ireland (HRI), Brian Kavanagh, lamented the lateness of the TCA, which was signed eight days before horses were slated to travel for breeding purposes.[55] While the month of January is quiet in terms of racing and sales, it is a pivotal time for the breeding industry. UK- and EU-based mares come to Ireland to be covered by Irish stallions.[56] The TIBSG welcomed the TCA and gratefully acknowledged that the EU would recognise the General Stud Book which means that from 1 January all racing and breeding stock are consider 'registered', and as noted above, there are less formalities required in the movement of registered equines.[57] The TIBSG exercised a word of caution and requested that movements be limited in the first two weeks of January 2021.[58]

On 1 January 2021, the EU no longer recognised UK transporter authorisations resulting in a standstill of heavy vehicles as drivers lacked the required documentation. Aside from delays in transport and the increase in associated costs, the issue of Value Added Tax (VAT) arises. VAT is payable or a security deposit is required for temporary exports; for example, for a horse travelling for a race or to be covered, the VAT rates differ between the UK and the ROI.[59] While the VAT can be reclaimed and the security deposit repaid on the return of the horse to their country of origin, it is an added layer of administration and cost.[60] A 'temporary admission procedure' meant that Irish trainers could be VAT exempt in the run up to Cheltenham.[61] Ciara Dillon, BDO Ireland's Head of Food/Drink and Agri-Business, explains that there are two ways in which Irish-based horses can travel to the UK: 'the ATA Carnet which is often referred to as the "passport for goods",

55 RTÉ Sport, 'Brian Kavanagh: Covid-19 and Brexit to affect Irish impact at Cheltenham festival', *RTÉ Sport*, 24 January 2021, www.rte.ie/sport/racing/2021/0123/1191646-kavanagh-covid-and-brexit-to-affect-cheltenham-chances/.

56 Brian O'Connor, 'Brexit bound to disrupt transport of horses to and from Britain', *Irish Times*, 7 December 2020, www.irishtimes.com/sport/racing/brexit-bound-to-disrupt-transport-of-horses-to-and-from-britain-1.4429941.

57 BHA, 'Thoroughbred industries Brexit steering group statement: Free trade agreement welcome, short-term disruption still likely', 24 December 2020, www.britishhorseracing.com/press_releases/thoroughbred-industries-brexit-steering-group-statement-free-trade-agreement-welcome-short-term-disruption-still-likely/. The General Stud Book (GSB) has been maintained and published since 1791 by Weatherbys, 'History of the general stud book', www.weatherbys.co.uk/horses-racing/bloodstock-studbook/history-of-the-general-stud-book.

58 *Ibid*, BHA.

59 Emma Berry, '"Tough road ahead" for post-Brexit horse transport', *Thoroughbred Daily News*, 17 January 2021, www.thoroughbreddailynews.com/tough-road-ahead-for-post-brexit-horse-transport/.

60 *Ibid*.

61 Michael Verney, '"Don't get caught out"—Irish trainers warned to have documents ready ahead of post-Brexit Cheltenham', *Irish Independent*, 15 January 2021, www.independent.ie/sport/horse-racing/dont-get-caught-out-irish-trainers-warned-to-have-documents-ready-ahead-of-post-brexit-cheltenham-39974131.html.

while the other is a "temporary admission procedure" '.[62] Dillon advises trainers to have the proper paper work completed in a lead in time of four to six weeks before they plan to travel to the UK. A financial guarantee from a bank may be required, but in using these two methods, trainers should be able to avoid VAT.[63] She adds 'that such procedures "will work both ways" with the same rules applying when British horses are coming into Ireland'.[64]

The inspections and checks that will be required under Stages One and Three will add to the cost of transporting horses. Horses coming from the UK into the ROI are bound by EU requirements and, unlike the Stage One conditions in the UK where is are no specific BCPs, since 1 January, Dublin Airport, Shannon Airport, Dublin Port and Rosslare Port are the only routes in which UK horses can enter the ROI.[65] Horses from the UK must be exported to the ROI in accordance with customs' procedures.[66] Prior notification of at least 24 hours of a horse arriving in the ROI from the UK must be given and the importer must complete and submit Part I of a Common Health Entry Document (CHED-A) via the Trade Control and Expert System, New Technology (TRACES NT).[67] Horses must be accompanied by valid identification and a completed EHC issued by the UK authorities. Horses will be subject to both physical and documentary inspections at the BCP of entry. On passing the inspections, the decision is entered in Part 2 of the CHED-A and the operator is furnished with a hard copy.[68] Depending on the type of equine and the type of movement, there may be blood testing, residency and isolation requirements.[69] The document prepared by the Department of Agriculture, Food and the Marine (DAFM) does not refer specifically to registered horses. It is a general guidance on the free movement of equines between the UK and the ROI. The reference to certain types suggests that 3H such as racehorses would not be subject physical inspections, blood testing, residency or isolation periods. Such requirements would render the movement of racehorses for

62 *Ibid.* For an explanation of the ATA Carnet, see UK Government, 'Take goods temporarily out of the UK', www.gov.uk/taking-goods-out-uk-temporarily.

63 *Ibid.*

64 *Ibid.*

65 Department of Agriculture, Food, and the Marine, 'Brexit notice movement of equines between Ireland and the UK from 1st January 2021', 31 December 2020, https://assets.gov.ie/89287/331fffc5-5411-469e-a54f-818f87594976.pdf.

66 Revenue, 'Customs traders and agents', www.revenue.ie/en/customs-traders-and agents/brexit/index.aspx.

67 Department of Agriculture, Food, and the Marine (n 65). The Common Health Entry Document is based on Regulation (EU) 2017/625 of the European Parliament and of the Council on official controls and other official activities performed to ensure the application of food and feed law, rules on animal health and welfare, plant health and plant protection products. More information is available at https://webgate.ec.europa.eu/cfcas3/tracesnt-webhelp/Content/L_CHED-PP/Intro.htm.

68 Department of Agriculture, Food, and the Marine (n 65) 2.

69 *Ibid.* There is a guidance on ponies and donkeys, UK Government, 'Guidance: Export horses and ponies: special rules', www.gov.uk/guidance/export-horses-and-ponies-special-rules.

temporary export untenable. As the UK's 3H are based on EU conditions, it would seem that the DAFM guidance is mainly directed at non-registered horses and would be in line with the requirements of the UK Government's BOM on non-registered equines. There is much uncertainty at the moment, and clarification is still being sought in relation to an EU regulation and whether foals can be included on their mother's passport or whether they will need a separate EHC as non-registered equidae and will the foal be required to spend 30 days' quarantine from the date of their birth to the time they travel.[70]

10.4. After Brexit—what changes and what does not—Bipartite agreement with Northern Ireland

The border between the ROI and NI impacts upon the transfer of equines. Horseracing is an all-island activity. There are 26 racecourses on the island with two located in NI. From 1 January 2021, a bipartite agreement between the ROI and NI came into force which operates along similar lines as that of the TPA. The bipartite agreement excludes horses destined for slaughter and permits the free movement of horses between the two countries without the need for veterinary certification. The Protocol on Northern Ireland/Ireland gives cognisance to the special relationship between the UK and the ROI. In order to avoid a 'hard border' between NI and the ROI, the Protocol effectively means that NI is still part of the EU Customs Union in relation to the free movement of goods.[71] Horses constitute goods within the meaning of EU Law.[72] Customs controls are instead placed on goods coming from the UK to NI.

Every year, over 6500 horses travel across the Irish border primarily to take part in races and point-to-point meetings.[73] In light of the Northern Ireland/Ireland Protocol

70 Article 23 of Commission Implementing Regulation (EU) 2015/262 of 17 February 2015 laying down rules pursuant to Council Directives 90/427/EEC and 2009/156/EC as regards the methods for the identification of equidae (Equine Passport Regulation) Text with EEA relevance, OJ L 59, 3.3.2015, pp. 1–53. See also Thoroughbred Breeders' Association, 'TBA Brexit FAQs for Breeders', 21 January 2021, p. 1, www.rossdales.com/assets/files/TBA-Brexit-FAQs-for-thoroughbred-breeders-120121.pdf.

71 It remains part of the customs territory of the UK, Article 4 of the Protocol on Northern Ireland/Ireland, https://assets.publishing.service.gov.uk/government/uploads/system/uploads/attachment_data/file/840230/Revised_Protocol_to_the_Withdrawal_Agreement.pdf. Article 18 (5) provides that after four years after the transition period, the Northern Ireland Assembly may decide to continue with the agreement or decide to terminate it.

72 There is no definition of goods under the Treaty on the Functioning of the European Union (TFEU); however, the Court of Justice of the European Union (CJEU) defined goods in Case 7–68 *Commission of the European Communities v Italian Republic* ECLI:EU:C:1968:51, at para. 428, 'products which can be valued in money and which are capable, as such, of forming the subject of commercial transactions'.

73 *Economic Impact of Irish Breeding and Racing* (n. 36) 57.

and the cessation of the TPA, the Department of Agriculture, Environment and Rural Affairs (DAERA) in NI and the DAFM in the ROI concluded a Bipartite TPA. NI thus 'maintains regulatory alignment with the EU on the application of Sanitary and Phytosanitary Measures and that European Commission rules on movement and identification of equines continue to apply'.[74] Equines can travel over the border without the need for veterinary certification. The movement of equines from NI to the UK will continue as it was. However, the date on which the registered equine left NI to compete in an event or race in the UK ('temporary export') will need to be documented. If the equine returns within 30 days to NI/EU, the date is needed for the EHC, which exempts the equines from blood testing when re-entering NI/EU.[75]

A pre-importation notification from DEFRA's IPAFFs is required for equines that are moving from NI to the UK via Dublin Port.[76] A DAERA issued EHC is also required. In line with the BOM, registered equines will not be subjected to testing for certain diseases, nor will they be required to satisfy any isolation or residency requirements in advance of their importation into the UK.[77]

The BOM applies to horses travelling from the ROI to the UK, as outlined above. For horses moving from NI to UK, neither veterinary certification nor pre-importation notification is required. However, horses travelling from the UK to NI will need an EU EHC and pre-notification on TRACES NT 24 hours in advance.[78] This is also required of registered equines returning from racing/competition or cultural events in the UK.[79] Testing, isolation and residency requirements are applicable in certain circumstances as explained by DAERA.[80] For equines entering NI, there are specific points of entry, namely Belfast and Larne. These points of entry apply to both registered and unregistered equines. There is a pre-notification required in advance of arrival through the TRACES-NT.[81] Regulation 2015/262 on equine passports is referred to in Annex 5 of the Northern Ireland/Ireland Protocol and will be applicable in the same way as it was under the TPA and EU Law.[82]

Article 227 (1) of Regulation (EU) No 952/2013 of the European Parliament and of the Council of 9 October 2013 laying down the Union Customs Code (recast) provides that 'Union goods may be moved from one point to another within the customs territory of the Union, and pass through a country or territory

74 Department of Agriculture, Environment and Rural Affairs, 'Equine end of transition Q&As', www.daera-ni.gov.uk/articles/equine-end-transition-qas.
75 *Ibid.*
76 *Ibid.*
77 *Ibid.*
78 *Ibid.*
79 *Ibid.*
80 *Ibid.*
81 *Ibid.*
82 Commission Implementing Regulation (EU) 2015/262 of 17 February 2015 laying down rules pursuant to Council Directives 90/427/EEC and 2009/156/EC as regards the methods for the identification of equidae (Equine Passport Regulation) text with EEA relevance, OJ L 59, 3 March 2015, pp. 1–53.

outside that customs territory, without any change in their customs status'.[83] This allows for what is known as a 'land bridge'. It means that:

> Britain can be used as a 'land bridge' between Ireland and France, and horses travelling between those countries will not have to go through check points at the border but will require an Intra Trade Animal Health Certificate. Horses travelling between the UK and the EU will require an Export Health Certificate for each journey.[84]

An Intra Animal Health Certificate (ITAHC) is processed via the TRACES. According to the DAFM Animal Health Division, the '[g]eneration of the ITAHC or DOCOM on TRACES will serve as advance notification to UK government of these animals entering GB. Separate notification via UK system IPAFFS will not be required'.[85]

10.5. After Brexit—what changes and what does not—Bipartite agreement with France

On 1 January 2021, a bipartite agreement on the movement of equidae between the ROI and France came into force. It follows the terms of the TPA and requires that 3H be accompanied by a DOCOM. HRI welcomed the news that an agreement had been concluded in December 2020.[86]

Although the TPA ceased to apply from 31 December 2020, the conclusion of the two bipartite agreements has quelled some of the uncertainty that existed in the lead up to the UK leaving the EU on 1 January 2021. Coupled with the 'land bridge' procedure, there are alternatives to the movement of racehorses between the three countries, albeit with increased costs and formalities.

10.6. After Brexit—what changes and what does not—The EU's Animal health law

The TIBSG, in its discussions on the impact of Brexit, identified three main priorities, one of which related to the TPA. It advised that the free movement of the

83 OJ L 269, 10 October 2013, pp. 1–101. The Regulation was recast, and the latest version is from 1 January 2020 and can be accessed at http://data.europa.eu/eli/reg/2013/952/oj.

84 Berry (n 59).

85 Department of Agriculture, Food and the Marine Animal Health Division, 'Trader notice export of equine animals from Ireland to the United Kingdom', AHD_TN 02/2020, 31 December 2020, p. 4, www.lhi.ie/wp-content/uploads/2021/01/Trader-Notice-TN-_02-2020_Brexit_Equine-_Vers-1-003.pdf.

86 Horse Racing Ireland, 'HRI welcome clarity on post-Brexit land bridge movement', 18 December 2020, www.hri.ie/content/press-office/press-releases/hri-welcome-clarity-on-post-brexit-land-bridge-movement/.

thoroughbred horse within the EU be maintained, which would necessitate the continued application of the TPA. This, however, was not possible. The TIBSG along with several international federations, including the FÉI and International Federation of Horseracing Authorities (IFHA), established a task force group in 2020, the International Horse Sports Confederation (IHSC) Task Force for Brexit and EU Animal Health Law.[87] This taskforce has been in discussions with the European Commission in relation the creation of a new 3H status that would conform with the EU's Animal Health Law, which came into force on 21 April 2021.[88] The Animal Health Law consolidates a number of current 'interrelated basic acts' that were introduced on a sector-by-sector basis.[89] The UK will need to either comply with the Regulation under the conditions required for third countries or will be required to have protections equivalent to those outlined in the Regulation.[90]

The Regulation would have replaced the TPA even if Brexit had not occurred and applies to the EU Member States and third countries subject to certain conditions. An amendment to the Animal Health Law Regulation to include 3H status would be an alternative route for the free movement of high-health equines between the EU and Britain. The British Thoroughbred Industry is engaged in ongoing discussions with the British government on the impact of the EU's Animal Health Law on the movement of British racehorses to and from the EU. There has been no decision as of yet as to whether 3H status horses will be included in a future amendment of the Regulation.

10.7. After Brexit—what changes and what does not—Future directions

The IHSC Task Force for Brexit and EU Animal Health Law produced a 14-page dossier in October 2020 wherein possible solutions were promulgated including the use of digital passports.[91] The dossier is called *Protecting the EU Equine Industry and Equine Health and Welfare: Solutions to frictionless movement of high health horses—competition, training, sales and breeding—across the EU and between the EU*

87 The FÉI, IFHA and other federations created the International Horse Sports Confederation (IHSC) in 2013 which brought the racing and equestrian bodies together under an umbrella group, International Horse Sports Confederation, 'IHSC Press Release—Equine governing bodies seek to secure industry future in EU-UK withdrawal agreement', 9 October 2020, www.ifhaonline.org/Default.asp?section=Resources&area=0&story=1071/.

88 Regulation (EU) 2016/429 of the European Parliament and of the Council of 9 March 2016 on transmissible animal diseases and amending and repealing certain acts in the area of animal health ('Animal Health Law') (Text with EEA relevance) OJ L 84, 31.3.2016, pp. 1–208.

89 For a summary of the Regulation see: European Commission, 'The EU animal health law', https://ec.europa.eu/food/animals/health/regulation_en.

90 BHA (n 32).

91 This dossier is available as a pdf on the FEI website: https://inside.fei.org/fei/your-role/veterinarians/biosecurity-movements/intl-movements.

and the UK.[92] It made a number of suggestions including a comprehensive Free Trade Agreement (FTA) between the UK and the EU that would preserve the free movement of 'high health equidae and the temporary movement of essential, skilled people (grooms, trainers, riders, jockeys, veterinarians, etc.)'.[93] It highlighted the economic value of horseracing/equestrian to the European economy and the effect of the Brexit on jobs in the industry:

> The annual economic value of the combined sport horse/equestrian, horseracing and breeding industries in Europe is €52.1 billion per annum. Direct full-time equivalent jobs total 210,000 and in excess of 500,000 direct and indirect jobs are reliant upon the racing and sport horse/equestrian industries.[94]

It proposed the following solutions:

1. Digital passport which includes the identity, vaccinations and medical records, movement, and ownership (including change of ownership) which provides competent authorities of the EU Member States with all the information and health guarantees they require;[95]
2. The inclusion of 3H status horses into the EU Animal Health Law which includes A-list third countries; and[96]
3. Regional agreements which guarantee traceability and biosecurity, for example the TPA and the agreement France has with the Benelux countries.[97]

Another option would be for a CTA for Registered Horses to be concluded between the three signatory states of the TPA. Using CTA that exists between the ROI and the UK as a template, a MOU could be concluded between the ROI, France and the UK with a view to extending it to other Member States that are impacted by Brexit and its effect on horse movements.[98]

10.8. After Brexit—what changes and what does not—Conclusion

In the lead up to the UK leaving the EU, there was much debate as to the effect it would have on the TPA. The discourse vacillated between whether the TPA could be redrafted to allow for the UK as a third country to remain part of it, or

92 *Ibid.*
93 *Ibid.*, p. 3.
94 *Ibid.*
95 *Ibid*, p. 6.
96 *Ibid.*, p. 7.
97 *Ibid.*
98 *Protecting the EU Equine Industry and Equine Health and Welfare* refers to Italy, Germany, Spain and the Netherlands as incurring economic losses in the horse industry, p. 3.

whether it would become invalid and the movement of horses between the ROI and the UK and France and the UK would be beset by health certification and pre-import notifications. Until late 2020 there was still much uncertainty. However, in December 2020 it became clear that the TPA would cease to exist from 1 January 2021 and that the movement of equines would become increasingly cumbersome with import controls being imposed.

The real effects of Brexit have yet to be quantified, and most areas of life have been impacted; the horceracing industry is but one. While it generates a huge amount of money for the exchequer in the UK and ROI, its significance may have been become blurred in the protracted negotiations that lead to the UK withdrawing from the EU. Another period of extension in light of COVID-19 was expected by some and perhaps the hope of another few months of a transition period resulted in the seriousness of the situation not being appreciated. The TCA was ratified on 30 April and came into force on 1 May 2021.

The EU Animal Health Law came into force on 21 April 2021. Relations between the UK and the EU have been fraught with tension in the aftermath of the UK officially leaving the EU. The post-Brexit relationship between the UK and the EU has been marred by internecine conflict that has culminated in attempts by the UK to alter the terms of the Northern Ireland/Ireland Protocol including the request to remove the Court of Justice of the European Union as the final arbiter in the Northern Ireland/Ireland Protocol.

The bipartite agreement between the ROI and NI is a much-welcomed development; however, it rests on the precarious Northern Ireland/Ireland Protocol. For the foreseeable future, the movement of 3H to the UK will be subject to extra formalities, and while there are guidance notes on the applicable provisions, there is still much precariousness and disconcertment amongst those involved in the industry. It will take time for the new procedures to be fully understood and it will be a system of trial and error until more coherent guidance from the relevant ministries of the DAMF, DAERA and DEFRA are published.

Bibliography

Donnellan, D. (2016) Glanders in horses: Biosecurity precautions taken at the Rio Olympics. *Global Sports Law and Taxation Reports*, 7:4, 20–23.

Chapter 11

Scottish sport, Brexit and cultural relations

Grant Jarvie

11.1. Introduction

Sport in Scotland is a devolved matter resulting from the powers delivered to Scotland through the Scotland Acts of 1998, 2006 and 2012. Scottish sports people participate in significant European sports events such as the European Champions League (football) and the Ryder Cup (golf). Scottish Universities access funding for sports research through European Erasmus funding. The Scottish sports transfer market trades with European sport. Scotland in sporting terms is often referred to as a footballing nation or the home of golf because of its historic role in the sporting world. Scotland as a sub-state nation that is part of the United Kingdom (UK) defers to the United Kingdom parliament on matters of foreign policy. The decision of the UK parliament to leave the European Union (EU) adds a further layer of cultural complexity to which Scottish sport has had to adapt. Should the impact of Brexit indirectly lead to an independent Scotland, the consequences for the Scottish sporting landscape might be greater than had originally been envisaged.

While brands and assets like Johnnie Walker Blue Label whisky, smoked salmon, shinty, Highland Games, golf, historic castles and scenery project heritage, others like BrewDog, Skyscanner, Rockstar North, Nova Innovation, esports and gaming project Scotland's dynamic future. There are those that bridge both heritage and innovation like the new V&A Dundee, the late Andrew Fairlie's two-Michelin star restaurant at Gleneagles, but also modern outdoor sports like mountain biking, innovative bids for major sporting events and making greater use of the sports knowledge exchange that is contained with Scotland's high performing university sector. How Scotland can achieve the appropriate balance of heritage and future will definitely be a critical factor in delivering on its national, UK and international objectives whatever the future landscape unfolds. The importance of sport as a cultural asset working harder on behalf of Scotland needs to be fully grasped in the post-Brexit period.

The reality of a sport in a devolved sub-state is not straightforward and consequently it is timely to examine the impact of leaving the EU on Scottish sport.

DOI: 10.4324/9781003162803-15

Scottish sport, Brexit and cultural relations suggests that (i) like other parts of the United Kingdom sport in Scotland will be impacted upon as a result of leaving the EU and that (ii) sport in Scotland is a cultural asset that Scotland will need to capitalise upon much more both in Europe and beyond Europe.

11.2. Scotland, Brexit and sport

11.2.1. General remarks

The UK left the EU on 31 January 2020 following on from the UK Government and the EU agreeing to forge a deal on their future partnership. From 1 January 2021 this new relationship with the EU came into effect.[1] There will be an impact upon many, if not all, of the areas of public life in Scotland including changes to the Scottish sporting ecosystem from professional sports to grassroots and volunteering. Mygov.scot writing on the 15 January 2021 warned of threats to sport in terms employment, funding and transport while carrying a specific set of warnings about horse racing and other equestrian sports in Scotland given that Brexit has an effect on the movement of horses in and out of EU countries.[2] With an annual attendance of about 208,000, horse racing is one of the most widely followed sports in Scotland after football.[3] Four of the five (Ayr, Haddington, Hamilton, Kelso and Perth) existing Scottish race venues were established by the beginning of the 19th century.[4] In 2018, the economic impact of the sport in Scotland was estimated to be in the region of £51.1 million per annum.[5] The impact on horse racing in Scotland, as a result of leaving the EU, is seen to be primarily in two areas: the wider performance sector and horse owners in general.

The Scottish Government was the first administration in the UK to set out a substantive policy response to Brexit in December 2016. On 24 December 2020, the UK Government and the EU announced agreement on core elements of a future relationship. While the former protested that this was the end of an auld and valued alliance the later heralded the departure as a new beginning. The Scottish Government argued that Brexit was against the overwhelming wishes of the majority of Scottish people who had voted to remain in the EU while the UK Government argued that the majority of the British people had voted to leave the EU. The Scottish Government's assessment of the UK withdrawal agreement predicted that the consequences for Scotland would be that Scottish GDP would

1 Mygov.scot, 'Sport in Scotland after Brexit', 15 January 2021, www.mygov.scot/brexit-sport/ (accessed 15 February 2021).

2 *Ibid.*

3 D. Carr, 'Racing makes "substantial contribution" to Scottish economy—report', *The Racing Post*, 13 August 2019, www.racingpost.com/news/racing-makes-substantial-contribution-to-scottish-economy-report/395024 (accessed 15 February 2021).

4 Kay and Vamplew (2000), p. 159.

5 Carr (2019) (n 3).

be 6.1% lower by 2030; the 6,900 companies operating in Scotland that exported goods to the EU and the 11,000 companies that were reliant on EU imports, as a result of a combination of higher costs, lost competitiveness and production and distribution delays would result in an adverse effect upon business; the Scottish services sector, which makes up 75% of the Scottish economy, would have to carry an increased level of risk; and the end to a freedom of movement of people meant that in a scenario of 50% less EU migration, Scotland's working population would decline by 2% and the proportion of children would decline by 12.8%.[6]

The vision of the national sports agency for sport in Scotland, Sportscotland, is that of an active Scotland where everyone benefits from sport.[7] Sport for All in Scotland, as is the case in the vast majority of countries, remains an aspiration rather than a reality. Removing further barriers to involvement in sport so that those on the margins of society have increased opportunities to enjoy what Scottish sport has to offer remains work in progress. However, any effort to promote sport as inclusive and for all must address the reality that the greater the disadvantage the worse the sport gradient. Thus, sport in Scotland while striving to open up opportunities operates within a context in which the underlying causes of poverty, inequality and access to sport are as much a systemic failing of a Scottish system in which inequality of condition, inequality of opportunity and inequality of capability impact upon any vision of sport for all.

There is a correlation between a nation's wealth and the number of infrastructure facilities that enable people to engage in leisure or competition sports (gymnasiums, playing fields, swimming pools, skate parks, fitness studios, facilities for outdoor sports, etc.) Scotland has invested heavily in sports facilities, but the landscape of Scottish sport will be changed as result of the decision to leave Europe. Sport is not protected by any form of statutory legislation that protects sport and recreation provision but rather such provision is left to the discretion of the 32 local authorities about what they see as adequate. Should the resilience of the Scottish economy be affected by leaving the EU then there would be a knock-on effect for sport at all levels.

At one and the same time Scottish port is part of global international landscapes that are present and strive to connect countries. Nearly every country in the world commits public resources to sport, and yet sport contributes to the gap between rich and poor.[8] For the first time ever has an international mandate been given to a country through the United Nations (UN)[9] to enable

6 Scottish Government, *Scotland's Place in Europe: Our Assessment of the Revised Withdrawal Agreement and Political Declaration* (Edinburgh: Scottish Government Publications, 2019), pp. 3–4.

7 Sportscotland, *Sport as a Way of Life: Corporate Strategy* (Glasgow: Sportscotland, 2019).

8 Jarvie (2019).

9 United Nations, *Transforming our World: The 2030 Agenda for Sustainable Development* (United Nations, 2015), https://sdgs.un.org/2030agenda (accessed 25 February 2021).

the 2030 Sustainable Development Goals.[10] Yet other resources are needed if the sport effort is to be enabled to win further freedoms for people in Scotland, and more generally. Scottish sports interdependence with wider political and economic trends and circumstances has been exposed further by the advent of the COVID-19 pandemic which has tested Scottish sports resilience at the same time that Scotland is experiencing the impact of leaving the EU. This is particularly the case for the most vulnerable people in Scotland. It is a simple fact that the UK Government failed to carry out any full equality impact assessment of Brexit. Such a task was undertaken by the Hepburn Report (2021) which concluded that for those already facing inequality, discrimination and/or social exclusion in Scotland, the consequence of leaving the EU meant that a further 137 potential impacts could be experienced.

While it is not the intention here to provide an account of the way in which Brexit has impacted upon every Scottish sport, the key areas of concern that have to date been identified are commented upon.

11.2.2. Scottish football

While several industries have been forced to come to terms with the new regulations introduced on 1 January, the debate over their lasting impact continues to unfold. Football is Scotland's number one national sport, and an analysis of the football transfers to and from Europe indicates that in the first post-Brexit transfer window, only 8 players moved from European clubs into Scotland and only three players moved from Scottish clubs to European clubs. Prior to Brexit Scottish football was used to the system where an EU national player could arrive in the UK and start playing for any club, at any level, without the club having to consider work permits or visas. Indeed, the arrival or influx of European players has often been cited as a reason for the fall in the number of Scottish players in the top level of football, but not just football since Rugby has perhaps benefited more from the labour migration of professional rugby players to and from Scotland.[11]

A specific worry concerned the movement of young footballers into Scotland from Northern Ireland. A FIFA amendment announced in December 2020 has allowed for the transfer of youth players between Northern Ireland, England, Scotland and Wales post-Brexit. The news eased fears that Northern Irish players aged 16 and 17 would not be able to move to other clubs across the water after the UK left the EU. FIFA acknowledged the UK consisted of four separate FIFA

10 Commonwealth, *Sport for Development and Peace and the 2030 Agenda for Sustainable Development* (London: Commonwealth Secretariat, 2015); Lindsey and Chapman (2017); UN (2015).

11 Williams (2020).

member associations and moved to ensure youth players could continue to transfer among the four.

> This amendment will apply generally to all situations where there are more than one association in the territory of a country and it will allow the transfer of players aged between 16 and 18 between those associations', said the FIFA council[12]'

The 'Brexit exemption' came as a relief to the IFA, whose traditional goal has been to move players to a professional club to Scotland and other parts of the UK at 16.

The new Immigration Rules, which applied from January 2021, meant that EU players have to qualify for visas.[13] This process involves two steps: (i) the player being endorsed by the appropriate sport's governing body. Each sport has their own rules for this, but Scottish football requires a certain percentage of international appearances which varies according to how highly the players' home country is ranked in the FIFA rankings and (ii) the individual player making a visa application. The implications of the new system being that (i) visas will be restricted to the top levels of sport. Clubs in lower leagues or amateur clubs looking to sign someone from the EU are unlikely to receive one of the limited endorsements available, and (ii) the process will take much longer even if the Home Office streamlined the visa process; it will still take a minimum of two to three weeks.[14] This may seem a short period, but compared to previous rules where an EU national could be signed and play the next day, it is a significant change. This means that there is likely to be a reduction in the number of EU nationals playing in Scotland, and even at the highest level there will be an increase in the amount of red tape around transfers of players in and out of Scotland.

In the words of one Scottish Premier League Club Head Coach from Hibernian Football Club:

> My understanding is that there is still to be a final decision made on how the criteria would work. If the same points system was applied to Scotland, I think it would make it more difficult to bring players in because by nature of the fees we could pay would be less for Internationals than players with less proven pedigree. The knock-on effect of that would be that more domestic players are given an opportunity then I don't think it is a bad thing—we have fairly Scottish core to our group anyway.[15]

12 BBC, 'Irish FA welcomes FIFA's post-Brexit youth transfer exemption', *BBC*, 5 December 2020, www.bbc.co.uk/sport/football/55188874 (accessed 24 February 2021).

13 Williams (2020).

14 *Ibid.*

15 P. Goodladd, 'Scottish clubs face "radical change" as Brexit changes signing rules for EU players', *BBC Scotland*, 18 December 2020, www.bbc.co.uk/sport/football/55360752 (accessed 15 February 2021).

11.2.3. The quest for major sporting events

Scotland has established itself as a being competitive in the international quest for hosting major sporting events. For a small country, it has had repeat business in terms of hosting major sporting events, with millions of people across the world tuning in to see the sporting action unfold in Scottish arenas and iconic venues. In recent times these have included The Ryder Cup 2014 at Gleneagles in Perthshire and the XX Commonwealth Games; followed by FIG Artistic Gymnastics World Championships in 2015, the UCI Track Cycling World Cup in 2016, the TOTAL BWF Badminton World Championships in 2017, the European Championships in 2018, the Solheim Cup 2019 and the scheduling of some of the finals of football's European Championships at Hampden Park, Glasgow for 2021. Scotland is expected to host the inaugural UCI Cycling World Championships in 2023. Unless the Scottish government adopts an event-driven strategy in which it provides incentives for events to be located in Scotland, perhaps supported by a Great Britain events strategy, the country could lose out as more events are staged in Europe.

11.2.4. Inequality, rights and a Scottish sports gradient

The Marmot review of health inequalities has long since argued that 'the link between social conditions and health is not a footnote to the "real" concerns with health but should become the main focus'.[16] The Marmot review talks of a health gradient in which inequalities of health demonstrating the presence of a social gradient in health outcomes associated with the unfair distribution of the social determinants of health. Such a logic also applies to Scottish sport and the spectre that the economic impact of Brexit plus a reduction of rights protection together runs the danger of impacting further upon the unequal access to sport for those experiencing poverty in Scotland.

Furthermore, there are likely to be legal impacts of Brexit across equalities groups, including the impact of sport with the diminution to rights and protections. At a general level, all equalities groups are likely to experience the loss of the EU Charter of Fundamental Rights—which guarantee a freestanding right to non-discrimination in sport—and recourse to the rulings and case law of the European Court of Justice. Equalities groups are also likely to feel the widespread loss of European Structural and Investment Funds (ESIF). The European Structural Investment Funds have contributed to sporting and recreation infrastructure in the Highlands and Islands, for example, through support for the establishment of the University of the Highlands and Islands. It is as yet unclear whether equalities groups will continue to be funded in the same way, and at the same level, through the UK's proposed post-Brexit Shared Prosperity Fund.

16 Marmot (2010), p. 4.

The impacts of Brexit will be gravest for people who face multiple inequalities. For instance: a disabled EU woman on a fixed-term contract, a minority ethnic low-income single mother, a man with a mental health disability who is homeless and has substance abuse problems, or a young, care-experienced member of the LGBTQIA+ community.[17] People with several protected or personal characteristics who face multiple disadvantages will likely face the deepest socioeconomic impacts and the widest forms of discrimination in the sport and physical activity workplace as well as the broader Scottish society at large. It is these groups that the Scottish Government should consider focusing on first and foremost, to mitigate any adverse effects of Brexit, as they are also the groups least likely to be resilient to changes.

Take, for example, the Scottish para sports community. Scotland has been at the forefront of some of the most progressive sports provision for para sport in Europe. The Scottish Football Association Para Football Board is the first in Europe to have a national football association develop a Para Football Board. The National Para Sports Centre that opened in 2016 at Inverclyde is also a beacon of light in Europe in terms of what can be done. Yet despite such provision and progress, the para sports community needs to be represented more. Nineteen percent of the Scottish population have a disability.[18] Only 20% of people with disabilities take the recommended level of physical activity compared to 52% of non-disabled people.[19] Only 7% of children with a disability in mainstream school have two hours/periods of quality physical education per week. Successful societies are inclusive societies and sport can act as a way to help bring communities together. Yet, universal access to Scottish sport remains a work in progress. While social characteristics are protected under the provision of The 2010 Equalities Act, social class, poverty and geography are still significant barriers to sport in Scotland that should not be ignored, nor should the reduction of rights levers that were provided through Europe and have been removed as a result of Brexit.

Furthermore, former Heart of Midlothian and Scotland defender Andy Webster gave the name to the Webster ruling on the status and transfer of players established under article 17 of FIFA's regulations. Article 17 was created by FIFA and the European Union to give professional players the same rights as other EU workers. Webster became the first footballer to invoke article 17 and released himself from his contract with Hearts in 2006. Will such rights for sports workers be protected to the same level within any new arrangements that are put in place?

A key message here and perhaps one that is being made for the first time in relation to Scottish sport is that the relationship between poverty, inequality and Scottish sport is a relationship that produces a sports gradient that exists in both a socioeconomic and geo-spatial sense in Scotland: a sports gradient which is likely

17 Hepburn (2021).
18 Jarvie (2019).
19 *Ibid.*

to be affected by Brexit and in particular the human rights levers that can be used to protect the those involved in disability sport.

11.2.5. Student sport, research and knowledge exchange

The funding of European research projects through Erasmus funding have promoted scientific and technological advance, collaboration and knowledge exchange between Member States; its discontinuation will, therefore, exclude Scottish Universities. These have included sports research streams of funding open to Scottish Universities in collaboration with European partners.

Almost €650 million of Horizon 2020 funding has been secured by Scottish organisations since 2014, and over 2,000 Scottish higher education students have taken part in Erasmus Plus each year. It said Scotland proportionally sends more students and attracted more Erasmus participants from Europe than any other country in the UK.[20] The first dedicated sports budget allocated specifically to the exchange of knowledge through sport in Europe was the equivalent of £7 million per year. The British Council Erasmus Plus funding for sports collaboration and exchange is one such income stream that has disappeared.

11.2.6. The spectre of independence and reduced funding

What if the Brexit result leads to an independent Scotland? The arguments about Scottish sport aired during the 2014 Scottish referendum could come back into play. The degree of UK sport funding allocated to Scotland through the Barnett formula or UK Lottery funding would come under increased scrutiny. The Welsh First Minister has already called for a more equitable agreement. The likelihood being that less money could be made available to Scotland because unlike with the Smith Agreement, which came into play following the 2014 Scottish independence referendum, it is unclear if Scottish sport and other areas of public life would be protected by no detriment clauses that protected Scotland within the Smith Agreement. A distinct worry would be the potential of less funding being made available to sport and physical activity as a result of the spectre of independence that was directly or indirectly influenced by Brexit.

Yet, while the challenge of Brexit has brought challenges to Scottish sport, it has also brought opportunities that need to be realised.

11.3. Scottish sport as a cultural asset

Since 2005, Scotland has committed at least £3 million per year towards funding international development work. This was initially focused on Malawi, to reflect

20 BBC, 'Brexit: Erasmus withdrawal huge blow for Scotland', *BBC*, 28 December 2020, www.bbc.co.uk/news/uk-scotland-55466439 (accessed 24 February 2021).

150 years of collaborative development between the two countries. From 2007 the budget expanded, with £9 million for projects in sub-Saharan Africa and South Asia, and yet again from 2017 where Scotland increased its International Development Fund (IDF) to £10 million a year. All of Scotland's international development work contributes to the sustainable development goals and the fight against poverty, injustice and inequality internationally and within the framework of the UN Sustainable Development Goals. Existing bilateral partnerships with Malawi, Zambia, Rwanda and Pakistan work across borders to address shared challenges in pursuit of the SDGs. In January 2021, the Scottish Government published the results of the joint bilateral review of Scottish-Irish relations and a road map for events up to 2025. Scottish Government Offices have been established in Beijing, Berlin, Brussels, Dublin, London, Ottawa, Paris and Washington.

The potential of Scottish sport to act as a cultural asset has still yet to be fully realised. The specific recommendations outlined in 2019 Review of Scottish Sporting Landscape[21] still have to be advanced. The report specifically pointed to the fact that Scottish sport should be supported to develop its potential as a soft power asset to advance Scotland's cultural relations. Sport sits within the health portfolio but there is an argument to be made for it to be at the heart of a new global narrative about Scotland. An intervention is required that would balance Scotland's enviable sporting heritage—golf, curling, bowls, football, shinty, Highland Games and Gatherings—with an ambitious sports diplomacy and cultural relations strategy that wins friends, influence and business for Scotland: an intervention that values sport as much as other soft power assets such as education and digital technology. The advent of Brexit has only further served to underline the fact that Scotland needs to optimise every tool that it has at its disposal to help with cementing and advancing Scotland's influence, attractiveness, capacity and capability to win international friends and partners.

The British Council's review of Scottish soft power potential[22] specifically points to Scotland's strong sporting culture in football, rugby, tennis and golf, and that Scotland should urgently consider employing sports diplomacy tools such as engaging in friendly matches or exchanges with Dubai, Qatar and the US.

Soft power maybe seen as the pursuit of Scottish influence through attraction; it is different from cultural relations. Soft power and cultural relations are different things and should not be confused. If soft power is the pursuit of influence through attraction, cultural relations is the creation of the conditions for sustainable collaboration between like-minded countries for mutual benefit.[23] Both of these are essential; there is often overlap between them, but they are different, and they

21 Jarvie (2019).

22 British Council, *Gauging International Perceptions: Scotland and Soft Power* (Edinburgh: British Council Scotland, 2019).

23 British Council, *Cultural Relations for the 21st Century. Report by International Cultural Relations Ltd for the British Council* (London: British Council, 2020).

require different strategies, arrangements and skill sets. Soft power shapes perceptions and preferences while cultural relations enable long-term partnerships and support reputational resilience.

Creating the conditions for a resilient world is not something that Scotland or any one country can do on its own, for it requires not only commitment but multiple countries to commit to thinking and acting for the long-term common good. Thus, for example country x or y might recognise that soft power strategies have to have a clear purpose and that such recognition – which might include enhancing country x or y's reputational resilience while fostering cultural relations with other like-minded countries – would help to enable such an outcome. More effective cultural relations could help to reduce the risk of major conflicts due to misunderstanding or no understanding between different countries, communities and/or groups.

A recent study notes glumly that 'there is no universally agreed definition of cultural relations'.[24] Cultural relations dawdles at the edges of public diplomacy and soft power and loiters at one end of the full spectrum of diplomacy. The phrase describes the whole infinitely various fabric of unofficial international contacts between people and institutions around the world, and it is something that the world of sport practices in abundance and which Scotland as a self-claimed sporting nation has as a tool in its international cultural relations locker; but it fails to use it as strategically as it could.

As the name suggests, cultural relations seek to create a relationship. The medium of exchange is culture, and what is created is a relationship, something that should be mutual but is not always mutual. Scottish sport is not always afforded the same status as other aspects of culture, and confusion continues to exist about what should and should not be included in cultural missions and visits. The role of the arts and music has long been recognised and celebrated in European culture as a valuable social tool. Scottish sport should be afforded the same status or parity of esteem as other facets of culture in Scotland's international strategies and portfolios. Such debates about elitist and exclusive definitions of culture pervaded the sociology of sport literature in the 1980s and 1990s,[25] but they still pervade Scottish Government approaches to culture and the configuration of ministerial portfolios. While Scottish sport is readily acknowledged as having an important part to play within ministerial health portfolios, there remains work to be done for mutual parity of esteem to be afforded sport within Scottish cultural portfolios. For the world of cultural relations sport raises a number of important questions? Can sport offer a sustained continuum of solidarity, shared practice and international fellowship? Can the cultural gatekeepers embrace a more complete world and definition of culture? How can cultural relations use sport as a tool to help build and

24 British Council, *Cultural Value: Cultural Relations in Societies in Transition (A Literature Review)* (London: British Council, 2018).

25 Jarvie (2006), pp. 66–72.

sustain long-term mutual relations and conversations? Such questions are not for Scotland alone to answer but they certainly needed answering if Scotland is to realise the potential of sport in a joined up Government rather than one that simply affords Scottish Government funding through primarily the health budget.

The potential of sport to make a difference, carry a message, deliver statements on a scale that few other areas of public life can, support movements (including interracial movements) provide a platform for social and political advocacy as well as support a new generation of sporting activists should not be underestimated. It is widely acknowledged that sport is an uneven socioeconomic and geopolitical resource but what should also be acknowledged is the choices around how countries choose to harness sport not just as a soft power tool but as part of a broader social contract that works for outcomes not just within countries but between countries. The sports proposition is a real one. It builds bridges for countries because it is a pillar of connection; its popularity, scale and reach are real; and it can assist with building resilience, reconciliation and rehabilitation.[26]

If you have a tool that is a language and has characteristics of scale, popularity and reach, then why should Scotland's sports governing bodies, non-governmental organisations and arm's length sports agencies not be funded to use it or exploit it fully to build mutuality and trust that works for the common good. If Scottish sport is to advance its case for the contribution that it can make to the common good, then what is required is a flexible normative framework that intentionally delivers outcomes and spaces that work in politically smarter ways. This proposition builds upon suggestions made by Bell, Pospisil and the British Academy that spaces are desperately needed to open up the possibility of dialogue involving the interests of more than one group, state or community.[27] Such spaces could be provided through Scottish sport being used to advance cultural relations.

When talking about Scottish sport, cultural relations and the common good means that sport is recognised as being part of a set of commitments and practices aimed at using public power to deliver public goods to people, regardless of their personal identity, political affiliation and/or geographic location. Sport should be valued as enabling better cultural relations as a cost-effective social tool and resources through which conversations can take place between countries, communities and individuals. In this way Scottish sport can position itself in spaces where, for example, transitional justice is being forged.[28] Thus, sport, cultural rela-

26 Cardenas (2013).

27 Bell (2017); J. Pospisil, *UN Review Process: Politics and International State and Peacebuilding*, Briefing paper 9. Political Settlements Research Programme (Edinburgh, Scotland, 2016: Edinburgh University), www.politicalsettlements.org/wp-content/uploads/2017/09/2016_BP_9_Pospisil_UN-Review-Processes.pdf (accessed February 21, 2021); British Academy (2017) Navigating inclusion in peace settlements: Human rights and the creation of the common good. British Academy: London, UK.

28 R. Duthie, 'Justice mosaics—How context shapes transitional justice in fractured societies' (2017), www.ictj.org/justice-mosaics-report (accessed 21 February 2021).

tions and the common good might be best understood as a project of ongoing political construction, rather than a pre-commitment to any one or new political order or utopian ideal.[29]

The challenge for Scotland is a tough one for it requires the cultural gatekeepers to be less aloof about what is seen as culture, diplomats to be less aloof about the contribution sport can make, and it requires many countries, communities and individuals to work across contexts to seek mutuality and forge and extend the common good. Scottish sport is not just a commodity or tourist attraction for it can be an immensely powerful vector of change, value, principle, solidarity, a symbol, means and arena through which a plurality of views can be listened to.

A key message here is that Scotland while it sees itself as a sporting nation it has yet to fully actualise or comprehend the value of the cultural asset that is sport. In a post-Brexit world in which Scotland as a sub-state nation does not hold the levers of foreign policy it should wake up to the rich soft power and cultural relations asset that it is gifted through sport.

11.4. Conclusion

There are few aspects of Scottish public life that are untouched by Brexit. It has already triggered a multitude of different avenues of negotiation at a time when stability and economic growth are the much-needed order of the day. Sport in Scotland is not immune from consequences of Brexit. The material and cultural vitality of Scottish sport is still responding to the shifting landscape that offers both threats and opportunities. The combined effects of the threats to the rules-based international order and the potential impact of Brexit mean that Scotland faces a challenging international context. With the triple complexity of a pandemic—Brexit and constitutional challenges all happening at once—it is tempting to conclude that public life in Scotland faces a perfect storm. To ensure that Scotland is prepared to meet these challenges, Scottish policymakers need to ensure they have the capability and capacity to engage effectively with international audiences and potential global partners in pursuing their international priorities.

References

Bell, C. (2017) *Unsettling Bargains? Power-Sharing and the Inclusion of Women in Peace Negotiations*. New York: UN Women.

Cárdenas, A. (2013a): Peace-Building Through Sport? An Introduction to Sport for and Peace. *Journal of Conflictology*, 4:1, 24–33.

Hepburn, E. (2021) *Brexit: Social Inequality Impacts*. Edinburgh: Scottish Government Publications.

Jade, M. (2017) *The Concept of the Common Good*. Edinburgh: University of Edinburgh working paper.

29 Jade (2017).

Jarvie, G. (2006) *Sport, Culture and Society*. London: Routledge.
Jarvie, G. (2019) *A Review of the Scottish Sporting Landscape*. Edinburgh: Scottish Government Publications.
Kay, J. & Vamplew, W. (2000) Horse-racing. In: Jarvie, G. & Burnett, J. (eds) *Sport, Scotland and the Scots*. East Linton: Tuckwell Press, pp 159–173.
Lindsey, I. & Chapman, T. (2017) *Enhancing the Contribution of Sport to the Sustainable Development Goals*. London: Commonwealth Secretariat.
Marmot, M. (2010) *Fair Society Healthy Lives*. London: The Marmot Review.
Williams, S. (2020) The impact of Brexit on sports law. *Morton Fraser*, 9 October. www.morton-fraser.com/knowledge-hub/impact-brexit-sports (Accessed 15 February 2021).

Chapter 12

Regulating the labour market for professional footballers

Post-Brexit challenges for Swiss football

Zahid Mustafi and Emmanuel Bayle

12.1. Introduction

Can a small country like Switzerland, with a population of just 8.5 million, create itself a niche in European football, home to most of the world's top leagues? In contrast with Europe's 'big five' football nations,[1] where football is by far the most popular spectator sport, Swiss football faces strong competition from ice hockey, both economically and in terms of popularity. For example, mean attendance at Swiss ice hockey matches during the 2018–2019 regular season was 6,950 (87.5% of stadium capacity) compared with 11,273 (55.6% of stadium capacity) for football.[2] What is more, Switzerland has German-speaking, French-speaking and Italian-speaking regions, each with its own social and cultural characteristics, so sports coverage is fragmented and expensive due to the need to translate content into these three languages.

12.1.1. Late professionalisation

Football professionalised much later in Switzerland than in most other European countries, and the process began quite slowly. Although it started in the late 1970s, by the 1986–1987 season Switzerland's first division still had only one fully professional team, Grasshopper Club Zurich; and the winners of the league title, Neuchâtel Xamax, had just six professional players in its 22-man squad. In fact, Swiss football was in a truly chaotic situation in the late 1980s and penalised by a number of factors: the championship was unattractive; players had a variety of legal statuses (professional/semi-professional/amateur); there was little investment in youth training, and match attendance was poor.[3] Nevertheless, the next

1 Big five' is the term used to describe Europe's leading football leagues: England, France, Germany, Italy, Spain.

2 RTS.ch, 'National League: on frôle les 7000 spectateurs de moyenne, 2019', 6 March 2019, www.rts.ch/sport/hockey/lna/10266007-national-league-on-frole-les-7000-spectateurs-de-moyenne.html (accessed 20 February 2021).

3 (Berthoud et al., 2016).

DOI: 10.4324/9781003162803-16

few years saw Swiss clubs gradually come into line with other European countries, where professionalism was the norm.

Another weakness in Swiss football was that most of the country's top clubs in the early 1990s relied on financial support from wealthy patrons. Consequently, many clubs found themselves in financial difficulty when their patrons were forced to reduce or withdraw their support following a major slump in the country's real-estate market in the mid-1990s. The Swiss Football Association (ASF) and Swiss Football League (SFL)[4] realised that they needed to take action to protect clubs and the national side. Their response was to invest massively in training and to restrict the number of foreign players in each club's squad in order to ensure that Switzerland continued to produce high quality players and that these players would be given sufficient match time. Nevertheless, some top-flight clubs went bankrupt in the 2000s, and others decided to give up their status as associations in order to become limited companies. In order to improve the quality of play and attract fans to matches, in 2003 Switzerland's football authorities completely restructured the professional championship. The first division was renamed the Super League and reduced to 10 clubs; the second division became the Challenge league. At the same time, the SFL made it mandatory for Super League clubs to become limited companies.[5]

12.1.2. Research question and methodology

Even though Switzerland is not a member of the European Union (EU), it has, like Iceland and Norway, signed a number of bilateral cooperation agreements with the EU that impact football.[6] Consequently, Swiss football is bound by the 1995 *Bosman* ruling, which paved the way for a revolution in both the sporting and economics side of European football. These legislative considerations have combined with the particularities of the Swiss context to shape the evolution of Swiss football over the last 25 years. Indeed, unlike clubs in other leagues, which earn huge sums from broadcasters, Swiss clubs suffer from a lack of international exposure and therefore receive little revenue from TV rights. Because they do not have the means to

4 Swiss Football League: 'The ASF's Swiss Football League (SFL) is an association under articles 60 and subsequent of the Swiss Civil Code (CC). The SFL is a section of the Swiss Football Association (ASF). The SFL's purpose is to: a) promote football in Switzerland, especially non-amateur football and elite junior football; b) protect its members' common interests; c) organise non-amateur football and corresponding competitions in Switzerland.' Statutes of the ASF's Swiss Football League, 2020.

5 Swissinfo.ch, 'Fussball: Der Verein hat ausgedient, die AG ist in', 22 October 2003, www.swissinfo.ch/ger/fussball-der-verein-hat-ausgedient-die-ag-ist-in/3580000 (accessed 16 February 2021).

6 Switzerland signed bilateral agreements with the European Union in 1999. 'The bilateral agreement on the free movement of people between Switzerland and the countries of the European Union will apply to sport as of 1 June 2004. Prior to this date, each team could have only five foreign players on the field at any one time (seven on the matchsheet). Henceforth, there will be no limits on players from the EU. Restrictions will apply only for non-EU players (five on the field, seven on the matchsheet).' Swissinfo.ch, 'Accords bilatéraux: la révolution du sport suisse', 23 January 2004, www.swissinfo.ch/fre/accords-bilatéraux-la-révolution-du-sport-Swiss/3734510 (accessed 16 February 2021).

buy expensive foreign players (the most expensive player bought between 2003 and 2020 cost €4.7 million), they have had to focus on training young Swiss players, an approach that is widely supported by the ASF and SFL with the aim of strengthening the national team. As a result, the Swiss championship has built a reputation as an excellent nursery for young players and is seen as a fertile recruiting ground for clubs in the big five championships. Hence, young locally trained players are not just valuable assets on the field of play, they also play an important role in the economics of Swiss football, as selling players provides clubs with an additional source of revenue that (partly) compensates for the meagre income they receive from TV rights.

The present study examines the way in which Switzerland's football clubs and governing bodies achieved this, taking into account the fact that, under its agreements with the EU, Switzerland is bound by European rules on the free movement of labour. So, what are the foundations of Swiss football's economic model, and how has it evolved since 1995? We addressed these questions by using a database of training and transfers by Super League clubs between 2003 and 2020 to determine the strategies Swiss clubs have adopted with respect to selling players. We begin by identifying the labour market rules and regulations governing player transfers. We then show that Switzerland's football authorities introduced rules to ensure that clubs continue to train young players and give them match experience, thereby creating a large pool of players from which to select the national team. These rules, which have consequences for both players and clubs, underlie two different strategies. First, they enable the league to ensure its championship continues to be truly 'Swiss' and increases playing opportunities for homegrown players by allowing only five foreign players on the field at any one time. Second, they have resulted in training becoming an important element in the economic model followed by Swiss clubs, as training allows clubs both to strengthen their teams by bringing through young players and to increase their income by selling locally trained players.

12.2. Labour market regulation and legislation

Europe's football championships are less tightly regulated than North America's major sports leagues,[7] and each country applies its own rules. In fact, Europe's football leagues, including the Swiss league, are becoming increasingly deregulated. Because all of Europe's leagues include a mechanism for relegation/promotion,[8] a club's performance on the field of play directly impacts its financial performance. There are no caps on salaries or transfer fees and no set redistribution of revenues between owners and players. Nevertheless, there are some differences in the rules each league sets for its championship. Switzerland's football authorities completely restructured its top two divisions in 2003, renaming them the Super League (first division) and the Challenge League (second division) and reducing the number of teams to 10 (Super League) and 16 (Challenge League). A further reduction in the

7 Andreff (2007).
8 *Ibid.*

size of the Challenge League to ten teams in 2012 was accompanied by the abolition of the promotion-relegation playoff between the ninth-placed Super League club and the second-placed Challenge League club. This measure was designed to reduce the risk of two Super League clubs being relegated each season and to make it harder for Challenge League clubs, most of which are not highly professionalised, to attain the top division. It also protected clubs that had the potential to compete in European competitions. Nevertheless, the relegation/promotion playoff was reinstated in 2018. These changes were made as part of a process to increase commercial revenues by making Swiss football more attractive[9] and, at the same time, to create a sort of semi-closed league. In addition, UEFA introduced its own rules on issues such as financial fair-play and homegrown players that take precedence over national rules, notably for clubs involved in UEFA competitions.

These rules raise questions for clubs, particularly with respect to transfers and players' origins. Indeed, transfers have become such essential components of clubs' economic and sporting models that disputes over transfer rules have been taken to Europe's highest courts. Most famously, in 1995 the European Court of Justice handed down its '*Bosman* ruling,' which gave players the right to move to any new club at the end of their contracts without their old club receiving compensation and banned restrictions on the number of foreign EU players within national leagues. By allowing rich clubs to sign many more of the continent's best players, the ruling has created huge imbalances between teams both within national championships and in European club competitions. Realising that these imbalances could adversely impact its competitions, in the mid-2000s UEFA introduced a 'homegrown players' rule to increase the equity between clubs.[10] Homegrown players are 'those who, regardless of their nationality, have been trained by their club or by another club in the same national association for at least three years between the age of 15 and 21. Up to half of the locally-trained players must be from the club itself, with the others being either from the club itself or from other clubs in the same association.' UEFA introduced the new rule in three phases, starting with the 2006/07 season, when clubs had to include at least four homegrown players in the squads 25 of players they entered for European competitions. This minimum number was increased to 6 out of 25 for the 2007/08 season and then to 8 out of 25 from the 2008/09 season.[11]

9 (Berthoud et al., 2016).

10 "UEFA's rule aims to encourage the local training of young players and increase the openness and fairness of European competitions. It also aims to counter the trend for hoarding players, and to try to re-establish a 'local' identity at clubs."

11 'From 2008/09, clubs in the UEFA Champions League and UEFA Europa League required a minimum of eight homegrown players in a squad limited to 25. These rules are also in force in several national leagues across Europe. Clubs have no obligation to put a certain number of homegrown players on the field of play, or on the matchsheet. They are entirely free in their team and matchday squad selection.The UEFA rule contains no nationality conditions whatsoever because within the EU such conditions are illegal (following the Bosman ruling). The European Commission stated that the UEFA rule was legal in a statement in May 2008, and that a review would take place in 2012.' UEFA, Protection of young players, www.uefa.com/insideuefa/protecting-the-game/protection-young-players, 2019.

Table 12.1 Rules on homegrown and foreign players applied in the Big Five Leagues and Switzerland's Super League (in 2021)

Players' origins (25 players)	*Bundesliga (Germany)*	*La Liga (Spain)*	*Ligue 1 (France)*	*Premier League (England)*	*Serie A (Italy)*	*Super League (Switzerland)*
National players	Min. 12 German players	-	-	-	-	-
Non-EU players	-	Max. 3 non-EU players[1]	Max. 4 non-EU players	Non-EU players must have played in 30-75% of their national team's international matches during the last two years[2]	Max. 3 non-EU players. 2+2 rules.[3]	Max. 5 Foreign players on the field at the same time[4]
Homegrown players[5]	4+4 rules[6]	-	-	8 homegrown players	4+4 rules[7]	8 homegrown players

1 Goal.com, 'Explained: How many foreign players are Real Madrid, Barcelona & each La Liga team allowed?' 17 August 2019, www.goal.com/en-gb/news/explained-how-many-foreign-players-are-real-madrid-barcelona/1kzy86sp6t2ex1qzhuvygusdwj (accessed 8 February 2021).

2 Pre-Brexit system: Players from non-European countries had to have played a certain percentage of their national team's matches, with the percentage depending on their country's FIFA ranking: 30% of international matches if the country is ranked in the top 10; 45% if it is ranked between 11th and 30th; 75% if it is ranked lower than 30th.

3 'Clubs with 0 or 1 non-EU players can recruit foreign players with no constraints up to the maximum authorised number (3). Clubs with two non-EU players can buy another two with no constraints, as long as one of these players replaces one of their existing foreign players. Finally, clubs with more than two non-EU players at the end of a season can buy two more players from outside Italy as long as one replaces an existing foreign player and the other meets the national team constraint. The national team constraint means that the player must have been selected for five of his national team's matches, including at least two matches in the last year.' Gianluca Zanfi, 'Liste serie a 2019/20: extracomunitari, vivai e italiani squadra per squadra', 29 June 2019, www.eurosport.it/calcio/serie-a/2018-2019/liste-serie-a-2019-20-extracomunitari-vivai-e-italiani-squadra-per-squadra_sto7347571/story.shtml (accessed 6 January 2021).

4 'Homegrown players include a) all players with Swiss or Liechtenstein nationality; b) all players who are citizens of a country that was a member of the European Union or the European Free Trade Association on 1 January 2007.' Swiss Football League, " *règlement sur la qualification des joueurs, Règlement de compétition de la SFL", Directives d'application de la liste des contingents*. 2019

5 There are sometimes differences in the way different football associations define homegrown players and how they apply their definition. For example, Germany and Italy apply UEFA's rule: four players trained locally by the club and four players trained by a club within the same association. English clubs do not differentiate between players as long as they were trained by a Football Association club for at least three months before they reached the age of 21. In Switzerland, the SFL defines a locally trained player (article 168, rules of the game) as: 'A locally trained player is one who—independently of his age—was registered with an ASF club for three full seasons (not necessarily consecutive) or for a period of 36 months between his 15th and 21st birthday.' This definition is similar to the one used in England.

6 DFL: 'Mindestens 12 deutsche Profis und Local-Player-Regelung', www.dfl.de/de/hintergrund/transferwesen/local-player-regelung/ (accessed 25 February 2021).

7 Federazione Italiana Giuoco calcio, COMUNICATO UFFICIALE N. 83/A.

Since 2010, clubs involved in European competitions have had to abide by a general rule on financial fair-play that UEFA introduced in order to prevent clubs spending more than they earn. Table 12.1 summarises the rules on players' origins used to regulate the football labour market in the big five leagues and in Switzerland, whose strategy with respect to training differs greatly from the strategies adopted by the big five.

As football's world governing body, FIFA sets general regulations with which national federations must comply. In the case of the status and transfer of players, FIFA's regulations do not contain any obligations or restrictions on transfers between countries, so national federations can set their own limits on the number of homegrown or non-EU players in their leagues. For European federations, these rules most also be compatible with agreements signed by European Union Member States and other members of the European Economic Area (EEA),[12] and with European laws, especially those governing the free movement of workers. Consequently, the last remaining quotas[13] mostly concern players from South America, North America, Oceania and some Asian countries.[14] In Switzerland, rules to promote training and regulate the movement of players were introduced in stages, starting in the mid-1990s, and have focused on encouraging clubs to train local players.

12.3. Training and transfers in Swiss football, 1995–2021: a four-phase evolution

As shown in Figure 12.1, Switzerland's football landscape has evolved greatly since the 1995 *Bosman* ruling, largely as a result of the training-based strategy adopted by the sport's governing bodies and top-flight clubs. The first phase involved developing youth training in order to improve the national team and ensure that clubs continued to field Swiss players. Phase two involved showcasing these players via matches with the national team and during European competitions with their clubs. Clubs would then be able to sell their best players to clubs in the big five countries and thereby earn much-needed income that could be invested in local transfers and used to underpin the clubs' economic models. Despite working well until around 2018, a combination of factors, many external to football, have led to a decline in the effectiveness of Switzerland's strategy.

12 The Cotonou Agreement is the overarching framework for EU relations with African, Caribbean and Pacific (ACP) countries. It was adopted in 2000 to replace the 1975 Lomé Convention.

13 Goal.com, '¿Cuántos extracomunitarios tienen Real Madrid, Barcelona y los equipos españoles, y cuántos permite La Liga?' 5 October 2020, www.goal.com/es-mx/noticias/cuantos-extracomunitarios-tienen-real-madrid-barcelona-y-los/gmr6eic8usdt17dj1l7f6bpy9 (accessed 10 February 2021).

14 Alyce Anthony, 'Since the Bosman ruling, football has moved into a system in which borders no longer exist', *Ecofoot*, 1 February 2019, www.ecofoot.fr/premium-interview-loic-ravenel-consequences-arret-bosman-football-europeen-4483/ (accessed 9 November 2020).

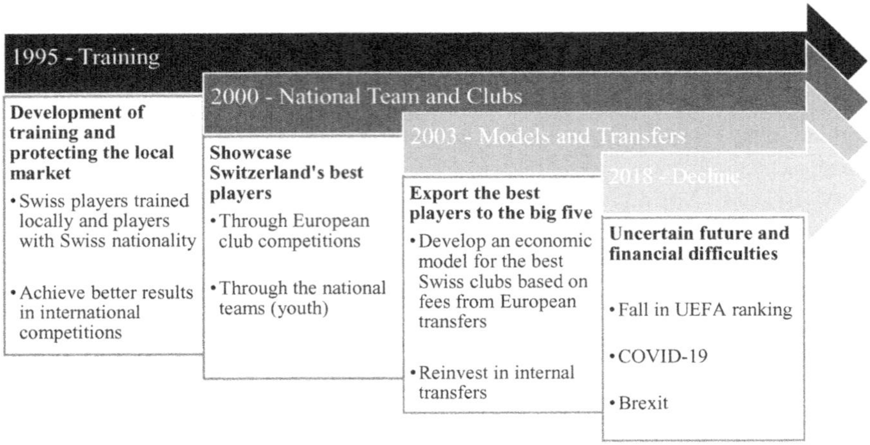

Figure 12.1 The four phases in the Swiss model, 1995–2020

12.3.1. Training

The commercialisation of sport entered a new era in the 1990s.[15] Aware of football's rapidly growing popularity and media potential, new companies decided to invest in football, mostly through sponsorship contracts. The ASF felt that some of these new revenues should be used to train young players. Marcel Mathier, the ASF's president from 1993 to 2002, explained this decision: 'At the time, professional football was not interested in training. I was worried that this money would be wasted, so we decided to direct 50% of investment into training.'[16] This policy had two main objectives: to improve the results obtained by Switzerland's national team and by Swiss clubs and to ensure Switzerland continued to be able to compete against Europe's leading football nations. A series of poor results by the youth and senior national teams, combined with weak coaching for young players and a lack of professional coaches, led the ASF to introduce coaching diplomas for all its member clubs. The ASF extended this measure to professional clubs in 1998–1999 via a new 'training label,[17]' implemented by the SFL, under which clubs that met certain criteria relating to youth training received subsidies from the ASF. These subsidies accounted for a large proportion of the ASF's

15 Bourg and Gouguet (2005).
16 (Berthoud et al., 2016).
17 'It imposes requirements that must be met before subsidies are awarded. They are linked to the specifications for technical staff (technical manager, talent manager, training manager, pre-training manager, forward coach(es), fitness coach(es)). These criteria are continually monitored by the SFL/ASF's Training Commission. This label applies to the elite junior categories M14, M15, M16, M18 and M21.' SFL, *'fondement d'une formation promise au succès.'*

budget.[18] In parallel, steps were taken to regulate the market in players by limiting the number of foreign players each club could include in its squad. This rule forced Swiss clubs to invest in training in order to ensure they had enough high-quality homegrown players but still enabled them to strengthen their squads by recruiting some talented foreign players. Encouraging performances by Switzerland's youth and senior national teams in the early 2000s, together with the exposure clubs received by competing in European competitions, opened up a variety of sources of revenue for Swiss clubs.[19] The ASF and SFL realised that new rules were needed in order to ensure clubs would allocate some of these resources to training local players, who would be eligible to play for the national team, rather than just using them to buy players abroad. Thus, as of the 2007/2008 season, Super League clubs have had to apply UEFA's homegrown players rule, under which at least 6 members of each club's 25-player squad must be homegrown. Only five foreign players were allowed on the field at any one time, but a club's matchsheet could include 18 non-homegrown players (this number has since been reduced to 17). The minimum number of homegrown players in each squad was increased to eight as of the 2008/09 season, but the number of foreign players allowed on the field did not change (see note 10). These new rules directly impacted both the national team and clubs, as they meant homegrown players, especially young players, were given more playing time in the Super League according to Figure 12.2.[20]

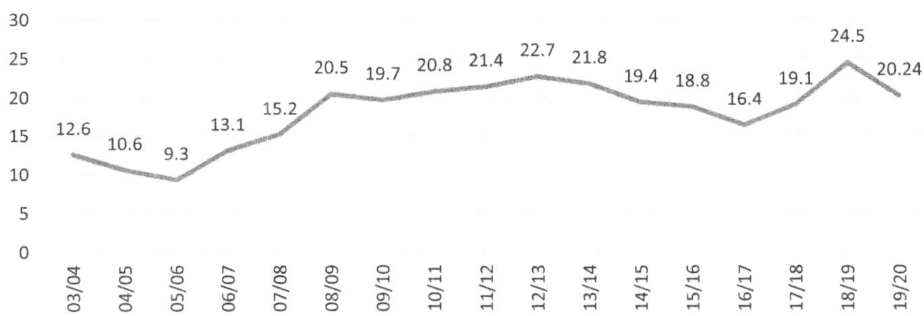

Figure 12.2 Playing time (percentages) for homegrown players since 2003

18 Berthoud, et al., (2016).

19 FC Basel is the Swiss club that benefits most from this shop window, as its recent domination of the Swiss championship (11 titles since the 2003–2004 season, including eight successive titles between 2010 and 2017) means that it competes in the Champions League and /or Europa League nearly every season.

20 RTS.ch, 'Super League: les joueurs formés au club n'ont jamais autant joué', 14 October 2020, www.rts.ch/sport/football/11640267-super-league-les-joueurs-formes-au-club-nont-jamais-autant-joue.html (accessed 19 November 2020).

12.3.2. National teams and clubs

12.3.2.1. National teams

Although one of the ASF's main goals was to strengthen Switzerland's national teams by investing in training and by ensuring Swiss players got to play for their clubs, rather than just sitting on the bench, the youth and senior national teams have not always fulfilled the ASF's hopes according to Figure 12.3. Switzerland currently lies 16th in FIFA's ranking (January 2021).[21]

Switzerland obtained its highest FIFA ranking in 1994 thanks to its performance in that year's World Cup finals. However, this ranking did not truly reflect the quality of Swiss football, and the country's results fell sharply immediately after the World Cup. In fact, Switzerland did not qualify for another major international tournament until Euro 2004, where it performed poorly and was eliminated in the first round. Nevertheless, the ASF's policy of improving training and developing young talent, introduced in the mid-1990s,[22] quickly bore fruit and its youth and senior national teams' results began to improve in the early 2000s.

For example, the Under-17 team won the European Championship in 2002 and the World Cup in 2009, while the Under-21 team reached the finals of the European Championship in 2011. Nine members of this Under-21 team graduated to the senior national side, which qualified for the World Cup finals in 2014 and 2018 and for the European Championship in 2016. Although the senior team did not progress further than the round of 16 in any of these competitions, playing in major international competitions was an excellent shop window for young Swiss players. In fact, showcasing Swiss football and Swiss players was one of the goals behind Switzerland's 1990 bid to host the 1998 World Cup. Despite failing

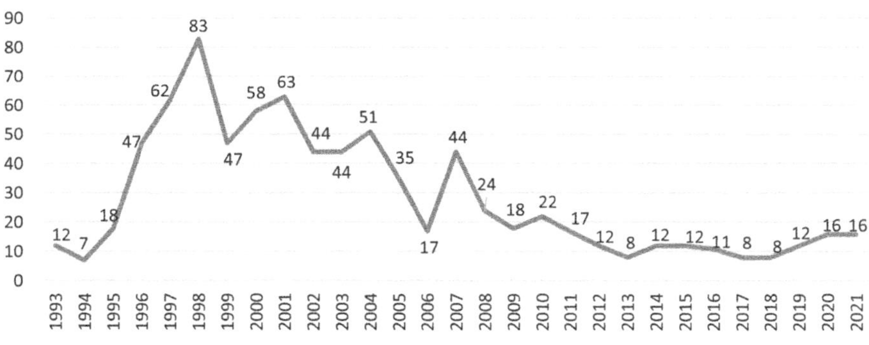

Figure 12.3 FIFA ranking of Switzerland's Senior National Team

21 FIFA rankings are based on each national team's results in official matches (friendly and competition matches).

22 Swiss Football Association: *Concept de promotion de la relève*, 1995.

to obtain the World Cup, the ASF bid for and obtained the 2002 U21 European Championship and the 2008 senior European Championship, Euro 2008, which gave international exposure to Swiss players whose clubs did not qualify for European club competitions.

12.3.2.2. Swiss clubs

The professionalisation of Swiss football began quite late. Even the largest clubs did not begin to professionalise until the end of the 1970s, and the process was slow. At first, team shirts were not allowed to bear sponsors' logos, and players' salaries were capped and local transfers of players were limited. However, the arrival of experienced foreign coaches and a few foreign players, attracted by Swiss clubs' performances in European competitions during the 1980s, boosted the professionalisation process. At first, some clubs managed to attract wealthy patrons who provided the resources they needed in order to compete against other European teams, but this source of funding was greatly reduced when Switzerland's real estate market slumped in the 1990s, impacting owners' ability to invest in their clubs. This decrease in funding could not have occurred at a worse time, as European football was also coming to terms with the repercussions of the 1995 *Bosman* ruling, which removed most constraints on the freedom of movement of EU players, thereby allowing richer clubs to recruit more star players. The previous quota system, which had restricted the number of foreign EU players clubs could recruit, had meant that Swiss clubs had still been able to afford star players in the 1980s and 1990s. The *Bosman* ruling also coincided with an explosion in TV revenues due to the emergence of pay-per-view channels,[23] which meant that Europe's largest clubs now had a lot more money to buy top players. In contrast, Swiss clubs felt little benefit from this unprecedented increase in TV revenues and some clubs, including Lausanne-Sport and Genève-Servette, went bankrupt in the early 2000s. If Switzerland's clubs were to bounce back, they had to find other sources of income. At the end of the 1990s, nine of the then 12 clubs in Switzerland's first division expressed the desire to become limited companies, a legal form that was made obligatory for all Super League clubs in 2003.

FC Basel was one of the first clubs to make this change. Thanks to a major investment from its new patron, the club was able to build a new stadium and draw up an economic model that enabled it to dominate the Swiss championship for a decade. As a result, it consistently qualified for European competitions, where it often punched above its weight (Europa League semi-finals 2012/2013, Europa League quarter-finals 2013/2014, Champions League round of 16 2011/2012–2014/2015–2017/2018). Competing in these competitions became a major source of revenue for FC Basel, which was the only Swiss club capable of competing against Europe's best in the early 2000s. In fact, Basel won 56% of the

23 Bourg and Gouguet (2012).

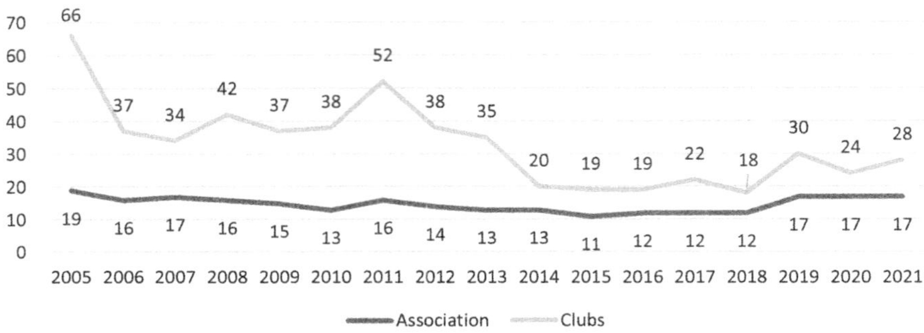

Figure 12.4 UEFA season association and club coefficients[1]

1 "The association club coefficients are based on the results of each association's clubs in the five previous UEFA Champions League and UEFA Europa League seasons. The rankings determine the number of places allocated to an association (country) in forthcoming UEFA club competition." https://fr.uefa.com/memberassociations/uefarankings/country/#/yr/2021, 2021.

points won by Swiss clubs in European club competitions at this time. In recent years, BSC Young Boys have emulated Basel's success, and the exposure gained in Europe has allowed it to make some highly profitable transfer deals. Other Super League clubs have found it difficult to follow in Basel and Young Boys' footsteps and have had to rely on local exposure. Nevertheless, some of them have managed to obtain very favourable terms when selling locally trained players to other Swiss clubs.

12.3.3. An economic model underpinned by transfers

12.3.3.1. Super League clubs' economic model, 2019

According to Andreff and Staudohar, football clubs have followed two types of financial model: the Spectators—Subsidies—Sponsors—Local model (SSSL), followed throughout football from 1960 to 1995, and the Media—Merchandising—Magnates—Market—Global (MMMMG) model, which arose from a market dynamic in which revenues from the SSSL model became insufficient to cover clubs' increasing expenditure.[24] However, only Europe's top championships containing its biggest clubs were able to adopt the MMMMG[25] model. Smaller footballing nations, including Switzerland, have continued to follow the SSSL model, with each country having its own specificities. Swiss clubs, for example, no longer receive true direct subsidies, and their economic model is not completely different

24 Andreff and Staudohar (2000).
25 Andreff (2000).

from the MMMMG model adopted by the big five countries, although the sums involved are much smaller. This is most obvious in the case of TV rights, which account for 53% of revenues for Premier League clubs, 34% for Bundesliga clubs, 42% for La Liga clubs, 47% for Serie A clubs and 37% for Ligue 1 clubs,[26] but which make up only 13% of revenues for Super League clubs. In addition, the sums involved in the big five countries are much larger than in Switzerland: in 1995–1996, the Swiss league earned just CHF1 million from TV rights, whereas the Premier League's contract for 1992–1997 was worth £191 million. Under its most recent TV contract (2017–2021), Switzerland's ten Super League clubs shared CHF24.1 million, and the ten Challenge League clubs shared CHF6.6 million, much less than the £1.7 billion[27] available to the 20 clubs in the Premier League. The resulting gulf in finances has led Swiss clubs to seek alternative sources of funding, most notably from training and selling players. This has been a successful policy for many of Switzerland's Super League clubs, which obtain a substantial percentage of their budgets (approx. CHF20 million[28]) from international transfer fees. As shown in Figure 12.5, Transfers have therefore become an essential part of the Swiss model.

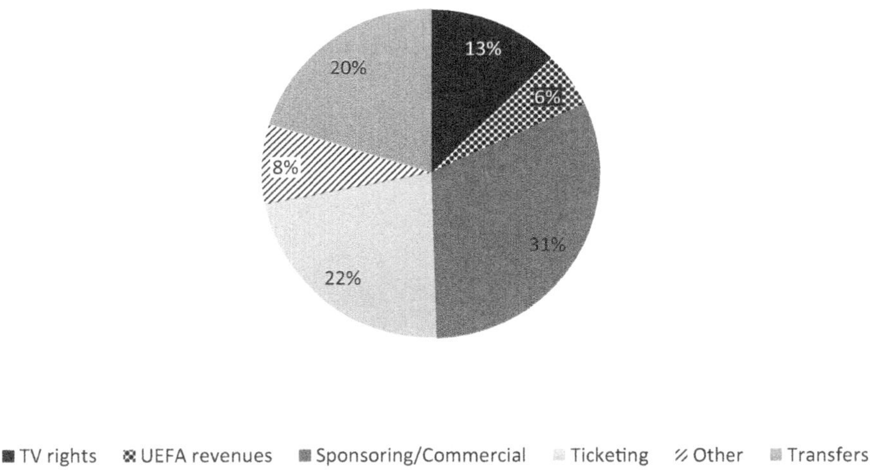

Figure 12.5 **Contribution of transfers to the economic model adopted by Swiss clubs**

26 UEFA, The European Club Footballing Landscape, Club licensing benchmarking report, financial year 2018.

27 Owen Gibson, 'Sky and BT retain Premier League TV rights for record £5.14bn', *The Guardian*, 10 February 2015, www.theguardian.com/football/2015/feb/10/premier-league-tv-rights-sky-bt (accessed 10 December 2020).

28 €18,240,000 euros (based on the exchange rate on 27 February 2021).

12.3.3.2. International transfers

The clubs with the highest revenues, and therefore the ability to spend the most on players, are those in the big five countries. Since the 2003–2004 season, 150 Swiss players have joined clubs in the big five (67 have gone to Germany, 32 to Italy, 23 to France, 19 to England and 9 to Spain). Most of the transfers involving sales of players (92%) have been to top division clubs, but this was the case for only 56% of loan transfers[29] and 34% of free transfers.

As shown in Figure 12.6, Germany's Bundesliga is the most popular destination for Swiss players, as geographical proximity and a shared language make it much easier for them to adapt to the new environment, and the close ties Swiss clubs have forged with German clubs have created a climate of trust. Serie A, Ligue 1 and the Premier League are less popular but are still important destinations. In contrast, very few Swiss players have moved to La Liga. The annual number of transfers has remained quite stable, especially in the case of Germany.

According to Figure 12.7, Germany is the largest importer of Swiss players, so, unsurprisingly, most of the income Swiss clubs earned from transfers between June 2003 and August 2020 came from Germany (€171.77 million), far ahead of England (€36.35 million), France (€17.83 million) and Italy (€9.15 million). Spanish clubs spent the least (€0.8 million) on Swiss players

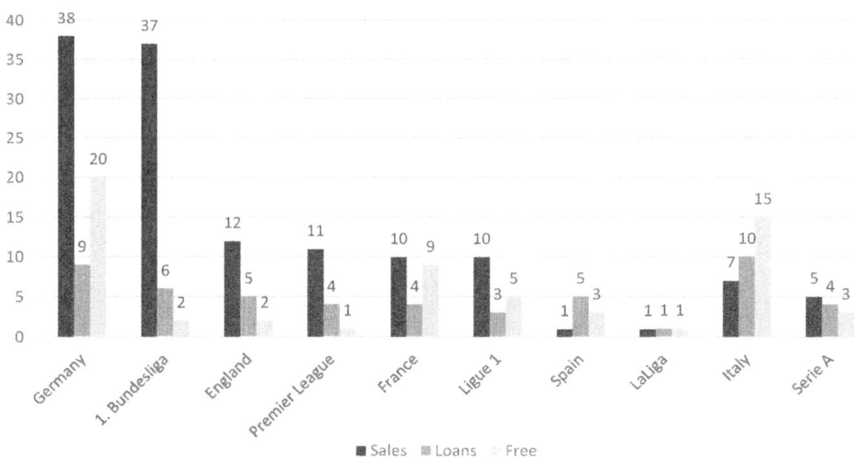

Figure 12.6 Type of transfers of Swiss players to the big five[1]

1 Transfermarkt.com.

29 Although some loans involve payments (the receiving club pays compensation to the lending club for the duration of the loan), these cases are categorised as 'loans' in the present study.

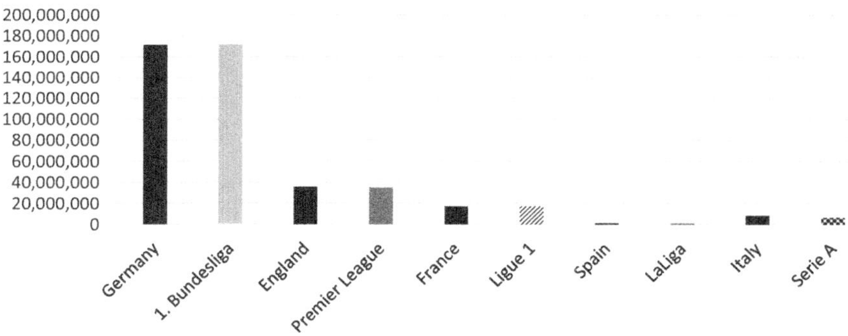

Figure 12.7 Sums earned from transfers (sales) to the big five countries

Table 12.2 Type of transfers and destinations of Swiss Super League players between 2003 and 2020[1]

Type of transfer	*Super League*	*Challenge League*	*Amateur League*
Sale	52 (€22.96 million)	10 (€1.3 million)	-
Loan	132	250	62
Free transfer	96	167	68
Youth/training	-	-	35
Total	**280**	**427**	**165**

1 Transfermarkt.com, 2003–2020.

during this period. Nevertheless, these revenues are shared by only the small number of Swiss clubs that manage to sell players to the big five countries. Because European competitions provide the best shop window for players, FC Basel has sold the most players to these countries (52% of total sales to the big five).

12.3.3.3. Local transfers

Most transfers involving Swiss players in the Super League are to another club in Switzerland. Of the 872 players transferred within Switzerland by a Super League club between 2003 and 2020, 280 joined another Super League club, 427 moved to a Challenge League club and 165 joined an amateur club. Super League clubs form the backbone of this local market, as they spend much more than clubs in lower divisions, even if some Super League clubs do not have the financial resources to buy players unless they are cheap. This is also the case for Challenge League clubs. Consequently, clubs tend to use loans or free transfers (e.g. to acquire players at the end of their contracts) to strengthen their teams without spending money. Clubs may also send some players to one of their elite-level amateur teams in order to gain experience (see Table 12.2).

12.3.4. Decline

As the difference in revenue compared with the big five countries has continued to grow, Swiss clubs have found it increasingly difficult to make an impact on European competitions. These poorer results have led to Switzerland slipping down the UEFA ranking, which makes it more difficult for Swiss clubs to qualify directly for European competition group stages. A particularly poor showing by Swiss clubs in 2018/2019, their worst performance in European competitions for ten years,[30] led to a drop in Switzerland's UEFA club coefficient. As a result, the number of European places allocated to Swiss clubs has been reduced from five to four (which is still an exceptionally high percentage—40% of Super League clubs—compared with other European leagues), and these clubs now have to go through more qualifying rounds.

The COVID-19 pandemic has also had a major impact on the finances of Swiss clubs, which are estimated to have lost both CHF100 million in earnings from the 2000–2021 season[31] and a significant amount of media exposure. These losses have compounded the problems of a championship that was already struggling. Indeed, some clubs have sought greater financial security by selling all or part of their stock to foreign investors. For example, FC Thun sold part of its stock to a Chinese group in 2019, and Grasshopper Club de Zurich was sold in 2020 to a Chinese conglomerate, whose founder already owns Wolverhampton Wanderers. Even FC Basel is facing financial difficulties, having declared a loss of almost CHF20 million before COVID-19 hit.[32]

Training remains a key component of the Swiss economic model, as it allows clubs to strengthen their squads by producing high-quality homegrown players and to increase their revenues by selling some of these players to foreign clubs. However, it is difficult for Swiss clubs to showcase their players if they are eliminated in the early stages of the Champions League and Europa League. Consequently, there is a risk that Swiss football will stagnate and no longer be able to

30 Valentin Schnorhk, 'Le foot suisse doit retrouver sa place en Europe', *Arcinfo*, 3 March 2019, www.arcinfo.ch/articles/sports/football/le-foot-Swiss-doit-retrouver-sa-place-en-europe-824946 (accessed 10 November 2020).

31 Battista Derchi Giovanni & Oyon Daniel, 'Les clubs de football face à la nécessité de réduire leurs charges', *LeTemps*, 11 August 2020, www.letemps.ch/sport/clubs-football-face-necessite-reduire-leurs-charges (accessed 6 January2020).

32 RTS.ch, 'Super League: FC Bâle a perdu 20 millions en 2019', 2 June 2020, www.rts.ch/sport/football/11370855-super-league-le-fc-bale-a-perdu-20-millions-en-2019.html (accessed 23 October 2020).

compete with Europe's top teams and that the resulting drop in the standard of play will also penalise the national team.

12.4. Discussion and perspectives

12.4.1. The four-phase evolution of Swiss football, 1995–2021

The evolution of Swiss football since the 1995 *Bosman* ruling can be divided into four phases. The first phase involved expanding training for young local players and imposing limits on foreign players in order to ensure homegrown players were able to play for their clubs. These two measures were designed to improve the national team's results and to improve the standard of Swiss club football. A series of impressive results by the national youth teams quickly showed that these measures were bearing fruit. Phase two began in 2003 when the SFL completely restructured the Swiss professional championship (newly named, Super League) into a semi-closed league. The resulting stability in the composition of the Super League means that Switzerland's top clubs have an excellent chance of qualifying for European competitions while continuing to receive a large proportion of the league's revenues (TV rights and sponsorship). Hence, clubs have more resources for developing training, for which they receive strong support from the ASF. However, Swiss clubs have struggled to make an impact in Europe in the last few seasons: Even FC Basel, which has won more than half of Switzerland's European competition points, is no longer doing as well in European competitions. As a direct result of this, Switzerland has slipped down the UEFA ranking and has lost one of its five European qualifying places. The reduction in revenues from European competitions, combined with low TV revenues, which are not likely to increase greatly, has severely impacted many clubs' finances. Now that the COVID-19 pandemic has further compounded these difficulties, more Swiss clubs might be forced to open up their shares to foreign investors.

12.4.2. Outlook: Brexit and its consequences for Swiss clubs

Following the United Kingdom's withdrawal from the EU, the English Football Association (FA), in consultation with the Premier League and English Football League (EFL), has introduced new government-approved rules on transfers of European players (December 2020). Under these rules, Premier League and EFL clubs can no longer buy foreign players below the age of 18 (FIFA regulations). Premier League clubs are also limited to buying at most three U21 players in each transfer window, starting in January 2021, and a maximum of six U21 players per season. In addition, European players will have to obtain a work permit, just like other foreign players. Work permits will be granted according to a points system based on the number of international matches played (youth and senior teams), the number of minutes played for their club in its national championship and in European competitions, and the 'quality' of the selling club, assessed in terms of the championship in which it plays, its league position and how far it progresses in European competitions. Work permits are granted automatically to players with the required number of points, and an appeals system has been set up to consider the cases of players who are just below the threshold. David Baldwin, the EFL's chief executive, noted: 'The objective of the EFL throughout this process has been to ensure EFL clubs continue to have the opportunity to sign players from overseas to enhance the quality of their playing squads.' According to the FA's statement, 'The system meets the joint objectives of the Premier League, EFL and the FA allowing access to the best players and future talent for clubs, as well as safeguarding England teams, by ensuring opportunities for homegrown players.' For the Premier League's chief executive, Richard Masters: 'Continuing to be able to recruit the best players will see the Premier League remain competitive and compelling and the solution will complement our player development philosophy of the best foreign talent alongside the best homegrown players.'[33] Nevertheless, the new rules, which came into force on 1 January 2021 but which will be reviewed prior to the summer transfer window, are certain to impact what is the world's most popular and richest championship.

English clubs were the second largest importers of Super League players between 2003 and 2020, spending more than €36.35 million. So how will the new rules affect the economics of Swiss football? Will transfers such as Albian Ajeti's move to West Ham (for €8.7 million) still be able to happen in 2021?[34] These are important questions for Swiss clubs, many of which depend on transfers to balance their budgets. Despite the depreciation of the pound compared with the Swiss franc, any lost income from transfers to England could have a major impact on the economics of Swiss football, already weakened by COVID-19, the paucity of TV rights and the inability to earn large sums from sponsorship and ticketing.

However, the FA's new rules could also help Swiss clubs hold onto their best young players for longer: previously, the attractiveness of the big five countries had tempted many players to leave Switzerland while they were still too young. According to Drut and Guégan, 'It is perfectly possible to imagine that TV rights and sponsorship contracts in other championships will increase due to the greater concentration of talent.'[35] Why not hope that keeping homegrown talent in Switzerland will improve the standard of play in the championship and enable clubs and the league to increase their revenues? This is a possibility that could be very positive in the long term.

33 TheFA, 'Plan agreed on entry requirements for overseas players in england post-brexit in 2021', 1 December 2020, www.thefa.com/news/2020/dec/01/gbe-points-based-system-launched-011220 (accessed 28 January 2021).

34 Maguire, Kieran, 2016, 'Brexit et football: quels changements pour la Premier League et le marché des transferts?' www.goal.com/fr/news/31/angleterre/2016/06/24/24992952/brexit-et-football-quels-changements-pour-la-premier-league (accessed 20 January 2021).

35 Drut and Guégan (2018). (Translation: Mustafi & Bayle.)

However, in the short term, English clubs may well turn to the other big five countries for players, especially France, the largest source of overseas players in the Premier League, whose clubs spent €1.25 billion on French players between 2010 and 2019.[36]

References

Bibliography

Andreff, W. (2000) L'évolution du modèle européen de financement du sport professionnel [The evolving European model of Professional sports finance]. *Reflets et perspectives de la vie économique*, 39:2, 179–196.

Andreff, W. (2007) Régulation et institutions en économie du sport. *Revue de la régulation*. http://journals.openedition.org/regulation/1274 (Accessed 27 February 2021)

Andreff, W. (2017) Le modèle économique du football européen. *Pôle Sud*, 47:2, 41–59.

Andreff, W. & Staudohar, Paul, (2000) The evolving European model of professional sports finance. *Journal of Sports Economics*, 1:3, 257-276.

Berthoud, J.; Quin, G. & Vonnard, P. (2016) *Le football Suisse, des pionniers aux professionnels*. Lausanne. Presses polytechniques et universitaires romandes.

Bourg, J.F. & Gouguet, J.J. (2005) *Économie du sport*. Paris: La Découverte.

Bourg, J.F. & Gouguet, J.J. (2012) II. La mondialisation des marchés du sport. In: Bourg, J.F. (ed) *Économie du sport*. Paris: La Découverte, pp. 37–57.

Drut, B. & Guégan, J.B. (2018) *Mercato: L'économie Du Football Au XXIe Siècle*. Paris: Bréal.

FIGC. Statuto Lega Italiana Calcio Professionistico. Federazione Italiana Giuoco Calcio, COMUNICATO UFFICIALE N. 83/A.

Swiss Football League. Directives d'application de la liste des contingents (February 2021).

Swiss Football League. Règlement de compétition de la SFL (February 2021).

Swiss Football League. Règlement sur la qualification des joueurs de la SFL (November 2020).

Swiss Football League. Statuts de la Swiss Football League de l'ASF (August 2020).

UEFA. The European club footballing landscape. Club licensing benchmarking report, financial year 2018.

Webography

Anthony, Alyce (2019) Depuis l'arrêt Bosman, le football est entré dans une logique où les frontières n'existent plus. *Ecofoot*, 1 February. www.ecofoot.fr/premium-interview-loic-ravenel-consequences-arret-bosman-football-europeen-4483/(Accessed 9 November 2020).

Battista Derchi Giovanni & Oyon Daniel, 'Les clubs de football face à la nécessité de réduire leurs charges', *LeTemps*, 11 August 2020, www.letemps.ch/sport/clubs-football-face-necessite-reduireleurs-charges (Accessed 6 January 2020).

Dekonik, 'Basile, Foot: le Brexit, une saignée de plus pour les clubs français', *Les Echos*, 26 December 2020, www.lesechos.fr/industrie-services/services-conseils/foot-le-brexit-une-saignee-de-pluspour-les-clubs-francais-1276574 (Accessed 4 January 2021).

36 Dekonik, 'Basile, Foot: le Brexit, une saignée de plus pour les clubs français', *Les Echos*, 26 December 2020, www.lesechos.fr/industrie-services/services-conseils/foot-le-brexit-une-saignee-de-plus-pour-les-clubs-francais-1276574 (accessed 4 January 2021).

DFL: Mindestens 12 deutsche Profis und Local-Player-Regelung. www.dfl.de/de/hintergrund/transferwesen/local-player-regelung/ (Accessed 25 February 2021).

The FA, 'Plan agreed on entry requirements for overseas players in england post-brexit in 2021', 1 December 2020, www.thefa.com/news/2020/dec/01/gbe-points-based-system-launched-011220 (Accessed 28 January 2021).

Football.ch. Concept de promotion de la relève de l'Association Suisse de Football. www.football.ch/portaldata/28/Resources/dokumente/fr/05_juniors_promotion_de_la_releve/5._Concept_de_Promotion_de_la_rel_ve.pdf (Accessed 25 November 2020).

Gibson, Owen (2015) Sky and BT retain Premier League TV rights for record £5.14bn. *The Guardian*, 10 February. www.theguardian.com/football/2015/feb/10/premier-league-tv-rights-sky-bt?/(Accessed 10 December 2020).

Goal.com (2019) Explained: How many foreign players are real Madrid, Barcelona & each La Liga team allowed? 17 August. www.goal.com/en-gb/news/explained-how-many-foreign-players-are-real-madrid-barcelona/1kzy86sp6t2ex1qzhuvygusdwj (Accessed 8 February 2021).

Goal.com. (2020) ¿Cuántos extracomunitarios tienen Real Madrid, Barcelona y los equipos españoles, y cuántos permite La Liga? 5 October. www.goal.com/es-mx/noticias/cuantos-extracomunitarios-tienen-real-madrid-barcelona-y-los/gmr6eic8usdt17dj1l7f6bpy9 (Accessed 10 February 2021).

Maguire, Kieran (2016) Brexit et football: quels changements pour la Premier League et le marché des transferts? www.goal.com/fr/news/31/angleterre/2016/06/24/24992952/brexit-et-football-quels-changements-pour-la-premier-league (Accessed 20 January 2021).

RTS.ch (2019) National League: on frôle les 7000 spectateurs de moyenne, 2019, 6 March. www.rts.ch/sport/hockey/lna/10266007-national-league-on-frole-les-7000-spectateurs-de-moyenne.html (Accessed 20 February 2021).

RTS.ch (2020) Super League: les joueurs formés au club n'ont jamais autant joué, 14 October. www.rts.ch/sport/football/11640267-super-league-les-joueurs-formes-au-club-nont-jamais-autant-joue.html (Accessed 19 November 2020).

RTS.ch, 'Super League: FC Bâle a perdu 20 millions en 2019', 2 June 2020, www.rts.ch/sport/football/11370855-super-league-le-fc-bale-a-perdu-20-millions-en-2019.html (Accessed 23 October 2020).

Swiss Football League, SFL Label de formation, "le label, fondement d'une formation promise au succès"(n.d.). www.sfl.ch/fr/sfl/promotion-de-la-releve/label-de-formation/ (Accessed 28 January 2021).

Swissinfo.ch (2003) Fussball: Der Verein hat ausgedient, die AG ist in, 22 October. www.swissinfo.ch/ger/fussball-der-verein-hat-ausgedient-die-ag-ist-in/3580000 (Accessed 16 February 2021).

Swissinfo.ch (2004) Accords bilatéraux: la révolution du sport suisse, 23 January. www.swissinfo.ch/fre/accords-bilatéraux-la-révolution-du-sport-suisse/3734510 (Accessed 16 February 2021).

Transfermarkt.com. Super league. www.transfermarkt.fr/raiffeisen-super-league/startseite/wettbewerb/C1 (Accessed 2020–2021).

UEFA (2019) Protection of young players, 5 March. www.uefa.com/insideuefa/protecting-the-game/protection-young-players/(Accessed 28 November 2021).

UEFA (2021) Country coefficients, 2 February. www.uefa.com/memberassociations/uefarankings/country/#/yr/2021 (Accessed 26 January 2021).

Valentin Schnorhk, 'Le foot suisse doit retrouver sa place en Europe', Arcinfo, 3 March 2019, www.arcinfo.ch/articles/sports/football/le-foot-Swiss-doit-retrouver-sa-place-en-europe-824946 (Accessed 10 November 2020).

Zanfi, Gianluca (2019) liste serie a 2019/20: extracomunitari, vivai e italiani squadra per squadra. *Eurosport,* 29 June. www.eurosport.it/calcio/serie-a/2018-2019/liste-serie-a-2019-20-extracomunitari-vivai-e-italiani-squadra-per-squadra_sto7347571/story.shtml (Accessed 6 January 2021).

Chapter 13

Brexit and global sport power Europe

Borja García and Henk Erik Meier

13.1. Introduction

The single market represents the most salient presence of the European Union (EU) in the international system.[1] The EU has been characterised as a great 'market power'[2] effectively shaping global regulation.[3] The EU's success has been attributed to the size of its internal market and comparative advantage in regulatory capability. However, Young has challenged the EU's image as an influential global regulator by claiming that the EU's success hinges on the regulatory capability of its interlocutors and congruence with their preferences.[4]

With regard to sports, along with the United States, the EU has acquired a reputation for being one of the few public authorities to influence sport governance and regulation.[5] While there is hardly a well-defined EU agenda to global sport regulation but rather issue-specific activities, García and Meier found evidence that the EU failed to fully exploit its actual structural power due to low policy cohesion and competence conflicts between Member States and EU institutions.[6] Indeed, Geeraert has highlighted that the EU, in some instances, has acted as a regulator of sports governance, but with a relatively low impact.[7] He has also explained how, under certain conditions, public authorities (including the EU) have managed to affect global sports governance by reducing the power of sport governing bodies, most notably in cases such as doping;[8] but even in those cases, the overall scorecard is relatively modest and the efficiency of those regulatory efforts is questionable.

1 Dür and Zimmermann (2007).
2 Damro (2012).
3 Bach and Newman (2010).
4 Young (2009, 2011).
5 Geeraert and Drieskens (2015), Meier and García (2015).
6 García and Meier (2016).
7 Geeraert (2016).
8 Geeraert and Drieskens (2021).

DOI: 10.4324/9781003162803-17

In view of this debate, in this chapter we seek to explore the extent to which Brexit could further weaken the EU's position in global sport governance. Great Britain is not only the birth land of most modern sports, but also one of the biggest and most dynamic sports markets in the world. As the EU's structural power is to be substantially reduced by Brexit, the prospects for the EU as global sports power might be further reduced. Moreover, Great Britain represented a specific model of sport governance, which had immense influence on global sport policy-making. British governments traditionally practice a liberal approach, which respects the autonomy of sport. Sport was defined as the private sphere of free citizens, who created and supported a strong and vibrant grassroots sports movement. Hence, it might be conceivable that after Brexit, dirigiste approaches to sport governance might be strengthened.

13.2. Is there a global sport power Europe?

Scholars have presented a number of complementary rather than competing propositions for explaining the EU's success as global regulator:

1. Market size. Since the EU represents the world's biggest internal market and is the largest exporter and importer of goods and services,[9] it enjoys 'structural power' in world trade allowing the EU to globalise its regulatory standards;[10]
2. Regulatory capacity and cohesion. According to Bach and Newman, the EU's success as global regulator results from its superior regulatory capacity.[11] Thus, the EU's character as a 'regulatory state' creates a comparative advantage providing 'tools to set market rules internationally as well'.[12] However, whereas Bach and Newman (2007) deem regulatory cohesion to be beneficial, it has been emphasised that low cohesion might strengthen the EU's bargaining position in case the EU is on the defensive because the EU's high threshold for internal agreements prevents EU negotiators from making concessions;[13]
3. Regulatory politics. According to the 'regulatory politics' approach, an interplay of domestic and global factors accounts for the rise of the EU as global regulator.[14] Hence, the fundamental tension between rules designed to perfect the single market and the global competitiveness for producers outside that market[15] can only be reconciled by uploading EU standards;[16]

9 Young (2011), Young and Peterson (2013).
10 See Dür and Zimmermann (2007), Meunier and Nicolaïdis (2006).
11 Bach and Newman (2007).
12 *Ibid.*, p. 828.
13 Meunier and Nicolaïdis (2006), Young (2011).
14 Kelemen (2010), Kelemen and Vogel (2010).
15 Smith (2011).
16 Jacoby and Meunier (2010).

4 Political opportunity structure. Young has stressed that previous research neglected that the EU's success depends not only on the EU's regulatory capability but also on (a) the regulatory capability of its interlocutor(s), and (b) how the EU's regulatory preferences align with those of non-EU governments.[17]

In addition to these rather general features, García and Meier identified some peculiarities of global sport regulation, which reduced the EU's efficacy:[18]

1 Strong market segregation. Only the Olympics and football (soccer) may claim global popularity. Whereas North America and Europe represent the two biggest sport markets,[19] even here market power is segregated. Between 2010 and 2012, European markets accounted for 22 per cent of the broadcasting income of the International Olympic Committee (IOC) whereas North America accounted for 55.9 per cent.[20] In contrast, 49.6 per cent of the Fédération Internationale de Football Association (FIFA)'s broadcasting income in 2012 and 2013 came from Europe but only 10.5 per cent from North America.[21] Yet, global revenues for soccer are higher than combined revenues for all US sports, such as Formula 1 racing, tennis and golf;[22]
2 Diffuse character and low capability. International sport governance has been diffuse and shaped by organisational rivalries, for example between the IOC and the International Federations (IFs), which govern the distinct sports. Moreover, the IFs share governance responsibilities with a broad range of stakeholders (leagues, clubs, athletes, organisers, etc.). Additionally, sport has been perceived as an autonomous sphere where political interference should be avoided.[23] The EU's ambitions to impose regulatory standards are likely to be perceived as a particularly interventionist or 'deep trade agenda' challenging incumbent regulatory authorities[24] because global professional sport relies on a complex and interwoven set of regulations. Thus, the EU might have to deal with interlocutors of only restricted regulatory capability and hostile to any public intervention;[25]
3 Clash of policy agendas and low cohesion. While professional sport represents an entertainment industry, Europeans perceive it as a much larger and

17 Young (2011).
18 García and Meier (2016).
19 PWC [Price Waterhouse Coopers] (2011) Changing the Game: Outlook for the Global Sports Market to 2015. New York: PWC. www.pwc.com/gx/en/industries/hospitality-leisure/changing-the-game-outlook-for-the-global-sports-market-to-2015.html.
20 IOC (2013) Olympic Marketing Fact File. Lausanne: IOC, p. 27.
21 FIFA (2013) Financial Report. Zürich: FIFA, p. 100.
22 A.T. Kearney, *The Sports Market: Major Trends and Challenges in an Industry full of Passion* (Chicago: A.T. Kearney, 2011), www.atkearney.com/documents/10192/6f46b880-f8d1-4909-9960-cc605bb1ff34.
23 Chappelet (2010).
24 Damro (2006), Young and Peterson (2006).
25 García and Weatherill (2012).

> deeper grassroots movement relying on volunteering and creating social capital. Hence, sport's hybrid character has given rise to a political agenda critical of market-oriented sport regulation.[26]

In their study on global sports power Europe, García and Meier analysed four regulatory issues in which the EU had to confront international sport governing bodies.[27] These issues were anti-doping, professional athletes' rights as employees, professional athletes' privacy rights, and consumer protection with regard to sport advertisement and sponsoring. It is important to note that these regulatory issues are not part of a systematic agenda on global sport policy, but were treated as fairly isolated dossiers. Three of the regulatory issues, that is, free movement of football players, privacy of athletes and ban on tobacco sponsoring in sport events, emerged only as unintended spill-overs of other EU policies.[28] For the four issues analysed, García and Meier found that the efficacy of the EU as global regulator of sports was rather low. The EU failed to achieve policy cohesion on major issues due to concerns about competence creeping by the EU at the expense of the Member States, unresolved policy dilemmas and conflicting economic interests of the Member States.[29] García and Meier concluded by claiming that low regulatory capacity prevented the EU from making the best use of its structural powers; this was particularly problematic with regard to the EU's agenda to protect the sport industry's integrity, which is threatened by corruption as well as match-fixing. Most striking was that even in the face of an 'objective' to address governance failures within FIFA, the initiative to fight blatant corruption within FIFA was taken by US judicial authorities and not by the EU, which represented so far the most important market for international soccer.[30]

Given that integrity of sport, that is, the promotion of good governance, combatting corruption, match-fixing and doping, is still one of the main areas of the Commission in the area of sport, the remainder of the chapter will discuss how the EU's efficacy in international sport policy-making with regard to these issues might develop.

13.3. Potential tensions between UK and EU after the Brexit

13.3.1. General remarks

In this section, we analyse some of the most pressing regulatory issues that the EU is currently facing in the area of sport, and we discuss the extent to which Brexit

26 Croci (2009), Parrish (2003).
27 García and Meier (2016).
28 *Ibid.*
29 *Ibid.*
30 *Ibid.*

might affect EU policies in those areas. As pointed out in the existing literature (e.g. García and Meier, 2016), the comparison of dossiers is the most illustrative way to competently analyse EU regulatory efforts towards sport. This is so because, despite having a soft competence on sport recognised in Article 165 TFEU, the EU is precluded by this very same article from adopting harmonising policies. That is to say, the EU cannot adopt a single coherent regulatory policy on sport, unlike in other areas such as environment, transport or telecommunications. Hence the need to adopt a comparative case-by-case approach in this section, mirroring very much the policy process of EU sport policy.

In this section we will contrast the position of the EU and the UK in relation to good governance and corruption in sport, match-fixing and doping. We have restricted our choice to these three issues due to the space available in this chapter and their salience in the ongoing European Union workplan for sport.

13.3.2. Good governance and corruption in sport

Governance and corruption are longstanding issues in the regulatory agendas of public authorities vis-à-vis sport organisations. It is well documented in the academic literature that one of the main reasons for increased regulatory efforts of national governments and EU institutions alike was a perception that sport bodies were unable to effectively deal with the emergence of new stakeholders in sport[31] and widespread mismanagement and corruption, as exemplified by the often cited Salt Lake City scandal that engulfed the IOC in the selection of the North American city to host the 2002 Winter Olympic Games.[32]

Indeed, good governance in sport has been one of the main areas of attention of EU sport policy even before it was formalised through the adoption of Article 165 TFEU. The European Commission (2007) White Paper on Sport[33] dedicated a whole section to governance issues. Once Article 165 TFEU was adopted and an EU sport policy formalised, governance and/or integrity of sport have featured in the priorities of the successive work plans designed by the Council and the European Parliament.[34] The EU has been active in the area of sport governance; however, it has always stopped shy of any type of direct regulation, not least because Article 165 TFEU prevents it to do so in principle. The reasons behind such behaviour could be summarised in a combination of lack of direct strong competence, political sensitivity of sport as a policy issue, and the strong lobby of sport organisations to maintain their so-called autonomy and their definition of what they conceive to be the European model of sport. As a result, the actions of EU institutions on sport governance are divided in three groups: soft legislative

31 Chappelet (2016).
32 Wenn et al. (2011).
33 European Commission (2007) White Paper on Sport. 11.7.2007. COM(2007) 391 final.
34 García et al. (2018).

action such as Council conclusions, funding of civil society projects through the sports chapter of Erasmus+, and a structured dialogue and consultation with sports stakeholders.

The interest of the EU in sports governance is clearly exemplified in its constant presence as a priority of the different 3-year EU work programmes on sport. The most relevant policy outputs are a deliverable by a Council Expert Group on Good Governance group that defined principles of good governance in sport, Council conclusions on good governance in sport, and a pledge board on good governance in sport.[35] The latter is a not very well-known soft-policy instrument where sport organisations can voluntarily make public their commitment to good governance principles.

Whereas the governance of sport and wider sport integrity issues feature in the agenda of the structured dialogue between the EU and sporting organisations, the EU sports forum or presidency priorities and conclusions for sport, the overall result in terms of direct legislative regulation is extremely low. In that respect, it has been only the application of EU law what has had a far more direct impact once again, as it did in the past. For example, the recent examination of the International Skating Union's rules on eligibility to participate in international competition by the European Commission and the General Court of the European Union clearly suggested the need to police the double role of sport federations as both governing bodies and competition organisers. At the time of writing this case is still on appeal to the Court of Justice of the European Union (CJEU), but should the CJEU sustain the General Court's judgment, we will find ourselves again with an example in which the direct application of generic and wider EU law to sport has a more direct effect than the outputs of the so-called EU sport policy.

The struggles of the EU to be an effective global regulator of sport governance, except through the direct application of EU law, compare to the more direct actions of the UK at the national level. Although the United Kingdom, true to its liberal and small-state tradition, does not have an excessively intrusive sport policy, it has been recognised how it took an increasingly more active role since the early 1990s and, especially, the arrival of Tony Blair's Labour government.[36] Linked to the increased levels of public funding to sport, the UK government devised a modernisation programme for sport organisations, which was designed and policed by its implementing agencies, UK Sport and Sport England. The initial stages were linked to self-assessment and to the organic development of good governance practices in sport. Whereas there was no direct regulation, the links to funding and to the expectations that the government had of sport organisations acted as a very powerful instrument to induce initial changes.

The UK government took an even stronger approach, although still short of direct regulation, with the adoption of the overtly prescriptive 2017 Code for

35 *Ibid.*
36 Houlihan and Lindsey (2013).

Good Governance in Sport.[37] The code was part of the Government's 2015 wider sports policy, titled 'Sporting Future—A New Strategy for an Active Nation', demonstrating the relevance that governance has as one of the priority areas of sport policy in the UK as well.[38] The Code is, again, linked to funding. It is outside the scope of this paper to analyse the content of the Code in detail. It is enough for our purpose here to consider that the Code establishes several governance-related criteria that sport organisations must comply with when they apply for government funding. The requirements are more stringent for those organisations applying for bigger levels of funding. As a result of the introduction of the code, some prominent UK sport federations had to reform their decision-making structures in order to comply with the requirements and continue receiving funding.[39]

Whereas the UK government claims to involve sport organisations and to consult wider with stakeholders in the design of both its 2015 framework sport policy document and the 2017 Code for Good Governance in Sport, the balance of power in this case is clearly more favourable to the government, unlike in the case of the European Union. It is curious to see that in both cases the public authorities have refrained from direct regulation, and probably for very similar reasons: Any regulation of sport might be so politically sensitive than the risks can outweigh the advantages, unless dealing with a clearly defined problem that transcends to the public opinion. However, the reliance of British sports organisations on governmental funding is a weak link that the government can use to pursue its governance agenda without the need of a direct intervention. In this respect, Brexit can exacerbate this tendency. Quite clearly, one of the drivers of the Brexit agenda pursued by Boris Johnson's Conservative government was to obtain complete regulatory independence from the EU, and to deviate from EU's regulatory standards as they see fit. The UK will have even a stronger capacity to regulate and delineate governance standards that could go further than those agreed at EU level. This does not have to be the case necessarily, but it is safe to affirm that the UK government will have more tools at its disposal, should it decide to press ahead. The EU, on the other hand, finds itself between a rock and a hard place, as it does not have the same level of competencies and, moreover, needs to balance the policy preferences of 27 Member States, besides juggling the demands of sports stakeholders with more self-regulatory autonomy and less financial dependence.

However, the British government is likely to face a dilemma in that respect. On the one hand, any UK government will always face the traditional deregulatory and liberal tradition of the country, very much oposed to public regulation. On the

37 UK Sport, *A Code for Sports Governance* (London: UK Sport, 2017), www.uksport.gov.uk/resources/governance-code

38 Department for Digital Culture Media and Sport, *Sporting Future—A New Strategy for an Active Nation* (London: Department for Digital, Culture, Media & Sport, 2015), www.gov.uk/government/publications/sporting-future-a-new-strategy-for-an-active-nation.

39 L. Scott, 'Tokyo 2020 Olympics & Paralympics: UK Sport asks government for exceptional funding', *BBC Sport*, 5 May 2020, www.bbc.co.uk/sport/52544576

other hand, and perhaps more importantly for our purpose here, the post-Brexit UK is looking for an agenda to regain a prominent role in global geopolitics once it has left the European Union. The ability to be a global power on its own was one of the messages that appealed to the Brexit voters. Global Britain was one of the slogans of the Conservative government during the Brexit negotiations.[40] In that search for a Global Britain (irrespective of what this concept might mean to different audiences), the government is looking to use sport as a tool of diplomacy and soft power. Indeed, the government has set up a budget to help British sport organisations bid for and host major sport competitions;[41] this will add to the already existing budget supporting Olympic athletes in their pursuit of medals.[42] The hosting of major sport events and the participation in those competitions can only be done under the auspices of the respective federations and governing bodies, which might have demands in exchange. Thus, the objective of using sport as one of the tools to situate post-Brexit Britain in the global stage could actually reduce any appetite for governance-related regulation that might be challenged by either national or international sport governing bodies.

13.3.3. Doping

The fight against doping has dominated much of the debate on public sport policies and public regulation of sport, especially since the well-known Festina cycling team scandal. The discovery of doping equipment during a custom inspection of the team's hotel at the 1998 Tour de France proved the 'widespread, systematic and organised' character of doping and, perhaps more importantly, the failure of the existing anti-doping regime,[43] that was lead until that moment by the International Olympic Committee and international sport federations. This perception of ineffectiveness against doping led several governments to threaten with direct regulatory action. Despite the IOC hosting a World Conference on Doping in Sport in Lausanne in 1999, distrust and dissatisfaction with the IOC amongst national governments had assumed such a dimension that public authorities wanted stronger action.[44]

Several Western governments used the conference to reap competences from the IOC and created the World Anti-Doping Agency (WADA) in 1999.[45] WADA represents a public-private partnership funded and controlled by the sport

40 Daddow (2019), Turner (2019).

41 BBC Sport, 'World Cup 2030: UK and Republic of Ireland associations back UK government support for bid', *BBC Sport*, 2 March 2021, www.bbc.co.uk/sport/football/56241637.

42 J. Halliday, 'Brutal but effective: Why team GB has won so many Olympic medals', *The Guardian*, 15 August 2016, www.theguardian.com/sport/2016/aug/15/brutal-but-effective-why-team-gb-is-winning-so-many-olympic-medals.

43 Hanstad et al. (2008).

44 *Ibid.*

45 DeFrantz (2008).

movement and governments on the base of parity. Whereas the IOC's anti-doping regime was of pure private character, WADA has a solid base in international law and has a much more aggressive mandate.[46] Geeraert and Drieskens have pointed out that the creation and development of WADA into the supreme anti-doping authority is an instance where public authorities have regained some regulatory authority that was initially delegated to sport organisations.[47]

Whereas doping is indeed a constant presence in the agenda of EU sport policy, the EU has not developed a common anti-doping policy in the traditional sense. Most of the debates are focused on the positions of the EU towards WADA, the representation of the EU in WADA, and the position in the discussions within the Council of Europe's Ad Hoc European Committee for the World Anti-Doping Agency (CAHAMA). There have also been some attempts to investigate doping in amateur sport. The European Commission highlighted the importance of combating doping in amateur sport, arguing that the use 'of doping substances by amateur athletes poses serious public health hazards and calls for preventive action, including in fitness centres'.[48] Hence, the Commission declared its intention to 'support transnational anti-doping networks, including networks focusing on preventive measures targeting amateur sport, sport for all and fitness'.[49] This support came in the form of funding for two projects on doping and the fitness industry between 2011 and 2012, that were part of the 2010 preparatory actions in the area of sport.

Coinciding with the Festina scandal, doping was high in the EU political agenda. The European Council underlined 'its concern at the extent and seriousness of doping in sports, which undermines the sporting ethic and endangers public health', calling for decisive response at EU level.[50] Building on the support at the highest political level, the European Commission launched a 'Community support plan to combat doping in sport',[51] which provided funding for two years of anti-doping projects and research to combat doping in sport.[52]

Following the creation of WADA, for a number of years the Commission and the incumbent Council Presidency occupied the seats of the EU in WADA's board. After two years, however, the Commission withdrew as WADA was 'not prepared

46 Hunt (2011), p. 87.

47 Geeraert and Drieskens (2021).

48 European Commission (2011) Communication: Developing the European Dimension in Sport, 18.1.2011, COM(2011) 12 final, p. 4.

49 *Ibid.*, p. 6.

50 European Council (1998) Vienna European Council—11 and 12 December 1998—Presidency conclusions, www.consilium.europa.eu/uedocs/cms_data/docs/pressdata/en/ec/00300-R1.EN8.htm, p. 96.

51 European Commission (1999) Communication from the Commission to the Council, the European Parliament, the Economic and Social Committee and the Committee of the Regions: Community support plan to combat doping in sport. COM(1999) 643 final, 1 December, Brussels: Commission of the European Communities.

52 Vermeersch (2006), p. 4.

to take decisions which are necessary to reconcile the WADA budgetary rules with Community financial rules'.[53] From this point EU Member States decided to coordinate their political and financial input towards WADA within the context of the Council of Europe,[54] but still retaining an EU flavour. For example, the EU sport ministers coordinate their position within the Council of Ministers, or they elect one European representative for WADA's board. Interestingly, the Council of Ministers has also delegated to the Commission the representation of the EU in CAHAMA meetings.

However, despite this rather heavy involvement in anti-doping and in WADA, academic observers have been critical of EU anti-doping regulation, considering that the EU has failed to develop a 'comprehensive EU anti-doping policy'.[55] It is true that anti-doping is a permanent point in the EU sport policy agenda. It features in the priorities of the work plan, and EU ministers for sport do coordinate their positions towards WADA. The role of the EU and European governments in the creation of WADA is undeniable. However, the extent to which they can now affect the decisions of the agency and its policies is more questionable. This was, for example, exemplified in the row between WADA and the EU on data protection issues.[56]

Following Brexit the positions of the United Kingdom and the EU in relation to doping are not likely to change much, though. The UK will be competent to design its own anti-doping policy. However, that was already the case pre-Brexit. The UK will face severe limitations, though, as it is bound now by its commitment to the WADA, the World Anti-Doping Code and the UNESCO convention against doping that gave level footing to the code. Whilst being an important sports power, the UK will now have to deal with WADA and anti-doping on its own. It will not be able to reap the benefits of collective action and coordination within the Council of Ministers. The UK will have now to coordinate its positions within the Council of Europe as one single actor. Whereas it might gain freedom to set a policy, it might lose leverage to see its policy preferences represented in the two key bodies: Council of Europe and WADA itself. The European Union, on the other hand, is likely to continue with a similar approach. It does have a representation and some input into global regulation against doping, but as discussed, the real effect of that position has been questioned. Brexit is unlikely to change this given the approach of the EU towards doping regulation has demonstrated to have a high level of path dependency and inertia. From time to time, there have surfaced questions as to the real effectiveness of the current set-up headed by WADA, but so far the agency has responded with increasing tightening of the code and increased activism in high

53 European Commission, *Community Funding of the Operating Budget of the World Anti-doping Agency Has Been Ruled Out. IP/01/1727* (Brussels: Commission of the European Communities, 3 December 2001).

54 Vermeersch (2006).

55 *Ibid.*, p. 5.

56 García and Meier (2016).

profile cases, such as the Russian state-sponsored doping. WADA has picked up prominent disputes with the IOC and other international federations to highlight its independence. Whereas the Russian scandal could have been another high-level focusing event[57] for the EU to increase its regulatory anti-doping efforts, this has not been the case. This indicates that, as mentioned, so far inertia is more prevalent in this field of EU sport policy.

13.3.4. Match-fixing

The final area of sport regulation that we discuss in this chapter is match-fixing or, as it is often known, the fight against the manipulation of results in sport competitions. This is, similar to doping, an area of interest that emerged through a number of scandals, rather than proactive policy entrepreneurship of the European Union (or any other government, for that matter). Match-fixing gained prominence due to a number of unsavoury and high-profile scandals, such as the 2006 Calciopoli scandal in Italian football,[58] which brought corruption in sport to the top of the news and political agendas. Furthermore, major police enquiries[59] certainly provided governments in the EU and beyond further indication about the major scale of the issue, with such investigations linking criminal activity to Asia and analysing how these match-fixing activities had centred around European football competitions.

In the context of the EU sport regulation, match-fixing first appears mentioned in the European Commission's communication on sport, where it promised to 'cooperate with the Council of Europe in analysing the factors that could contribute to more effectively addressing the issue of match-fixing at national, European and international level'.[60] The Hungarian presidency of the EU in 2011 brought the issue of match-fixing to the table of EU sport ministers, which was since then ever present in the meetings of the sports ministers and the EU work plans for sport.

The issue of match-fixing gained in importance to the extent that the EU sports minsters tried to develop a common strategy that could send a regulatory intent, even within their limited competences. However, during the Cypriot EU presidency of 2012, it was apparent that the diverging interests of Member States, especially those with a prominent gambling industry such as Malta, were making any regulatory attempt very difficult, if not impossible. These constraints have meant that it has actually been, once again, the Council of Europe that was the

57 Kingdon (1995).

58 S. Kuper, 'Azzurri's quest consoles nation rocked by scandals', *Financial Times*, 6 July 2006, www.ft.com/cms/s/2/6129251e-0de3-11db-a385-0000779e2340.html#axzz3PMjylxy9.

59 See Europol, 'Results from the largest football match-fixing investigation in Europe', *europol.europa.eu*, 6 February 2013, www.europol.europa.eu/content/results-largest-football-match-fixing-investigation-europe

60 European Commission (2011) Communication: Developing the European Dimension in Sport, 18.1.2011, COM(2011) 12 final, p. 12.

institution taking the initiative in developing a policy against match-fixing in Europe. The Council of Europe's Enlarged Partial Agreement on Sport (EPAS) is an intergovernmental organisation in which most but not all the EU Member States are members. The Council of Europe, through EPAS, started to deal with match-fixing issues back in 2008, which in a way also created a first mover advantage and provided the CoE with an institutional memory, knowledge and inertia that the EU did not have, in spite of the intergovernmental nature of the CoE and its lack of direct regulatory power.

As a result, on 28 September 2011, the CoE adopted a recommendation which invited EPAS to undertake a feasibility study on a legal instrument that could combat match-fixing in Europe. This has crystalised in the development and final adoption of the so-called Macolin Convention, a short title for the Council of Europe Convention on the Manipulation of Sports Competitions. As such, CoE conventions are legal international instruments, but these need to be signed, ratified and implemented by the CoE Member States through their internal legislation. The Macolin Convention entered into force in September 2019. At the time of writing this chapter, the convention had been ratified by Norway, Portugal, Ukraine, Moldova, Switzerland, Italy and Greece: that is to say, only by three EU Member States. The EU, as an international organisation, has not signed the convention yet.

Match-fixing, similar to doping, is yet another example of the limitations of the EU as a regulator of global sport. Despite the major salience of match-fixing as a policy issue, as demonstrated by the many times it has been discussed in meetings and documents, the reality is that the EU has not a fully-fledged match-fixing policy. It might even be adventurous to concede the EU has developed a coherent strategy in this area, other than recognising the importance of match-fixing and the need of multi-stakeholder coordination. However, when it comes to the links of match-fixing that could affect the gambling industry, it has not been possible to find common ground.

Brexit could perhaps facilitate agreement once the UK is not sitting at the table in EU institutions, especially given the relevance of the betting industry in the UK and the cultural prevalence and importance of betting itself in British culture. However, there are still other Member States, such as the Republic of Ireland and Malta, that will pursue similar agendas, albeit without the support now of one of the major Member States. However, it seems clear now that, following the adoption of the Macolin Convention, the CoE has increased even more its centrality in this debate. It is also important to highlight that Article 165 TFEU clearly calls for cooperation with the CoE in EU sport policy. Hence, both institutions need not to be seen as being in a turf war.

13.4. Conclusion

In this chapter we have discussed the role of the European Union as a regulator of global sport. We analysed the EU regulatory powers that could be employed to set standards and policies in the sport industry. A lack of policy coherence, existing institutional inertia and the clear opposition of sport stakeholders greatly reduce the regulatory agency of the EU in the area of sport. This is unlikely to change with Brexit, as we have seen in the comparative analysis of three major areas of interest in EU sports policy, namely the governance of sport, the fight against doping and the fight against match-fixing.

The governance of sport is the area in which Brexit opens a window of opportunity for the EU to adopt a more proactive role, but for this to happen Member States need to find a consensus on the application of EU law to sport or the development of a more active regulatory action through EU sport policy. In our view, Brexit could reduce the leverage of the UK in this area, even when the Conservative government has made a clear of point of Brexit being a departure from EU regulatory standards. However, the eagerness of the UK to use sport as a tool of soft power and diplomacy is likely to link the fate of the British government to the demands of international sport organisations.

The regulatory agency of the EU in the fight against doping was strong in the early stages of the creation of WADA. The common approach of the EU helped Europe to maximise impact. However, the need to operate through the Council of Europe and WADA's own development has reduced the regulatory impact of the EU after the creation of WADA. Indeed, the EU cannot be said to have a clearly defined and fully-fledged anti-doping policy, according to academics. Given the existing policy inertia, this is unlikely to change with Brexit. The EU will retain, though, the benefits of its common actions, something that the UK will need now to navigate on its own. This should not be seen as insignificant.

A similar conclusion can be reached in relation to match-fixing because it follows similar policy dynamics. The regulatory impact of the EU in this area is diluted by the diverging policy preferences of Member States, the ongoing dynamics that favour action within the Council of Europe and the complex network of stakeholders involved (from sport organisations to police agencies). This is perhaps the area in which Brexit could help to find some common ground in reaching agreement amongst Member States once the policy preferences of the United Kingdom are not on the table any more. However, the adoption of the Macolin Convention and the reticence of the remaining (small) Member States will not make this easy.

Although it is still early days, Brexit is unlikely to have a major effect on the EU's regulatory power in sport. The structural set up of EU sport policy and the policy inertia and path dependency of the application of EU law and policy to sport greatly reduce the margin of actions for EU institutions.

References

Bach, D. & Newman, A.L. (2007) The European regulatory state and global public policy: Micro-institutions, macro-influence. *Journal of European Public Policy*, 14:6, 827–846.

Bach, D. & Newman, A.L. (2010) 'Governing Lipitor and Lipstick: Capacity, Sequencing, and Power in International Pharmaceutical and Cosmetics Regulation'. *Review of International Political Economy*, 17:4, 665–695.

Chappelet, J.L. (2010) *Autonomy of Sport in Europe*. Strasbourg: Council of Europe Publishing.

Chappelet, J.L. (2016) From Olympic administration to Olympic governance. *Sport in Society*, 19:6, 739–751.

Croci, O. (2009) Taking the field: The European Union and sport governance. In: Tömmel, I. & Verdun, A. (eds) *Innovative Governance in the European Union: The Politics of Multilevel Governance*. Boulder, CO: Lynne Rienner, pp. 139–157.

Daddow, O. (2019) GlobalBritainTM: The discursive construction of Britain's post-Brexit world role. *Global Affairs*, 5:1, 5–22.

Damro, C. (2006) The new trade politics and EU competition policy: Shopping for convergence and co-operation. *Journal of European Public Policy*, 13:6, 867–886.

Damro, C. (2012) Market power Europe. *Journal of European Public Policy*, 19:5, 682–699.

DeFrantz, A. (2008) Which rules? International sport and doping in the 21st century. *Houston Journal of International Law*, 31, 1–26.

Dür, A. & Zimmermann, H. (2007) Introduction: The EU in international trade negotiations. *Journal of Common Market Studies*, 45:4, 771–787.

García, B.; de Wolff, M. & Yilmaz, S. (2018) Issue framing and institutional constraints in EU agenda-setting: An analysis of European Union sport policy. *Journal of Contemporary European Research*, 14:1, 23–29.

García, B. & Meier, H.E. (2016) Global sport power Europe? The efficacy of the European union in global sport regulation. *Journal of Common Market Studies*, 55:4, 850–870.

García, B. & Weatherill, S. (2012) Engaging with the EU in order to minimize its impact: Sport and the negotiation of the Lisbon treaty. *Journal of European Public Policy*, 19:2, 238–256.

Geeraert, A. (2016) *The EU in International Sports Governance: A Principal-Agent Perspective on EU Control of FIFA and UEFA*. Houndmills: Palgrave Macmillan.

Geeraert, A. & Drieskens, E. (2015) The EU controls FIFA and UEFA: A principal—agent perspective. *Journal of European Public Policy*, 22:10, 1448–1466.

Geeraert, A. & Drieskens, E. (2021) The dynamics of de-delegation: A principal—agent explanation of the reversal of private authority in international sport governance. *Public Administration*, 99:1, 156–170.

Hanstad, D.V.; Smith, A. & Waddington, I. (2008) The establishment of the world anti-doping agency: A study of the management of organizational change and unplanned outcomes. *International Review for the Sociology of Sport*, 43:3, 227–249.

Houlihan, B. & Lindsey, I. (2013) *Sport Policy in Britain*. London: Routledge.

Hunt, T.M. (2011) *Drug Games: The International Olympic Committee and the Politics of Doping, 1960–2008*. Austin, Texas: University of Texas Press.

Jacoby, W. & Meunier, S. (2010) Europe and the management of globalization. *Journal of European Public Policy*, 17:3, 299–317.

Kelemen, R.D. (2010) Globalizing European union environmental policy. *Journal of European Public Policy*, 17:3, 335–349.

Kelemen, R.D. & Vogel, D. (2010) Trading places: The role of the United States and the European Union in international environmental politics. *Comparative Political Studies*, 43:4, 427–456.

Kingdon, J.W. (1995) *Agendas, Alternatives and Public Policies*, 2nd edition. New York: Harper Collins Publishers.

Meier, H.E. & García, B. (2015) Protecting private transnational authority against public intervention: FIFA's power over national governments. *Public Administration*, 93:4, 890–906.

Meunier, S. & Nicolaïdis, K. (2006) The European union as a conflicted trade power. *Journal of European Public Policy*, 13:6, 906–925.

Parrish, R. (2003) *Sports Law and Policy in the European Union*. Manchester: Manchester University Press.

Smith, M.P. (2011) 'Single Market, Global Competition: Regulating the European Market in a Global Economy'. *Journal of European Public Policy*, 17:7, 936–953.

Turner, O. (2019) Global Britain and the narrative of Empire. *The Political Quarterly*, 90:4, 727–734.

Vermeersch, A. (2006) The European Union and the fight against doping in sport: On the field or on the sidelines? *Entertainment and Sports Law Journal*, 4:1, 1–12.

Wenn, S.R.; Barney, R. & Martyn, S.G. (2011) *Tarnished Rings: The International Olympic Committee and the Salt Lake City Bid Scandal*. Syracuse: Syracuse University Press.

Young, A.R. (2009) Confounding conventional wisdom: Political not principled differences in the transatlantic regulatory relationship. *British Journal of Politics and International Relations*, 11–4, 666–689.

Young, A.R. (2011) The rise (and fall?) of the EU's performance in the multilateral trading system. *Journal of European Integration*, 33:6, 715–729.

Young, A.R. & Peterson, J. (2006) The EU and the new trade politics. *Journal of European Public Policy*, 13:6, 795–814.

Young, A.R. & Peterson, J. (2013) 'We care about you, but': The politics of EU trade policy and development. *Cambridge Review of International Affairs*, 26:3, 497–518.

Part V

Conclusion

Chapter 14

European Union law and the regulation of sport in the United Kingdom after Brexit

The mediative effect of international sports regulations

Simon Boyes

14.1. Introduction

The referendum of June 2016, the departure of the United Kingdom from the European Union in January 2020, and the commencement of new arrangements between the United Kingdom and European Union at the end of 2020, have led to and will continue to have an impact on the regulation of sport in the United Kingdom.

The formal end of the application of European Union law within its borders has significant consequences for the regulation of sport in the United Kingdom. Since the landmark judgment in *Union Royale Belge des Sociétés de Football Association v Bosman*,[1] European Union law and its institutions have had a significant influence on the regulatory structures of sport within the Member States, including in the United Kingdom.

The most obviously prominent amongst these impacts have been in relation to the European Union law prohibition on discrimination based on nationality. However, there has been a range of effects in the United Kingdom, consequent on the country's withdrawal from the treaties. While much attention has been given to these changes, little consideration has been given to the ongoing impact of European Union legal principle in the United Kingdom in the post-Brexit era.

This chapter seeks to highlight and to explore these ongoing aspects and to assess the probable nature of the relationship going forward.

The chapter begins with a brief outline of the impact of European Union law on the regulation of sport in the United Kingdom during the period of its membership, before considering the broad changes given effect by Brexit, including an assessment of the formal residue of European Union law, given effect by the United Kingdom withdrawal legislation and the future relationships established. It then seeks to explain the influence of European Union law on sport's regulatory schemes. This will encompass the shaping effect of the Union's institutions—particularly the Court of Justice and Commission—as well as consideration of the

1 Case C-415/93 [1995] ECR I-4292

DOI: 10.4324/9781003162803-19

application of European Union law principles by sports' own dispute resolution fora, notably the Court of Arbitration for sport.

Finally, the chapter will identify those strands of European Union law which have filtered through sports global regulatory structures to have an ongoing impact within the United Kingdom, even after Brexit.

14.2. The United Kingdom and the European Union after Brexit

The story of the European Union law and the regulation of sport in the United Kingdom is, by-and-large the same as in each of the other Member States. As a Member State throughout the period in which sport has been actively considered by the European Union's institutions, the United Kingdom has felt the full effect of the relevant legal developments over that time. As a Member State the effects of European Union law on sport have been direct and, as a consequence, little thought has been given to the extra-territorial effects of European Union law on sports regulation.

The United Kingdom's departure from the European Union marks, in theory at least, a break with the legal principles which have held sway within the jurisdiction since the country joined the, then, European Economic Community in 1973. The Trade and Cooperation Agreement (TCA) concluded between the two parties does away with much of that content, although there is some degree of continuity in some areas. However, it is notable that the TCA omits any ongoing provisions pertaining to free movement of persons or, indeed, non-discrimination, in contrast to many of the partnership and cooperation agreements which the European Union shares with other third countries.[2] Similarly, although there are level playing field commitments in the agreement, there are no directly comparable competition law provisions with those to be found in the European Union treaties themselves. As such, this means that the major treaty provisions, which have had the greatest effect on sport, no longer apply in the United Kingdom and have not been retained in the TCA.

The United Kingdom has, however, retained some elements of European Union law.[3] In large part this is a practical necessity born of the sheer volume of European Union law directly applicable in the United Kingdom prior to Brexit and the impracticality of enacting domestic legislation in the time scales concerned. This means that European Union law retains some residual influence in the United Kingdom, as does the domestic legislation enacted to give effect to, for example, Directives. These national United Kingdom measures are ostensibly domestic in nature but are, however, ultimately the product of the European Union's

2 Although note the provisions relating to settled status of those having exercised their rights of free movement prior to Brexit.

3 Sections 2–4 European Union (Withdrawal) Act 2018

legislative processes. Perhaps the best example of this with consequence for sport is the Competition Act 1998, which largely mirror the competition law principles set out in the European Union Treaties.[4]

While European Union law does retain some lingering effect, as a consequence of these continuity provisions, the reality remains that, removed of its obligations to respect these principles as a European Union Member State, there is a strong likelihood that there will be amended or repealed over time.

Similarly, while the Withdrawal Agreement (WA) between the parties makes provision for post-Brexit judgments of the Court of Justice of the European Union to remain relevant, the reality is that the United Kingdom's adherence to European Union law will be frozen in time. If these new measures are enacted and implemented, there will be an inevitable and continuing drift between the European Union and United Kingdom.

The result—the two parties forging their own future path—means that the influence of European Union law in the United Kingdom will inevitably wane over time. From the perspective of sport and sports regulation, it is likely that any lingering effect by these means will be minimal at best. While some retained measures will, of course, interact with sport at some level, there are no obvious examples of retained law which will have a significant and sustained impact on sport itself. However, despite this, there are strong arguments that sport in the United Kingdom will experience an ongoing, substantial influence from European Union law, despite Brexit.

The immediate effect of the United Kingdom's withdrawal from the European Union is most prominent in the context of rules relating to restrictions on the ability of foreign nationals to participate in professional sport domestically. Perhaps the most notable feature of the impact of European Union law on sport was the significant liberalisation of nationality-based restrictions. This was, of course, a consequence of the application of Article 45 of the Treaty on the Functioning of the European Union, which outlaws such discrimination. This was, too, extended by the subsequent cases of *Deutscher Handballbund eV v Kolpak*[5] and *Simutenkov v Ministerio de Educación y Cultura*[6] to include relevant partnership and association agreements between the European Union and third countries.

The immediate impact of the inapplicability of European Union law in the context of the United Kingdom has been the immediate move towards re-introduction of measures aimed at limiting participation based on nationality. Notably, the football authorities, particularly in England, have seen this change as an opportunity to require higher levels of participation from domestic nationals in their professional leagues.

4 See, for example, *Hendry v World Professional Billiards and Snooker Association* [2002] ECC 8
5 Case C-438/00, [2003] ECR I-4135
6 Case C-265/03, [2005] ECR I-2579

A similar impact has been noted in respect of the capacity to recruit new players, particularly in the context of professional team sports.[7] The end of free movement between the United Kingdom and the Member States of the European Union has meant that a much higher bar must be met before a player can take up employment with a club in the United Kingdom. This is, in large part, a consequence of the application of work permit and visa requirements to would-be athletes seeking professional engagement in the United Kingdom.[8] This has, in effect, placed incoming European Union citizens in the same position as potential employees from any other nation-states, and vice versa.

The removal of these obligations relating to both free movement and nationality-based discrimination are high profile examples of the impact of the withdrawal of the United Kingdom from the European Union, and the accompanying elimination of the effects of European Union law. The general view in this respect has been that Brexit, therefore, brings an end to the European Union's influence on the regulation of sport in the United Kingdom. This is certainly true in a direct sense; as noted above, the new relationship between the United Kingdom and the European Union contains little which is likely to have a significant, ongoing impact on the regulation of sport. However, this does not account for the indirect means by which European Union law may continue to influence sport in the United Kingdom, given its extensive influence over the regulation of global sport during the last three decades.

14.3. The extra-territorial effect of European Union law

Although ostensibly confined to the territories of its Member States, European Union law has demonstrated capacity for significant reach beyond that, in the case of sport.

In the first 'sports' case to reach the Court of Justice of the European Union—*Walrave and Koch v Union Cycliste Internationale*[9]—the capacity for external reach was amply demonstrated in the context of a challenge to purportedly discriminatory eligibility rules. The Court emphasised the applicability of European Union law, even to situations governed by regulatory bodies based outside of its Member States—in this case the International Cycling Union, based in Switzerland. It did so not on the basis that it was not material from where the rule or restriction emanated, but that its affect could be located within the European Union. In a similar way, it also demonstrated the capacity to impact on sports events taking place in jurisdictions outside of the European Union Member States. In the case of *Walrave*

7 Perry and Steenson (2019).
8 *Immigration Rules Appendix M: sports governing bodies*, Sports governing bodies for Tier 2 (Sportsperson) and Tier 5 (Temporary Worker—Creative and Sporting) applications.
9 Case C-36/74, [1974] ECR 1405

this involved the International Cycling Union World Championships, taking place in Spain which was not—at the time—a Member State. It also established that European Union law would be applicable to not only public authorities, but also self-regulatory bodies such as international sports federations, the Court of Justice noting that to do otherwise could effectively neutralise efforts to achieve the free movement of persons.

Although, perhaps, not in itself hugely significant, the case nonetheless paves the way for the much greater impacts which rolled out of the judgement in *Bosman*. In particular, it provided clarification on these important points concerning the reach of European Union law, which, in the context of the *Bosman* judgment, assumed a much greater significance.

The *Bosman* case will be familiar to most but, in brief, the key elements of the judgment are that football's transfer system, which limited the capacity of professional players to move to another club once their contract with their previous employer had expired, and rules limiting the number of foreign players in a squad or team amount to a breach of European Union law, which is now embodied in Article 45 TFEU.

This contrasts with the effects of similar litigation in national jurisdictions. In England, George Eastham challenged football's retain and transfer system as being in unlawful restraint of trade.[10] Although, in part, success was limited to national boundaries and had no international impact. This limitation on the practical capacity of national law to effect change in sports regulatory systems was emphasised by the case of *Cooke v Football Association*.[11] Here, the claimant footballer sought a transfer between Irish and English clubs. FIFA regulations imposed requirements on any player seeking a transfer between clubs in different national associations, to the end that they were required to obtain the grant of a transfer certificate from the originating association before he would be permitted to register with the new club, in a new association. In *Cooke*, the claimant was unable to obtain this certification from the Football Association of Ireland, and his transfer to an English club was refused by the English Football Association as a consequence. Although ultimately successful in the litigation, and in spite of the trial judge's observation that if FIFA's regulations were contrary to English law, then the Football Association would simply have to withdraw from the organisation, there was no withdrawal and FIFA's regulations remained intact and unrevised.

This is noteworthy in juxtaposition to *Bosman* and what followed, in that the latter effected the emergence of the European Union as a regulatory rival to the international sports federations, which previously had been largely free from any meaningful challenge. This was of course most notable in the context of football, with the European Commission seemingly empowered by the Court of Justice

10 *Eastham v Newcastle United Football Club* [1963] 1 Ch 413
11 *Cooke v Football Association* (1972) The Times, 24 March

determination in *Bosman*. The Commission had demonstrated only a limited interest in sport prior to the case, having been concerned with the development of the 3 + 2 rule following on from the litigation in *Dona v Mantero*,[12] and in the commercial sphere, competition law problems relating to ticketing for the 1990 FIFA World Cup, hosted by Italy.[13]

In spite of the clear nature of the ruling in *Bosman*, FIFA, football's world governing body, sought to resist the consequences of the judgment. In particular, it claimed that the Member States of the European Union amounted to only a tiny part of its global jurisdiction, and as such it is unacceptable that a globally approved set of a regulations could be challenged by such a relatively small section of its membership:

> FIFA has noted with disappointment the decision taken by the European Court of Justice regarding the case of Jean-Marc Bosman.
>
> FIFA points out that the decision affects only 18 of the 193 national associations affiliated to the world body. The current transfer system is based upon the Statutes and Regulations which have been duly approved by all the FIFA member associations and has proved to be effective, and is therefore not cast into doubt by today's decision.
>
> FIFA will study what adaptations UEFA may need to consider as far as the 18 affected European associations (of a total UEFA membership of 50) are concerned.[14]

Notably, in the context of this chapter, the *Bosman* judgment itself was not as extensive as might have been first imagined. While the rules relating to non-discrimination were much expanded because of *Bosman*—it was no longer permissible to discriminate against a professional sports person on grounds of nationality—this by and large had an effect limited to European Union Member States and their citizens. Similarly, the prohibition on transfer fees for out of contract players was only applicable to European Union nationals seeking a transfer between clubs in different European Union Member States; there was no legal imperative to deploy a similar rule to transfers involving third country nationals or those occurring between clubs within the same Member State.

The expansion of what has become known as the *Bosman* free transfer to apply at a domestic level only occurred following significant pressure from players and players unions and against the background of threats of further litigation. Most noticeable in this respect was the clean lodged by Hungarian professional

12 Case C-13/76 [1976] ECR 1333

13 92/521/EEC: *Commission Decision of 27 October 1992 relating to a proceeding under Article 85 of the EEC Treaty* (IV/33.384 and IV/33.378 - Distribution of package tours during the 1990 World Cup).

14 'FIFA Reaction to Bosman Case Decision' FIFA Media Release, 15 December 1995

footballer, Tibor Balog.[15] Hungary was not at that time a Member State of the European Union; consequently, the easing of restrictions had not been extended to Hungarian and other third country nationals playing professionally in European Union Member States. Balog claimed that the continuation of this restriction on his capacity to move, despite his contract having ended, was anti-competitive as being an alleged breach of what is now Article 101 TFEU. Having reached the Court of Justice by way of a preliminary reference, Balog's case was withdrawn shortly before Advocate General Stix-Hackl was due to deliver her opinion. The rules were amended in such a way as to encompass all professional players, irrespective of nationality.

The ultimate consequence of the interaction between European Union law and football's transfer system was the introduction of a reformed regulations on the status and transfer of players by FIFA. These regulations came into effect globally in 2001, not just within the jurisdictions of European Union Member States. Thus, the decision in *Bosman*, and the involvement of the European Commission in formative aspects of these international regulations, gives emphasis to the significant impact of European Union law on the regulation of a global sport, such as association football. What is notable is that, at the time, the effect of this ruling should have been limited only to the Member States of the European Union—at that time numbering only 15. It is true, too, that the capacity to move freely at the end of a contract required by European Union law after *Bosman*, applied only to those movements across borders between European Union Member States.[16] However, following *Bosman* the European Commission pursued a much more pro-active approach to the regulation of sport, in particular football. The Commission suggested that the whole of football's transfer system, not only those aspects caught by the judgement of the Court of Justice, was in breach of elements of European Union law. Although there exists no specific case law or legislation in this regard, the Commission had a clear influence on the development of football's transfer system in the aftermath of *Bosman*. This is because the transfer system ultimately adopted by FIFA did not just take effect in the Member States of the European Union; but, driven by the need in sport for a level playing field, as a means of facilitating fair competition, the scheme shaped by the *Bosman* judgment and the intervention of the European Commission has taken effect on a global basis. In essence what has happened is that the European Union, because of its

15 Case C-264/98 *Tibor Balog v ASBL Royal Charleroi Sporting Club*, case withdrawn; see as a further example of, ultimately, withdrawn litigation effecting regulatory change Case C-243/06 *SA Sporting Pays du Charleroi and G-14 Groupement des clubs de football européens v FIFA* OJ C 2121, 2 September, p. 11; and effecting change which is subsequently approved, Case COMP/37.124, see 'Commission closes investigations into FIFA rules on players' agents' IP/02/585 18/04/2002; Case T-193/02, Piau v Commission [2005] ECR II-209; Case C-171/05, Piau v Commission [2006] ECR I-37.

16 Morris et al. (1996).

geopolitical strength, has been able to externalise its own principles and standards, effectively amplifying their effects beyond the *de jure* limits of its legal system.[17]

This demonstrates the reach of European Union law beyond its own boundaries, including the capacity to impact in far distant jurisdictions. This is perhaps best emphasised by a case which came before the Court of Arbitration for Sport in 2005, brought by the Uruguayan football club Peñarol.[18] Peñarol became involved in a dispute with Paris St Germain after they claimed a transfer fee for two players who had signed for the French club. Peñarol had attempted to unilaterally extend the contracts of these two players, Cristian Rodriguez and Carlos Bueno, in accordance with the rules of their own national federation, but in contravention of those required by FIFA's new regulations. During the case, Peñarol argued that the rules of the Uruguayan federation should take precedence over FIFA's rules as amended by agreement with the European Commission, Uruguay, of course, not being a Member State of the European Union. In finding in favour of Paris St Germain, the Court of Arbitration for sport noted the importance of the universal applicability of such rules, and that as a result the *FIFA Regulations on the Status and Transfer of Players* overrode the competing Uruguayan domestic principles. This clearly demonstrates the significance extraterritorial reach of European Union law, as mediated through these regulations.

In the context of Brexit this exemplifies the lingering impact of European Union law in the United Kingdom through these regulations. While the United Kingdom was a Member State of the European Union at the time these events took place, the effect is no less significant as a result of its withdrawal. So, while United Kingdom has formally resigned its membership of the European Union, and is no longer subject to its legal regime, it does nonetheless continue to be impacted, albeit indirectly, by these regulations, so clearly influenced by European Union legal principle. Given that these events have taken place during the United Kingdom's membership of the European Union this may be regarded as being relatively insignificant; however, the European Commission, and European Union law more generally, continue to have an effect on sports regulations and international federations, which will inevitably have an impact in the United Kingdom.

European Union law does not only have a formative role through these successful challenges. As well as sports regulatory issues arising in the context of litigation and enforcement, there are numerous examples of the European Union, and this legal system operating in a cooperative rather than confrontational fashion. This is evident in two major respects. First, this can be identified through litigation and demands for enforcement which have sought to co-opt European Union legal

17 See, as a further example of the capacity of European Union institutions to effect regulatory change on global sports operations, Case COMP/36.638, see 'Commission closes its investigation into Formula One and other four-wheel motor sports' IP/01/1523 Date: 30/10/2001.

18 TAS 2005/A/983 & 984 *Club Atlético Peñarol v Carlos Heber Bueno Suarez, Cristian Gabriel Rodriguez Barrotti & Paris Saint-Germain.*

principles as a means to challenge or overturn existing regulatory provisions, but which have failed. Second, it can be seen in the supportive, indeed collaborative, approaches adopted by the European Union institutions towards regulatory measures of which it is supportive.

In respect of the first, there was a sense, following *Bosman*, that European Union law provided a cure-all for any aggrieved claimants who might find aspects of sports regulations objectionable or restrictive. However, two cases in the immediate aftermath of *Bosman*, *Deliège*[19] and *Lehtonen*,[20] demonstrated that European Union law would not be overly interventionist, as long as sports regulators respected its overarching principles. Two cases provide further examples. The first of those, *Bernard*,[21] concerned the compatibility of football's rules pertaining to financial compensation for the training and development of young players, which flows from the aspect of the *Bosman* judgment which means that it remains possible for football clubs to obtain monetary compensation for young players, trained by the club, who are nonetheless out of contract. In this case the Court of Justice of the European Union demonstrated its willingness to accept restrictions which could be justified as being consistent with European Union law. In particular, both Advocate General Sharpston and the Court itself accepted that legitimate objectives pursued in a proportionate manner could be regarded as justifiable despite appearing on their face to breach European Union legal principles. In the context of competition law, a would-be challenge to the Financial Fair Play rules imposed in European club football by UEFA could establish very little traction either with the Commission, or through the judicial process before the Court of Justice.[22] Indeed, the Commission has appeared to be a willing supporter of these measures.[23] Perhaps most notably, the Court of Justice effectively approved sport's anti-doping rules in *Meca-Medina and Majcen v Commission*.[24] There is little doubt that, had this cased forced reform of those regulations, the impact would have been global in nature.

The second instance of this formative, collaborative approach has been fostered by the introduction, in 2009, of Article 165 TFEU. Article 165 provides the European Union with a soft law competence in relation to sport; this has the consequence of restricting European Union action two measures of a complimentary,

19 Cases C-51/96 and C191/97 *Deliège v Ligue Francophone de Judo et Disciplines Associées ASBL* [2002] ECR I-2549.

20 Case C-176/96 *Jyri Lehtonen & Castors Canada Dry Namur-Braine v Fédération Royale Belge des Sociétés de Basketball ASBL* [2000] ECR I-2681.

21 Case C 325/08 *Olympique Lyonnais SASP v Olivier Bernard and Newcastle United.*

22 Case C-299/15 *Striani & Others*, ECLI:EU:C:2015:519; CASE AT.40105 UEFA *Financial Fair Play Rules*.

23 European Commission and UEFA, *Joint Statement*, 21 March 2012, https://ec.europa.eu/competition/sectors/sports/joint_statement_en.pdf (accessed 23 April 2021).

24 Case T-313/02, *Meca-Medina and Majcen v Commission* [2004] ECR II-3291; Case C-519/04 P, *Meca-Medina and Majcen v Commission* [2006] ECR I-6991

coordinating or supporting nature. Most notably, Article 165 TFEU is limited in providing power only to promoting and fostering cooperation, meaning it is entirely facilitative in nature. The work undertaken to develop what has become known as the 'European Dimension in Sport', has seen the European Union engage with sport on a collaborative basis across a wide range of areas. These range from anti-doping, trafficking, athlete training and education, safety and security at sports events, accessibility to sports organisations and events for the disabled, and the promotion of women's access to leadership positions in sport.

Much of the above illustrates the predominance of football as a vehicle for European Union law. However, European Union law, particularly competition law, has begun to be pervasive in sports more broadly. This is most notable in the extent to which sports premier dispute resolution body, the Court of Arbitration for Sport, has been engaged in the application of European Union competition law in cases which have been brought before its panels. This is not a new phenomenon, having first arisen in relation to a challenge brought against a UEFA rule limiting multiple ownership of football clubs participating in the same European club competition.[25] These are, however, issues which have grown in both prominence and frequency in the context of disputes arising before the Court of Arbitration for Sport.

While the deployment of European Union law in cases before the Court of Arbitration for Sport is not a given,[26] it has become increasingly integrated within the body of law deployed by the CAS. It has dealt with relatively fundamental European Union legal principles, such as the direct effect of Directives,[27] the interpretation on FIFA Regulations on the Status and Transfer of Players in the light of European Union free movement of persons principles,[28] the compatibility of arbitration proceedings with European Union competition law,[29] consideration of the validity of UEFA's 'home grown player' rule,[30] the applicability of European Union partnership agreements in the context of national team selection[31] and the Charter of Fundamental Rights of the European Union[32] However, this also runs to cases in

25 CAS 98/2000 *AEK Athens and Slavia Prague v UEFA*, award of 20 August 1999; see also, Case COMP/37.806 'Commission closes investigation into UEFA rule on multiple ownership of football clubs' IP/02/942 27/06/2002.

26 See, for example, CAS 2019/A/6345 *Club Raja Casablanca v Fédération Internationale de Football Association (FIFA)*, award of 16 December 2019.

27 CAS 2017/A/5051 *Jarmo Ahjupera v Ujpest 1885 Futball Kft*, award of 29 September 2017

28 CAS 2016/A/4903 *Club Atlético Vélez Sarsfield v The Football Association Ltd., Manchester City FC & Fédération Internationale de Football Association (FIFA)*, award of 16 April 2018.

29 CAS 2014/A/3561 & 3614 *International Association of Athletics Federation (IAAF) & World Anti-Doping Agency (WADA) v Marta Domínguez Azpeleta & Real Federación Española de Atletismo (RFEA)*, award of 19 November 2015.

30 CAS 2012/A/2852 *S.C.S Fotbal Club CFR 1907 Cluj S.A. & Manuel Ferreira de Sousa Ricardo & Mario Jorge Quintas Felgueiras v Romanian Football Federation (FRF)*, award of 28 June 2013.

31 CAS 2009/A/1788 *UMMC Ekaterinburg v FIBA Europe e. V.*, award of 29 October 2009

32 CAS 2008/A/1485 *FC Midtjylland A/S v Fédération Internationale de Football Association (FIFA)*, award of 6 March 2009.

which the CAS effectively stands as proxy for European Union institutions in the wholesale application of competition law provisions.[33]

14.4. Conclusions: European Union law and the regulation of sport after Brexit

Despite Brexit, the regulation of sport in the United Kingdom has not been cut entirely adrift of the impact of European Union law. There remain residual 'legacy' effects, stemming from nearly five decades of membership, during which the influence of European Union law has grown exponentially, and time in which it has had at least a partial shaping effect on domestic sports regulation. Neither does the United Kingdom's withdrawal from the European Union amount to a 'line in the sand' beyond which no further effects will be felt. Although there are immediate and obvious consequences—the end of free movement being the most prominent—the influence of European Union law extra-territorially is much more wide-ranging and subtle than just that.

The formative and reformative impact of the European Union, through both law and institutional action, takes effect at a global level. The European Union, therefore, plays a key role in supervising and steering the global sports regulatory environment in a range of key areas.

Even after Brexit, the United Kingdom is by no means isolated from these effects; the regulation of sport continues to operate in a global context, perhaps more so than any other sector it is characterised by cross border interactions of one sort or another.

Thus, the well-established but still growing role of the European Union in both adversarial and collaborative engagements with sport will continue to effect the regulation of sport in the United Kingdom, irrespective of the severing of formal links after Brexit.

References

Morris, P.E.; Morrow, S.H. & Spink, P.M. (1996) EC law and professional football: Bosman and its implications. *Modern Law Review*, 59:6, 893–902.

Perry, K. & Steenson, M. (2019) A post-Brexit impact: A case study on the English premier league. *Harvard Journal of Sports & Entertainment*, 10:1, 7–59.

33 CAS 2007/A/1287 *Danubio FC v Fédération Internationale de Football Association (FIFA) & FC Internazionale Milano S.p.A.*, award of 28 November 2007.

Chapter 15

Conclusion

Sport regulation between Brussels effect and Brexit dividend

Jacob Kornbeck

15.1. Introduction

Through its contributions written by authors with expertise in a wide array of areas of law and policy, this book set out to explore regulatory legacies and challenges which are likely to affect the sport sector as a consequence of Brexit. What have the chapters revealed about such legacies and challenges? What is the extent of the retained Union law in the UK, and to what extent and in what ways will Brexit upend existing practices and arrangements in sport? Has the regulatory capacity of the EU been underrated in the field of sport—as the Introduction suggests that it may often have been within more generic British policy circles—and what would the implications of such a finding be? And finally, what sort of EU regulation used to condition the functioning of British and European sport: regulation of a direct, sport-specific kind, or rather generic regulation which happened to affect sport as well, alongside other sectors (horizontal effects)? These are the questions which will be addressed in this Conclusion, by identifying what the 13 substantive chapters of this book have revealed about the regulatory legacies of 47 years (1 January 1973 to 31 January 2020) years of British EC/EU membership, and what challenges can be expected from its discontinuation.

15.2. Regulatory legacies and challenges identified

First, under the heading 'Introduction,' *Jacob Kornbeck* argued, in Chapter 1, that the regulatory aspects of the 'Brexit and Sport' theme deserve a book in their own right. He went on to show that British decision-makers seem, more often than not, to have ignored the impact of Community/Union regulation, preferring to treat Europe as an intergovernmental 'block' with rules enshrined in 'deals' rather than in law. Yet at the same time, EU regulation constituted a powerful argument for the 'Leave' camp. To frame the discussion further, *Alexander Brand, Arnout Geeraert and Arne Niemann* have, in Chapter 2, revisited European (dis-)integration theories with a view to establishing their pertinence to the 'Brexit and Sport' theme. For although the majority of chapters were written by colleagues from the

DOI: 10.4324/9781003162803-20

legal community, the ambition was always that the book should be equally relevant to political scientists and other social scientists, as well as to the practitioners of sport policy and sport politics. Comparing the different schools of integration theory, Brand, Geeraert and Niemann foresee a significantly declining level of EU-UK transactions, reminding also that UK decision-makers rarely wanted the Union to be in the driver's seat in the policy and politics of sport. Due to the spillover generated by decades of integration, neofunctionalism would suggest some non-disintegrative impulses flowing from Brexit, while supporters of Liberal intergovernmentalism might look for attempts by actors, on either side of the Channel, to reconnect in spite of Brexit, because they would see this as being in their own best interest. Postfunctionalists, on the other hand, might question to what extent sport can become a policy field like any other, while the authors conclude that the ultimate test case with which to ascertain the effect of Brexit on sport policy and politics would be some sort of EU-UK showdown over a sport-related issue. However, they do not regard such a scenario has especially likely.

Second, as regards the applicable 'Rules,' including but not limited to enforceable Union law, *Stefaan Van den Bogaert* has discussed the end of free movement after Brexit with a specific focus on football in Chapter 3. His chapter shows how important free movement law has been to the development of EC/EU sports law and, recognising that Brexit is an unprecedented event in the history of the Union, tries to gauge the likely outcomes of the UK's withdrawal. Estimating that these may still be early days, where effects are difficult to assess, underscores that free movement is generally perceived as one of the greatest achievements of the EU integration process. As this achievement has now been discontinued as far as the UK is concerned, the Premier League might suffer significantly from the absence of direct access to the vast European recruitment pool of football players. He finds the new requirement system for overseas players to be detailed and complex, demanding additional paperwork and administrative costs and signifying a decrease on players recruited from Europe. On the other hand, Brexit could also entice clubs to invest more in home-grown talents, making the game 'more English' again. A similar caesura cannot be found in the subject matter of Chapter 4. Quite on the contrary, *Andrea Cattaneo* has demonstrated that the EU approach to State aid in sport has consistently distinguished between aid supporting structures and activities matching acknowledged public policy objectives (qualifying for flexibility) and aid to professional clubs (calling for a stricter interpretation of the applicable rules). Cattaneo has shown a concordance between the findings made by European competition authorities and courts, on the one hand, and their British counterparts, on the other. Under the terms of the TCA, he expects the applicable law to remain fairly stable, although only the future can tell whether the UK will, after all, wish to diverge from the EU line. For while convergence is likely to persist in the short term, this might cease to apply in the long term. Recent disputes related to Olympic Stadium tenancy issues demonstrate the sensitivity of such subsidies. In a similar vein, in Chapter 5, *Leanne O'Leary*, while acknowledging that the post-Brexit situation puts the UK at liberty to reorient the direction of its employment law and policy, subject only to the level playing field provisions in the TCA, the effect for individual employment rights, including the determination of employee and worker status, will only become apparent as the EU and UK trade relationship develops. While the UK may enshrine a new definition of 'worker' in new legislation, there are no indications that this would imply any sport-specific changes, while any new EU rules would be of no effect in the UK. Because industrial relations are already regulated by national law, the effect of Brexit on trade unions should be nil, whereas possible future legislation repealing the Human Rights Act 1998 would definitely make itself felt, especially if it were to limit the right to collective bargaining and strike action, as well as litigation by trade unions, within an already restrictive British regime on collective labour rights. A far more unambiguous assessment of the expected effects of Brexit was provided, in Chapter 6, by *Seema Patel*, in her exploration of equality and human rights in relation to athletes' sex and gender. While here, too, effects will take time to unfold, Patel recognises that minority rights protection may well be diminished in the absence of the protection offered, in the pre-Brexit context, by Union primary and secondary law, by the Charter of Fundamental Rights (CFA) as well as through their interpretation by the EU courts. The legacy of British EU membership is seen as substantial, and it cannot be taken for granted that continued British membership of the Council of Europe will ensure the sustainability of the status quo level of protection.

Third, with regard to 'stakeholders,' any assessment of the expected or likely effects of Brexit will, by necessity, vary from one case to another. In Chapter 7, *Walter S. Palmer* recounted his experience as a trade unionist representing professional athletes in European Social Dialogue specialised on sports occupations. Palmer stresses the British colleagues' significant experience from national social dialogue and also 'the high opinion that UK representatives had of their labour relations system in sport, despite its obvious shortcomings.' He finds that their departure must have left a void, wondering which national traditions (French, German, Scandinavian or other) will fill the gap. Palmer considers the possibility of a more pro-active role to be played by the EU, in the future, holding sports organisations to account over issues of governance and the rule of law, while he also allows for the possibility of an increasingly confident UK engaging willingly with international sports organisations. Much remains to be seen, Palmer concluded, bearing in mind that the sport sector comprises three different occupational sub-sectors: professional sport, not-for-profit sport and 'active leisure.' For these occupations, European Social Dialogue was limited to a pilot phase, so far, although it might be reinvigorated; whereas the Dialogue continues in the field of professional football. At any rate, the EU legacy appears considerable. Chapter 8, by *Stephen Weatherill*, provides an example of a sport in which the reintroduction of nationality-based restrictions, hitherto forbidden under Union law, is bound to unfold important repercussions. Weatherill emphasises that the British Parliament is at liberty to pass any legislation it now sees fit, meaning that even the current arrangements could change radically. Current restrictions on the granting of work permits for professional players from Europe have the potential to damage British clubs and to weaken them relative to European clubs. On the other hand, Weatherill speculated that lobbying activities could be expected which would aim shake off these new restrictions to make British clubs more competitive again, in relation to their European rivals. In Chapter 9, *Richard Parrish* has shown that, in the case of cricket, which is far less reliant upon recruitment from Europe, the situation varies considerably from that of football. Since 1 January 2021, 'Bosman' (i.e. EU) and 'Kolpak' (i.e. EEA and associated states) players can only be registered with the English Cricket Board (ECB) if the can demonstrate settled or pre-settled status in the UK. Parrish has also revealed how Union law continues extending protection to players from discrimination based on nationality, such as in the Court's recent *Biffi* judgment; although Parrish has noted that the Court did, on that occasion, consider necessary and proportionate restrictions potentially permissible. If anything, the case of cricket serves as an illustration of how variable the financial and other interests of different sports can be.

Fourth comes the dimension of 'Geography,' which in some instances might also have been referred to using the term 'geopolitics.' In her investigation into the transfer of racehorses between the United Kingdom, Ireland and France, in Chapter 10, *Laura Donnellan* has explained how a tripartite agreement (TPA) was used to facilitate these transfers and how its disappearance was a direct consequence of Brexit. As the absence of a solid legal base meant that transports would be fraught with red tape in the shape of health certification and pre-import notifications, the annulment of the TPA has faced stakeholders in the equine sector with considerable challenges. The substantial economic value of the industry does not seem to have warranted any special treatment to protect its interests within the larger Brexit framework, whereas a Bilateral Agreement between Ireland and Northern Ireland would appear to remedy some of the worst shortcomings; although, depending on the Northern Ireland/Ireland Protocol, Donnellan found its position 'precarious.' Another example of the geography of Brexit in the field of sport is discussed by *Grant Jarvie* in Chapter 11. Jarvie has shown that Brexit is likely to affect not only Scottish elite sport but also Scottish community and amateur sport in various ways and to varying degrees. The abrupt changes brought by Brexit represent both threats and opportunities, while Grant has emphasised the combined effects of the threats to the rules-based international order and the potential impact of Brexit. Scotland therefore faces a challenging international context, with the 'triple complexity of a pandemic, Brexit and constitutional challenges' including the possibility of a future Scottish referendum regarding secession from the UK. In their account of the strategies developed by Swiss football clubs in response to their country's place outside the European Union, in Chapter 12, *Zahid Mustafi* and *Emmanuel Bayle* have shown that Swiss clubs have declined since the 1995 ECJ *Bosman* ruling. While a few first-tier clubs have good prospects for participating in European competitions and for earning from centrally marketed TV transmission rights, they are not generally in position to have an impact on European football. Declining revenues have made their situation gradually more difficult.

One likely effect of Brexit would be that fewer Swiss-trained players are likely, under the new British immigration rules, to find employment in the UK. This in turn could improve the standing of Swiss clubs, who have hitherto been exposed to hard competition over players from the 'big five' European countries, and it might also make it easier for Swiss clubs to use home-grown Swiss talent. The final 'Geography' contribution was Chapter 13 by *Borja García* and *Henk Erik Meier*. Under the title 'Brexit and Global Sport Power Europe,' they have discussed the role of the European Union as a regulator of global sport. Drawing on insights from the EU's involvement in international debates and processes regarding the governance of sport, anti-doping and match-fixing, Garcia and Meier acknowledged a certain potential for a more proactive role which the EU could play, while also taking note of the limitations which have manifested themselves so far. A consensus would need to be found among Member States regarding the application of Union law, even if the authors consider it possible that the leverage of the UK could be diminished by Brexit, although the potential of British soft power and sport diplomacy should not be underrated. On balance, they drew the conclusion that the regulatory impact of the EU has often been diluted by the diverging policy preferences of Member States, the ongoing dynamics that favour action within the Council of Europe and the complex network of stakeholders involved (from sport organisations to police agencies). They have also speculated that the departure of the UK from the EU might, here like in many other policy areas, provide the Union with an opportunity to find common ground where British reticence may have had a restraining effect in the past.

Fifth and last comes the 'Conclusion' part of this book. Prior to the present Conclusion, Chapter 14 by *Simon Boyes* has delved in the question of which role can be expected for European Union law in the United Kingdom after Brexit. Boyes has been speculating about the 'the mediative effect of international sports regulations,' pointing to 'residual, "legacy" effects, stemming from nearly five decades of membership; during which the influence of European Union law has grown exponentially, and in which time it has had at least a partial shaping effect on domestic sports regulation.' This implies a reaffirmation of the perpetually dynamic nature of the integration process, including for the Union as a legal community. Notwithstanding the obvious impacts from Brexit, such as the cessation of the applicability of free movement rules, the 'formative and reformative impact of the European Union, through both law and institutional action,' will, according to Boyes, continue to take effect at a global level. The EU will thus continue 'supervising and steering the global sports regulatory environment in a range of key areas,' and the UK cannot reasonably expect to be insulated from these effects.

15.3. EU regulation: underestimated in the sport sector?

The observation made in the Introduction—that British decision-makers seem, more often than not, to have underrated the legal and regulatory nature and capacity the Community or Union—may apply to the generic British-European relationship;. Yet, for the specific purposes of our assessment of the sport sector as a case study in Brexit-related challenges, it does not seem plausible that the same bias would be replicated. Rather, 'EU and sport' debates seem to have been concerned with Community and Union law for a very long time, and the regulatory reach of the EC/EU appears to have been visible to most actors over several decades; instead, it appears to have been at the forefront of many debates, and the material presented by contributors to this book confirms that regulation as at the heart of the sport sector's interface with British EU membership, and hence also with Brexit.

Prior to the entry into force of the Lisbon Treaty (2009), no Treaty article mentioned sport specifically. That non-specific rules of Community law could nevertheless affected sport indirectly was a possibility to be factored in, although one which was recognised only by some academic authors.[1] Sports governing bodies (SGBs) (and public authorities as well) seem to have favoured a 'don't ask, don't tell' approach. Since the 1974 *Walrave* ruling[2] of the Court, it had been established Community law that Treaty provisions certainly applied to their activities to the extent that they constituted economic activities. With its restriction to 'purely sporting' aspects of sport, the Court had left a fair amount of ambiguity which SGBs, understandably and legitimately,[3] took as an indication that there must be areas of *lex sportiva* which would qualify for insulation from the reach of the Treaty. We now know that this is not the case, but only because of the Court's 2006 ruling in *Meca Medina*,[4] in which the Court had set aside a judgment handed down by

1 Weatherill (2016) quotes Weatherill (1989) as well as Giltay Veth (1978) and Ubertazzi (1976) cited therein. We could also refer to Westerkamp (1980) in an effort, at the very least, to demonstrate that categorical myopia was not warranted with regard to the possibility that the private rules of SGBs, in various fields, might be incompatible with Community law, and that its applicability might go far beyond the confines of causa *Walrave* and, finally, that the distinction between economic and non-economic dimensions of sport might not, in the end, insulate SGBs and their rules, *per se*, from the reach of Community (later Union) law. Or to Deselaers (1998) who pointed to the applicability of antitrust law, three years after *Bosman* (where AG Lenz had acknowledged the possibility in principle without the Court using its insights in its judgment, which was based on free movement rules), yet five years before *Meca Medina* (where the Court finally adjudicated its first sports case based on antitrust rules).

2 Judgment of the Court of 12 December 1974. B.N.O. Walrave and L.J.N. Koch v Association Union cycliste internationale, Koninklijke Nederlandsche Wielren Unie and Federación Española Ciclismo. Reference for a preliminary ruling: Arrondissementsrechtbank Utrecht—Netherlands. Case 36–74. ECR 1974 01405. ECLI:EU:C:1974:140.

3 As recognised e.g. by Egger and Stix-Hackl (2002), p. 84. (Christine Stix-Hackl (1957–24 October 2018) served as First Advocate General of the Court (2000–2006) and Alexander Egger was, at the time of writing the paper cited, her legal assistant (*référendaire*).

4 Judgment of the Court (Third Chamber) of 18 July 2006. David Meca-Medina and Igor Majcen v Commission of the European Communities. Case C-519/04 P. ECR 2006 I-06991. ECLI:EU:C:2006:492.

the Court of First Instance (now the General Court),[5] which in turn had largely replicated the doctrine favoured by SGBs. Intermittently, in *Bosman*,[6] the Court had made the (until then) most dramatic incursion into the ambit of privately regulated sporting practices: an incursion which SGBs had been unable to anticipate, as they had been continuously banking on their ability to deploy considerable lobbyistic influence, reaching out to political decision-makers at all relevant levels.[7] Following *Bosman*, after a short period of denial, SGBs had decided to shift tack and 'join them' rather than 'beat them,' developing an approach which sought common ground with EU institutions, rather than challenged the legitimacy of their role.[8] This more conciliatory approach was a rational response to the failed attempts to have far-reaching exemptions for sport written into the Treaty, at the time when the Convention on the Future of the European Union (2001–03) was preparing a draft Constitutional Treaty. Although the Constitution was ultimately rejected by French and Dutch voters, it is noteworthy that text on sport included in the 'Freiburg Draft' of 2003 did not survive into the final text.[9] As opaque as many of these debates may have appeared to outsiders, the essence remained one of a rather pedestrian simplicity: the reach of the 'autonomy' of SGBs as private regulators and the relevance of the proclaimed 'special characteristics' (or 'specificity') of sport. While the latter became part of the language of the Treaty (Art. 165 TFEU) post-Lisbon, it has usually failed to produce the effects expected by SGBs, such as in judgments clarifying the application of free movement (*Bernard*[10]) or State aid rules, be it in relation to State aid via preferential tax treatment;[11] land transactions and land use decisions under municipal and

5 Judgment of the Court of First Instance (Fourth Chamber) of 30 September 2004. David Meca-Medina and Igor Majcen v Commission of the European Communities. Case T-313/02. ECR 2004 II-03291. ECLI:EU:T:2004:282.

6 Judgment of the Court of 15 December 1995. Union royale belge des sociétés de football association ASBL v Jean-Marc Bosman, Royal club liégeois SA v Jean-Marc Bosman and others and Union des associations européennes de football (UEFA) v Jean-Marc Bosman. Reference for a preliminary ruling: Cour d'appel de Liège—Belgium. Case C-415/93. ECR 1995 I-04921. ECLI:EU:C:1995:463.

7 Parensen (1998).

8 García and Weatherill (2012).

9 Weatherill (2017), pp. 144–145.

10 Judgment of the Court (Grand Chamber) of 16 March 2010. Olympique Lyonnais SASP v Olivier Bernard and Newcastle UFC. Reference for a preliminary ruling: Cour de cassation—France. Case C-325/08. ECR 2010 I-02177. ECLI:EU:C:2010:143.

11 See Commission Decision (EU) 2016/2391 (SA.29769) of 4 July 2016. OJ L 357, 28 December 2016, pp. 1–16.—Judgment of the General Court (Fourth Chamber) of 26 February 2019. Athletic Club v European Commission. Case T-679/16. ECLI:EU:T:2019:112.—Judgment of the General Court (Fourth Chamber) of 26 February 2019. Fútbol Club Barcelona v European Commission. Case T-865/16. ECLI:EU:T:2019:113.—Judgment of the General Court (Fourth Chamber) of 26 February 2019. Athletic Club v European Commission. Case T-679/16. ECLI:EU:T:2019:112.—Judgment of the Court (Fifth Chamber) of 4 March 2021. European Commission v Fútbol Club Barcelona. Case C-362/19 P. ECLI:EU:C:2021:169.

regional planning authority;[12] or through financial guarantees,[13] to sport.[14] In one case (*Biffi*[15]), it even produced the exact opposite effect, as the Court deducted that precisely *because* sport is special and has the potential to facilitate people's social integration into their local community, it is of particular importance that its rules should not discriminate against European nationals participating in competitive amateur sport.

15.4. EU sport regulation: direct or indirect?

As we have seen in the preceding paragraph, the horizontal effect of rules enshrined in EC/EU legislation extraneous to, but applicable to, sport has a very long history as a source of consternation and occasional annoyance among sports organisations. Between direct sport regulation and policy (Art. 165 TFEU), and indirect regulation and policy (based on various other Treaty provisions), the indirect version is always bound to affect the sport sector most profoundly, already because the post-Lisbon sport policy framework (Art. 165 TFEU) is one which the Treaty (Art. 6 TFEU) does not allow to use for adopting any legally binding rules. An explicit HEPA policy based on a 2013 Council Recommendation may represent the highest level of EU soft law available;[16] yet it is nevertheless not very effective in changing national practices, away from tradition medals—and events hosting–driven policies, towards more policies targeting ordinary citizens more directly and effectively.[17] The same HEPA policy goals may be pursued more effectively via eligibility rules in EU funding programmes[18] or distinctions made in Commission decisions based on competition law,[19] including in the field of State aid[20] (representing a far bigger volume

12 See Commission Decision (EU) 2016/2393 (SA.33754) of 4 July 2016. OJ C 358, 29 December 2016, pp. 3–24.—Judgment of the General Court (Fourth Chamber) of 22 May 2019. Real Madrid Club de Fútbol v European Commission. Case T-791/16. ECLI:EU:T:2019:346.

13 See Commission Decision 2017/365 (SA.36387) of 4 July 2016. OJ C 365, 2 March 2017, pp. 12–37.—Judgment of the General Court (Fourth Chamber) of 12 March 2020. Valencia Club de Fútbol, SAD v European Commission. Case T-732/16. ECLI:EU:T:2020:98.—Judgment of the General Court (Fourth Chamber) of 20 March 2019. Hércules Club de Fútbol, SAD v European Commission. Case T-766/16. ECLI:EU:T:2019:173.—Judgment of the General Court (Fourth Chamber) of 12 March 2020. Elche Club de Fútbol, SAD v European Commission. Case T-901/16. ECLI:EU:T:2020:97.—Commission v Valencia Club de Fútbol and Spain. Case C-211/20 P (pending).

14 For a discussion of all cases, see Kornbeck (2021b).

15 Judgment of the Court (Third Chamber) of 13 June 2019. TopFit e.V. and Daniele Biffi v Deutscher Leichtathletikverband e.V. Request for a preliminary ruling from the Amtsgericht Darmstadt. Case C-22/18. ECLI:EU:C:2019:497.

16 Kornbeck (2018b).

17 Kornbeck (2021a).

18 Kornbeck (2018a).

19 García et al. (2017).

20 Kornbeck (2019b, 2021b).

of cases than the fields of antitrust and mergers). This reality of sport being affected by Community/Union law without being addressed specifically by it was framed two decades ago, by Walter Tokarski & Dirk Steinbach,[21] at a time when a 'common-market coalition' versus a 'sociocultural coalition'[22] were competing for discursive power over EC/EU sports law and policy. The direct/indirect dichotomy is as relevant in 2021 as it was in 2001.

The dichotomy has been phrased differently by different authors. In taking stock of developments leading up to 2003 (the Constitutional Treaty still had not been rejected by French and Dutch voters), Richard Parrish made assumptions about possible future developments aimed at 'reconciling sport and law'[23] through the 'birth' of 'EU sports law.'[24] In so doing, Parrish introduced a distinction between 'sports and EU law,' essentially consisting in applying Single Market legislation to sport which 'did not create a discrete area of sport law,'[25] and 'EU sports law and policy'[26] proper, through 'bureaucratic measures,' 'legislative measures,' 'ECJ jurisprudence' as well as 'Commission quasi-jurisprudence.'[27] Stephen Weatherill, for his part, distinguished between the 'negative law' of the Union, including free movement and competition rules,[28] as opposed to its 'positive law' in the shape of soft law based on Art. 165 TFEU.[29] Yet Weatherill also warned that the 'calculatedly vague aspects' of this article suggested that the 'openness is deliberate,' with the vagueness requiring 'the elaboration of institutional practice.'[30] Whether a policy of strategic ambiguity has been applied is a matter for future historians to decide. It seems, however, that Community/Union has been relatively successful in acting as a supranational sports regulator, albeit in a limited number of areas (the limited impact on anti-doping governance illustrates the limitations inherent to its approach) (see Chapter 13 by *García & Meier*).

> The EU can claim some credit for these shifting governance styles. It has successfully managed to export its own approach to policymaking, which requires the consultation of affected parties and relevant stakeholders, to the sport system. // From the promotion of good governance principles, to the competence expressly granted to the EU to promote cooperation between bodies responsible for sport, to the impact of the activity of the Commission and

21 Tokarski and Steinbach (2001), pp. 69, 89–90; cf. Tokarski et al. (2004), pp. 62; Tokarski et al. (2009), pp. 48, 79; Van den Bogaert and Vermeersch (2006).
22 Parrish (2003), p. 250.
23 *Ibid.*, p. 160.
24 *Ibid.*, p. 197.
25 *Ibid.*, p. 205.
26 *Ibid.*, p. 207.
27 *Ibid.*, pp. 206–211.
28 Weatherill (2017), pp. 57–64.
29 *Ibid.*, pp. 64–67.
30 *Ibid.*, p. 66.

> the judgment of the Court of Justice, the EU has progressively shifted the hierarchical nature of the sports governance system towards more horizontal and inclusive approach. The sports pyramid is a different shape as a result.[31]

In pre-Lisbon times, it may be true that the general population almost only knew about the 'indirect' blend of Community regulation and policy,[32] while it is equally true that is was 'more spectacular' than the 'direct' variant,[33] while even today the general population may not be very aware of the role of the EU as a sport regulator. Yet this may owe more to the fact that a regulatory model relying largely on horizontal application effects is bound to be less vertical and more horizontal in nature, even if a certain limited 'horizontalisation' has taken place over time (with Art. 165 TFEU the most visible result of this process).[34] In relation to Brexit, the relative invisibility may have led to sport not being taken into account very often in the Brexit negotiations: an impression arising from reading the process and output of these negotiations, but also one which would require a more specific, empirical assessment for a more outspoken analysis to be feasible.

15.5. EU sport regulation: Brussels effect or Brexit dividend?

If EU regulation is relevant, as affirmed above, this insight prompts the question of what effects (whether beneficial or detrimental) can be expected to ensue once Brexit has been enacted. Acknowledging a 'Brussels effect' necessarily implies the conceptual possibility of a 'Brexit dividend' to be reaped by escaping the regulatory reach of the EU: a realisation imposing itself regardless of the observer's own views and preferences as regards the desirability of EU membership versus EU exit.[35]

In a series of empirical-legal research projects undertaken over half a decade, Anu Bradford and her colleagues at Columbia University have shown that the European Union is far more than a 'paper tiger': its regulation in such areas as competition policy, antitrust law, data protection and the regulation of the digital economy has a great following worldwide, and often more than that of the USA. They have found the global reach of the Chicago School's influence on antitrust to be rather limited,[36] as opposed to the ordoliberalism of the EU approach.[37] The Australian privacy lawyer Graham Greenleaf has demonstrated a massive influence

31 Cattaneo and Parrish (2020), pp. 157–158, at 422.
32 Tokarski et al. (2004), p. 61.
33 Groll (2005), p. 95.
34 Kornbeck (2006).
35 I am indebted to Ardi Kolah for allowing me to use this concept originally formulated in an earlier version of his proposal for doctoral research at Queen's University Belfast (QUB) regarding a thesis on data protection law in Northern Ireland versus the Republic of Ireland.
36 Bradford et al. (2020).
37 Bradford and Chilton (2018), Bradford et al. (2019).

of EU data protection law worldwide, and particularly in South East Asia,[38] and Anu Bradford has posited the existence of a 'Brussels effect.'[39] Bradford observed a 'deeply underestimated aspect of European power that the discussion on globalisation and power politics overlooks,' yet with a 'tangible impact on the everyday lives of citizens around the world.'[40] In many cases, the 'Brussels effect' can be traced back to companies' and countries' desire to gain access to the sizeable and lucrative Single Market of the EU:

> When assessing the value of market access, foreign corporations also consider the adjustment costs that are necessary to enter the market. A foreign producer will have an incentive to comply with the importing jurisdiction's strict standard when the benefits of market access outweigh the adjustment costs. The larger the strict importing market and the lower the adjustment costs relative to the benefits of market access, the more likely that adjustment will take place. In the case of consumer goods, the benefits of market access are determined by the number and affluence of potential consumers of that product as well as by the opportunity costs of forgoing those consumers. These opportunity costs are particularly high when demand in the corporation's home market or in alternative third markets is limited. The adjustment costs can consist of initial setup costs and recurring compliance costs. They vary with the significance of cross-border differentials that determine the degree of adjustment and various other compliance costs associated with market access, including licenses or approval processes.[41]

As Bradford readily admits, the Brussels effect has not been equally strong in all sectors, and EU values and human rights have not been equally well exported to all regions of the world.[42] Yet, this finding does not as such invalidate the 'Brussels effect' in those areas where it has come to bear. It is equally important to avoid liberal pipedreams about an EU being always and everywhere wed to multilateralism,

38 Greenleaf (2012, 2018, 2021).

39 Bradford (2013, 2020).

40 Bradford (2013), p. 1: 'Contrary to [an identified] prevalent perception, this Article highlights a deeply underestimated aspect of European power that the discussion on globalisation and power politics overlooks: Europe's unilateral power to regulate global markets. The European Union sets the global rules across a range of areas, such as food, chemicals, competition and the protection of privacy. EU regulations have a tangible impact on the everyday lives of citizens around the world. Few Americans are aware that EU regulations determine the makeup they apply in the morning, the cereal they eat for breakfast, the software they use on their computer, and the privacy settings they adjust on their Facebook page. And that's just before 8:30 AM. The EU also sets the rules governing the interoffice phone directory they use to call a coworker. EU regulations dictate what kind of air conditioners Americans use to cool their homes and why their children no longer find soft plastic toys in their McDonald's Happy Meals.'

41 *Ibid.*, p. 12.

42 *Ibid.*, p. 58.

while it may instead be 'selectively supporting multilateralism in areas where it lacks unilateral power.'[43] The extent to which its State aid rules have been infused into its bilateral trade agreements of the 'second generation' (post-2006) varies considerably and shows a direct correlation with the bargaining strength of its opposite numbers: the prospect of missing access to a more lucrative market has taught EU negotiators not to overplay their hand.[44] Yet these and similar limitations cannot diminish the importance of the very real impact which the 'normative market Europe'[45] has had in many fields:

> The EU's regulatory clout shows that the EU can be a superpower without a super state. [. . .] The more the EU bolsters the authority of the UN Security Council, the more the EU can constrain the exercise of unilateral power by the United States. But when it comes to the regulation of global markets, the EU can go it alone and is hence less concerned about pursuing multilateral institutional cooperation.[46]

If EU is 'already a superpower and, importantly, a superpower of a meaningful kind,'[47] this is largely due to the primacy and direct of Union law: the quasi-statehood of the Union in those areas of policy and regulation where Member States have conferred upon the Union, substantial and meaningful powers habitually reserved for sovereign states. It may be a superpower without a state, a model of governance without a government,[48] a proto-state without a country or a polity without a *demos*, yet the impacts are often astonishingly concrete in the real world. This is the reason why the reach of European law has been resented in some quarters, and not only for emotional and symbolic but also for very practical reasons. Brexit was and is not only about regaining a feeling of control, as evidenced in the rather costly decision to reintroduce the old British blue passport—which to the chagrin of some nostalgic people, did no resemble the pre-1980s model very much, in part because International Air Transport Association (IATA) requirements made alignment with the burgundy EU passport inevitable. But Brexit is also about regaining sovereignty over policies and standards, some of which risks seriously disrupting the level playing field vis-à-vis the EU. All of this confirms that the EU is not a paper tiger; yet what do these insights mean in the field sport? For

43 *Ibid.*, p. 66.
44 For a discussion, see Neumann (2019).
45 See Geeraert and Drieskens (2016), as well as the overview of 'normative power' or 'normative market' scholarship, starting with Manners (2002), as well as for an application of this explanatory model to the case of sport.
46 Bradford (2013), p. 66.
47 *Ibid.*, p. 67.
48 For a negative application of this theoretical concept, in an analysis of the political governance of the Eurozone crisis, see Heise (2012). For a more neutral application to the case of sport, see Kornbeck (2020a).

we ought to remind ourselves that the regulatory effects of Union law are variable and sector-dependent.

A 'Brexit dividend' has been promised in various fields of regulation, with a UK relieved of the purported shackles of EU regulation being set to bounce with renewed energy towards unheard of levels of growth and dynamism.[49] Critical scholars have started looking for areas of regulation in which a dividend could be suspected (for those adhering to extreme neoliberal views[50]), as lower standards would make the UK more competitive than the EU, including social policy[51] or public procurement,[52] while others have pointed out that the loss of opportunities offered by EU membership might offset (the countervalue of) any such dividend, such as in regional development (through the disappearance of EU regional grants).[53] While the chapters in this book have illustrated some of the actual as well as potential effects of discontinuing EU regulation in the British sport sector (effectively the 'Brussels effect'), future research could also look more specifically into the (expected, imagined or merely possible) gains and losses, when British sports are able to follow deviating regulatory models (the 'Brexit dividend').

However, Brexit effects can be felt not only within organised, professionalised and commercialised sports, but also within amateur and community sports (see e.g. Chapter 11 by Jarvie). As the subsequent section will show—in a less scholarly and more personal way—they can also be felt outside the sport sector itself, yet within a sector related to sports, such as the sport science branch of academia.

15.6. *Obiter dictum:* Brexit and sport science departments in UK higher education institutions

Whether in journal articles, monographs or edited books, introductions often serve to delineate a topic as much as to identify the topic itself: defining such ground as the text does not aim to cover, as much as ground to be covered. In this context, the present Conclusion would be incomplete without mentioning a chapter which was dear to my heart but which had to be abandoned, by its authors, for reasons which are directly Brexit-induced and deeply saddening. Initially, three European colleagues employed at two different UK universities had submitted the following abstract which we had agreed on as a basis for them to write their chapter:

> Amid a context of neoliberal forces, enhanced labour mobility, increasingly fierce educational competition and a globalised marketplace, the United

49 For a generic discussion, see e.g. Rosamond (2020), p. 1095.

50 For an academic discussion of the Leave camp's reliance on neoliberal thought, including ideas from the Mont Pélerin Society, see Hölscher and Howard-Jones (2021).

51 Stewart et al. (2020).

52 Sanchez-Graells (2021).

53 Jessop (2018), p. 1742.

Kingdom's universities have made evermore substantive investments into internationalisation. Such activities have included growing and fortifying transnational research networks and collaborations, resourcing satellite campuses in emergent and strategically significant market zones, undertaking lucrative student recruitment drives, and remodelling curricula to broaden course content, appeal and engagement with wider audiences. Notwithstanding long-held global reputations and prestige, in these processes, higher education (HE) providers in the UK have not been able to be complacent. While, for example, the influx of international recruitment to the nation remains high (c.500,000 international students per year), the consistent flow of student migration is vulnerable. As both Brexit (the focus of this chapter) and, more recently, COVID-19 impacts and demographic downturns in undergraduate intake cohorts have shown, Universities' reliance on robust internationalisation strategies and structures remains important. Approaches and understandings about the values of internationalisation, invariably, differ across and within UK HE. Subsequently, not all the effects, risks and opportunities of internationalisation are borne out equally among HE members.

In this chapter, we focus on the domain of sport-related studies, specifically the Sport Management subject area, where the UK has maintained its international leadership and dominance. To note, 41 of the UK's Sports departments rank in the global top 300 Sport Science Schools and Departments (Shanghai International Rankings, 2018)[54] and sport management student recruitment, research and collaborative activity remains fundamental to this status. Sport studies—with its emphasis on the popular and periodic nature of elite and mass-participatory sport, and on related areas of physical activity, human performance, health, leisure and recreation—remains a vibrant landscape. Nonetheless, as we investigate, like elsewhere the onset of and processes associated with Brexit has [worked and] does work against this growth and potential. In the first instance, by: 1) inhibiting the free-movement and financially amiable conditions EU students currently enjoy; 2) complicating and thwarting valuable opportunities for international student work placements (a fundamental component of UK Sport Management offerings); 3) adversely affecting the appeal and ability of the UK to attract and recruit high calibre international and EU academic staff; and, 4) collaborative research enterprise. Drawing on extant data sets, document analysis and personal reflections, we examine the interconnected trinity of international student recruitment, European staff resource, and research networking. Ultimately, we suggest that, in the absence of foreseeable UK government and policy change, the current epoch affords ideal opportunities to sustain transnational

54 See Statistics for Shanghai Ranking's Global Ranking of Sport Science Schools and Departments 2018, https://www.lebde.org/Special-Focus-Institution-Ranking/Statistics-for-Sport-Science-Schools-and-Departments-2018.html (accessed 22.10.2021)

advocacy for unity and stronger lobbying within HE for international investment, sustainability and security.

My colleagues had intended the following structure for their paper:

8. Brexit, Higher Education and UK Sport Management futures: realities, opportunities and possibilities
8.1. Intro: The internationalisation of sports studies within the UK
8.2. International student recruitment
8.3. EU work placements
8.4. Attraction and retention of international employees.
8.5. Research grants/collaboration.

This definitely looked like a promising chapter: one which I was looking forward to receiving. All authors had asked to submit by 1 March 2021, at a time when the early stages of the COVID-19 (Coronavirus) pandemic made many colleagues more productive than usual. This was to change as 2020 ebbed out and 2021 commenced and, while a few authors submitted in February, the vast majority could not meet the deadlines, with many sharing very personal stories of teleworking conditions, in many cases with young children studying online. I agreed to numerous extensions, with many colleagues insisting that this was exceptional for them, which I knew it was. Of the three anonymous colleagues who had agreed to write the higher education chapter, one withdrew from the project while the remaining two colleagues still wished to contribute. Increasingly, these two colleagues came to feel the stress of surviving in post-Brexit British academia, and felt it impossible to address the relevant issues on scholarly terms. One lost his long-term academic position but managed to find a new post at another British university, while the other colleague stuck to their extant post. It was agreed that they could submit a personal essay rather than a fully neutral academic paper. Yet while they both coped, in various ways, their problems were directly Brexit-related and Brexit-induced: evidence of the mechanisms which they had set out to describe and analyse in their planned Chapter 8. On 20 April 2021, however, I received a deeply saddening email message including the following remarks:

> I am gutted to inform you that this is not the news you would like to hear unfortunately. And we are equally disappointed by that . . . Under the current circumstances of extreme teaching overload in a—new to us institution—teaching new material, we are unable to produce a high standard contribution. [. . .] Having been forced to change employer in the middle of a pandemic after 12 year at [name of university] and at the same time having to write about a topic such as Brexit that is sentimentality heavy for us, it is just too much to handle.
>
> We do not want to delay further the publication of the book. We were honoured by your invitation to form part of this adventure and we feel really sorry that we cannot under these circumstances produce a good outcome.

> Our students are extremely stressed in this climate of COVID-induced remotely teaching, and they keep asking us for more and more tutorials for the dissertations, and we are inundated by additional meetings, extra tutorials, and more and more support that we have been asked to provide them. We tried to get some time and energy to focus on our chapter but line managers have clearly asked us to prioritise our students for the next couple of months. Our sincere apologies again Jacob, but under these circumstances we are not able to have a clear 'author' mind and produce a good standard manuscript. Apologies for letting you down this time. We hope that you will understand that this is not what we have hoped either.

And also:

> Another aspect that particularly has affected me is the withdrawal from Erasmus + sport programme. As you probably know our previous University was one of the first to have benefited by the 'Participatory actions for sport' programme back in 2009–2010 and which I led on behalf of my ex-School. Since then I was able to lead three more successful Erasmus + Sport programmes as CI in partnership with other European colleagues. These solid and synergies benefit mutually my British University as they provided the means to collect some valuable data that later on were transformed in scientific articles and constituted the base for further research and professional practise funding.
>
> Unfortunately, first the uncertainty and later on the confirmation of the [nefarious] news regarding Brexit affected negatively long-established collaborations with valuable EU partners who progressively ceased from asking to collaborate with us.
>
> It's a shame for the openness of the scientific spirit that has dominated British academia over the centuries. My previous department has already lost two magnificent scholars who have now moved to other EU countries to continue their brilliant career.
>
> Me too since Brexit happened. I have been approached by two EU Universities, and I am currently thinking seriously to accept an offer to move to a very well-established EU institution who is willing to recruit me.

I asked my colleagues for permission to quote—anonymously, of course—from their email message, and I decided to bring it as part of the present Introduction. There is no better illustration that these two colleagues had defined a truly valuable contribution for this book; it would have been authentic, instructive and significant, even if it had been presented in a possibly less scholarly style. May this also serve as a reminder that academics are human beings and citizens, too, as well as partners, parents and much else. Even if we believe in disinterested scholarship—and the present editor is someone with a clear preference for the 'sine ira et studio' defined by Tacitus,[55] as opposed to the positionality of today's identity politics, social justice and critical theory paradigms—personal testimonies can definitely be enriching, including at the heuristic and epistemological one. There is much to learn from Brexit, including on the European side where adjustments may also be needed.[56] The present book does not include a chapter on the effects of Brexit on British higher education in the thematic field of sport science and related disciplines, although it could have—and should have. Their personal recount largely confirms what has been reported in mainstream research by psychologists specialising on well-being in the workplace, regarding effects which Brexit may have upon European workers;[57] which in turn seem to vindicate insights gained from research in the fields of social policy[58] and social work.[59]

15.7. Concluding remarks

As this Conclusion has shown, the chapters of the present book have revealed various degrees and constellations of regulatory legacies and challenges which, in the wake of Brexit, are making themselves felt in the sport sector, or which can be expected to do so over the coming months and years. While the resulting image is a patchy one—with every field of regulation presenting its own peculiarities and with each sport being a microcosm of its own—it is fair to say that all chapters have demonstrated a significant legacy of 57 years of British EU membership, while the challenges arising from its discontinuation are variable. In contrast to the examples from mainstream British policy-making provided in the Introduction, claims that the regulatory capacity of the EU had been underrated in the field of sport would be entirely unwarranted; rather, the ability of the Union to affect the sector would appear to have been observed and taken into account by the relevant actors early on and, from then on, continuously. Finally, and with reference to dichotomy proposed by Tokarski and colleagues in the early 2000s,[60] what has affected British sport up until 2020—and what may continue to do so even beyond 2020–21, if we are to believe Simon Boyes (Chapter 14)—is not the explicit and direct brand of EU sport regulation and policy (based on Art. 165 TFEU and with a rather modest regulatory potential) but rather the horizontal effect of rules extraneous to the sector but nevertheless applicable to it. This effect has been observable since the Court's 1974 *Walrave*[61] ruling and manifested itself again in 2019, in a most

55 Tacitus, Annals I.1.
56 Bourgeot (2020).
57 Weinberg et al. (2020).
58 Hantrais (2019).
59 For a rich account of Polish working women's experiences with British social services, see Duda-Mikulin (2019).
60 Tokarski and Steinbach (2001).
61 Judgment of the Court of 12 December 1974. B.N.O. Walrave and L.J.N. Koch v Association Union cycliste internationale, Koninklijke Nederlandsche Wielren Unie and Federación Española

impressive way in the context of its *Biffi*[62] ruling, as a renewed illustration of the power of the horizontal effect of Union law.[63]

What this book could not provide, *inter alia*, would have been empirical studies of the interplay between British negotiating strategy and style; generic Brexit policy choices and negotiation outcomes; and the outcomes specifically achieved (or not) in the policy field of sport. If the UK in general—and the financial industry in the City of London in particular[64]—feared becoming the 'rule-taker' of Europe, then it would nevertheless seem probably that it would have applied differentiated strategies and styles, from one sector to another. In May 2021, in the wake of the forced landing of an EU flight in Minsk, Belarus, the UK was eager to use its brand-new HMS Queen Elizabeth full-size aircraft carrier as a backdrop for a press conference of Nato Secretary General Jens Stoltenberg and Nato top brass, including two senior officers of the Roland Navy and the RAF. While this media performance may be interpreted as a nod to the USA as well as an affirmation of British exceptionalism in a European context (France having then only one full-size carrier, and one commissioned a full 20 years earlier),[65] the speech of First Sea Lord Admiral Tony Radakin used extremely inclusive language, emphasising that the UK had not chosen to be on its own. Yet British Brexit negotiators deployed strategies and tactics which did not always (if at all) match the analysis and advice of civil servants, military officers and other experts and professionals. Their approach to Europe was largely a reflection of domestic politics and, as a study based on confidential interviews with British leaders,[66] has shown, symptomatic of typically Anglo-Saxon, adversarial politics generated by majoritarian electoral systems and an absence of coalition governments: the exact opposite of the consensus-seeking EU.[67] Scholarship from

Ciclismo. Reference for a preliminary ruling: Arrondissementsrechtbank Utrecht—Netherlands. Case 36–74. ECR 1974 01405. ECLI:EU:C:1974:140.

62 Judgment of the Court (Third Chamber) of 13 June 2019. TopFit e.V. and Daniele Biffi v Deutscher Leichtathletikverband e.V. Request for a preliminary ruling from the Amtsgericht Darmstadt. Case C-22/18. ECLI:EU:C:2019:497.

63 Lindholm and Parrish (2020).

64 James and Quaglia (2020).

65 See the article Secretary General visits HMS Queen Elizabeth on NATO exercise Steadfast Defender. 27 May. 2021. Last updated: 27 May. 2021 20:28, www.nato.int/cps/en/natohq/news_184210.htm, as well as the video clip included.

66 Martill and Staiger (2021).

67 *Ibid.*, p. 272: Our discussion above has highlighted a number of ideational factors, broadly specific to the UK, which can be said to have contributed to the British decision to adopt a hard bargaining strategy, including an individualist ideology, adversarial political culture, weak socialisation into European norms, misperceptions of bargaining power, and pre-existing 'divide and rule' routines: First, the nature of the UK's democratic institutions and, in particular, the 'Westminster model' of parliamentary democracy inculcates an adversarial form of politics which—when it impinges on international negotiations—works against the British norm of cautious diplomacy. Second, neither the British elite nor public have internalised the normative aspects of European identity, leading to a widespread and pervasive view of the EU—and the negotiations—as a transactional and

the UK has focused on possible connections between the UK's experience of running the world's biggest empire and its reluctance to join the EC/EU as an ordinary member,[68] on the steady decline in global influence from the 1956 Suez crisis and until Brexit[69] or on the reluctance of Theresa May, as a Prime Minister, to choose a more consensus-driven negotiating style.[70] While some 'Remainer' or 'Remoaner' literature may be biased by liberal ideas and unable to grasp more complex motivations and behaviours on the part of Brexiters, as well as those who simply had to implement the relevant decisions, a worthy research task would consist in investigating how sport chapters of Brexit were negotiated, as compared with other areas of regulation and policy. Was sport neglected or not? If it were, this would be a striking finding for a country whose sport sector—or 'industry' as it is often called in the UK—has been so successful and contributed to massively to wealth and jobs creation, private and public sector revenue, as well to projecting a positive image of the UK (what in the 1990s was known as 'Cool Britannia'). Neglecting sport would, in the case of the UK, be tantamount to neglecting a seldom and valuable heirloom. Such research would, however, clearly be for empirical researchers from the social sciences to conduct because, while document analysis would no doubt be essential, it would need to be supported by interviews. This in turn raises the question what Brexit means for 'EU sport studies',[71] 'EU sports law studies'[72] and 'EU sport politics/policy/policy studies.'[73]

Returning to the safe ground of regulation, as investigated in this book, our chapters could not cover all potentially relevant aspects of EU regulation. The most obvious case of omission may be that of competition policy and antitrust law, where an administrative complaint brought by two athletes against the International Skating Union's (ISU) selection rules triggered a highly visible Commission

zero-sum endeavour. Third, perceptions of Britain's bargaining power have been far greater than an objective rendering of UK capabilities would endorse, reinforcing the belief that hard bargaining is an appropriate strategy. Indeed, the misestimation is clear in multiple respects: British influence is routinely overstated, unviable alternatives to a deal regularly cited, and the extent of domestic cohesion over-emphasised. Fourth, partisanship matters, and the conservative ideology of statecraft, ascendant in British politics in the aftermath of the referendum has favoured forceful bargaining strategies and valorised the perception of strength as tools for achieving a distributionally beneficial outcome. Fifth, the negotiations have been characterised by a fall-back on pre-existing routines based around the success of divide-and-rule strategies in previous rounds of negotiations, reinforced by a belief that EU unity would fail to hold.

68 See e.g. Sanghera (2021).

69 Stephens (2020).

70 Seldon and Newell (2020).

71 Kornbeck (2013).

72 Boyes (2012); Weatherill (2010, 2017, 2018).

73 Lösche (2010).

decision,[74] which was tried by the General Court on 16 December 2020.[75] An appeal has been brought against this ruling (by ISU, not the Commission) before the Court,[76] all of which confirms that antitrust remains one of the most relevant areas of EU regulation in relation to the sport sector.[77] That the EU possesses such power by virtue of the Treaty is significant for, as a US author notes in an introduction to global sports law, antitrust may be the single most effective remedy against excessive powers wielded by sports governing bodies (SGBs).[78] An antitrust chapter would have seemed a natural addition to the present book, yet not all that seemed desirable could be achieved in the end, especially as the editor and his publisher agreed that the book ought to be published in 2021 to avoid obsolescence. The second most natural candidate for a chapter, which was not secured in the end, would have been a chapter on data protection, which could have been expanded to comprise other (not necessarily digital) aspects of privacy. In anti-doping, data protection is a field of regulation in which the EU has made it clout felt, especially in the years 2008–2014, when the present editor was the Commission's one and only full-time anti-doping coordinator.[79] Brexit challenges in the field of anti-doping (arguably in area in which the EU has not had much of an impact, as recognised by García and Meier in this book)[80] and other aspects of integrity protection, including corruption[81] could certainly deserve an assessment in their own right. The same applies, *mutatis mutandis*, to a more generic discussion of the protection of human rights and fundamental rights;[82] intellectual property and sports image rights;[83] transfers, sports agents and the protection of athletes and players who are minors;[84] the promotion of health-enhancing physical activity (HEPA) as a substitute to traditional public policy in the field of sport and

74 Decision C (2017) 8240 final. Commission Decision of 8.12.2017 relating to proceedings under Article 101 of the Treaty on the Functioning of the European Union (the Treaty) and Article 53 of the EEA Agreement Case AT.40208—International Skating Union's Eligibility rules (Only the English text is authentic). http://ec.europa.eu/competition/antitrust/cases/dec_docs/40208/40208_1384_5.pdf

75 Judgment of the General Court (Fourth Chamber, Extended Composition) of 16 December 2020. International Skating Union v European Commission. Case T-93/18. ECLI:EU:T:2020:610.—For a discussion of the Commission decision challenged before the General Court, see e.g. Kornbeck (2019a), Pijetlovic (2018), Szcyszak (2018b).

76 International Skating Union v Commission. Case C-124/21 P (pending). Appeal brought on 26 February 2021. OJ C 163, 3 May 2021, pp. 19–21.

77 For an authoritative summary, see Pijetlovic (2018), Szyszczak (2018a, 2018b).

78 Ross (2021), pp. 80–83.

79 For a more unbiased account than the present editor might be able to provide, see Waddington (2010). See also Kornbeck (2018a, 2020b).

80 For a summary, see Anderson (2018).

81 Schenk (2018).

82 Boyes (2018).

83 Coors (2018).

84 De Marco (2018).

the potential to use the HEPA paradigm as a corrective and alternative to traditional sports policies driven by the desire to earn medals for nation-states and/or to host international events;[85] sustainable financing;[86] volunteering;[87] EU funding programmes for community sport; as well as the prevention of stadium violence.[88]

The 'Europeanisation' of sport has not happened in isolation from macro-level trends affecting the modus operandi of sports, at different levels, both inside and outside the European Union. As a result, 'EU sports law' has developed as a recognisable sub-discipline.[89] Over the past half-century, such trends have included democratisation, commercialisation, professionalisation, commodification and politicisation.[90] At different stages of this era, the Community/Union has engaged with sport in various ways, sometimes (as in the case of ECJ/CJEU/TFI/GC[91] case law) actually confirming these trends instead of applying the brakes on them. Yet the 'Europeanisation' of sport (whatever it means in practical terms) is not free from being influenced by such trends as populism, or indeed by Brexit.[92] The veracity of such realisations is confirmed by insights such as those furnished in the chapters of this book.

References

Anderson, J. (2018) The EU's role on doping in sport. In: Anderson, J.; Parrish, R. & García García, B. (eds) *Research Handbook on EU Sports Law and Policy*. Cheltenham: Edward Elgar, 79–97.

Anderson, J.; Parrish, R. & García García, B. (eds) (2018) *Research Handbook on EU Sports Law and Policy*. Cheltenham: Edward Elgar.

Bourgeot, R. (2020) Brexit adds to Europe's need for economic rebalancing and technological impetus. In: Bongardt, A.; Talani, L.S. & Torres, F. (eds) *The Politics and Economics of Brexit*. Cheltenham: Edward Elgar, pp. 181–203.

Boyes, S. (2012) Sports law: Its history and growth and the development of key sources. *Legal Information Management*, 12:2, 86–91.

Boyes, S. (2018) Human rights at the intersection of EU law and sport. In: Anderson, J.; Parrish, R. & García García, B. (eds) *Research Handbook on EU Sports Law and Policy*. Cheltenham: Edward Elgar, 120–138.

Bradford, A. (2013) The brussels effect. *Northwestern University Law Review*, 107:1, 1–68.

Bradford, A. (2020) *The Brussels Effect: How the European Union Rules the World*. Oxford: Oxford University Press.

85 Kornbeck (2018b)
86 Ó'Conaill (2018).
87 Partington (2018).
88 Tsoukala (2018).
89 Boyes (2012), Miège (2017), Weatherill (2017), Anderson et al. (2018), Cattaneo and Parrish (2020).
90 Scheerder (2020).
91 European Court of Justice, Court of Justice of the European Union, Court of First Instance (1989–2009), General Court (2009-present).
92 Porro et al. (2020).

Bradford, A. & Chilton, A. (2018) Competition law around the world from 1889 to 2010: The competition law index. *Journal of Competition Law & Economics* 14:3, 393–432.

Bradford, A.; Chilton, A. & Lancieri, F. (2020) The Chicago school's limited influence on international antitrust. *University of Chicago Law Review*, 87:2 (2020), 297–313.

Bradford, A.; Chilton, A.; Linos, K. & Weaver, A. (2019) The global dominance of European competition law over American Antitrust law. *Journal of Empirical Legal Studies*, 16:4, 731–766.

Cattaneo, A. & Parrish, R. (2020) *Sports Law in the European Union*. Alphen aan den Rijn: Kluwer (International Encyclopaedia of Laws, Sports Law—Suppl. 80).

Coors, C. (2018) Harmonisation and diversity: Trends and challenges in European sports image rights law. In: Anderson, J.; Parrish, R. & García García, B. (eds) *Research Handbook on EU Sports Law and Policy*. Cheltenham: Edward Elgar, 228–245.

De Marco, N. (2018) Transfers, agents and minors. In: Anderson, J.; Parrish, R. & García García, B. (eds) *Research Handbook on EU Sports Law and Policy*. Cheltenham: Edward Elgar, 382–409.

Deselaers, W. (1998) Sportverbände und Europäisches Kartellrecht. *Wirtschaft und Wettbewerb (WuW)*, 48:10, 947–954.

Duda-Mikulin, E.A. (2019) *EU Migrant Workers, Brexit and Precarity: Polish Women's Perspectives from Inside the UK*. Bristol: Policy Press.

Egger, A. & Stix-Hackl, C. (2002) Sport and competition law: A never-ending story? *European Competition Law Review*, 23:2, 81–91.

García, B.; Vermeersch, A. & Weatherill, S. (2017) A new horizon in European sports law: The application of the EU state aid rules meets the specific nature of sport. *European Competition Journal*, 13:1, 28–61.

García, B. & Weatherill, S. (2012) Engaging with the EU in order to minimise its impact: Sport and the negotiation of the treaty of Lisbon. *Journal of European Public Policy*, 19:2, 238–256.

Geeraert, A. & Drieskens, E. (2016) Normative market Europe: The EU as a force for good in international sports governance? *Journal of European Integration*, 39:1, 79–94.

Giltay Veth, J.P. (1978) Uitsluiting van buitenlandse voetballers: mogelijk binnen de EEG? *Nederlands Juristenblad*, 53:504–513.

Greenleaf, G. (2012) The influence of European data privacy standards outside Europe: Implications for globalization of convention 108. *International Data Privacy Law*, 2:2, 68–92.

Greenleaf, G. (2018) 2017–2018 further update to graham Greenleaf's Asian data privacy laws—trade and human rights perspectives, 15 November. https://ssrn.com/abstract=3285086.

Greenleaf, G. (2021) How far can convention 108+ 'globalise'? Prospects for Asian accessions. *Computer Law & Security Review*, 40:105414, 1–12.

Groll, M. (2005) *Transnationale Sportpolitik. Analyse und Steuerungsansatz sportpolitischer Interaktionen*. Aachen: Meyer & Meyer Verlag (Sportforum; 14).

Hantrais, L. (2019) *What Brexit Means for EU and UK Social Policy*. Bristol: Policy Press.

Heise, A. (2012) Governance without government. *International Journal of Political Economy*, 41:2, 42–60.

Hölscher, J. & Howard-Jones, P. (2021) Brexit: The lure of the neoliberal thought collective. In: Andreff, W. (ed) *Comparative Economic Studies in Europe: A Thirty-Year Review*. Cham: Palgrave Macmillan, pp. 171–189.

James, S. & Quaglia, L. (2020) Rule maker or rule taker? Brexit, finance and UK regulatory autonomy. *International Political Science Review*, November. doi:10.1177/0192512120967380

Jessop, B. (2018) Neoliberalization, uneven development, and Brexit: Further reflections on the organic crisis of the British state and society. *European Planning Studies*, 26:9, 1728–1746.

Kornbeck, J. (2006) Sport und EG/EU—Ein horizontales oder vertikales Thema? Eine Zwischenbilanz der ersten dreißig Jahre (1974–2004). *Sport & Gesellschaft*, 3:1, 81–103.

Kornbeck, J. (2013) The normality of EU sport policy studies: Disciplinary locus in political science, sport science or elsewhere? *Acta Universitatis Carolinae—Kinanthropologica*, 49:1, 5–16.

Kornbeck, J. (2018a) An exemplary illustration of the distinction between private life and data protection (Art. 7–8 CFR): The ECHR's joint decision in FNASS v France and Longo v France (Art. 8 ECHR). *Journal of Data Protection and Privacy*, 2:2, 116–130.

Kornbeck, J. (2018b) Health-friendly sport policy: An emerging soft law doctrine. In: Anderson, J.; Parrish, R. & García García, B. (eds) *Research Handbook on EU Sports Law and Policy*. Cheltenham: Edward Elgar, pp. 49–78.

Kornbeck, J. (2019a) Specificity, monopoly and solidarity in the European commission's ISU (International Skating Union) decision: Anything new under the sun? *Journal of European Competition Law & Practice*, 10:2, 71–79.

Kornbeck, J. (2019b) State aid and access to sport—lessons for VAT law? *European State Aid Law Quarterly*, 18:2, 138–156.

Kornbeck, J. (2020a) *Die Konsolidierung des Politikfelds Sport durch die Europäische Kommission (2001–2011). Konstitutionalisierung, Spill-Over oder Regieren ohne Regierung?* Wiesbaden: Springer.

Kornbeck, J. (2020b) Foreword. In: Sloot, B. van der; Paun, M.A. & Leenes, R. (eds) *Athletes' Human Rights and the Fight against Doping: A Study of the European Legal Framework*. The Hague: T.M.C. Asser Press (ASSER International Sports Law Series), pp. vii–xviii.

Kornbeck, J. (2021a) Droit dur ou droit mou? L'Union européenne et la promotion des APS. *Jurisport*, 216, 39–41.

Kornbeck, J. (2021b) Spanish professional football clubs: How salient is the exact nature of the aid provided? *European State Aid Law Quarterly*, 20:1, 120–138.

Lindholm, J. & Parrish, R. (2020) Horizontal direct effect of Union citizenship and the evolving sporting exception: TopFit, *Common Market Law Review*, 57:4, 1283–1304.

Lösche, P. (2010) Sportpolity, Sportpolitics und Sportpolicy als theoretische Annäherung an eine Sportpolitikwissenschaft. In: Tokarski, W. & Petry, K. (eds) *Handbuch Sportpolitik*. Schorndorf: Hofmann (Beiträge zur Lehre und Forschung im Sport; 172), pp. 11–28.

Manners, I. (2002) Normative power Europe: A contradiction in terms? *Journal of Common Market Studies*, 40:2, 235–258.

Martill, B. & Staiger, U. (2021) Negotiating Brexit: The cultural sources of British hard bargaining. *Journal of Common Market Studies*, 59:2, 261–277.

Miège, C. (2017) *Sport et droit européen*. Paris: L'Harmattan.

Neumann, F. (2019) *Export des europäischen Beihilfenrechts. Eine Analyse der Europäisierung des internationalen Subventionsrechts durch bilaterale Handelsabkommen*. Wiesbaden: Springer.

Ó'Conaill, S. (2018) Sustainable financing in football and the EU. In: Anderson, J.; Parrish, R. & García García, B. (eds) *Research Handbook on EU Sports Law and Policy*. Cheltenham: Edward Elgar, pp. 246–260.

Parensen, A. (1998) Die Fußball-Bundesliga und das Bosman-Urteil. In: Tokarski, W. (ed) *EU-Recht und Sport*. Aachen: Meyer & Meyer, pp. 70–150.
Parrish, R. (2003) *Sports Law and Policy in the European Union*. Manchester & New York: Manchester University Press.
Partington, N. (2018) Volunteering and EU sports law policy. In: Anderson, J.; Parrish, R. & García García, B. (eds) *Research Handbook on EU Sports Law and Policy*. Cheltenham: Edward Elgar, pp. 98–119.
Pijetlovic, K. (2018) European model of sport: Alternative structures. In: Anderson, J.; Parrish, R. & García García, B. (eds) *Research Handbook on EU Sports Law and Policy*. Cheltenham: Edward Elgar, 326–359.
Porro, N.R.; Martelli, S. & Testa, A. (2020) Introduction: Sport and the citizens of a disenchanted Europe. In: Porro, N.R.; Martelli, S. & Testa, A. (eds) *Sport, Welfare and Social Policy in the European Union*. London: Routledge, 1–6.
Rosamond, B (2020) European integration and the politics of economic ideas: Economics, economists and market contestation in the Brexit debate. *Journal of Common Market Studies*, 58:5.1085–1106.
Ross, S.F. (2021) *Advanced Introduction to Global Sports Law*. Cheltenham: Edward Elgar.
Sanchez-Graells, A. (2021) The UK's green paper on post-Brexit public procurement reform: Transformation or overcomplication? *European Procurement & Public Private Partnership Law Review*, 16:1, 4–18.
Sanghera, S. (2021) *Empireland: How Imperialism Has Shaped Modern Britain*. London: Viking.
Scheerder, J. (2020) Conclusion: Established models of European sport revisited from a socio-politological approach. In: Porro, N.R.; Martelli, S. & Testa, A. (eds) *Sport, Welfare and Social Policy in the European Union*. London: Routledge, pp. 153–168.
Schenk, S. (2018) Integrity of sport. In: Anderson, J.; Parrish, R. & García García, B. (eds) *Research Handbook on EU Sports Law and Policy*. Cheltenham: Edward Elgar, pp. 431–445.
Seldon, A. & Newell, R. (2020) *May at 10: The Verdict*. Devizes: Biteback Publishing.
Stephens, P. (2020) *Britain Alone: The Path from Suez to Brexit*. London: Faber & Faber.
Stewart, K.; Cooper, K. & Shutes, I. (2020) What will 'taking back control' mean for social policy in the UK? Brexit, public services and social rights. *Journal of European Social Policy*, 30:4, 509–517.
Szyszczak, E. (2018a) Application of EU competition rules to sport. In: Anderson, J.; Parrish, R. & García García, B. (eds) *Research Handbook on EU Sports Law and Policy*. Cheltenham: Edward Elgar, pp. 261–283.
Szyszczak, E. (2018b) Competition and sport: No longer so special? *Journal of European Competition Law & Practice*, 9:3, 188–196.
Tokarski, W.; Petry, K.; Groll, M. & Mittag, J. (2009) *A Perfect Match? Sport and the European Union*. Aachen: Meyer & Meyer.
Tokarski, W. & Steinbach, D. (2001) *Spuren. Sportpolitik und Sportstrukturen in der Europäischen Union*. Aachen: Meyer & Meyer.
Tokarski, W.; Steinbach, D.; Petry, K. & Jesse, B. (2004) *Two Players—One Goal? Sport in the European Union*. Aachen: Meyer & Meyer.
Tsoukala, A. (2018) Violence at sporting events. In: Anderson, J.; Parrish, R. & García García, B. (eds) *Research Handbook on EU Sports Law and Policy*. Cheltenham: Edward Elgar, pp. 139–156.
Ubertazzi, G.M. (1976) Le domaine du droit communautaire. A propos de l'arrêt Walrave, Union cycliste internationale. *Revue trimestrielle de droit européen*, 635–647.

Van den Bogaert, S. & Vermeersch, A. (2006) Sport and the EC treaty: A tale of uneasy bedfellows? *European Law Review*, 31:1, 821–840.
Waddington, I. (2010) Surveillance and control in sport: A sociologist looks at the WADA whereabouts system. *International Journal of Sport Policy and Politics*, 2:3, 255–274.
Weatherill, S. (1989) Discrimination on grounds of nationality in sport. *Yearbook of European Law* 9: 55–92.
Weatherill, S. (2010) Bosman changed everything: The rise of EC sports law, the past and future of EU law. In: Poiares Maduro, M.P. & Azoulai, L. (eds) *The Classics of EU Law Revisited on the 50th Anniversary of the Rome Treaty 2010*. Oxford & Portland, OR: Hart Publishing, pp. 480–487.
Weatherill, S. (2016) The Lex Sportiva and EU law: The academic lawyer's path before and after Bosman. In: Duval, A. & Van Rompuy, B. (eds) *The Legacy of Bosman: Revisiting the Relationship between EU Law and Sport*. Den Haag: T.M.C. Asser Press & Heidelberg: Springer, pp. 233–250.
Weatherill, S. (2017) *Principles and Practice in EU Sports Law*. Oxford: Oxford University Press.
Weatherill, S. (2018) Sources and origins of EU sports law. In: Anderson, J.; Parrish, R. & García García, B. (eds) *Research Handbook on EU Sports Law and Policy*. Cheltenham: Edward Elgar, pp. 6–23.
Weinberg, A.; Antoniou, A.S. & Cooper, C.L. (eds) (2020) *Brexit in the Workplace: A Psychology of Survival?* Cheltenham: Edward Elgar, pp. 58–79.
Westerkamp, G. (1980) *Ablöseentschädigungen im bezahlten Sport*. Münster: Dissertation University Münster.

Index